KU-640-061

The politics of home draws attention to the multiple relocations that take place in literatures in English in the twentieth century by examining these texts' investment in the notion of "home." Rosemary Marangoly George examines contemporary literary theory, colonial and postcolonial narratives on belonging, exile and immigration, to argue that literary allegiances are always more complicated than expected and yet curiously visible in formulations of "home." She demonstrates how, in the twentieth century, the practices of global English challenge the very logic of organizing literatures in accordance with national boundaries. Reading Englishwomen's narration of their success in the Empire against Conrad's account of colonial masculine failure, R. K. Narayan alongside Fredric Jameson, contemporary Indian women writers as they recycle the rhetoric of the British Romantic poets, Edward Said next to M. G. Vassanji and Jamaica Kincaid, and Conrad through Naipaul and Ishiguro, *The politics of home* explores the privilege that underlies both feeling at home and travel.

Rosemary Marangoly George is an Assistant Professor, Literatures in English and Cultural Studies, at the University of California, San Diego. She has published in *Cultural Critique, differences, Novel* and other academic journals.

The politics of home

PR 9081 GEO

QMW Library

23 1156785 6

)1

2

{

J3

1 / MAY 2UU4

THE POLITICS OF HOME

Postcolonial relocations and twentieth-century fiction

Rosemary Marangoly George
University of California, San Diego

CAMBRIDGE
UNIVERSITY PRESS

QMW LIBRARY
(MILE END)

Published by the Press Syndicate of the University of Cambridge
The Pitt Building, Trumpington Street, Cambridge CB2 IRP
40 West 20th Street, New York, NY 10011–4211, USA
10 Stamford Road, Oakleigh, Melbourne 3166, Australia

© Cambridge University Press 1996

First published 1996

Printed in Great Britain at the University Press, Cambridge

A catalogue record for this book is available from the British Library

Library of Congress cataloguing in publication data

George, Rosemary Marangoly.
The politics of home: postcolonial relocations and twentieth-century fiction.
p. cm. Includes index
ISBN 0 521 45334 8 (hardback)
1. English literature – Foreign countries – History and criticism.
2. English literature – Developing countries – History and criticism.
3. Commonwealth literature (English) – History and criticism.
4. Politics and literature – History – 20th century. 5. National characteristics in literature.
6. Emigration and immigration in literature. 7. Nationalism in literature.
8. Immigrants in literature. 9. Home in literature. I. Title
PR9080.G46 1995   820.9 – DC20
95–9777 CIP

ISBN 0 521 45334 8 hardback

TAG

Contents

Acknowledgments   *page* ix

Prologue. All fiction is homesickness   1

1   Home-countries: narratives across disciplines   11

2   The authoritative Englishwoman: setting up home and self in the colonies   35

3   The great English tradition: Joseph Conrad writes home   65

4   Nostalgic theorizing: at home in "Third World" fictions   101

5   Elite plotting, domestic postcoloniality   131

6   "Traveling light": home and the immigrant genre   171

Epilogue. All homesickness is fiction   199

Notes   203

Index   251

Acknowledgments

I would like to thank my colleagues at the Department of Literature, University of California, San Diego, for their support and encouragement over the last four years. Much of this book was researched and written through summer grants provided by the Academic Senate Committee on Research, UCSD, in 1993 and 1994. For their intellectual engagement with my work long after I graduated from Brown University, I am deeply indebted to Neil Lazarus and Ellen Rooney. I would also like to thank Nancy Armstrong, Michael Davidson, Frances Foster, Masao Miyoshi, Louis Montrose, and especially Robert Scholes, for their specific cautions and encouragement on this project. I am grateful to Lisa Lowe not just for her careful reading of sections of this book but for her sustained interest in my professional wellbeing. Several of these above named colleagues have read versions of various chapters, and their insights have saved me from making many big and small blunders along the way. Others who have read sections of this book and whose suggestions have greatly enhanced the final product include Judith Halberstam, Chandan Reddy, Roddey Reid, Michael Ryan, Rajeshwari Sunder Rajan, Susie Tharu, Quincy Troupe, and Elizabeth Weed. Special thanks are also due to my friends and fellow-travelers, John Lowney, Pam Hardman, Yuko Matsukawa, Andrew Morrison, Aparajita Sagar, Mark Sanders, and Sudha Swaminathan. Research assistance from Mehnaz Ghaznavi at UCSD is gratefully acknowledged.

This book would not be what it is without the detailed and insightful comments made by Gauri Viswanathan, the Cambridge appointed reviewer for this text. My editors at Cambridge, Kevin Taylor, Josie Dixon, and Linda Bree have my gratitude for their flexibility and constant confidence in the project. I also thank Polly Richards, my copy editor at Cambridge, and Karen Van Ness at UCSD for preparing the index. Permission to reprint from *differences* and *Cultural*

Critique where earlier and shorter versions of chapters 6 and 2 were first published is gratefully acknowledged.

Finally, I want to thank the Marangoly family, especially my siblings, for their amused disbelief mingled with pride, and for allowing me to use the cover picture despite their misgivings. Thanking Badri in a sentence is difficult but I do it here – for having no misgivings ever. I dedicate this book to them, S. G. Badrinath and the Marangoly family, living with (and on occasion, far from) whom has enabled me to write with greater clarity about home.

Prologue. All fiction is homesickness

> Philosophy is really homesickness; it is the urge to be at home everywhere.
> Novalis

> At times home is nowhere. At times one only knows extreme estrangement and alienation. Then home is no longer just one place. It is locations.
> bell hooks

Over the course of the last hundred or so years, the concept of home (and of home-country) has been re-rooted and re-routed in fiction written in English by colonizers, the colonized, newly independent peoples and immigrants. What is attempted in these pages is an examination of a central aspect of the novel in English, its investment in the notion of "home," in a project that does not restrict itself to an exclusive consideration of either "first world" or "third world" fictions. Under the auspices of "global English," this project examines the ways in which a host of different fictions re-present the ideologies of "home" and thus initiate the movement from English Literature to literatures in English. Bringing global English into the discussion challenges the very logic of a literary field and of an academic discipline that has hitherto been organized into two or three compartments: English Literature (i.e. from the British Isles), American Literature (US Literature), and World Literature (in English and in translation). These are, of course, vigorously contested categories, but "global English" alters the terms of contestation even when the texts under consideration remain the same. I will argue that an examination of the concepts and structures we recognize as "home" in the context of global English generates a reassessment of our understanding of belonging – in the English language as much as in spaces we call home.

The word "home" immediately connotes the private sphere of patriarchal hierarchy, gendered self-identity, shelter, comfort, nurture and protection. Realist novels in English in the last hundred years have

I

situated themselves in the gap between the realities and the idealizations that have made "home" such an auratic term.[1] As imagined in fiction, "home" is a desire that is fulfilled or denied in varying measure to the subjects (both the fictional characters and the readers) constructed by the narrative. As such, "home" moves along several axes, and yet it is usually represented as fixed, rooted, stable – the very antithesis of travel.

While this is primarily a study that moves among fictional texts, it is also about homes in culture, about travel away from home, about traveling homes, about home-countries, and about the travel of literary texts and of literary theory. James Clifford has stated that "[o]nce traveling is foregrounded as a cultural practice then dwelling, too, needs to be reconceived – no longer simply the ground from which traveling departs, and to which it returns."[2] Dwellings, homes, home-country: given the variations on the practices that would qualify as "home-making", both in and out of fiction, it would be counter-productive to insist on any one overarching formula for "home." And yet, in order to begin, I will put forward some formulations that will be fleshed out, substantiated, and on occasion even overturned in the chapters that follow.

What are the dimensions of "home"? I would like to suggest that the basic organizing principle around which the notion of the "home" is built is a pattern of select inclusions and exclusions. Home is a way of establishing difference. Homes and home-countries are exclusive. Home, I will argue, along with gender/sexuality, race, and class, acts as an ideological determinant of the subject. The term "home-country" in itself expresses a complex yoking of ideological apparatuses considered necessary for the existence of subjects: the notion of belonging, of having a home, and a place of one's own. And yet, in the very reference to a "home-country" lies the indication that the speaker is away from home. This distance from the very location that one strives to define, is, I believe intrinsic to the definition that is reached. The politics of location come into play in the attempt to weave together a subject-status that is sustained by the experience of the place one knows as Home or by resistance to places that are patently "not home." "Location" in the context of this study suggests the variable nature of both "the home" and "the self," for both are negotiated stances whose shapes are entirely ruled by the site from which they are defined. Locations are positions from which distance and difference are formulated and homes are made snug.[3]

Given the global history of British imperialism, any literary consideration of the word "home" in the twentieth century must pay attention to the changing status of English as it becomes a world language.[4] Does "home" change in its significations when articulated from different locations? Does "Home" as said in British India signify differently from "Home" as pronounced in British Africa? And once independence from the British is gained, does this English word, as used in newly formed African and Asian nations and in their literatures, undergo a radical re-orientation of geographical, psychological and material connotations? Studies in global nationalisms and/or in literary studies have not adequately addressed these issues. In this book, I look at the literatures produced from some of these locations and read them for their representations of the everyday imagining of home and country. My aim is to read more than the domestic into representations of the home, to keep location from being reduced to a geographic place on the map and politics from being reduced (or elevated) to nationalism.

In *Imagined Communities: Reflections on the Origin and Spread of Nationalism*, Benedict Anderson exposes the complex intertwining of all the texts (especially "print-commodities,") that are read in a society with the popular imagining of that community.[5] In the global literature I have chosen to work with, the (re)writing of home reveals the ideological struggles that are staged every day in the construction of subjects and their understanding of home-countries. The search for the location in which the self is "at home" is one of the primary projects of twentieth-century fiction in English. This project may get obscured or transcended as the narrative unfolds, but it is never completely abandoned. It is in this context that I read all fiction in terms of homesickness.

Considerations of the space marked "home" have for the most part been read as the terrain of conservative discourses. "Home" has been abandoned to its clichés. And yet, in recent times, there have been several successful attempts to theorize homes and domesticity as more than the place and pursuit of private individuals.[6] I would like to contribute to this branch of interdisciplinary scholarship that works toward a deconstruction of the opposition that has traditionally been maintained between four points: the private and the public spheres; the two genders; the colonizer and the colonized; and the west and the rest of the world, especially their respective literatures. Our ways of reading the trope of "home" in literature in English sometimes subverts and at other times enforces these binarisms. For instance, the divide maintained between colonizer and colonized by terms such as "the colonial subject" needs to be rethought. The usual practice is to read "colonial subject" as referring exclusively to "those subjected to colonialism."[7] Global literature in English as interpreted in these pages compels us to see *all* those subjects constructed by colonial and imperial ideologies in circulation in their location as "colonial subjects." Such a definition would include both subjects of the colonizing race as well as those of colonized races. Considering both locations (that of colonizer and that of colonized) *simultaneously* guarantees that a recognition of the collaboration between the two groups remains central to the analysis. The heterogeneity of colonial subjects belonging to colonized races is such that expanding the category to include those colonizers who are implicated in imperial and colonial enterprises does not render the category imprecise or unproductive. This simultaneity accounts for subjects who share a history of colonialism, without making the claim that all colonial subjects are identical: it is a strategy that intervenes in the construction of binarisms.

And yet binarisms are essential for the purposes of definition. Homes and nations are defined in the instances of confrontation with what is considered "not-home," with the foreign, with distance. Ultimately then, distance in itself becomes difference. Thus, for instance, it is in the heyday of British imperialism that England gets defined as "Home" in opposition to "The Empire" which belongs to the English but which is not England. It is under colonial occupation that African nationalists in the region called Rhodesia begin referring to their country as "Zimbabwe," a location that will come into being *after* "one man, one vote" becomes a reality in that country. As these brief examples demonstrate, it is hard to theorize notions like home or location except when specific historical and/or literary settings are taken into account. And yet, when literary texts are under consideration, the use of a common global language persuades us that indeed "home" is literally spelled the same the world over. Translations are not deemed necessary from English to English nor from realist novel to realist novel.

Over the last two centuries, the novel in the west has been read as having as its focus: love, courtship, seduction, female subjectivity, the home and domesticity. As such, the novel has often been interpreted as being, like its mainly "feminine" consumer, outside or irrelevant to the workings of the national destiny. With the advent of colonial fiction, however, this literary genre's implication in events of nation and empire can no longer be ignored. In fact, imperial literature can be read as the imagining of one's (domestic) ideology in an expanded space. Whether the motivation behind such imaginative expansions amount to domestication, love, seduction or rape varies from text to text. What becomes clear however, with the advent of the imperial novel is that the tales and tasks of homemaking (understood to be gendered female) are not very different from the tales and tasks of housekeeping on the national or imperial scale (usually gendered masculine).

Fiction in English by the colonized (or the once colonized) is manacled to "English Literature" in myriad ways. And yet, at the very outset, I will insist that to read global literatures in English as a gift bequeathed by erstwhile colonizers is to begin at a dead end. There is, of course, the common language – at first imposed and then shared. The form of some of the fiction in English by writers from the colonies also relies heavily on English literary traditions. This symmetry does not always extend to the contents of the fiction. For the colonized to raise their voices is to change the contents of the English novel, even if their first utterances are in "His Master's Voice." Writing alongside nationalist movements and the concomitant resistance to imperialism, the colonized use these same literary tools to assert a subject position for themselves and for the communities they wish to represent – a subject position that draws its validity and energy from a new engagement with the space that can now belong exclusively to "our people."

The literatures in English by colonial subjects (British and colonized races) work hard to further specific and differently motivated patriotic projects. However, as I will demonstrate in the chapters that follow, twentieth-century literature in English is not so concerned with drawing allegories of nation as with the search for viable homes for viable selves. Literature (even that which is written at the height of nationalist struggles) does not relate the exact same story that nationalism does. Nationalist movements narrate one story, literature creates its home through tangential locations. Literature may thus serve also as a site for resistance to dominant ideologies like nationalism. Hence Ayi Kwei Armah's *The Beautyful Ones Are Not Yet Born* and Ama Ata Aidoo's *No Sweetness Here* are both set against the backdrop of Ghanaian independence, yet the narratives are different from each other and from non-literary discourses produced from that site. In a very different context, George Orwell's writing, with its loyalty to England undermined by a recognition of the violence of Empire, is emblematic of this simultaneous capitulation and resistance to the ideologies of nation and empire. As the chapters that follow will demonstrate, "home" and "home-country" are used to articulate a whole range of political stances – radical, reactionary and revolutionary. They can, of course, also be completely bland terms for those subjects for whom "home" or "feeling at home" is always a given, under all regimes.

What all this indicates is that homes are not neutral places. Imagining a home is as political an act as is imagining a nation. Establishing either is a display of hegemonic power. Similarly, having all these markers laid out for one to step into as part of a naturalized socialization process is an indication of the power wielded by class, community and race. Reading within a context of global English exposes the political anchors of language, literature and space. The chapters that follow attempt to examine the broadest implications of the term "home" as present in various literatures in English. The attempt is to capture in one frame the dynamic fashion in which a particular fiction formulates its ideological stance on the concept of home. I have chosen to focus on certain literary instances in which the very notion of the home undergoes substantial revision.

I begin the first chapter by noting that traditional readings of nationalism cannot fully account for the processes by which diverse subjects imagine themselves at home in various geographic locations. Recent developments in the scholarship on nationalism and the writing on homes and subjecthood in other discourses are then brought together. Finally, in an attempt to rethink the links between the self and the home I turn to the promising examination of this equation in contemporary feminist theory.

In the second chapter, I work with novels and home-management guides written by Maud Diver, Flora Steel and others, to examine the impact on the British female subject of managing homes in the empire in the early twentieth century. The argument is that the colonial occupation of the Indian sub-continent established one of the primary arenas in which an identifiable group of English women first achieved the kind of authoritative self associated with the modern female subject – "the full individual" that Elizabeth Fox-Genovese sees as the desired goal of feminism in capitalist societies. The English home in the colonies was represented in these texts as an empire in miniature. More interesting and unexpected in this discourse is the representation of the empire as an expanded domestic space peopled by masters and servants. Given that their work of household supervision was valued for its contributions to the imperial cause, these English women in the colonies were closer to the position of national subject than their sisters back home – even those struggling to win the right to vote.

Turning to a consideration of Conrad's masculine representations of home and nation, I attempt to read his strangely "unreadable" politics. Is his work no more than the conservative and panic-stricken writing of an aristocrat who saw all kinds of terrors in women, domesticity and the working class, or was he an iconoclast whose fiction took apart the bourgeois ideals of the sacred home, chaste femininity and social order? Is he one of Perry Anderson's "white emigres" who buttress the dominant ideology's worship of home by capturing its elusive, illusionary dimensions in fiction?[8] Or does Conrad's writing attempt to alert the English of the dangers that menace their fetishized understanding of England as "Home"? This chapter assesses the polar oppositions in Conrad's work by examining the contesting binarisms that the narrative in *Almayer's Folly*, *Lord Jim* and *Heart of Darkness* constructs in order to produce coherence. I then argue for a repositioning of Conrad's writing that takes him out of his usual literary category (Modernism) and reads his work in relation to other international writing produced in the English-speaking globe.

The next, mainly theoretical chapter makes the transition to contemporary fiction and the politics of reading such texts. It attempts to destabilize the position of tacit influence occupied by Fredric Jameson's "Third World Literature in the Era of Multinational Capitalism" in the writing on and especially in the teaching of postcolonial literature in the west.[9] The attempt to fix "third world" literatures in nationalist moments and/or nationalist texts does them a disservice and yet it does give these texts, which Jameson calls "alien," a focus that renders them recognizable to western readers. In resisting the urge to be at home everywhere, this chapter argues for a revision in western theorizing on postcolonial literature.

This is followed by an examination of issues other than nationalism in Indian literature written in English: homes, religion, marriage, personal fulfillment and the burden of gendered subjectivity. Working with *The Dark Room* by R. K. Narayan, I demonstrate that the model recognized in the west as "The Third World Novel" (national allegory, despair after independence, horrors of gender inequality, community as core) is only one type of writing that has been mistaken for the whole. In the next chapter I examine novels by several prominent Indian women writers who write in the English language to argue that this writing in the language and diction of privilege may not be the radical, resistive act that is today automatically associated with the very term "postcolonial," but it reveals the complex writerly allegiances at work in such locations.

bject status of the immigrant, especially that of the non-
migrant to the west, forces another literary reinscription of
nd of home. In this final chapter, I reconsider the usual asso-
of immigrant fiction with the themes of loss, painful homelessness, nd the "less-than-whole" subject who longs for assimilation into
a national culture. With the aid of *The Gunny Sack*, M. G. Vassanji's
powerful novel on Indian immigrants in East Africa who relocate to
North America, I demonstrate that the immigrant genre is marked by
a curiously detached reading of the experience of "homelessness" as
well as by excessive use of the metaphor of luggage, both spiritual and
material. Do such belongings impede or facilitate belonging? Homi
Bhabha's theory of "DissemiNation," Jamaica Kincaid's *Annie John*
and Edward Said's *After the Last Sky*, are among the other texts on
immigration and exile that are deployed in this attempt to formulate
the characteristics of the immigrant genre.

Clearly, this is not an attempt to "cover" the entire English speaking
globe, nor will this book offer a systematic history of global English.
Instead, I envision this project as examining the construct "home-
country" in several distinct instances where the political, historical and
cultural location makes revisions necessary. The theoretical debate initiated in the first chapter continues in subsequent chapters. Two of the
chapters that follow examine the rhetoric of home in the writings of
women of privilege – in the first instance provided by English women,
privileged by race and in the case of Indian women writers, privileged
by class. Other chapters examine masculine readings of "Home": the
figure of Conrad as a troubled outsider/insider is problematized by the
representation in Vassanji's text of joyous international homelessness. I
do not wish to imply that every situation in the fiction of those who
have been colonized or of the immigrant can be read as variations on
similar events in the realm of the colonizer. Yet, in each of these
instances, both halves of the formula "home-country" are made to
take on weight that they do not bear when considered independently.
Ultimately, I would like to see both "first" and "third" worlds implicated (albeit differently implicated) in the term "the postcolonial,"
rather than have it refer specifically to the non-west.[10] Such a move, I
will argue, may set the stage for considerations of the non-west in an
arena where both sides are not held down by the always already
assigned central and marginal positions. Acknowledging a common
history of colonialism implicates both margins and center in the future
course of this history. Under this revised rubric of postcolonialism, one

could genuinely be confused about which location (the one-time colonizer or the one-time colonized) takes on the center and which the margin in the arena of cultural politics. Certainly in assessing the literature produced from these locations one finds that often the marginal (for example: women and domesticity in *Heart of Darkness*, England in *Annie John*) takes over the center.

What, then, is home? How do we travel from Novalis' "urge to be at home everywhere" to bell hooks' "home is nowhere"? And what lies beyond this impasse? One distinguishing feature of places called home is that they are built on select inclusions. The inclusions are grounded in a learned (or taught) sense of a kinship that is extended to those who are perceived as sharing the same blood, race, class, gender, or religion. Membership is maintained by bonds of love, fear, power, desire and control. Homes are manifest on geographical, psychological and material levels. They are places that are recognized as such by those within and those without. They are places of violence and nurturing. A place that is flexible, that manifests itself in various forms and yet whose every reinvention seems to follow the basic pattern of inclusions/exclusions. Home is a place to escape to and a place to escape from. Its importance lies in the fact that it is not equally available to all. Home is the desired place that is fought for and established as the exclusive domain of a few. It is not a neutral place. It is community. Communities are not counter-constructions but only extensions of home, providing the same comforts and terrors on a larger scale.[11] Both home and community provide such substantial pleasures that have been so thoroughly assumed as natural that it may seem unproductive to point to the exclusions that found such abodes.

This prologue brings together the many concerns that provided the impetus for this study. The rest of the book addresses the formulations put forth here and attempts to complicate the assumptions that underlie much of what is suggested in these initial pages. I have been enabled in my own analysis by the work of practitioners in the fields of feminism, gender studies, Marxism, postcolonial theory, cultural studies and semiotics. However, the novels that I read for this project are the cultural texts from which I have derived the greatest pleasures of theory and praxis. These novels serve as the ground for this study.

CHAPTER I

Home-countries: narratives across disciplines

"What's Home Got to Do With It?"
Biddy Martin and Chandra Mohanty

Today, the primary connotation of "home" is of the "private" space from which the individual travels into the larger arenas of life and to which he or she returns at the end of the day. And yet, also in circulation is the word's wider signification as the larger geographic place where one belongs: country, city, village, community. Home is also the imagined location that can be more readily fixed in a mental landscape than in actual geography.[1] The term "home-country" suggests the particular intersection of private and public and of individual and communal that is manifest in imagining a space as home. Home-country, while widely used in travel documents, personal narratives and fiction, is not quite the object of nationalism as it is usually understood.

At the different levels of discourse that a culture engenders, the notion of physical or spiritual home-country is variously announced: as a heritage as well as a place where *some* persons were/are/or will be "at home." These utterances and assertions are routinely categorized as: personal, local, communal, and/or national affiliations. These affiliations are held apart as separate mutually conflicting claims or they are co-opted to satisfy the requirements of the specific narrative that is unfolding at any given location. In this chapter, I will document some of the readings of "home" formulated in various academic locations. The narratives are not similar, yet common to the rhetoric of "Home" in most disciplines, is an ahistoric, metaphoric and often sentimental story line. In fact, fictionality is an intrinsic attribute of home. The homes that are constructed through these texts are multifarious experiences and desires which are at best vigorously interrogated, frequently unchallenged, and never quite rejected. I will examine the overlapping constructs of home and nation to sug-

gest that while the nation is the object and subject of nationalist narratives, literary narratives are more centrally concerned with the idea
of home. Finally, I turn from psychoanalytical and other readings to
current feminist theorizing for direction in my project of pulling the
rug from under a comfortable and singular understanding of home.

COLONIALISM AND NATIONALISM AS NARRATIVES ON PLACE

The pitfalls of seeing nationalist movements as the only ideological
frame through which one can imagine a space as home, can best be
demonstrated by examining the classic mid twentieth-century western
texts on nationalism.[2] Western studies of nationalism, more often than
not, begin with a study of the origins of nationalism. Having located
the origins of nationalism in late eighteenth-century Europe, these
narratives go on to read all subsequent nationalisms as so many variations of the same model based on the same principles. When nationalism arises in the non-European parts of the globe it is read as a
"borrowed" event. Hence the tenuousness if not the failure of these
nationalisms (when measured against the dimensions of the model) is
predicted as well as located in the borrowedness of the concept itself.
In such a situation it is futile to use the terms of classic nationalism in
an inquiry into global representations of the self and home because
the terms are always loaded. Hence, the voicing of desires for
"Home" in the non-western world has for the most part been
declared nonexistent or at least unreadable *except* as further manifestations of a (borrowed) nationalistic fervor.

Reading home as articulated in global English *through nationalism*
can be a productive enterprise only if the terms of nationalism are
radically rethought. Beginning with *Imagined Communities: Reflections on
the Origins and Spread of Nationalism* written by Benedict Anderson and
first published in 1983, there have been a number of revisions to the
traditional ways of reading nationalistic events as well as a whole new
array of events that are deemed nationalistic. The most significant
development is Partha Chatterjee's replacement of the notion of
"borrowed" nationalism with the carefully nuanced assessment of
"derivative" nationalism in *Nationalist Thought and the Colonial World:
A Derivative Discourse*.[3] In his introductory chapter, "Nationalism as a
Problem in the History of Political Ideas," Chatterjee carefully examines the western discourse on nationalism and the problem of derivative

nationalisms in non-European colonial countries. He enters "the field of discourse, historical, philosophical and scientific, as [if it were] a battleground of political power."[4] Reading the ideological history of Indian nationalism within this discourse of power, Chatterjee demonstrates that "Indian nationalism" is derivative but different, not just from European models but also different at different stages in its own history.

Despite the shared rhetoric, anti-colonial nationalism operates from an impetus that is antagonistic to precisely its host body, colonial nationalism. And yet "Home" is articulated along similar lines in both discourses: it is the sentimentalized and pure cultural center. If, as Douglas Porteous claims, "home [is] the territorial core" of all societies then it becomes useful to examine how this territory is made to fit into the larger maps of nations and of empires.[5] When is the word "home" shrunk to denote the private, domestic sphere and when is the "domestic" enlarged to denote "the affairs of a nation"? This fluidity of meaning cannot be appreciated unless we are willing to rethink cultural boundaries. Writing on Palestinian women's everyday redrawing of the spaces marked as home/the street, as inside/outside, Mary Layoun proposes that we account for this fluidity of assigned space by reading nationalism as narrative; as stories that are not just spoken and written but acted out as well.[6] Nationalism, Layoun insists, "tells a story by articulating (presumably) linked elements. Not by chance, it also constructs and privileges its own narrative perspective" (p. 411). Layoun goes on to argue that:

The rhetoric of nationalism as narrative persuades and convinces its audience(s) – its implied readers and listeners – of the efficacy and desirability of its terms and of the "natural" relationship between those terms. Its appeal derives not just from the letter and word of truth and order (as "grammar"), but *with* letters and words in the sense of persuasion and likely possibility (as rhetoric). (p. 411)

The logical extension to this suggestion that nationalism is plotted along a literary path author(iz)ed by certain select persons is the proposition that "we can bring to bear on narratives of nationalism the critical and theoretical insights of analyses of literary narratives with their considerations of narrative voice, time, and space, emplotment, of closure and strategies of containment" (p. 413). If we were to read nationalism in this literary fashion, it would be easier to understand why certain counter-narratives fall by the wayside.

In the context of anti-colonial nationalist narratives the desired "happy ending" is of the newly independent nation. The anti-colonial bent of such nationalist narratives imposes this single denouement that complicates and suppresses other story lines. Sara Suleri has referred to "the encounter of colonialism and the emergence of nationalism" as "secret sharers in an act of cultural transcription so overdetermined as to dissipate the logic of origins, or the rational framework of chronologies."[7] It is in this context that nationalism leads to the interpretation of diverse phenomenon through one glossary, thus erasing specificities, setting norms and limits, lopping off tangentials. I would like to consider what happens to disparate and local expressions of feeling at home when they are translated into the rhetoric of nationalism.

The urge to generalize on "home" as represented through various global English language texts is very strong because we have access to these utterances in a language that we can understand without the acknowledgment of difference that translation would impose.[8] Translation can be seen as the attempt to impose a common interpretation via a common language – to move texts to a common ground. And yet, nationalism (one such common ground) can account only in nationalist terms for the processes by which diverse subjects imagine themselves at home in a specific geographic location.[9] An anecdote from *Homecoming* by Ngugi Wa Thiong'o provides us with a demonstration of the "unsystematic" fashion in which a place is recognized as home as well as the way in which the event is translated into the dominant narrative of nationalism. Ngugi writes,

One day I heard a song. I remember the scene so vividly: the women who sang it are now before me – their sad faces and their plaintive melody. I was then ten or eleven. They were being forcibly ejected from the land they occupied and sent to another part of the country so barren that people called it the land of black rocks. This was the gist of their song:

> And there will be great joy
> When our lands comes back to us
> For Kenya is the country of black people.
> And you our children
> Tighten belts around your waist
> So you will one day drive away from this land
> The race of white people
> For truly, Kenya is a black man's country.

They were in a convoy of lorries, caged but they had one voice. They sang of a common loss and hope and I felt their voice rock the earth where I stood literally unable to move.

Their words were not the platitudes of our university philosophers who use words as shields from life and truth: these women had lived the words they spoke. There was at once a fatalistic acceptance of the inevitable and also a collective defiance. "We shall overcome," they seemed to say. The women had taken a correct political stand in the face of an oppressive enemy.[10]

One cannot but notice the blatant romanticizing and masculinizing ("Kenya is a black man's country") that Ngugi performs on the women's text in the course of his translation. In nationalist discourses all articulation of "home" are drawn into one commonality of time and space. This harnessing of diverse discursive trajectories on "belonging" is as much a process of genericism as of gentrification: in analyses with a nationalist agenda, all desires for "home" are elevated by being addressed to and met by the prescribed happy ending. Ngugi's presentation of "the gist" of the women's song is quite "translated" into the discourse of nationalism even while he admires their "correct" political stance for being different from the "platitudes" of the bourgeois intellectuals. Yet in spite of our inability to have the anecdote outside or prior to Ngugi's nostalgic re-presentation of it, one can glimpse an instance of imagining a place as home which is articulated in an event that evicts the subject from that very space.

Whether one is working with cultural discourses in the Euro-american context or in the context of once-colonized countries there is a pressing need to separate nationalism at the level of elite scholarship, political rhetoric, jurisprudence and state-building from the imagining of a place as one's home that functions on the everyday level of ordinary people as they write and live ordinary lives. While thinking in terms of home and nationalism may occur simultaneously in cultural productions, the two events are often parallel or tangential to each other. This point is illuminated by Edward Said's promising analysis of the notion of place:

The readiest account of place might define it as nation...But this idea of place does not cover the nuances, principally of reassurance, fitness, belonging, association, and community, entailed in the phrase *at home* or *in place*.[11]

Here, Said moves beyond the traditional notions of "place = unit of national space," and "any association with place = patriotism/nationalism." At the everyday level of discourse, nationalism as we know it becomes too restrictive a term because it devalues (or else gentrifies) ordinary, everyday, subaltern, "non-official" experiences of home. Mary Layoun insists that the "every day struggles and choices of ordinary folk, their attempts to come to terms with and sometimes to change the shape of a dominant narrative have too often been minimized by critical consideration" (p. 413). She goes on to make an even more crucial point:

And yet they [ordinary folk] too – and not just the states or leaders who speak in their names – engage in both theorizing about and acting in the narrative(s) of the nation. While this process should neither be effaced from consideration nor, conversely, treated with nostalgia and overvalorized, there are moments when this everyday experience of parts of the nation/people truly confounds the dominant definition of the national narrative and, sometimes, offers more pragmatic and flexible alternatives to dominant national constructions. (pp. 413–14)

Is the concept of "home" (in global literature in English) one such "pragmatic and flexible" alternative to "dominant national constructions"? What would qualify a subject as a part of "ordinary folk"? The class affiliations of most writers from outside the Euroamerican globe who produce literature in English would automatically cancel their categorization as "ordinary folk." And yet, their fiction serves to blur distinctions and categories of nationalism, and to make the understanding of "home" as a purely private place and of "nation" as a public arena, wholly inadequate. Fiction, as we will see in the chapters that follow, puts the discourse of nationalism to uses other than that of nation building.

In *The World, the Text and the Critic* Edward Said draws a distinction between the two kinds of affinity that an individual can hold. I would like to use his distinction between "filiation" and "affiliation" to further my examination of the relations between formal nationalistic articulations and the thinking of a place as home. Theorizing primarily in the context of late nineteenth and early twentieth century writers, Said calls "filiation" the ties that an individual has with places and people that are based on his/her natal culture; that is, ties of biology and geography. "Affiliations," which are what come to replace filiations, are links that are forged with institutions, associations, communities and other social creations. The movement is always from filiations to affiliations.[12] This replacement of one type of ties with the other is read as "a passage from nature to culture" so that:

a filial relationship was held together by natural bonds and natural forms of authority – involving obedience, fear, love, respect, and instinctual conflict – the new affiliative relationship changes these bonds into what seem to be transpersonal forms – such as guild consciousness, consensus, collegiality,

i.e. filial relationship with one's mother
affilial relationship with one religion...?

professional respect, class, and hegemony of a dominant culture. The filiative scheme belongs to the realm of nature and "life," whereas affiliations belongs exclusively to culture and society.[13]

The language used in this passage could be read metaphorically so that it cites the usual location of what could loosely be called "home" as a filiation within discourses of affiliation that define "ties" in terms of larger arenas like nations. In Said's theory it is vital to maintain the distinction between the two levels of affinities; as a result, the more local "tie" is *necessarily* read as the more personal and private "natural" bond.[14] Yet, to read this passage from Said's text alongside the following passage from Jomo Kenyatta's writing on the effects of colonialism on Gikuyu culture would suggest that neither filiations nor affiliations are ever "natural":

When the European comes to Gikuyu country and robs the people of their land, he is taking away not only their livelihood, but the material symbol that holds family and tribe together.[15]

Kenyatta sees this taking away of land as the "one blow which cuts away the foundations from the whole Gikuyu life, social, moral and economic."[16] For Kenyatta then, rebuilding this sense of "homeland" requires more than the efforts of official nation building after independence. There is no "natural" link between a place and a people: instead there are links that are forged or forgotten on both material and spiritual levels. Yet, what is primarily reconstructed is just such a "natural" link with a place. The discourses that construct "home" in the contexts of colonialism and postcolonialism suggest that ultimately both affiliations and filiations are learned, created, recalled and/or forgotten in everyday history. A necessary alteration to propositions like Said's would be to see "filiations" as those bonds that are naturalized as "natural" through the discourses that differentiate them from those bonds that are naturalized as "artificial" or as "affiliations."

What we have in the many discourses that situate home in opposition to wider public spaces is a sense that "homes" and the desire for such spaces are "natural" urges common to all humans at all times. What the hyphen in "home-country" makes explicit are the ideological linkages deemed necessary for subjects who are at home in a social and political space and even more acutely for those who are, because of geographic distance or political disenfranchisement, *outside* their "legitimate" space. Home-country and home resonate differently from different locations for different subjects and often even for the same subject at different locations. And yet while the actual cultural practices change

apidly and dramatically, the desired ideals that such practices are mod-
elled after are much slower to change. Hence, in this current global
moment of rethinking nation and nationalism, there may be an added
desire to keep the idea of "home" and "community" intact.

Like several other scholars working in the area, Chandra Mohanty
has declared that: "[w]ith the rise of transnational corporations which
dominate and organize the contemporary economic system, however,
factories have migrated in search of cheap labor, and the nation-state
is no longer an appropriate socioeconomic unit for analysis."[7] As a
result, Mohanty goes on to add, contemporary postindustrial societies
like Europe and the US "invite cross-national and cross-cultural
analyses for explanation of their own internal features and socioeconomic constitution. Moreover, contemporary definitions of the "third
world" can no longer have the same geographical contours and
boundaries" (p. 2). Given this dramatic instability of large categories
like "nation", "first world/third world," the inclination to maintain
the smaller units like "home," "the family" and "community"
increases. For example, in contemporary Hollywood interpretations
of home and family, the desire for the comforts that these places
undoubtedly provide has led to representations of such spaces as elastic, unendingly accommodating and ultimately big enough to hold
everyone. Even alternative productions such as Ang Lee's *The Wedding
Banquet* follow the Hollywood prescription. A New York love story of
a gay couple, a green card marriage, a pregnancy, two fathers, one
mother, two happy grandparents, *The Wedding Banquet* provides just
such a soothing narrative.

At the risk of implying a universal humanism, I will suggest that if
any common pattern can be traced in the many versions of home that
contemporary cultures provide us with, it is one of exclusions. Homes
are not about inclusions and wide open arms as much as they are
about places carved out of closed doors, closed borders and screening
apparatuses. When different groups or individuals jostle each other to
establish a space as their own, as an exclusive manifestation of their
subjecthood, this struggle can become as urgent as keeping oneself
alive. As a result, "home" becomes contested ground in times of political tumult either on the level of power struggles at a national communal stage or at the interpersonal familial level. The chapters in this
book will examine several such projects of self-preservation as well as
the ways in which signs of such struggle are (often incompletely)
erased in the formulations of "home" in global English.

THE SELF AT HOME

The conflation of home and self is one of the threads that runs through the examination of "home" in the discourse produced by such different disciplines as literary theory, architecture, sociology, political science, geography, philosophy and psychology. In this section I will analytically explore some of these discussions, not comprehensively, but with the intention of reading various texts alongside and against each other. The focus returns inevitably to literary and related cultural texts.

While the issue of "homelands" or "home-countries" is raised primarily in the discourse on nationalism and other so-called masculine, public arenas, the issue of "home" and the private sphere is usually embedded in discourses on women. In literature and literary theory, until quite recently, most considerations of the home have occasioned examination of the status of women. The association of home and the female has served to present them as mutual handicaps, mutually disempowering. Hence, the woman is incapacitated because she is "tied" to the home, and the home is shelter for the incapacitated. For men, both women and the home provide momentary escape and respite, but to linger too long at these comforts is to be lost. This analysis could apply as easily (albeit differently) to a novel like *Heart of Darkness*, published in 1899 by Joseph Conrad, to *Sons and Lovers*, published in 1913 by D. H. Lawrence, or to *Wife*, published in 1975 by Bharati Mukherjee. In these texts, the representation of the physical and psychic spaces called "home" serve as sites of both potential subversion and containment.

It is in psychoanalytical texts that this equation of home and self occurs most frequently and in some complexity. Carl Jung developed a thesis that explicitly reads an individual's home as the "universal archetypal symbol of the self."[18] In *Memories, Dreams and Reflections*, an autobiographical text, Jung recounts his dream of himself as a house which he proceeded to explore in the same dream. Jung's "dream house" unfolds in careful chronological correctness − his passage through its rooms and levels takes him from an upper storey salon "situated" in the eighteenth century to a lower level set in the fifteenth century, and further down a level to a floor that invoked the mediaeval period, from there to a cellar set in the Roman period and finally to a prehistoric cave below the cellar and from there to the earth itself which is the common ground beneath all houses, or in

Jungian terms, the collective unconscious. In Jung's interpretation of this rather scripted dream the movement through the house mimics the history of the psyche's development:

> It was plain to me that the house represented a kind of image of the psyche
> – that is to say, of my then state of consciousness, with hitherto unconscious
> additions. Consciousness was represented by the salon...The ground floor
> stood for the first level of the unconscious.[19]

Later in this autobiography, Jung writes about building his house in Bollingen on Lake Zurich along the lines of the house plan revealed to him in his dream:

> At first I did not plan a proper house, but merely a kind of primitive one-
> storey dwelling. It was to be a round structure with a hearth in the center
> and bunks along the walls. I more or less had in mind an African hut where
> the fire, ringed with stone, burns in the middle, and the whole life of the
> family revolves around this centre. Primitive huts concretise an idea of
> wholeness, a familial wholeness in which all sorts of domestic animals like-
> wise participate. But I altered the plan even during the first stages of build-
> ing, for I felt it was too primitive. I realized it would have to be a regular
> two-storey house not a mere hut crouched on the ground.[20]

The dangers of such a close equation of home and the self are clear in the passages quoted above. The suggestion is that the style of one's dwelling place parallels the development of one's psyche. Here, Jung's rejection of what he sees as the African hut as too primitive for him, is, given his equation of house and psyche, a rejection of a corre-sponding "African psyche" as too primitive for him. Hence, in build-ing his dream-house in material terms, Jung sees moving beyond this apparently singular and timeless African hut as a manifestation of his moving beyond the primitive in himself. Here as elsewhere, the equa-tion of the self and the home is not an ideologically innocent associa-tion – it is predicated on a comparison with a home and a self that is perceived as static, basic, unadorned, less than adequate. And yet the (racial) political reverberations of home design are attested to as purely psychoanalytical data.

Gaston Bachelard, Clara Cooper, David Sopher, Yi-Fu Tuan, E. Relph, Douglas Porteous and more recently Adrian Forty and Witold Rybczynski, all stress the proximity of home and self-identity.[21] Humanist geographers like Tuan, Relph and Bachelard are especially concerned with the emotional responses that places produce in people and their work can be seen as "an exception to geography's mas-culinist uninterest in the home."[22] In her feminist assessment of the limits of geographic knowledge, Gillian Rose defines humanist geography as a "humanist conceptualization of place" (p. 41). Of humanist geographers, Rose writes, "places for them were locations which, through being experienced by ordinary people, became full of human significance. Humanistic geographers tried to recover the ways in which places were perceived, arguing that it was impossible to make sense of the social world unless academics listened to the interpretations of those who lived in it" (p. 41).

Following the publication of Bachelard's *The Poetics of Space*, the consensus seems to be that "home" and "non-home" are the basic divisions of geographic space, just as "self" and the "non-self" or "Other" represent the basic divisions of psychic space. What is striking about most of these articulations on the various aspects of the home is the absence of any kind of ambivalence about the assertions made or any recognition of the sweeping assumptions beneath the theses on home. This lack or oversight can perhaps be accounted for by the overriding assumption that the home is a given – a space that is already marked out in symbolic and material dimensions for the occupant. Hence, the confidence of these statements from the opening lines of Porteous' essay "Home: The Territorial Core":

Home provides both the individual and the small primary group known as the family with all three territorial satisfactions [identity, security, stimulation]. These satisfactions derive from the control of physical space, and this control is secured by two major means. The personalization of space is an assertion of identity and a means of ensuring stimulation.[23]

Read, for instance, alongside accounts of child abuse and other forms of domestic violence, Porteous' definition of this territory as "an assertion of identity and a means of ensuring stimulation" takes on terrifying proportions. The last passage in David Sopher's "The Landscape of Home" is equally at ease with the notion of home as a stable, easily identifiable and universally available item:

Peace be upon Robert Frost, but home is not where they have to take you in, it is where they want to take you in. The landmarks of home are the signs that one is welcome. Most of us in academic life know that wherever we may be living, we are to some degree, in the biblical phrase, "strangers in a strange land." Yet the signs in the landscape are there to read, and they can tell us that we are, after all, at home.[24]

Sopher's momentary delving beneath cliches, only to return to their soothing, solid familiarity is characteristic of this discourse. It is almost as if the very word "home" evokes an aura of safety and stability.

"Home-bases" Tuan insists in *Space and Place*, are "intimate places to human beings everywhere" (p. 147). This scholarship works toward buttressing this sense of "well-being" and security that has come to mean "home". Tuan's *Topophilia: A Study of Environment, Perception, Attitudes and Values*, coins a word ("topophilia") for the sentimental attachment that people have to places.[25] Topophilia is visual pleasure and sensual delight as well as "the fondness for place because it is familiar, because it is home and incarnates the past because it provokes pride of ownership and creation" (p. 247).

Gillian Rose argues that the universalization and idealization of the comforts of home in this discourse is the logical outcome of a "feminization of place". With masculinity as the implicit norm of geographic discourse, place is understood as a maternal woman (nurturing, natural) and hence geographic knowledge is constructed on a foundation provided by the relationship of this (masculine) subject with the mother which is predicated on "the exclusion of women (among others) from the geographical" (p. 62).

Rose's astute reading of the feminization (or more specifically the mothering) of place is retraced along the axes of psychoanalysis, architecture and literature in Anthony Vidler's *The Architectural Uncanny: Essays on the Modern Unhomely*. In the first section of his book, Vidler presents "[t]he perpetual exchange between the homely and the unhomely, the imperceptible sliding of cosiness into dread" as setting the parameters for much of the discussion on homes in nineteenth and twentieth-century western cultural discourses on the subject. However, this "dread" is primarily the dread of the "feminine." Beginning with the nineteenth-century trope of the haunted house, Vidler goes on to analyze the responses to the discovery of the ruins of Pompeii, and from there to consider work across several disciplines – Freud, Schelling, F. T. A. Hoffman, Melville, Poe, Walter Pater, Adorno and Le Corbusier among others. Vidler reads Freud's "uncanny" as the primary example of this "sliding of cosiness into dread" that underlies the notion of home. In Freudian terms, this "uncanny" stems from old, familiar experiences that are repressed and then emerge in the present as transformed anxieties. Vidler suggests that "the impossible desire to return to the womb, the ultimate goal represented by nostalgia, would constitute a true 'homesickness'" (p. 55). Vidler quotes the following passage from Frued's writing to substantiate his reading:

It often happens that neurotic men declare that they feel that there is something uncanny about the female genital organs. This *unheimlich* place, however, is the entrance to the former *Heim* [home] of all human beings, to the place where each one of us lived once upon a time and in the beginning... In this case too, then, the *unheimlich* is what was once *heimisch*, familiar: the prefix *un* is the token of repression. (p. 55)

Elsewhere in Vidler's book this association between homes and wombs is elaborated upon by other readings of (s)mothering: as in the images of being buried alive provided by the Pompeii excavations and by Freud's insistence that the fear of being buried alive by mistake is the repressed fantasy of "intra-uterine existence."[26] Homes, wombs and tombs take on a proximity that is tenable only within psychoanalytical discourse. The feminization of the home to the exclusion of women in this discipline substantiates Rose's reading of geographical texts. Ultimately what such gendering of place does is to further "naturalize" the notion of "Home" resulting in its categorization alongside "natural phenomena" like birth and death. Nature is of course to be understood as a construction of culture and yet "home" moves from being perceived as property to become a part of the life cycle. As in Tuan's celebration of "pride of ownership and creation," the economics disappear when "home" reappears as a natural formation.

The blurring of the distinctions between women, creativity and property is a trademark of patriarchal societies. Tracts on home design, decorum and other guidebooks for women in the nineteenth and early twentieth century exhibit a similar identification of women and homes. The home was believed to be an expression of the personality of the "woman of the house," and often it stood in as a metaphor for her body. The woman's job was to decorate and maintain her home as she did her mind, personality and body.[27]

If one indulges in this identification of home with subject identity, then a brief examination of the representation of homes in the colonial novels can be very illuminating. Using for the moment the metaphors of these texts such as the use of the word "native" to signify all non-westerners, one notes that while much is written about the English home in the colony, representations of the "native" home are sketchy. Hobsbawm notes that some cities in the colonies during the age of empire, 1875–1914, had populations greater than large European cities of the time.[28] And yet the colonial novel does not acknowledge the large number of "native" homes that would, of necessity, have been established in the cities. Instead, "native dwellings" are either ramshackle huts, palaces that are disproportionately large or simply "ruins" inhabited by people. A classic example is provided by the opening passage in Forster's *A Passage to India* where the city of Chandrapore is "scarcely distinguishable from the rubbish that it [the Ganges] deposits so freely...Houses do fall, people are drowned and left rotting, but the general outline of the town persists, swelling here, shrinking there, like some low but indestructible form of life."[29] In *The Indian Metropolis: A View to the West*, architectural historian Norma Evenson draws our attention to a section from Rudyard Kipling's 1893 poem, "The Song of Cities," in which he laments the decline of the city of Madras, India: Kipling compares the city to "– a withered beldame now,/Brooding on ancient fame."[30] Evenson notes that in 1893, Madras was a fairly young city which had never been, as Kipling's poem claimed, "crowned above queens" in a glorious past. It was simply that Madras did not follow the urban plan usually identified with cities of its size and was hence perceived as a city in decay and decline.

In the colonial text, the "native subject" as manifest in the representation of the native home is either a "lack" or an "excess." Hence we are led to believe that the absence of a "self/home" that resembles the "self/home" born of western individualism signals the absence of alternative notions of subjecthood. There are no "ordinary" subjects; just faceless, outhoused "boys" or excessively bejewelled or painted rajahs and chiefs. It is significant that the novels written by Indian sub-continentals and Africans in the postcolonial era, often establish as their protagonist, the ordinary citizen with his/her sometimes modest, but nevertheless potent notions of home.[31]

If the home stands not just for one's representations of oneself but for what others see of one, then it is doubly important to pay attention to the status of those without homes either because of economic circumstance or political disenfranchisement. Furthermore, what of those homes or selves that are not recognized as such because they are deemed inappropriate or inadequate? An everyday example would be that of the mobile home park in present day USA which is always set at the very edge of a town or suburb. Such parks are seen as violating the "true" image of the neighborhood and its occupants are often coded as "transients," a term which one is invited to read as "unstable." Or consider the black shanty towns in South Africa or the slums in urban India that are routinely torn down because they are interpreted not as homes but as spaces where non-subjects live in "informal circumstances."[32]

Under colonialism, the "native" exists as another kind of "subject": one who is a subject of the colonial race. This is, in itself, a condition that excludes subject status as those in control of colonial discourses know it. In "The Subject and Power," Michel Foucault draws attention to the two ways of reading the word "subject":

> There are two meanings of the word *subject*: subject to someone else by control and dependence, and tied to his own identity by a conscience or self-knowledge. Both meanings suggest a form of power which subjugates and makes subject to.[33]

The concept of the subject must be further problematized if it is to be used productively in different scenarios. Are these "two meanings" mutually exclusive? Can one be subject to someone else and tied to one's own identity at the same time? Or are such multiplicities a luxury or simply a difficult stance to maintain because it would require that one resist the oppressive definitions of that *someone else* to whom one is subject?[34]

Problematic as the concept of the subject is, I would like to use it as an evaluative tool for the measure of recognition given to various peoples, genders, and classes in the cultural texts that I examine. My justification is that in a world-view where subjecthood is the only measure of equal worth, criticism of such a world-view should not exempt itself from adopting a "strategic" use of the notion of "subjectivity" (to refashion Spivak's use of the term "strategic positive essentialism"). Much of the resistance from contemporary practitioners of theory in the west to using the subject as a trope stems from its history in the west as a part of liberal humanism. Claiming subject status for those who have been denied this privilege dramatically alters this history. There is no way that the non-subject's or subaltern's claiming of subject positions for herself can be read as "business as usual" in the world of liberal humanism.[35]

"HOMESICK WITH NOWHERE TO GO"

In recent years feminist criticism has once again taken up the issue of home and its usefulness as a concept and as a place from which to launch feminist transformations of culture. In this section I intend to read a few crucial feminist essays on this topic and trace the ways in which they read and respond to each other. Several issues underlie my examination. What does home signify in contemporary western feminisms? Where does home end and community begin? What happens to the equation of home and self in feminist accounts? How do feminist readings of space account for the overlap between home,

community and nation? What are the politics of location in these
texts? Last, and most importantly for the purposes of this book, what
are the literary implications of such feminist rereadings of the home?
Responses to these questions are scattered through the remainder of
this chapter and through the book.

Biddy Martin and Chandra Mohanty begin their very influential
1986 essay "Feminist Politics: What's Home Got to Do with It?" by
stressing "the importance of not handing over notions of home and
community to the Right."[36] The challenge as they see it, is "to find
ways of conceptualizing community differently without dismissing its
appeal and importance" (p. 192). Martin and Mohanty examine how
subjects are constituted by their relationship with "home." Their argument is as powerful as is Foucault's argument that the subject is constituted by sexuality.[37] The Martin and Mohanty essay is particularly
concerned with Minnie Bruce Pratt's account of the process of recognizing herself as a subject who is molded by her experience of "home."
Written in 1984, Pratt's "Identity: Skin Blood Heart"[38] serves as a
starting point for Martin and Mohanty's examination of –

the configuration of home, identity, and community; more specifically, in the
power and appeal of "home" as a concept and desire, its occurrence as a
metaphor in feminist writings, and its challenging presence in the rhetoric of
the New Right.[39]

What Martin and Mohanty share with the other scholars who have
written on the home and whose work has been discussed earlier in
this chapter, is their assumption that identity is shaped by the individual's experience of home. But the radical difference of the Martin
and Mohanty text lies in their exploding of the received notions of
"home" and the ambience of safety, security and individualism that
the word has gathered around itself.

Martin and Mohanty accelerate a process that they identify as beginning in Pratt's work, namely, the process of disassembling the notion of
"home." They read Pratt's essay as "constructed on the tension
between two specific modalities: being home and not being home."[40]

"Being home" refers to the place where one lives within familiar, safe, protected boundaries; "not being home" is a matter of realizing that home was an
illusion of coherence and safety based on the exclusion of specific histories of
oppression and resistance, the repression of differences even within oneself.[41]

Thus, to rephrase Robert Frost and David Sopher, home is neither
where they have to take you in nor where they want to take you in,

but rather the place where one is *in* because an Other(s) is kept out. Both the essays work at uncovering the violence, terror and difference that is repressed in everyday securing of a home. By locating herself outside the protective environs of southern, white, middle-class ideologies that she grew up in, and by trying to establish a home with her Jewish lover in a black, inner-city neighborhood, Minnie Pratt attempts to rethink "home" and in the process reformulate "community," for those for whom such privileges *are* givens.

What the work of Pratt, Mohanty and Martin does in the process of interrogating the conventional notions of home and community, is to interrogate the notion of "identity" itself – even those identities that are based on progressive political alliances. Pratt's careful articulation of why her associations with NOW, as well as her desire for a safe space for lesbians, were *limited by definition* is central to her thesis that those who have power and privilege have to lose the self constructed by such privilege in order to gain admittance to a world community. Pratt works her way to this stance by walking her reader through the many locations that she has entered, occupied, felt at home in and then rejected. Finding herself "homesick with nowhere to go," Pratt asks: "What is it exactly that we are afraid to lose?" What is to be lost is safety, protection, and the self that is constructed through these privileges. Pratt writes:

When we discover truths about our home culture, we may fear we are losing our self: our self-respect, our self-importance...we may fear that we will lose the people who are our family, our kin, be rejected by "our own kind"...we can go "too far."[42]

In her sophisticated analysis of "home" for those who have been granted the privilege, Pratt's text makes us question the entire project of subjecthood and feeling at home. Part of Pratt's intention seems to be to leave her essay "open-ended" and her choice of rhetorical style allows her to do so: faced with the rigor of operating from an unsettled self-identity/home, she ends her essay with "a dream...in waking life" of reconciliation with all those from whom she has been kept separate. Meanwhile she continues "to struggle with myself and the world I was born in." Home remains a desirable place. And yet, Pratt's advocation of struggle and of embracing the unfamiliar is the absolute antithesis of what has (and continues to be) known as "home" – the place of comfort and familiarity.[43] Pratt's essay demonstrates that home can no longer be as we know it.

Pratt's autobiographical essay is crucial to Caren Kaplan's articulation of a new "feminist poetics" that is based on the first world feminist critic's willingness to leave home in order to feel difference, displacement and "deterritorialization" more keenly.[44] In "Deterritorializations: The Rewriting of Home and Exile in Western Feminist Discourse," (1987) Kaplan uses Gilles Deleuze and Felix Guattari's construction of "Minor Literature," Pratt's essay, and Michelle Cliff's *Claiming an Identity They Taught Me to Despise* to elaborate on the processes by which western feminism can learn to practice the revolutionary art of "becoming minor."[45] "Becoming minor" or "reterritorialization without imperialism" requires that first-world critics "dare to let go of their respective representations and systems of meaning, their identity politics and theoretical homes."[46] For the first-world feminist critic, Kaplan insists, "the challenge at this particular time is to develop a discourse that responds to the power relations of the world system, that is, to examine her location in the dynamics of center and margins."[47] In a reflective passage Kaplan herself voices the cautionary statements that need to be made alongside such advocation of what elsewhere in her essay is dubbed "nomadism":

When first world critics advocate a process of "becoming minor" it is necessary to ask: where are we located in this movement of language and literature? What do we stand to gain? Do we have freedom of movement and where does this freedom come from? For example, I would have to pay attention to whether or not it is possible for me to *choose* deterritorialization or whether deterritorialization has chosen me. If I choose deterritorialization, I go into literary/linguistic exile with all my cultural baggage intact. If deterritorialization has chosen me – that is, if I have been cast out of home and language without forethought or permission, then my point of view will be more complicated...My caution is against a kind of theoretical tourism on the part of the first world critic, where the margin becomes a linguistic or a critical vacation, a new poetics of the exotic. One can also read Deleuze and Guattari's resistance to this romantic trope in their refusal to recognize a point of origin. Theirs is a poetics of travel where there is no return ticket and we all meet, therefore, en train.[48]

Several points need to be made here. First, cultural baggage is also carried by those whom "deterritorialization has chosen." There are no wanderers, however impoverished, however sudden their eviction, who are cast out empty-handed or empty-headed.[49] What is commendable is Kaplan's effort to devise a common agenda for all feminists regardless of their (race, class, geographic) location. She writes: "Exploring all the differences, keeping identities distinct, is the only way we can keep power differentials from masquerading as universals.

We will have different histories, but we will often have similar struggles."[50] What remains murky is how this new feminist poetics will proceed from poetics to making "the connections necessary to change prevailing power relations"?[51] Kaplan cautions against textual tourism and/or simple appropriation of the strategies of those who are already "minor." And yet this essay that begins with citations from Chela Sandoval's writing, followed by insights drawn from Gloria Anzaldua and Minnie Pratt finally ends with Michelle Cliff's discoveries about herself in *Claiming an Identity*. Cliff writes of a garden that is a "private open space."[52] Kaplan sees here a successful move to reterritorialization via writing. Hence she declares Cliff's garden:

a new terrain, a new location, in feminist poetics. Not a room of one's own, not a fully public or collective self, not a domestic realm – it is a space in the imagination which allows for the inside, the outside, and the liminal elements in between. Not a romanticized pastoral nor a modernist urban utopia – Cliff's garden is the space where writing occurs without loss or separation.[53]

The central question that needs addressing is whether "a space in the imagination" that allows writing "without loss or separation" can come into being without a corresponding change in the actual ordering of space? If this corresponding change cannot be brought about by emulation or by theoretical forays into the unfamiliar, then the first world critic has to leave her privilege behind as she searches for alternate ways of "becoming minor."

Kaplan states that "we all meet, en train" after claiming that Deleuze and Guattari's resistance to "a poetics of the exotic" is ensured by their "refusal to recognize a point of origin." I would argue that Kaplan's article is marked by a similar refusal to recognize points of arrival. And that this refusal, rather than serve as resistance to textual tourism reveals a desire to avoid or suspend the first-world critic's investment in homes of privilege and power rather than to relinquish them altogether. Where does this train stop? When Kaplan advocates "nomadism," she is suggesting that the train never stops. Kaplan does not indicate how this literary train ride between equals will be matched by corresponding reordering of power and privilege in everyday life. Yet if the train did stop would it bring the first-world critic back home? Kaplan would argue that it would not and cannot... at least not for practitioners of the new feminist poetics, because home would be different. It would be a "private open space."

Perhaps Kaplan's "en train" could be understood as a variation of what Chandra Mohanty has called a "temporality of struggle." In

"Feminist Encounters: Locating the Politics of Experience" (1992)
Mohanty presents the temporality of struggle as that "which disrupts
and challenges the logics of linearity, development and progress which
are the hallmarks of European modernity."⁵⁴ Mohanty elaborates:
"[i]t suggests an insistent, simultaneous, non-synchronous process
characterized by multiple locations, rather than a search for origins
and endings which, as Adrienne Rich says, 'seems a way of stopping
time in its tracks'" (p. 87). Read in the light of this theorizing by
Mohanty, it would seem that "points of arrival" are to be indefinitely
deferred as we engage in a politics of process and movement.

In a 1988 essay titled "Choosing the Margin as a Space of Radical
Openness" bell hooks suggests that the *diverse pleasures* of oppositional
political struggle "can be experienced, enjoyed even, because one
transgresses, moves 'out of one's place.' For many of us that movement requires the pushing against oppressive boundaries set by race,
sex and class domination. Initially then it is a defiant political gesture.
Moving, we confront the reality of choice and location."⁵⁵ Certainly,
Pratt's essay as well as the essay by Kaplan can be read within this
rubric... they are self-consciously transgressive as the subject chooses
to relocate herself. bell hooks presents the issue as a matter of *choosing*
to position ourselves either "on the side of the colonizing mentality"
or to "continue to stand in political resistance with the oppressed,
ready to offer our ways of seeing and theorizing, of making culture
towards that revolutionary effort which seeks to create space where
there is unlimited access to the pleasure and power of knowing, where
transformation is possible. This choice is crucial" (p. 15). Kaplan's
cautions must be reiterated here as a necessary corrective to hooks'
proposition on choice. Indeed Kaplan's deterritorialization can be
read as a parallel to bell hooks' transgressive moving "out of one's
place." But are the subjects addressed in the two articles identical?

Kaplan's "we" is primarily "the first-world critic" who wants to
"become minor" and hook's "we" constitutes those who are hailed by
her definition of the politics of location: "those of us who would participate in the formation of counter-hegemonic cultural practice to
identify the spaces where we begin the process of revision" (p. 15). In
the final pages of *Feminism and Geography*, Gillian Rose categorizes
much of the writing discussed here under the suggestive notion of
"the politics of paradoxical space." The paradox comes from articulations of geography and geometry that do not come "naturally" to the
writers and yet create "not so much a space of resistance as an

entirely different geometry through which we can think power, knowledge, space and identity in critical and, hopefully, liberatory ways."[56]
Clearly there is some overlap in the subject addressed in all these
feminist texts that attempt to theorize the need to move beyond one's
home into less safe, less comfortable spaces. And yet the differences
are what keeps any strategy from being perfectly viable for all subjects
at all times. What is called for then, is a coalition politics across difference of the kind advocated by Bernice Johnson Reagon in her
speech at the West Coast Women's Music Festival 1981 at Yosemite
National Forest in California.[57]

Reagon pares down the concept of home until it is no more than a
"barred room" – a place which is nurturing, nationalistic and open
exclusively to people like oneself. It is against this notion of home,
that Reagon advocates coalition. Her words were initially directed to
participants in a women's music festival:

We've pretty much come to the end of time when you can have a space that
is "yours only" – just for people you want to be there. Even when we have
our "women-only" festivals, there is no such thing...There is no hiding place.
There is nowhere you can go and only be with people who are like you. It's
over. Give it up. (p. 357)

Coalition work, Reagon stresses, is precisely the location that is not
home. To coalesce is to open the barred room to persons from different locations with different agendas, to be willing to risk losing one's
secure place. Reagon writes of the effects of such open-house events:

The first thing that happens is that the room don't feel like the room anymore. [Laughter] And it ain't home no more. It is not a womb no more.
And you can't feel comfortable no more...Inside the womb you generally are
very soft and unshelled. You have no covering. And you have no ability to
handle what happens if you start to let folks in who are not like you. (p. 359)

While Reagon's essay was intended as a critique of the organized
women's movement (and its perpetuation of "a myth that there is
some common experience that comes from just cause you're women,"
p. 360), its reverberations continue to be felt on a variety of political
projects that construct exclusive "homes" for its participants. Amongst
these political projects the one which is central to *this* book is the production of literary "homes" as well as the theoretical "homes" constructed by literary and cultural criticism. How does coalition building
function in the context of literary readings? How do we step out of literature's barred rooms?

Feminist readers have insisted on noting the ideological investments of both literature and literary criticism. As such feminists have always been deconstructive. The project of much feminist literary criticism has been to invade barred rooms and to create discomfort in masculine strongholds. Yet a corollary to such activism has been an insistence on "a room of one's own" – constructed not so much by certain influential feminist theorists or literary figures but by a few, seemingly inviolable, feminist *cult texts*. Counter readings that question the feminist narrative woven around texts like *Jane Eyre*, *The Yellow Wallpaper*, *A Room of One's Own*, or *Their Eyes Were Watching God* force discomforting but productive coalitions between feminism and other issues in cultural politics. Gender issues are forced to share the space they exclusively occupy in a strictly feminist reading with issues such as (homo)sexuality, race, class, and nationality. A brilliant example of such a coalition reading is provided by Susan S. Lanser's 1989 essay on *The Yellow Wallpaper* which radically challenged the definitive, *feminist* interpretation of this story of a young woman's descent into insanity.[58] After Lanser's rereading, this novella can no longer generate the angry, even exhilarating exposure of patriarchal oppression on the basis of which a certain feminism is learned and a corresponding feminist theory is formulated. Lanser claims "[a]lthough– or because – we have read 'The Yellow Wallpaper' over and over, we may have stopped short, and our readings, like the narrator's, may have reduced the text's complexity to what we need most: our own image reflected back to us." Part of this textual complexity that the narrator represses and what the feminist commentators have, according to Lanser, also refused to acknowledge is the racial and national ideology that would be immediately conjured up by the color yellow in the period when the story was written. Lanser writes:

If we locate Gilman's story within "the psychic geography" of Anglo-America at the turn of the century, we locate it in a culture obsessively preoccupied with race as the foundation of character, a culture desperate to maintain Aryan superiority in the face of massive immigrations from Southern and Eastern Europe, a culture openly anti-Semitic, anti-Asian, anti-Catholic, and Jim Crow...In California, where Gilman lived while writing "The Yellow Wallpaper," mass anxiety about the "Yellow Peril" had already yielded such legislation as the Chinese Exclusion Act of 1882. (p. 425)

Read within this "discourse of racial anxiety," the feminist theorizing generated by this story needs drastic revision. The yellow woman behind the wallpaper who so distresses, attracts and repulses the white narrator is the Other in a nationalist discourse. How then do we read the feminism inscribed by this text? The questions Lanser poses in her article are absolutely crucial:

Is the wallpaper, then, the political unconscious of a culture in which an Aryan woman's madness, desire, and anger, repressed by the imperatives of "reason," "duty" (p. 14) and "proper self-control" (p. 11), are projected onto a "yellow" woman who is, however, also the feared alien?....Might we explain the narrator's pervasive horror of a yellow color and smell that threaten to take over the "ancestral halls," "stain[ing] everything it touched" as the British-American fear of a takeover by aliens? (p. 429)

Lanser's reading of color politics in Gilman forces an acknowledgment of the existence of (in the course of its disruption and then demolition) a certain "barred room." In doing so through *The Yellow Wallpaper*, she compels us to rethink home and privilege as more than events in a universal, patriarchal time and space. Women, Bernice Reagon tells us, "have been organized to have our primary cultural signals come from some other factors than that we are women" (p. 361). "Women people" as she terms it have to coalesce in order to cross "our first people boundaries – Black, White, Indian, etc." (p. 361). Each of us, then, is a mini coalition in ourselves – yoking together sexuality, race, gender, class, and countless other ideologies – working toward locations where *all of me* could feel at home for the time being.

What, then, are we left with? Perhaps, a daily resisting of the safety proffered by safe places. Perhaps Mohanty's "temporality of struggle" and Rose's "paradoxical space." A continual stepping out of or transgressing of boundaries and a redrawing of private and public spaces as well as of global divides. A recognition of privilege when we have it and a recognition of those who do not have homes or communities that we are familiar enough with to recognize. One caution is essential here. Much depends on who comprises the "we" that I address at the beginning of this paragraph. Can this "we" include or speak for (and to) those persons for whom homes, homelands or even nationhood are still unrealized desires? Is it feasible then, beginning from Pratt's stance, to work toward a unilateral rejection of safe-homes?[59]

Perhaps it is time we examined varying notions of home to see what can be recycled in less oppressive, less exclusionary ways. In the next chapter, I examine an instance in which women claim national subject status for themselves on the basis of having successfully set up house in alien territory. In the following study of the impact on English women of successful home management in the late nineteenth and early twentieth century, I reconsider the issues raised in this chapter: namely, the place of the home in nation and empire, the confluence of the self and the home, feminist aspirations and domesticity, as well as the direct link between attaining subjecthood and the denial of the same to Others.

CHAPTER 2

The authoritative Englishwoman:
setting up home and self in the colonies

Don't return male stares...it is considered a come-on. Turning away haughtily and draping your shawl over your head will have the desired effect...if you get the uncomfortable feeling that he's encroaching on your space, chances are he is. A firm request to keep away – use your best memsahib tone – may help.

Advice to western women tourists,
India: a travel survival kit, 1990

Whatever their differences, women shared the experience of having been denied access to an authoritative self as women.

Elizabeth Fox-Genovese

In juxtaposing the above two quotations, my intention is to draw attention to the codes of authorization that are available to *some* women in *some* situations.[1] The self as "memsahib" is a role that is readily available to white women tourists today as it was to white women colonists yesterday. The two citations also disclose the marks of ruling ideologies on the social constructions of gender: for the English woman in the empire, colonialism provided an "authoritative self" whose vestiges can be traced even in a "travel tip" from the 1990s. What are the implications of these historical continuities?

In "Deterritorializations: The Rewriting of Home and Exile in Western Feminist Discourse," Caren Kaplan articulates the recent emphasis on the politics of location in some first world feminisms.[2] She works within and against the constructs of Deleuze and Guattari's theory of "deterritorialization," (which she interprets as the "moment of alienation and exile in language and literature") in order to describe "a new terrain, a new location, in feminist politics."[3] This deterritorialization or "becoming minor" requires that:

We must leave home, as it were, since our homes are often the sites of racism, sexism, and other damaging social practices. Where we come to locate ourselves in terms of our specific histories and differences must be a place with room for what can be salvaged from the past and what can be made new.[4]

35

As western feminists begin to formulate the ways in which leaving home could enhance their understanding of global links, in the attempt to practice "not imperialism but nomadism" (Kaplan's phrase), it would be profitable to turn to historic instances when western women have actually left home and set up house in alien territory and grappled with manipulating an alien language. English women in the British empire in the late nineteenth and early twentieth century serve as a useful and recent example of such excursions outside the home. Of course this is not a randomly chosen example. Rather, I will try to demonstrate that the sojourn of the "Englishwoman" (that unhyphenated subject equal to the "Englishman") in the empire, writes a crucial chapter in the history of the formations that we today know as western feminism. Given this earlier, empowering "travel" away from home in western women's history, one which was *also* represented by the women involved as "alienation and exile," the call for "nomadism" and other such counter-travel brings to the surface the very structures of both imperialism and/or tourism that are so deeply entrenched in western gestures of leaving home. The history of race and gender in the west make problematic any contemporary excursions into Other territories whose echoes of earlier similar gestures are wished away. In this context, Kaplan's suggestion that we use "what can be salvaged from the past" necessitates a return to this period in the past of western feminism.

This chapter will argue that the colonial occupation of the Indian sub-continent[5] established one of the primary arenas in which English women first achieved the kind of authoritative self associated with the modern female subject. It is in the colonies that nineteenth and early twentieth century English women become "the full individual" that Fox-Genovese sees as the desired goal of feminism in capitalist societies.[6] This authoritative self was defined against a racial Other (Indian women) in encounters that were located in space that was paradoxically domestic as well as public: the English home in the colonies.

Examining several popular novels and home management guides written by and about English women in the Indian empire, this chapter assesses the impact of imperialism on issues pertinent to English women's emancipation in this period. In these texts, the British empire was represented as an arena in which English women had hard tasks to perform and where the quality of that performance could buttress or jeopardize the imperial project. There was an assumption that the successful running of the empire required the womanly skills of household management. Most importantly, the imperial occupation of India allowed for the prescription of the domestic as the most fulfilling arena in which a modern female subject could operate. Hence, while in England in this period, this prescription was being vociferously challenged by some, the colonies provided a contemporary situation in which housework and home management were valuable national contributions. Clearly, the analysis in this chapter is not meant to account for *all* English and other European women in the Indian empire – many of these women were not mistresses of households ruling alongside the male British colonialist but worked as teachers, missionaries, maids and governesses, and as such were differently positioned in colonial society. However, the home management guides and novels examined in this chapter construct and address a generic English woman in the Empire who is imagined as a practicing memsahib or a young woman who has the potential and opportunity to be one. Despite differences of class and/or regional origin in Britain, differences in marital status and age, all British women were invited by these and other imperial texts to recognize themselves as English.[7] Also to be noted is the fact that the Indian women encountered in these English women's texts belong to certain specific communities, but are invariably presented as typical, generic Indian women.[8]

In *Desire and Domestic Fiction*, a study of novels and conduct books from eighteenth-century England, Nancy Armstrong presents us with a powerful argument:

such writing as the conduct books helped to generate the belief that there was such a thing as a middle class with clearly established affiliations before it actually existed. If there is any truth in this, then it is also reasonable to claim that the modern individual was first and foremost a female.[9]

Reading similar English conduct books and novels written in the Indian empire, about a century later, I would like to argue that the modern *politically authoritative* Englishwoman was made in the colonies: she was first and foremost an imperialist.

IMPERIALISM AND THE AUTHORITATIVE ENGLISHWOMAN

Our understanding of the status of female political and personal authority in this period is largely based on recent studies on the women's suffrage movement. Writing on the emergence of this movement in England, Ellen DuBois explains that since the "independent, virtuous citizen was entirely male in conception," ... "the labor of women, like that of servants, [was] obscured by (though necessary to) the appearance of men's independence."¹⁰ As a result, women's political contributions were thought to be indirectly but adequately represented through their husbands, fathers or brothers. The demand for women's direct political participation as articulated by the suffragettes was firmly resisted and ridiculed.

In "Imperialism and Motherhood" Anna Davin notes that the word "citizen," in the days when women did not vote, referred exclusively to men.¹¹ Women's only avenue for patriotic contributions to the well-being of the nation and empire was via motherhood. The quality of motherhood was seen as directly affecting the quality of the "future citizens" (read "male children") – which in turn determined the vigor of the imperial race. Davin quotes a passage from the December 1903 issue of the *Journal of Obstetrics and Gynaecology of the British Empire* which advocates teaching the skills of mothering to women:

by instruction leading to the improvement of the individual we shall aid in preserving women for their supreme purpose, the procreation and preservation of the race, and at the same time promote that race to a better standard, mentally and physically.¹²

Hence the only recognizable female *national* subject position in England at the time was that of "mother." The establishment of English homes in the colonies increased the avenues through which English women could directly contribute to the dominant national ideologies as well as earn recognition for their labor. And such contributions were rarely in the conventional category of "motherhood." In fact, most English mothers in the colonies sent their children back to England for schooling while themselves remaining behind with their husbands. Hence, while motherhood was deemed the most important and fulfilling role for women in England, English women imperialists stoically bore their separation from their children and earned praise for a maternal stance that was, in other circumstances, greeted with the highest censure.

In *"Am I that Name?": Feminism and the Category of "Women" in History*, Denise Riley notes that it is the classification according to gender, "and here the critical gender is female," that keeps "women" from becoming "human" – from achieving the status of "truly sexually democratic humanism".¹³ It is significant that most feminist commentary on European women in the nineteenth and early twentieth centuries does not consider the impact of imperialism on issues of authoritative selfhood and the move from "woman" to "human".¹⁴ One needs to consider what constitutes "authority" in these instances as well as who this lack of authority is measured against.[15] For, as Gayatri Spivak astutely states in "Three Women's Texts and a Critique of Imperialism":

what is at stake, for feminist individualism in the age of imperialism, is precisely the makings of human beings, the constitution and 'interpellation' of the subject not only as individual but as "individualist."...As the female individualist, not-quite/not-male, articulates herself in shifting relationship to what is at stake, the "native female" as such (*within* discourse, *as* a signified) is excluded from any share in this emerging norm.[16]

Spivak's account of female individualism makes imperialism a central feature of the making of the white female subject in nineteenth-century texts. Colonial occupation allowed for the continued evolution of this domestic female subject even as it seemed to disrupt the ideological and material requirements for domesticity. With the establishment of the English home outside England, there was a physical repositioning of the hitherto private into what had been considered the most public of realms – the British empire. The domestic, on which the effects of capital had been naturalized and neutralized over the decades of industrial and imperial expansion, was now being reconstituted outside England. This process of reconstitution, which began with the advent of imperial women to the colonies, resulted in a dramatic refiguration of England as home-country and of women as (national) subjects.[17] Consider the epigraph which sets the tenor of Maud Diver's study, *The Englishwoman in India* (1909):

What would India be without England, and what would the British Empire be without Englishwomen? To these women are due gratitude not only of their country but of the civilized world. Fearlessly the woman of British birth looks in the eye of danger. Faithfully and with willing sacrifice she upholds the standard of the King-Emperor – the standard of culture and of service to humanity.[18]

The imperial enterprise gives "of British birth" its significance in this instance. Of course the terms "faithful," "willing sacrifice," "culture" and "service" were commonly used in descriptions of women's contribution, but only in the context of the domestic world. The colonies offered a legitimate "public domesticity" to late Victorian and early twentieth-century English women that required the most imaginative skills of the home-maker and yet held out the promise of inclusion in (masculine) public life.

Writing on the construction of the category "woman" in this period in England in *Am I That Name? Feminism and the Category of "Women" in History*, Denise Riley coins the term the "social sphere" in order to

refer to a feminized area of operation which extended even into public space but which was in opposition to the "political" (masculine)
sphere. Working within the "social" realm, women "became both
agents and objects of reform in unprecedented ways" but these divisions also kept "women's issues" out of politics.[19] The "social" sphere
"provided the chances for some women to enter upon the work of
restoring other, more damaged, women to a newly conceived sphere
of grace."[20] Spivak extends this analysis by considering the impact of
such restoration on the female colonial subject. Working with Bronte's
Jane Eyre she asserts that the novel can be read as "an allegory of the
general epistemic violence of imperialism, the construction of a self-
immolating colonial subject for the glorification of the social mission
of the colonizer."[21] Colonialism extended the scope of the "social"
and allowed women to advocate and practice social reform quite
untouched by any acknowledgment of the violence of imperialism.
Hence, as later sections of this chapter will demonstrate, the glorification of the English woman as a "full individual" was daily re-estab-
lished by the encounters with Indian women who could then be
represented as such "self-immolating" female colonial subjects.

Ellen DuBois claims that the significance of the women's suffrage
movement rested precisely on the "fact that it bypassed women's
oppression within the family, or private sphere, and demanded instead
her admission to citizenship, and through it admission to the public
arena."[22] Elsewhere she argues that "suffragette militancy literally took
women out of the parlour and into the streets."[23] This bypassing of
the private sphere, according to DuBois, made the movement a prime
target for repression and ridicule. In contrast, the colonial space and its
discourses offered a public role to the white woman that was unmistakably public and yet, palatable to a patriarchal, imperial society in ways
that the demands of the "new woman" and suffragist were not. Novels
and home-management guidebooks written in the late nineteenth and
early twentieth century, by authors such as Maud Diver, Flora Steel
and Alice Perrin created a new and self-proclaimedly "modern" female
figure: the energetic, domestic, benevolent partner in the imperial
mission. In the course of these texts, these female colonizers fare much
better than the "New Woman" whose sense of self is informed by the
feminist notions in circulation in contemporary Europe and America.

In the colonies, the circumstances in which the ceremonies of public
and private were played out were vastly different from those in the
home-country. The distinctions between public and private, while they

were maintained, repeatedly broke down and had constantly to be redrawn. Hence, there was little escaping the artificiality of the separation of public and private spheres. Consider briefly the setting up of households in camps, when military and/or administrative work at borders required that officers live at the very outposts of empire for years on end. At camp, flimsy partitions were used to create the necessary aura of privacy, of separation between home and work. There was also the popular view that all of one's stay in India was an extended camping trip (undertaken for sport or military purposes or both!) In their letters, diaries and conduct books, housewives applauded themselves for their own and their servants' inventiveness in producing a semblance of domestic order out of the most meager resources.

Conventionally, the strongest link that has been made between English women and British imperialism is their status as consumers of the material benefits of this enterprise. Most scholars (feminist and otherwise) agree that there were, in the late nineteenth and early twentieth-century England, essentially two very different spheres within which the two genders operated – the public, masculine sphere of work and the private, domestic, female sphere.[24] Fox-Genovese writes that within capitalist systems the distinctions between production and reproduction, between subsistence and market, between public and private, acquire an increased hegemony because so many political and economic institutions enforce these distinctions.[25] Along with these distinctions came the increasingly rigid association of women with the private sphere so that eventually it was understood that this aspect of life was (and should be) outside of politics.

Housework done by housewives in this period was not classified as labor – it was non-productive because it did not command a wage. Fox-Genovese writes that "for women, their relative exclusion from [the] process of commodification went hand-in-hand with their exclusion from full individualism."[26] The English woman in the Indian empire however, was not merely decorating house and self but managing "base-camp." In this context, the work done by English women even when it was what had hitherto been defined as "house-keeping," is recognized as valuable labor. Hence, one could argue that given the acknowledgment of their labor contributions to the imperial cause, the English women in the colonies were further along the route to "full individualism" than women back home – even those struggling to win the right to vote. The novels and home management books that the imperial enterprise engendered were deeply concerned with the capac-

ity of the English woman to use and abuse this opportunity to function
as contributing national subjects alongside the English man.

MAKING THE MEMSAHIB

For these unrecorded heroines are a nation without a history. "Wives," *The
Englishwoman in India*

From about the mid nineteenth century there was a vast amount of literature, fictional and otherwise, written on English life in the Indian sub-
continent. A great number of these texts were written by English women,
who had spent varying amounts of time in the colony themselves. Their
audience was their fellow imperialists of both genders, at "Home" and in
the empire. The avowed aim of many of these "lady romancers," as
Benita Parry calls them, was to draw attention to the role played by
English women in the imperial endeavor. The novels, and the guidebooks
for English women in India articulate and accentuate the contributions of
women and their work towards the smooth operation of empire.

Analysis of the imperial novel in English as a legitimate literary genre
has appeared at various moments in the twentieth century within the
context of prevailing critical conventions. In 1949 Suzanne Howe published the first book-length analysis of this genre entitled *Novels of
Empire*.[27] This study notes the ways in which the "novel follows the flag"
into India, Indo-China, Africa, Australia and New Zealand. In a list of
thirty writers on "British India," Howe includes six women writers.
Noting that this fiction contains some of "the unhappiest books in the
language," Howe's humorous assessment is that "novels about India
provide more vicarious discomfort than anyone is entitled to."[28] Howe
claims that these novels subject the reader and protagonist to "the vast
boredom, the introspective torment, the 'hot dull vacancy' of Indian
life" before allowing both parties to return to an English setting.[29]
"Nowhere in literature" Howe writes, "is Home spelt with a larger capital letter."[30] In this literature, England is represented as the originary
and ultimate destination of the narrative journey. And needless to say,
whether one is a character in the novel or an implied reader of it, one
needs to be "of British birth" to travel the whole route.

In 1972, Benita Parry's *Delusions and Discoveries* examined how India
was experienced and represented through the "lens of the British imagination" from 1880 to 1930. In considering how writers "reordered their
ideas and perceptions in fiction," Parry writes of the smugness with
which "Anglo-Indians" viewed their position in India.[31] But there is no

direct mention of gender issues or of the general complacency about
the status of English women. Parry sorts out the vast body of this fiction
into four categories. The first category, "romantic novelettes," considers
the work of five women writers, which is followed by "problem novels,"
and then by Kipling and Forster, each of whom occupies a category of
his own.[32] Of the first category, Parry writes:

> The romantic writers, whose novelettes are grouped together because they
> are virtually indistinguishable, reveal themselves rather than India, and are
> principally interesting as symptomatic of Anglo-Indian attitudes. The
> received opinions and automatic responses of the conformist Anglo-Indians
> are naively recorded, as is the neurotic concern with protecting their identity
> from pollution by strange, unwholesome and deviant India. What they did
> not know about India – and they knew very little – these writers guessed,
> and these guesses and half-truths uncover their obsessions and fantasies.
> Drawn from Anglo-Indian mythology and ministering to the community's
> conceit, theirs is both a calculated self-portrait and an unintended confession.
> Many of the lady-romancers' characteristics can equally be applied to Flora
> Anne Steel, but she has been treated separately both because she was so
> earnestly concerned with verisimilitude in her portrayals of India and because
> she had considerably more insight into the Anglo-Indian dilemma...
> Mrs. Steel's India, which is simultaneously clear-sighted and obstinately blind,
> accurate and preposterous, tolerant and self-righteous, suggests the chasm
> between empirical observation and the discernment of subjective truth.[33]

Phrases such as "guesses" and "half-truths," used to castigate the "lady
romancer", suggest that Parry believes that more was available to others
in the discourse than these women, with their implicitly limited talent,
could grasp or express. Why else would Parry call these on average
400 page long novels, "novelettes"? I would argue that the novels written by such women writers as Maud Diver, Alice Perrin and Flora
Steel, do speak a certain truth. These novels do represent the truth
about a specific "Real India" that they helped construct. Their India,
with all its "received opinions and automatic responses," its "obses-
sions and fantasies" was the reality inhabited by the British in India.[34]

"Whiteness" and "Englishness" in the discourse of Empire, and
again especially in its fiction, take on a power that only masculinity
and/or capital could command in the western world at the time. And
this results in a radical re-presentation of the heroines of such fiction
as desirable not just in terms of the literary conventions which require
that she be young and physically attractive, but *because* she is white
and English. Consider the introduction to Honor, the English heroine
of *Captain Desmond V.C.*, published in 1914, by Maud Diver:

In the clear light the girl's beauty took on a new distinctness, a new living charm. The upward-sweeping mass of her hair showed the softness of bronze, save where the sun had burnished it to copper. Breadth of brow, and the strong moulding of her nose and chin, suggested powers rather befitting a man than a woman. But in the eyes and lips the woman triumphed – eyes blue-grey under very straight brows, and lips that even in repose preserved a rebellious tendency to lift at the corners. From her father, and a long line of fighting ancestors, Honor had gotten the large build of a large nature; the notable lift of her head; and the hot blood, coupled with endurance, that stamps the race current coin across the world.[35]

Here and elsewhere in the novel, Honor is described as the optimal genetic flowering of her race. She falls in love with her eugenic equal, Captain Theo Desmond. His wife Evelyn, who is described at the outset as "a mere slip of womanhood," is presented as the epitome of everything a memsahib cannot afford to be (*CD*, p. 15). The plot details the ways in which Honor tries to make a true memsahib out of the flighty Evelyn. In the climax of the novel, Evelyn is shot and killed by "rebel natives" from the hill region that Desmond and his regiment were in the process of "subduing." Honor leaves for England. Desmond, who for some time before Evelyn's death has been in love with Honor, spends a year in mourning and traveling through Europe. He meets Honor in England and they acknowledge their love for each other.

Captain Desmond V.C. illustrates the complex use that is made of the English woman in the machinations of empire. There were two levels at which English women buttressed the empire: the first, which was overtly stressed by the fiction writers, was that of the managers of "base-camp," helpmates and partners in the imperial enterprise. The second level is the more covertly articulated use of the white woman's presence in the colonies as a rationalization for the "necessity" of the violent repression of colonized peoples. Honor, as "player," is the efficient memsahib, and Evelyn is the "pawn" whose death at the hands of the Afridis is used to justify the "punitive expeditions" that Desmond periodically undertakes over the course of the narrative.[36]

In 1917, Maud Diver published *Unconquered: A Romance*, a novel set in contemporary England, touching the same ideological registers as her novels set in India. The novel begins on the eve of the First World War.[37] Sir Mark Stuart Forsyth, a Scottish aristocrat who is the hero of the novel falls in love with the entirely unsuitable Bel Alison. Bel Alison, whose lack of a masculine last name is significant, is a woman of the world: "modern," shallow, sexy, she has been an actress, writer and feminist, among other fleeting vocations. Her devoted companion is the staunch feminist, "Harry," whose lesbianism is represented as a lightly veiled monstrosity.

Mark's mother and mainstay, Helen Forsyth, who is central in the novel, is the gracious, strong woman of (noble) character. Helen dislikes Bel and would rather Mark marry their common friend, the kind and gentle Sheila Melrose, who is also well born and well-bred. When war breaks out, Mark enlists to fight. Helen and Sheila cheer him on in contrast to the pacifist Bel who begs him not to enlist. Mark is declared first lost and then killed in action. However, he returns home after a period of convalescence in a convent in France. Because he is partially paralyzed Bel deserts him. She goes on to become an anti-war/feminist crusader. Sheila's steadfast adoration finally pays off when she gets her man, albeit physically much damaged.

Diver's narrative strategy in these novels is to define the ideal woman via negations: Sheila and Honor are everything that Bel and Evelyn are not. The fact that the men in both these novels make unhappy first choices when it comes to love and marriage is significant. In the course of their relationship with their first choice, the men in both novels see the contrast between the two women and despite owing their allegiance to the less deserving woman, offer it to the other. In *Emma*, Jane Austen writes: "How many a man has committed himself on a short acquaintance, and rued it all the rest of his life!" Diver, however, arranges for fortuitous narrative events that give the hero a second chance at choosing the ideal partner.

Like her novels set in India, Diver's *Unconquered* reads in part like a conduct book that is full of exhortations to "true womanliness" and "true manhood." Diver's characters serve as illustrations of the best and the worst of the two genders. It is interesting to examine her discourse on women and the etiquette of their movements within and between public and/or private space. Much emphasis is placed on the fact that Bel has no home and no parents. Her past is indeterminate and somehow more eventful than is deemed proper; she has lived in many homes with relatives, with friends, with "Harry" (whose love for her is "like a man's") and gossip is that she had even gone away with a married man for a weekend. She has lived abroad in indeterminate circumstances – in America, in India, on the continent; and much like the stereotypical rake, has seduced hapless lovers, leaving behind her several broken hearts.

Helen Forsyth, the hero's mother, is the female character most valorized by the text. Helen translates poetry but her main passion is the

revival of English arts and crafts through a revival of "home industries." Toward this purpose she has set up, on her estate, a crafts
colony which is peopled by local handicraft producers. Their supervision is what occupies her time when she isn't entertaining. One needs
to read Diver's novels set in India to appreciate how this portrait of
the cultured, benevolent lady of the manor is transferred to the
Indian setting *and democratized* in the sense that it is made available to
a wider class of English women in the colony. In India, one need not
be an aristocrat or be married to one, nor have an estate − a husband
with an official post, servants and a modest compound around one's
house are the only prerequisites for playing the grand lady.

Helen Forsyth's home is her arena of fulfillment as a woman and
as a nationally responsible citizen. Early in the text, we are introduced to her character through a tour of her home:

Yet, for all her activities and far-reaching aims, her true life had always been
centred in her home...the world's most strenuous workers found in her home
atmosphere, a refreshment and inspiration worth some sacrifice of activity to
preserve in an age of wholesale experiment in life, and art and religion. They
might rate her for living in a backwater; but, as their intimacy grew, they
realised that she was more vitally in touch than themselves with the world's
greater issues; that her uneventful days were rich in experience, informed by
a central purpose and an unshaken faith in certain abiding truths...
the room [her "sanctuary"] was...a friendly, intimate room, set in the bastioned
tower that dated from feudal times. But arrow-slits had long given place to
unlimited light and air; and, like all rooms that are loved and genuinely lived in,
it was quick with the personality of one who imparted something of herself to
the very chair she used and the books and pictures on her walls. These last
were few and individual; but of her books there was no end. (*UR*, pp. 39–40)

Helen Forsyth's "true life" is centered well within her (feudal, yet
refinished with "unlimited light and air") ancestral home. Here Diver
maintains that an intellectually and socially active woman whose life
is centered around her home occupies a vantage point from which
she can be "vitally in touch...with the world's greater issues." This
paean to domesticity on a grand scale is greatly enhanced when it is
located in the colonies. Here, the alien nature of the terrain makes it
a challenge for the most uninspired or resisting homemakers.

In *Unconquered*, when the war starts, the women characters have the
option of playing a visible public role. The contours of this role are
always defined by a focus on serving as supports to their men in
wartime. Hence the narrative applauds Helen and Sheila's efforts in
running an ambulance service for the injured in Boulogne, but Bel's

bitterness about the human losses of war and her anti-war public speaking engagements are met with authorial ridicule.[38] Diver's novels suggest that everyday events in the lives of English women living in India call for Helen Forsyth's and Sheila Melrose's *wartime* capacity for managing homes, house-guests and servants as adroitly as they nurse dying soldiers on the battlefront, ride, drive, shoot and give and take orders. When Desmond is wounded in a border skirmish in *Captain Desmond V.C.*, his wife Evelyn (like the beautiful Bel in *Unconquered*) cannot bring herself to accept the man's disfigurement. Honor is given the chief responsibility in nursing Desmond and she brings him back from the brink of death. And Evelyn displays her complete inadequacy as a good memsahib when she attempts to leave Desmond in his doctor's care and go to Muree, a hill-station, until Desmond is well enough to join her.[39] Goodness in a woman or a man in this discourse is measured by how well they bear up to the circumstances they find themselves in. "Circumstance," Diver writes elsewhere, "is, after all, the supreme test of character, and India tests a woman's character to the utmost."[40] The parallels between *Unconquered* and *Captain Desmond V.C.* illustrate the argument that the kind of "rising to the occasion" that war calls for in English women in England is similar to the *everyday* demeanor expected from the English woman in the Indian colony. Hence Diver draws our attention to Sheila's quiet ability to

face this inferno of pain and death and mental anguish without a sense of bitterness or rebellion [which] was more of an asset than she knew. It was, in fact, the keystone of her character, the secret of her spiritual poise. (*UR*, pp. 189–90)

It is consistent with the differences between Honor/Sheila and Evelyn/Bel that the women who have authorial approval see men's work of quelling enemies of the empire and nation as crucial, whereas both Evelyn and Bel keep urging their respective male partners to leave off fighting. Like Sheila in *Unconquered*, Honor expects Desmond to continue with the Frontier regiment even after he is wounded in a skirmish. To restrain men from the manly work of empire and nation is to hamper them and in this discourse only "the native" lacks restraint. Consider the following exchange between Desmond and Evelyn where he explains to her that a "punitive expedition" against the Afridis is imminent and necessary:

"No, no, Ladybird – you're going to be plucky and stand up to this like a soldier's wife, for my sake. The Frontier's been abnormally quiet these many months. It will do us all good to have a taste of real work for a change."
"Do you mean...will there be much...fighting?"

"Well – The Afridis don't take a blow sitting down. We have to burn their crops you see; blow up their towers; enforce heavy fines, and generally knock it into their heads that they can't defy the Indian Government with impunity. Yes; it means fighting – severe or otherwise, according to their pleasure."

"Pleasure! – It sounds simply horrible; and you – I believe you're *glad* to go!"

"Well, my dear, what else would you have? Not because I'm murderously inclined," he added smilingly. "Every soldier worth his salt, is glad of a chance to do the work he's paid for. But that's one of the things I shall never teach you to understand!" (*CD*, pp. 217–18)

This passage is among the many that mark Evelyn's wifely inadequacies. That no irony is intended in Desmond's account of burning the "enemy's" crops, or in his definition of "a taste of real work" is clear from one notable plot detail: it is at this point in the novel that Honor, who has been witness to the above exchange between husband and wife, discovers that she is in love with Desmond.

It is the inroads that Desmond's work makes into her private sphere that Evelyn most resents. The time and space marked home, which she expects to share exclusively with her husband, are invaded by his colleagues' use of their home as an extension of the work place and of work hours. In the following exchange between Evelyn and Honor which takes place early in the novel, the confidence with which Honor states her opinions displays how attune she is with the required deportment of English women and men wherever on the Empire they may be stationed.

Mrs. Desmond flung out her hands with a pretty, characteristic gesture... "I thought India was a lovely place *till* I came here. Theo warned me... But that didn't seem to matter, so long as I had him. Only I am so seldom *able* to have him. The regiment swamps *everything*. The men are always in uniform, and always at it: and the aggravating part is that they actually like that better than anything."

Honor laid her hand over the one that rested on her knee. She saw both sides of the picture with equal vividness.

"What a dire calamity!" she said gently. "I am afraid that on the frontier, if a man is keen, his wife is bound to stand second: and if only she will accept the fact, it must surely be happier for both in the long run."

Mrs. Desmond looked up at her with pathetic eyes. "But I don't *want* to accept the fact. I want to be first always; and I ought to be...But Theo seems to be the private property of half the regiment! There's his chief friend Major Wyndham, and the Boy, his subaltern, he thinks the world of them; and they seem to live in the house. Then there's a tiresome old ressaldar always coming over to do Persian with him..." (*CD*, pp. 18–19)

Here, it is worthwhile to note the proximity of Honor's position to the descriptions of hostessing responsibilities in Maud Diver's non-fictional text, *The Englishwoman in India*. In a chapter titled "Hostess and Housekeeper," Diver writes "Every Anglo-Indian wife is of necessity a hostess also in her own degree...– whatever her natural inclination, she must needs accept the fact that her house, and all that therein is, belongs in a large measure, to her neighbour also" (*EI*, pp. 48-9). Honor's long stay with the Desmonds is not interpreted by Evelyn as a similar intrusion. Rather, Honor's visit seems to reaffirm the existence of the codes of a public/private split where staying with a married women lends respectability to a single woman's sojourn abroad.

The contrast between Honor and Evelyn could be rewritten as a list of "dos and don'ts" for potential memsahibs.[41] It is no surprise that some of the best known colonial decorum and home-management guidebooks were written by English women who had already written several novels. Of these, the most popular one was written by Flora Anne Steel (who was also a prolific writer of fiction) and Grace Gardiner. Entitled *The Complete Indian Housekeeper and Cook* with a lengthy subtitle: "giving the duties of mistress and servants, the general management of the house and practical recipes for cooking in all its branches," this book's popularity can be gauged by the fact that it was revised and reprinted more than a dozen times between 1888 and 1917.[42] In the introductory chapter to this guide, the authors write:

Here [in India], as there [in England] the end and object is not merely personal comfort, but the formation of a home – that unit of civilization where father and children, master and servant, employer and employed, can learn their several duties. When all is said and done also, herein lies the natural outlet for most of the talents peculiar to women. It is the fashion nowadays to undervalue the art of making a home; to deem it simplicity and easiness itself. But this is a mistake, for the proper administration of even a small household needs both brain and heart. (*CIH*, p. 7)

Hence, setting up home in the Empire, because of the many challenges involved, once again made the "art of making a home," an occupation worthy of a woman with "brain and heart." Furthermore, in the empire, the need for constant creation of such "civilization" was urgently felt. Novel after novel suggests that it is the daily construction of the home-country as the location of the colonizer's racial and moral identity and as the legitimization of the colonizer's national subjecthood that made possible the carrying out of the work of empire. And, as Diver and others were quick to point out, it was on the home, this "unit of civilization," that the reputation of the entire civilizing project (as imperialism was often perceived to be) rested.[43] Thus Diver cautions,

It is a true saying – one that should never be far from the minds of English-women in India – that for the upholding of British prestige in the East, "far more credit is due to the individual men and women who have carried out in their lives the loftiest conceptions of English truth and virtue, than to the collective wisdom of the office in Downing Street." And in these days of unrest, when the most optimistic cannot shut their eyes to the decline of that prestige, through India's loss of confidence in our national strength, when the very loftiness of our justice and altruism bids fair to undermine our Empire, the individual man and woman may still, in their degree, help to defer or hasten a catastrophe that only a policy of power – just, yet unflinch-ing power – can remotely hope to avert. (*EI*, pp. 87–8)

Diver does not name the source that she cites in this passage but her own statements reword the sentiment without euphemism or lofty rhetoric. The "unrest" that Diver finds wearisome is a veiled reference to the increasingly vocal Indian demand for self-rule. Such an impend-ing "catastrophe" is reason enough for reiterating the responsibility of every English person to contribute to the maintenance of colonial power. Needless to say, Diver's methods of home management are based on a similar "policy of power – just, yet unflinching power." And the administration of this power was assigned to the memsahib.

HOUSEHOLD MANAGEMENT: "MAKE A HOLD"

If the English woman recognizes herself and is recognized as national subject only outside the national boundaries, then she becomes "of the master race" only in the presence of "the native" who will hail her as "memsahib" (literally, "madame boss"). The home is the pri-mary, and often the only, site where such encounters between white women and those of the colonized races take place.

In the absence of her children, the English woman sets out to disci-pline the "natives" in her compound – and we are repeatedly assured that these persons are no more than children requiring discipline. With her home and compound as her domain, the English woman's chal-lenge, her duty even, is to keep this strange and unmanageable territory under control. Her triumph is to replicate the empire on a domestic scale – a benevolent, much supervised terrain where discipline and pun-ishment is meted out with an unwavering hand. As with the empire, the territory of the home is already secured for the English occupant. Thus the English woman does not have to keep house as much as supervise the keeping of her house. A direct parallel can be drawn to Desmond's work in *Captain Desmond V.C.* which entails not the conquest of new territory but the maintenance of law and order. The English home in the colony thus represents itself as the empire in miniature. Diver writes:

In fine, if a woman wills to keep house successfully in India, she must possess before all things a large tolerance and a keen sense of justice, rare feminine virtues both, even in these days. She must train her mind to look upon petty falsehoods, thefts, and uncleanliness not as heinous offenses, but as troublesome propensities, to be quietly checked. Swift should she be also to recognize the trustworthy man, and to trust him liberally... (*EI*, p. 70)

The language is that of state craft and high diplomacy. The housewife is to aspire to the role of the politically astute leader who holds the reins of the empire in his hands, adept at knowing when to let them go slack and when to tighten the grip. Since these are "rare feminine virtues," only exceptional women can *man* the turbulent colonial house.

What is even more interesting and unexpected in this discourse is the representation of the empire as no more than an expanded version of the domestic arena. Thus Steel and Gardiner write:

We do not wish to advocate an unholy haughtiness; but an Indian household can no more be governed peacefully, without dignity and prestige, than an Indian Empire. (*CIH*, p. 9)

Time and time again, the colonial discourse, especially the texts written by women, represent the management of empire as essentially "home-management" on a larger scale. There are doors to be locked, corners to be periodically dusted, rooms to be fumigated and made free of pest, children (i.e. "natives") to be doctored, educated, clothed, disciplined, accounts to be kept, boundaries redrawn and fences mended.

Housekeeping in the colonies is often represented as an imperial military campaign. Writing of the need to follow a simple accounting system and a written inventory of food supplies, Steel and Gardiner note, "life in India always partakes of the nature of a great campaign" (*CIH*, p. 21). Hence, the daily supervision of servants is presented as "an inspection parade" which "should begin immediately after breakfast, or as near ten o'clock as circumstances will allow" (*CIH*, p. 8).

At the heart of all advice and every tip that this text offers is the attempt to inculcate the proper deportment of rulers – for the mistress rules alongside the master. Hence the first chapter of the Steel and Gardiner guide, "Duties of the Mistress," presents the domestic realm in terms of duties, rules, rewards and punishment:

The first duty of a mistress is, of course, to be able to give intelligible orders to her servants; therefore it is necessary she should learn to speak Hindustani...

The next duty is obviously to insist on her orders being carried out..."How is this to be done?"...The secret lies in making rules and *keeping to them*. The Indian servant is a child in everything but age...first faults should never go unpunished.

But it will be asked, How are we to punish our servants when we have no hold on their minds or bodies? – when cutting their pay is illegal, and few, if any, have any sense of shame. The answer is obvious. Make a hold (*ES*, pp. 3–4).

Citing their "own experience," the authors then go on to describe a system of fines and rewards that circumvent the rules that they themselves are subject to, even as they devise punishments for servants who break the rules! The trick is to engage servants at the lowest rate possible and then offer some extra as "buksheesh" conditional on good service.

From it [buksheesh] small fines are levied, beginning with one pice for forgetfulness, and running up, through degrees of culpability, to one rupee for lying. The money thus returned to imperial coffers may well be spent on giving small rewards: so that each servant knows that by good service he can get back his own fines... (*CIH*, p. 4)

As an example of another "kindly and reasonable device" to control "the obstinate cases" as well as "to show what absolute children Indian servants are," Steel and Gardiner suggest the forced administration of castor oil "on the ground that there must be some physical cause for inability to learn or to remember" (*CIH*, p. 4).

This is considered a great joke, and exposes the offender to much ridicule from his fellow-servants; so much so that the words, "*Mem Sahib tum ko zuroor kaster ile pila dena hoga*" [The Mem Sahib will definitely have to make you drink castor oil], is often heard in the mouths of the upper servants when new-comers give trouble. In short, without kindly and reasonable devices of this kind, the usual complaint of a want of hold over servants *must* remain true until they are educated into some sense of duty. (*CIH*, pp. 3–5)[44]

Such selections from the first three pages in the text are enough to understand the force with which Steel and Gardiner meet the object of their text – described in passing in the very first footnote which is a quick justification for their use of phonetic spellings of words from Indian languages:

The object of this book being to enable a person who is absolutely unacquainted with India, its languages and people, to begin housekeeping at once, the authors have decided on adhering throughout to purely phonetic spellings. (*CIH*, fn 1, p. 2)

[handwritten marginal note: Mussolini used these tactics too.]

Since the essence of housekeeping is the learning of imperial privilege, it is logical that this is the lesson that every chapter reinforces. Hence, as the above quoted footnote indicates, even the scattered citations from the languages or cultures of the Indians are represented only as means of improving the memsahib's "hold" on the native.

In her novels Diver presents language acquisition as an intellectual pursuit unique to the colonial situation. Honor marvels at Desmond's dedication to his work when she sees him struggling to improve his Persian language skills before he takes the administrative exam that would get him his promotion in the services. It follows then that she is eager to master various Indian languages whereas Evelyn is bored with the entire enterprise. Honor's knowledge of "*the* native language" is yet another charming indication of the overwhelming compatibility between her and Desmond. The mysterious, romantic, even spiritual (given that Desmond is a married man for most of the novel) bond between them rests on a bedrock of a shared imperial ideology – both proudly take up the burden of being English in the Indian Empire. And as "good" imperialists, their first task is the mastery of the language. In the context of colonialism, the language of imperial control and discipline is primarily the imperial languages – namely, English or French. "Native" language acquisition is represented in popular imperial discourses as motivated by an unpolitical, often purely aesthetic and linguistic, interest in an alien culture. However, these novels and home management guides demonstrate how "native" language acquisition enables the colonizer by allowing him or her a closer surveillance of the colonized group. In *The Englishwoman in India*, Maud Diver bluntly advocates the acquisition of the relevant "native" language by English women for the sole reason of administering power. She writes:

Surely, no sight could be more pitiful and ludicrous than that of a woman who has given place to wrath, and is powerless to put it into words; nor can such an one [*sic*] ever hope to keep a retinue of a dozen servants under control. (*EI*, p. 71)

No house, these management guides repeatedly insist, runs smoothly on its own accord. And yet, as with the Empire, the image that is conveyed *must be* one of ease of authority. The ultimate aim of house management as advocated in these guides is to erase the signs of supervision and struggle from the surface. Thus Diver writes:

for experience shows that the most successful housekeepers and hostesses are not found among the women whose minds, tongues and feet run incessantly upon household matters, but among those who – by hidden method and management – give a surface impression of large leisure, and of a mind free to give its undivided attention to the subject or the individual of the moment. (*EI*, pp. 54–5)

That Lady Helen Forsyth's leisure and radiant benevolence in *Unconquered* is born of centuries of feudal privilege is part of the ideological underpinnings of the culture that the novelist glosses over. However, in her guide to colonial India, Diver can clearly and repeatedly advocate that "a surface impression of large leisure" be secured "by hidden method and management." Imperial privileges, unlike those privileges created by class divisions in England, are unproblematically presented as available for all English subjects in the colonies.[45]

In *Colonizing Egypt*, a brilliant study of the everyday ways in which Egypt was transformed into a British colony in the late nineteenth century, Timothy Mitchell notes that because Michel Foucault's analyses focused on France and northern Europe, the colonizing nature of disciplinary power has been obscured from his analyses.[46] Mitchell brings to our notice the fact that the panopticon was a colonial device first used on the borders between Europe and the Ottoman Empire and then in colonial India. The panoptic principle as a means of household management was widely advocated by Steel and Gardiner as well as by Maud Diver in *The Englishwoman In India*. Sophisticated surveillance, of course required that the memsahib "learn not to *see* all that comes in the ways of her eyes; for with natives, as with children, the art of not seeing, practiced sparingly and judiciously, will go far to preserve domestic peace" (*EI*, p. 71). The language here is not as we might at first think of nursery rules but once again of state management. In the empire, indigenous populations were often represented as "unruly" children, a move that rendered juvenile the acts and aspirations of such peoples while also erasing the serious, meditated nature of their resistance. Managing a home and managing the Empire were ultimately part of the same project. In these difficult circumstances, "constant, personal supervision," writes Diver, is "the one weapon that can never fail" (*EI*, p. 35).

Supervision also included the regulation of the private life of servants. Steel and Gardiner place this job under the category of the "minor duties" of a mistress. There is no doubt in the minds of these writers that privacy is not a concern in Indian homes. Diver writes that this is so because "man, in his undeveloped state, [is] untroubled by a senseless passion for privacy" (*EI*, p. 131). In the interest of keeping "bazaar" illnesses and indecencies out of the household, Steel and Gardiner advocate that all servants be compelled to live in the compound. But this, they add

is no reason why they should turn your domain into a caravanserai for their relations to the third and fourth generation. As a rule, it is well to draw a very sharp line in this respect, and if it be possible to draw it on the other side of mother-in-law, so much the better for peace and quietness. (*CIH*, p. 4)

Hence, Englishwomen who want to "begin housekeeping at once," are here instructed to delineate, with "very sharp" lines, the familial bonds that they would find acceptable in their compound. Not surprisingly, the western nuclear family structure is the one deemed appropriate. The local practice of married couples living with their families is represented in this instance through the figure of the quarrelsome mother-in-law. Furthermore, Steel and Gardiner add, the mistress should enquire every day if there is any illness in the compound and "as often as possible – once or twice a week at least – she should go a regular inspection round the compound, not forgetting the stables, fowl-houses, & c." (*CIH*, p. 4). In the final instance then, the servants are no more than so much livestock requiring inspection.

Indian homes, if, as Diver puts it, "by courtesy they may be so called," are dim, lightless, segregated quarters that can be lighted up only by the introduction of western practices (*EI*, p. 131). In the place of homes, these writers find "dwellings" that are either ramshackle huts, palaces that are disproportionately large or simply "ruins" inhabited by people. Hence the "native" as manifest in the representation of his/her home is either a lack or in excess.[47]

My Indian Family: A Story of East and West Within an Indian Home, a novel in the form of a diary set in the 1930s, written by Hilda Wernher, a Scandinavian based in England, examines the intricacies of life in an Indian household.[48] The narrator and central protagonist is a middle-aged European woman who moves to India and into a Muslim household when her daughter Mary Ann marries Rashid, an Indian research scientist whom she met in England. The blurb on the book jacket of *My Indian Family* quotes from a *New York Times* review of the novel: "It is like a small window opened in the great haunted house of India to let in the sunshine and fresh air of Western comprehension."[49] The narrator presents herself as a blend of "western comprehension" with a sympathetic appreciation of things Indian.

And yet, despite this effort to understand specific nuances of Indian domestic and social arrangements, there is in *My Indian Family* the inevitable final rejection of most of it. The only solution is to "let in the sunshine and fresh air of western comprehension," and the only enlightened Indians are those amenable to these changes. Once again we have the lamenting of the lack of privacy in Indian homes, accompanied by an inability to recognize Indian interpretations of privacy.

The boundaries between the spaces assigned to two sexes, those which separate adults from children and the sahibs from the servants, are recognized and valorized only if they draw on European concepts of privacy. Hence the narrator finds unacceptable the Indian practice of children sharing beds or of entire families sleeping in courtyards in the hottest months of the year.

The only way of changing this sorry state of affairs in the Indian home is to work on the Indian woman. And yet there was no suggestion that any role but the purely domestic could fulfill the potential in Indian women. Diver writes:

The advanced woman of the West is apt to conclude over-hastily that the narrow, hidden life of her Eastern sister, with its lack of freedom, its limited scope for self-development and individual action, must needs constitute her a mere lay figure in the scheme of things; a being wholly incapable of influencing the larger issues of life; whereas a more intimate knowledge of facts would reveal to her the truth that, from that same hidden corner, and by the natural primal power of her sex, the Eastern woman moulds the national character far more effectively than she ever could hope to do from the platform or the hustings (*EI*, pp. 100–1).

Here then we have another example of the ideological continuance between the conservative view on the role of women in England and in her colonies. Thus, because of the "natural primal power of her sex," the Indian woman is most powerful when she operates from her home. The problem that needs to be eliminated is the fact that she is confined to a hidden corner instead of having the *entire* house as *her* territory. This is where her western sister has to step in to introduce her to her rightful domain and of course to point out to her that aspiring to any *larger* or more public space (perhaps of national dimensions as in the freedom struggle movement) was futile. What must be noted is that from the late nineteenth century onwards, contemporary Indian women who were accepted as role-models or at least well known, led very public lives as active participants in various social reform movements as well as in the national independence movement.[50]

"OUR EASTERN SISTERS": WHITE WOMAN'S BURDEN

In her landmark text *Ain't I a Woman?*, bell hooks writes of the brief moment in American history, in the late nineteenth century, when the sexism of white America was greater than their racism.[51] Her reference is to the white male advocation of granting the right to vote to black men before granting this right to white women. hooks notes that white women activists who had hitherto allied themselves with black political activists, withdrew their support and urged white men to allow "racial solidarity" to overshadow their plans to support black suffrage. In the English colonies and its many texts, there were very few if indeed any such moments when alliances between genders overshadowed racial solidarity. When overtures made by white women toward establishing such gender alliances failed, the conclusion reached was that Indian women themselves resisted self-improvement and liberation from domestic tyrannies. In *My Indian Family*, the narrator relates how she tries, unsuccessfully, to instill the "ladies first" principle at a formal tea-party with her Indian guests – a Mr. Jawarker and his two unnamed wives. What is specially noteworthy is how smoothly the knowledge of the Other is transformed into a means of dismissal of cultural differences. A full appreciation of the problematic nuances requires a lengthy citation:

True, we know that a Hindu woman considers it correct to serve her lord first and that, somehow, all Orientals have similar customs. But this is our house. We can stage an object lesson in different treatment of women, by serving tea in Western fashion...Mary Ann is pouring; I take the first cup to the senior, the second to the junior, now the ruling wife (the elder is said to live all by herself somewhere about their courtyard). Both ladies refuse, both motion me unashamedly to take the first cup to their joint lord. I remain adamant, saying that "West in," ladies come first. Mary Ann seconds me; Rashid says to the ceiling – he can't address ladies directly – that it is high time things were altered in this country. Mr. Jarwarkar, an educated man, laughs and says he'd like to try the new regime for once. But it's no use. Burri bai, seeing that I don't give in, rises, takes the cup from my hand and presents it ceremoniously to her unfaithful lord, thus carrying out to the letter the Code of Manu, as far as the conduct of wives is concerned. The same procedure is repeated over each dish. Man comes first. Again India has won the day (*MIF*, pp. 55–6).

The narrator's self-confidence is clearly demonstrated in this passage. What escapes her 'Other'wise careful reasoning is the fact that "ladies first" does not dramatically alter the gender inequalities present in a scenario where "man comes first." The encounter between white women and Indian women, in either's home, once again serves to underline the assumption of superiority that the English woman has of her status *as woman*.[52] Thus despite the occasional reference to Indian women as "our eastern sisters," there is no substantial alliance that is possible between the two groups of women. In this context, "again India has won the day" reverberates with the narrator's resignation at her failure to instill an English sense of female worth in her Indian guests.

As English writers (of both genders) were quick to note, the white woman's status in society was the norm, the yardstick by which "native" lack was measured.[53] Perhaps it is consequent that while in Europe at the time some women were struggling to win the right to vote, in the Indian Empire there was a comfortable belief that the white women's emancipation was a completed project – one only had to look at "native" women to know so. A chapter entitled "Eastern Womanhood" in Maud Diver's *The Englishwoman in India*, ends with:

In these days, too, when education behind the Purdah seems tending towards an ultimate lifting of the veil, it lies with the Englishwoman in India to prove, by the simplicity and uprightness of her own way of life, that a woman, being free in all things, may yet refrain from using her liberty as a cloak of vanity and folly; that tender womanliness and self-effacement may, and do go hand in hand with an unrestricted outlook upon the world at large; a fact that Orientals – the women no less than the men – are singularly slow to believe. (*EI*, pp. 88–9)

The contemporary white woman (circa early twentieth century) is emancipated and has achieved all that there is to achieve in terms of gender equality or self-development. Clearly, the right to vote is not what gender equality is measured by, for it is without this liberty that Diver finds her fellow country women – "free in all things." The case of the English women as imperialists, forces an adjustment of theorizing on authoritative selfhood and global sisterhood, because it brings in the critical component that is missing from such formulations about the "common humanity" of people – the historically continuous issues of race and power.

In her guide book, Diver repeatedly suggests that the ordinary English woman in India has the responsibility of her Eastern sisters in her hands:

Every mistress of a house has, within her compound, some scope for work in this direction. True she has only one female servant, but every man in her service is certain to possess a wife and family. For celibacy is an outcome of civilization, and the Hindu and Mohommadan have yet to discover its advantages. By means of this patriarchal system, then, any Englishwoman can find material ready to her hand, should curiosity or sympathy prompt her to take an active interest in the joys and sorrows of those sister-women whom chance has brought together within her gates. (*EI*, pp. 77–8)

"Curiosity," "sympathy" and "love" are all equally legitimate reasons to work one's designs on this "material ready to her hand."[54] Projects like the *Female Medical Aid Fund* started by Lady Dufferin allowed the Englishwoman entry into areas and events in Indian homes that would otherwise have remained unknown to them.[55] Maud Diver is effusive in her praise for this project because it indicates "the keen insight into native character and prejudice shown in all Lady Dufferin's dealings with India's inscrutable peoples" (*EI*, p. 93). And she quotes approvingly from the project's charter to further demonstrate Lady Dufferin's wisdom:

The end of ends underlying the whole splendid effort was "to carry help and alleviation into the remote chambers of zenanas and 'bibi-ghars,' behind whose jealously-closed doors no unrelated man might pass; and to which, if such assistance were to be taken, it must be by the hands of trained women; preferably women of like nationality and caste." (*EI*, p. 94)

Writing of the "foyer social," a government-sponsored educational and social welfare program for urban African women in Belgian Africa between 1946 and 1960, Nancy Rose Hunt details the many ways in which the program provided European women with the means and materials with which to reshape the domestic arrangements of the African women living in the colonial city of Usumbura, Ruanda-Urundi (present-day Bujumbura, Burundi).[56] The "house-visit" part of the program gave European social workers physical access to the students' private life and an opportunity to inspect, correct and applaud all signs of emulation of European domestic ideology.

Nor was this practice of inspection of the homes of one's "lesser sisters" confined to the colonies. From the late nineteenth century onward, in cities in England and France, a concerted effort was made by local authorities and women's volunteer groups to curb infant mortality rates and to generally improve the quality of the imperial race by monitoring the domestic life of the urban working-class population. A vital part of this supervision was carried out by "lady health visitors" who inspected working-class homes dispensing disinfection powder and hints to mothers on feeding, clothing, schooling of children, on dirt and on "the evils of bad smells" as well as urging "on all possible occasions, the importance of cleanliness, thrift and temperance."[57]

In the Indian colony, the practice of demarcating domestic and public space between the genders through the use of the purdah especially frustrated the English woman's attempts at reform.[58] Any resistance on the part of Indian women to such schemes was interpreted as the "evil result" of their "innate ideas and customs" (*EI*, pp. 96-8). Hence writing on the Dufferin Fund, Diver concludes: "[y]et despite all that money, tact, and stringent regulations could achieve, high-caste

Zenana women have shown no disposition to avail themselves freely of the medical skill placed at their disposal; possibly because female life is of no great value in the East" (*EI*, p. 98). Diver's conclusion implies that because female life is of no great value, *Zenana* women do not attempt to save themselves from death. Perhaps their faith in alternative methods of healing was stronger than their trust in the Dufferin fund, but this is not how Diver chooses to read the situation. Partha Chatterjee has argued that Indian nationalism "located its own subjectivity in the spiritual domain of culture, where it considered itself superior to the West and hence undominated and sovereign."[59] According to Chatterjee, domestic arrangements and women's issues were located within this spiritual domain. Hence, Chatterjee continues, Indian nationalism and social reform could not "permit an encroachment by colonial power into that domain" (p. 249). The reluctance to let Lady Dufferin and others work their reforms into Indian homes can be understood in light of Chatterjee's thesis that "reforms which touch upon the 'inner essence' of the identity of the community can only be carried out by the community itself, not by the state" (p. 251).

IN CONCLUSION

Writing about city planning in colonial Egypt, and the colonialists' apparent need to fix boundaries and to create order for instance by differentiating interior from exterior, Timothy Mitchell unintentionally provides us with an articulation of the project of the colonial novel as written by these women writers:

The world is set up before an observing subject as though it were the picture of something. Its order occurs as the relationship between observer and picture, appearing and experienced in terms of the relationship between the picture and the plan or meaning it represents. It follows that the appearance of order is at the same time an order of appearance, a hierarchy. The world appears to the observer as a relationship between picture and reality, the one present but secondary, a mere representation, the other only represented, but prior, more original, more real. This order of appearance can be called the hierarchy of truth...it is in terms of such a hierarchical division, between a picture and what it stands for, that all reality, all truth is to be grasped. The methods of ordering, distributing and enframing that create the division, therefore, are the ordinary way of effecting what the modern individual experiences as the really real.[60]

Mitchell's "picture" is that which is suggested by the "Egypt" exhibits at world exhibitions in Paris and other western metropoles in the mid to late nineteenth century. Travelers from Europe to Egypt expected, according to Mitchell, to walk from the exhibit to the truth "behind" it. The truths that they recognized in Egypt then, would be those which corresponded to the "preview" provided by the exhibit in Europe. One could argue that the novels and guidebooks by these women writers were similarly constructed and consumed. They were written and read as representations of the truth about British India and as such became self-fulfilling prophecies. The "preview" that the books provided thus becomes identical to the reality inhabited and represented by writers. For the author to have visited India did not necessarily add or subtract from the quality or success of the novels she wrote. Hence the phenomenon of writers like Ethel Dell, who wrote several very successful novels set in British India, the most famous being *The Lamp in the Desert*, without having left England. Her biographer notes that she got her information from other India-writers, among them Kipling and Maud Diver.[61]

What is remarkable about these novels and guidebooks is the confidence of the female authorial voice. The ideological proximity of this genre with the other discourses of imperialism constructs "the Englishwoman" – a female subject who is firmly anchored as a "full individual" through her racial privileges. Hence despite the dislocations (both geographic and linguistic) that these women experienced, their writing represents a coherent, unified bourgeois subjecthood.

Writing about *Men in the Sun*, a novella by the Palestinian writer Ghassan Khanafani, in her book *Travels of a Genre: The Modern Novel and Ideology*, Mary Layoun ascribes the fragmented, compartmentalized narratives that make up the story to the very quality of Palestinian life in exile.[62] Layoun declares: "For *Rajal fi al-shams* [*Men in the Sun*], there is little question of autonomous and unified subjects as the source of action and meaning."[63] The intermeshing of aesthetic value and ideology in the novels by the "lady romancers" works in ways that are fundamentally different from the workings of Khanafani's "contemporary Palestinian-Arabic novel in exile." Given the fundamental differences in the two experiences of "homelessness" and dislocation there is a sharp contrast in the type of narratives that the two discourses construct. For despite the fact that the English imperialists in India often represented themselves as exiled from their homeland, it is hard to justify the use of the term "exile" in this context today.[64] Yet, "Gender, Colonialism, and Exile: Flora Anne Steel and Sara Jeanette Duncan in India" an article by Rebecca Saunders published in 1989 explores this instance of what she sees as "women writing in exile."[65] Exile is not the same as manning one's post in the empire. The twentieth century has presented us with so many harrowing instances of exile that is experienced as extreme homelessness, refugee status in detention camps, constant fear of expulsion, that Saunders' application of the term here comes across as very facile. And yet this term is unproblematically used in contemporary scholarship to describe the situation of western women who are away from home.[66]

Looking at the novels by English women in the colonies in Layoun's terms, one finds here a literature where "unified and autonomous subjects" are always the source of action and meaning. These texts serve to translate the discomfort of dislocation into a means of self-aggrandization *even as* they record the Englishwoman speaking an alien language in an alien terrain. A rudimentary grasp of the "native" language (often just the imperative mode) is all the linguist equipment one needs to be marked as "White." Similarly, in these imperial romances, non-English characters are marked by a curious inability to master the English language or at least the correct British accent – a lack which is indicative of their less than whole subject-status.[67]

If, in the late nineteenth and early twentieth centuries, women writers in England (Virginia Woolf, for example) saw literary, aesthetic and even political distance between themselves and an easy understanding of the self within a community, such contradictions were erased in the colonies. Here "not belonging" was one's only avenue to unified and autonomous subject status. Being white and English was what marked the imperialist as the fortunate outsider. And as such, it was a status shared equally by English men and women and was therefore erased as a possible site of gender struggle. In 1929, when Virginia Woolf wrote her impassioned feminist manifesto calling for a "room of one's own," she needed only to have looked over to the everyday discourses inscribed by her country women in the empire. By 1929 the English wife in the colonies had enjoyed decades of greater political participation and greater personal authority than feminists and women modernists of the time in England. The memsahib was a British citizen long before England's laws caught up with her.[68]

I have tried to demonstrate that it was because of the autonomy afforded by their dislocation that "lady romancers" displayed a self-confident female voice not usually heard in the history and literature of English women in the England at the time. In these texts by English women, the representations of India, of Indians, and of the English in

India, owed much to the prevailing dominant ideology of imperialism but these texts also shaped this ideology especially as available to us in its literary fiction. Hence, one could argue that later novels, such as *Burmese Days* (1934), and to a certain extent, *A Passage to India* (1925), essentially follow the same romance plot in the same Indian setting with the same race and gender dynamics and ideological stances, though written by better known (canonical, male) writers. For instance, traces of Evelyn, the unhappy heroine of *Captain Desmond V.C.* can be found in Elizabeth Lackersteen, the heroine of *Burmese Days*. Mrs Moore figures abound in the novels of these women writers. Her mystical link with India and its people, made famous in Foster's novel, would already be familiar to readers of the imperial novel through their acquaintance with fictional middle-aged women who are central to the plot such as the narrator of *My Indian Family* and Lady Helen Forsyth in *Unconquered*. If we are to give over to these writers, or "lady romancers" as Parry chose to call them, their proper literary terrain, then we would have to read Orwell and Forster as writers in the imperial romance tradition or alternately, read Diver and others as practitioners of the realist/naturalist school.

In the next chapter I examine the work of Joseph Conrad who is the best known writer of (masculine) colonial romances. Conrad's novels are, however, usually classified as examples of early modernism. With his work the popular genre of the colonial novel moves into the rarefied regions of high art. His novels are familiar domestic tales set in alien territories. Hence Conrad's novels complicate the neat schematic of modernist literary territory by blending both high and low art. In doing this he travels beyond his compatriots whose novels record and recreate *either* the grappling with the difficulties of the familiar, the known world (upper-class London in Woolf, Dublin in Joyce) *or* the grappling with the difficulties of the unfamiliar, alien outposts of empire (Orwell in Burma, Diver in the Indian northwest frontier region). Conrad grapples with both and inscribes a horrifying truth: the different is the same/the same is different. In the process of exploring "the Jungle" he succeeds in making European metropoles, European ideals of domesticity, marriage, and femininity seem monstrous and threatening. In doing this he demolishes the cherished fetishes of the colonial romance genre that thrive in the novels and handbooks by Steele and Diver. The anxieties of race, nationality, gender and language that lie well below the surface of the colonial romance crisscross the surface of his text and disrupt narrative, dialogue, description, plot and characterization.[69] Reading these markings reveals Conrad's complex and idiosyncratic representation of English culture as utterly contaminated and yet, because it is the only civilization that he can recognize as such, worth saving from extermination.

Conrad's works bring the fiction of England up to date with other English political and cultural interventions in the world. His novels demonstrate Europe's massive dependence on the colonies, not just in economic terms, but also for self-sustenance and self-definition. Steel and Diver's writing created "successful" English women in the colonies who were rewarded with the status of English (authoritative) subjecthood. Conrad's texts created "failed" English (and European) colonial men who nevertheless earn the status of being "one of us" – and that, Conrad tells the reader, is ultimately all that matters.

CHAPTER 3

The great English tradition: Joseph Conrad writes home

> a book is a deed... the writing of it is an enterprise as much as the conquest of a colony.
>
> "A Glance at Two Books," Joseph Conrad

> "The trouble with the English is that their history happened overseas, so they don't know what it means."
>
> Whiskey Sisodia in *Satanic Verses*

In Joseph Conrad's novels the imperial romance genre is re-presented through literary maneuvers which we now identify as early modernist. Conrad brings the world map that was Europe's playing field at the turn of the century into his fiction in a singular fashion: the aegis of British imperialism is ever present and yet the viewpoint is not comfortably English. His is no longer the nineteenth-century tale set in exotic faraway places. Instead, Conrad takes the exploration of the alien, hitherto present in the adventure and romance tale, and subjects it to the scrutiny given by his contemporaries and predecessors to the most integral concerns of English domestic culture. His writing displays many of the inescapable contradictions and compromises that are present at the very sites from which global literatures in English are produced. Looking ahead to Salman Rushdie's *Satanic Verses* and to the astute comment made by a rather inebriated Whiskey Sisodia further underlines the singularity of Conrad's literary location: while his is certainly not the voice of the postcolonial critic, he does sense that England's history "happens overseas."[1] It is never a comforting tale that Conrad's favored narrator, Marlow, brings back to England. For Conrad's fiction examines the foreign, but only to make the most disturbing assessment of domestic culture. The sameness at the center of all social constructions of difference is "the horror" that his novels expose.

65

In recent years, both Terry Eagleton and Fredric Jameson have variously diagnosed Joseph Conrad's literary work as exhibiting symptoms of the modernist (and even post-modern) affliction of an absent center, a resonant silence at its core.[2] Much of this theorizing stems from an essay written in 1968 by Perry Anderson, which he has since updated.[3] In this seminal essay of 1968, entitled "Components of the National Culture," Perry Anderson located an "absent center" at the heart of twentieth-century British culture – a void marked and characterized by the lack of a classical sociology and a national Marxism, that is, by the lack of a total theory of the self or of the nation. Anderson argued that as a consequence there had been no "synthesis designed to capture the 'structure of structures'– the social totality as such" in Britain in the various disciplines of the first half of the twentieth century.[4] Instead, the void at the center of British culture generated a "pseudo center" – a "timeless ego" that was floated in discipline after discipline, arresting change, revolution and even self-examination.[5]

Anderson proceeds in this article to draw attention to "the white emigration" to England, from 1900 onward, of practitioners in all the major disciplines. As a result, he argues, the "crucial formative influences in the arc of culture" were exerted by these emigres who "powerfully flattered and enlarged in the convex mirror they presented to it...every insular reflex and prejudice" in the British intelligentsia.[6] According to Anderson, they "both reinforced the existing orthodoxy and exploited its weakness."[7] These emigres, for the first time, "systemized the refusal of system" thus codifying a national culture that had as its locus a pseudo-center.[8] One could see Conrad falling right into place in this category of "the white emigre," but whether he plays out the role of reinforcer of the existing orthodoxy that Anderson assigns to these foreign practitioners remains an issue of debate.

Following Anderson's lead, Terry Eagleton published *Exiles and Emigres* (1970), a brilliant reading of modernist literature in terms of the confrontation of the familiar with the alien. Eagleton's considerations of modernist literature in this study center around the problems "raised by the 'emigre' theme."[9] His opening sentence in the introduction reads:

If it is agreed that the seven most significant writers of twentieth-century English literature have been a Pole, three Americans, two Irishmen and an Englishman, then it might also be agreed that the paradox is odd enough to be studied.[10]

Eagleton goes on to argue that the kind of totality of vision that is available in the work of Romantic poets and the Victorian realists is not visible in the work of twentieth-century writers, except partially in the work of exiles (from the upper social classes) and emigres.[11] Similarly, Fredric Jameson argues in his "Field Day" essay that the "spatial disjunction" that resulted from colonial economic enterprise had "as its immediate consequence the inability to grasp the way the system functions as a whole." This condition of having a national literature that can "no longer be grasped immanently; [that] no longer has its meaning, its deeper reason for being, within itself" is according to Jameson the absent center of modernism. Modernism is marked by a lack that "cannot be made up or made good." Hence,

This new and historically original problem in what is itself a new kind of content now constitutes the situation and the problem and the dilemma, the formal contradiction, that modernism seeks to solve; or better still, it is only that new kind of art which reflexively perceives this problem and lives this formal dilemma that can be called modernism in the first place.[12]

Such historiographic analysis shifts critical attention from the usual categorizing of modernism that is circumscribed by stylistic qualifications to forcefully emphasizing the links between political geographies and the terrain covered by modernist fiction.

Conrad's fiction collapses both geography and genre: the different and the distant all crowd the pages of his novels to construct narratives that are part adventure story, part romance, part existential journey, part philosophical brooding on actions, desires, and motivations. And yet the overwhelming problematic that this fiction constantly returns to is that of finding home and of being hailed as "one of us" even as the narrative keeps the obstacles to such comforting closure in view. While Conrad's domestic fiction is deeply imbricated within imperial enterprises, his representations of home, family and the feminine, work on the tropes already present in the English novel tradition. This chapter attempts to rethink Conrad's position within this literary canon: he is taken out of his usual literary category (Modernism) and instead read in relation to other global literatures produced in the English-speaking world. In this new context that builds on the theorizing produced by Anderson, Eagleton and Jameson, rather than being a less than spectacular modernist, Conrad can be read as leading the literary genre of fiction in English into a global arena. This is demonstrated through analyses of *A House for Mr. Biswas* by V. S. Naipaul and *The Remains of the Day* by Kazuo Ishiguro that trace the links to Conrad as they become visible at various levels in the two novels. And finally, at every stage in this discussion, examinations of Conrad's manipulation of gender are woven in so that what is revealed at the heart of his masculine texts are terrifying feminine spaces.

In *Criticism and Ideology*, published six years after *Exiles and Emigres*, Eagleton writes:

At the centre of each of Conrad's works is a resonant silence: the unfathomable enigma of Kurtz, Jim and Nostromo, the dark, brooding passivity of James Wait in *The Nigger of Narcissus*, the stolid opacity of McWhirr in *Typhoon*, the eternal crypticness of the "Russian soul" in *Under Western Eyes*, the unseen bomb-explosion and mystical silence of the idiot Stevie in *The Secret Agent*, Heyst's non-existent treasure in *Victory*.[13]

While Eagleton lists only male characters as personifying this silence, I would like to argue that the resonant silences in Conrad's novels bear/bare the marks of *both* genders. In Conrad's fiction, silence, darkness, the vacuum or void is the enunciation of the feminized heart not just of the jungle but also of the civilized world. Hence we could revise Eagleton's list by adding: the silent spectacle of the Amazon and the obsessive sorrow of The Intended in *Heart of Darkness*, the clinging petulance of Jewel in *Lord Jim*, the terrible wrath of Winnie Verlock in *The Secret Agent*, the quiet conspiracies of Mrs. Almayer and Nina in *Almayer's Folly*.

However, the feminine in Conrad's novels can be read as more than a litany of the names of female characters. In its widest connotation, the feminine or feminized is that which is effaced in any show of masculinity.[14] Thus, when Eagleton writes,

The 'message' of *Heart of Darkness* is that Western civilisation is at base as barbarous as African society – a viewpoint which disturbs imperialist assumptions to the precise degree that it reinforces them.[15]

it is important to note that this "barbarism" is always gendered. While Eagleton prefers for obvious reasons to use the term "African society," in Conrad's fiction "the jungle" is the term used to metonymically refer to the world outside of Europe and North America. The horror of both jungle and civil barbarism comes from the fiction's insistence that at their "base" both jungle and civil worlds are feminine or at best exhibit a perverse masculinity. Hence the disturbance and/or reinforcement of imperialist assumptions that Eagleton sees held in precise balance in this novel are unsettled by the introduction of the issue of gender. Projecting the barbarous onto the "less than manly" woman *or man* allows for a clear tip in the scales in favor of "reinforcement of imperial assumptions."

Value, honor, individualism, work, are all represented in these novels as solidly masculine concerns – except that they are carved out of and against the terrain of the feminized or the "less than masculine" other races and lower classes. Neither white women or women and men of other races benefit from being the ground on which a figure like Tuan "one of us" Jim is erected.

Shifting the focus from gender to genre, one finds that the crisis at the center of these novels can be renamed as the crisis that ensues when the ideal of masculine heroism is revealed to be unattainable without restricting oneself to the terms of romance and/or adventure writing. Hence, in Conrad's novels, there are no male or female heroic characters like those who people novels written by Maud Diver, E. M. Forster and Flora Steel. Conrad's literary ambition was clearly not the modest one of furthering the romance genre. For him "a book is a deed...the writing of it is an enterprise as much as the conquest of a colony."[16] Writing more than the manly tale of the sailor at sea, Conrad created characters like Marlow, Jim and Nina Almayer, who could not be contained within the stock figures of "adventurous young man" or "beautiful maiden."

Conrad's novels often veil the inadequacy of storybook heroic masculinity by displacing the desire for such romantic idealism from the male to the female characters in the narrative. In *Lord Jim*, Jim's desire to be like a hero in a book is shattered by the Patna episode – but in Patusan it is resurrected in and transferred onto Jewel's adoration of Tuan Jim. *Heart of Darkness* ends with the Intended's insistence on a Kurtz of mythic proportions. For Kurtz, as for Marlow and Jim, at the end there is only "the horror" of (gendered) human inadequacy that has to be confronted. The suggestion is that the "feminized" have their illusions: they never inhabit the "real" world. The ambiguity and lack of closure that critics have noted in Conrad's depiction of imperialism also mark his depiction of the domestic arena.[17] Hence, one can ask whether Conrad was an iconoclast whose fiction deliberately took apart the bourgeois ideals of the sacred home, chaste femininity and social order. Or is his work no more than the conservative and panic-stricken writing of an aristocrat who saw all kinds of terrors in women, domesticity, the working class, and other races?

THE HOME AND THE WORLD: LATE VICTORIAN AND
EDWARDIAN ENGLAND

Writing on Dickens and the concept of home in his novels, Frances Armstrong argues that "the complexities of the Victorian concept of home can best be understood as the result of adult attempts to bridge, perhaps unconsciously, the growing gap between the home of childhood memory and the home of the present."[18] Armstrong maintains that in seventeenth and eighteenth-century England such attempts to bridge the gap between the remembered ideal and the real were unnecessary because successive generations lived in the same home or general location, in more-or-less the same circumstances. In the nineteenth century however, there was an overwhelming sense of rapid and irreversible changes in society that led to the sentimentalizing of the home. This sentimentalization, Armstrong argues "resulted from a refusal to examine too closely what home really was, lest its magic be revealed as humanly contrived, and the break with the past be shown to be complete."[19]

Few words in nineteenth-century English fiction are as charged with connotations as is the word "home."[20] In the preface to the 1870 best-seller, *The Complete Home*, Julia McNair Wright writes,

Between the Home set up in Eden, and the Home before us in Eternity, stand the Homes of Earth in a long succession. It is therefore important that our Homes should be brought up to a standard in harmony with their origin and Destiny.[21]

Whether the ideal home was located in the past of one's childhood or in the future form of a heavenly abode, what is noteworthy is that the home of the present was perceived as being somewhat lacking in its function as "Home." Such sentimentalism served the function of ideology, which Jorge Larrain has explained as "a solution at the level of social consciousness to contradictions which have not been solved in practice."[22]

Visions of the home are celebrated in novels such as *Mansfield Park*, *Vanity Fair* and *Jane Eyre*. However, the idyllic domestic tableau in almost any Victorian novel is usually secured and contrived out of an exclusion or repression of disruptive factors. For example, consider this paragraph from the concluding pages of *Vanity Fair*:

Lady Jane and Mrs. Dobbin became great friends – there was a perpetual crossing of pony-chaises between the Hall and the Evergreens, the Colonel's place. Her Ladyship was godmother to Mrs. Dobbin's child, which bore her name.[23]

Thackeray goes on to write about the two families, their sons who become good friends, go to Cambridge and fall in love and so on. But the very next paragraph begins with –"Mrs. Rawdon Crawley's name was never mentioned by either family..." An unreformed Becky Sharp (Mrs. Rawdon Crawley) has no place in the benevolently ordered domestic world that Thackeray wishes to leave with the reader at the end of his novel. Becky Sharp is firmly and almost brutally pushed out onto the fringes – foreign countries, desperate means and more schemes. In *Jane Eyre*, there is no illusion about the exclusions that make a family cohere – on the very first page, young Jane needs to be banished to a drafty window seat before Mrs. Reed and her children can arrange themselves before the hearth.

If one wants to locate the idealization of the home, of love, and of womanhood in the Victorian age, the single most important and per-haps most quoted, document is John Ruskin's "Of Queen's Garden." In *Sesame and Lilies*, Ruskin annunciates the Victorian ideology of home as follows:

This is the true nature of home – it is the place of Peace; the shelter not only from all injury, but from all terror, doubt, and division. In so far as it is not this, it is not home; so far as the anxieties of the outer world penetrate into it, and the inconsistently-minded, unknown, unloved, or hostile society of the outer world is allowed by either husband or wife to cross the threshold, it ceases to be home; it then becomes only a part of the outer world which you have roofed over, and lighted fire in. But so far as it is a sacred place, a vestal temple, a temple of the hearth watched over by Household Gods...so far as it is this...so far it vindicates the name, and fulfills the praise, of Home.[24]

This passage is especially interesting in its demonstration of the absolute confidence with which the notions of bourgeois universality are mar-shalled.[25] "In so far as it is not this, it is not home" writes Ruskin, thus negating the value or legitimacy of the homes and family life of the working class and of the lower rungs of the urban middle class.

And yet even a lowly clerk like Mr. Wemmick in *Great Expectations* can think of his moated, wooden cottage in Walworth amongst "a col-lection of backlanes, ditches and little gardens" as his little protected castle, where every night at nine o'clock, Greenwich time, the gun fires and the bridge is drawn up "with a relish and not merely mechani-cally," as an amused Pip notes. An English home in English fiction in the nineteenth and early twentieth centuries was more than a physical structure. Nor was it, as Wemmick's careful maintenance of an "office" and "home" self demonstrates, the exclusive domain of women. In the

Subjection of Women (1869), Mill records the masculine move to domesticity in the nineteenth century – a change from the coffee house routine of the bourgeois male in the eighteenth century. Mill explains the phenomenon as follows:

The association of men with women in daily life is much closer and more complete than it ever was before. Men's life is more domestic. Formerly, their pleasures and chosen occupations were among men, and in men's company: their wives had but a fragment of their lives. At the present time, the progress of civilization, and the turn of opinion against rough amusements and convivial excesses which formerly occupied most men in their hours of relaxation – together with (it must be said) the improved tone of modern feeling as to the reciprocity of duty which binds the husband towards the wife – have thrown the man very much more upon the home and its inmates, for his personal and social pleasures: while the kind and degree of improvement which has been made in women's education, has made them in some degree capable of being his companions in ideas and mental tastes.[26]

This passage is a rich nineteenth-century patriarchal checklist for the masculine requirements from "family life." The bringing about of this companionate marriage that Mill describes was a central theme in Victorian and Edwardian fiction. Conrad's novels, I will demonstrate, also dwell on these issues if only to display the vast gap between the ideal and the actual. The central concern of his fiction is the encounter between the familiar and the unknown – in courtship and marriage as in trade and adventure – but in the course of this exchange all of home culture is held up to scrutiny.

At the end of the long Victorian era of imperialism and expansion, while the rest of Europe witnessed profound intellectual and political upheaval, England alone remained, for the most part, stable and secure or as Perry Anderson puts it – "chloroformed."[27] Anderson quotes with great effect the opening paragraph from Roy Harrod's biography of John Keynes. This paragraph is reproduced here in its entirety because it is evocative of the solid world of the English intelligentsia before 1914.

If Cambridge combined a deep-rooted traditionalism with a lively progressiveness, so too did England. She was in the strongly upward trend of her material development; her overseas trade and investment were still expanding; the great pioneers of social reform were already making headway in educating public opinion. On the basis of her hardly won but now solidly established prosperity, the position of the British Empire seemed unshakeable. Reforms would be within a framework of stable and unquestioned social values. There was ample elbow-room for experiment without danger that the main fabric of our economic well-being would be destroyed. It is true that only a minority enjoyed the full fruits of this well-being; but the consciences of the leaders of thought were not unmindful of the hardships of the poor. There was a great confidence that, in due course, by careful management, their condition would be improved out of recognition. The stream of progress would not cease to flow. While the reformers were most earnestly bent on their purposes, they held that there were certain strict rules and conventions which must not be violated; secure and stable though the position seemed, there was a strong sense that danger beset any changes.[28]

Hence, Anderson argues, never seriously challenged from within, the dominant class and its intellectuals had no reason to contemplate or theorize their culture. By the end of the nineteenth century, this English upper class was master of a third of the world. The impact of this enlarged field of operation was felt on every aspect of the English national imagination. Raymond Williams notes that it is at around this time that, due to the prevalent imperial practices, the traditional relationship between city and country in England was completely rebuilt on an international scale.[29] He goes on to elaborate:

From about 1880 there was then this dramatic extension of landscape and social relations. There was also a marked development of the idea of England as "home", in that special sense in which "home" is a memory and an ideal. Some of the images of this "home" are of central London: the powerful, the prestigious and the consuming capital. But many are of an idea of rural England: its green peace contrasted with the tropical or arid places of actual work; its sense of belonging, of community, idealized by contrast with the tensions of colonial rule and the isolated alien settlement.[30]

Establishing the link between the pervasive fetishization of the home and capitalist expansion is easily done. One only has to read Victorian descriptions of the business world or of foreign travel to learn that home is where, in Carlyle's words "we cease the struggle in the race of the world, and give our hearts leave and leisure to love."[31] With the overseas success of the British empire, the "race of the world" took on a very literal meaning. After the Berlin conference in 1884, in which the African continent was parceled out to the several contending European powers, a new world order was established.[32] British literature, the left arm of imperial discourse, joined with anthropology to articulate the new pressures that were placed on the white man with the responsibility of this world on his shoulders. Travel, and that too through a hostile world, was represented as the very antithesis of being at home.

Conrad enters the arena of English literature at this very juncture – when the hurly burly of imperial scramble for colonies has quietened down and when intellectualizations of imperial feats and trials

are sought and read with interest. Conrad's literary works amply illustrate Walter Benjamin's maxim that every document of civilization is
at the same time a document of barbarism. However, it is just as difficult to read Conrad against the grain as it is to determine exactly
what Kurtz meant when he wrote "exterminate all the brutes" across
what was to be a "humanitarian" document. Conrad's literary interest is indeed with civilization and barbarism and "home" as deployed
in Conrad's novels strikingly points out the inadequacy of considering
one without the other.

Eagleton has described the "Conradian ideology" as itself "inter-
nally complex, compounded of elements of various ideological sub-
ensembles (of the "emigre", Merchant Code, Romantic artist and so
on) as well as of major elements of the dominant ideology (imperialism)."[33] Conrad's figure is the site of a multitude of complex ideologies: Polish, exiled with his parents to Russia, multilingual, gentleman,
shiphand, captain, writer, exile...the list of complementary and contradictory facets seems endless. His life was dominated by two powerful empires – Russia and Britain. As a member of a subject race for
the early part of his life and as a "resident alien" in his last thirty
years, Conrad was alert to the politics of location. It could be argued
that Conrad chose the sea, and later took to writing, as ways of avoid-
ing the suicidal, patriotic course of action taken by his father and
other relatives. Home then, was constructed either on board a ship
(i.e., outside national boundaries) or in the abstracted, contemplative
world of his writing.[34]

Conrad was apparently not very popular with his shipping mates –
they called him, ironically, "the Russian Count," because of his fop-
pish dress style and because of the obvious class difference between
this educated, multilingual foreign gentleman and the average ship's
officer. In *Conrad in the Nineteenth Century*, Ian Watt deals with the
question of how Conrad perceived his adopted nation, England:

Conrad's England, however, was primarily the England of the merchant
navy, and of a great literature; what Conrad really thought of the English
people – among whom he spent his shore leaves and subsequently settled
for the last thirty years of his life – is very difficult to know. The English may
not exactly be xenophobes, but they do not take quickly and warmly to foreigners. Brobrowski's letters certainly do not suggest that his nephew took to
his adopted countrymen easily or enthusiastically; and although what
Conrad later said about them was almost unexceptionally laudatory, we
must remember what politeness exacts from the guest, and how gratitude
exaggerates benefits.[35]

Watt goes on to add that what Conrad loved and admired in England were "the residues of the past, of the sailing ship, of the age of Palmerston and the Pax Britannica." Above all there was the "silent but passionate loyalty" of the British that Conrad cherished. Yet, Watt insists, Conrad never felt "at home" in England. Even when he could afford it he never bought a house – the ultimate symbolic and material declaration of belonging. Hence, either Conrad had an outsider's clear insight into the society in which he lived, albeit provisionally, for thirty years, *or* he was the eternal foreigner (a state that requires the active refusal of belonging), who drew on an understanding of England garnered from "a great literature" and from the past, and thus never moved beneath or beyond the cultural idealization of the domestic to an awareness of "the real conditions of existence."[36] Conrad articulated the nature of his divided allegiance between Poland and England to a fellow Polish expatriate in these terms – "Both at sea and on land my point of view is English, from which the conclusion should not be drawn that I have become an Englishman. That is not the case. Homo duplex has in my case more than one meaning. You will understand me. I shall not dwell upon that subject."[37] How do we interpret this declaration? Perhaps he is not so much Perry Anderson's "white emigre" as he is one of V. S. Naipaul's "mimic men." Naipaul's mimics are subjects who never quite escape the sentence of colonialism.[38] And yet mimicry, as Homi Bhabha has demonstrated in various essays, can be a potentially subversive stance. Of these mimic men, Bhabha writes: "He is the effect of a flawed colonial mimesis, in which to be Anglicized, is *emphatically* not to be English."[39] Bhabha goes on to elaborate: "[t]he *menace* of mimicry is its *double* vision which in disclosing the ambivalence of colonial discourse also disrupts its authority" (p. 129).

Other citations from Conrad's own writing put a decisive brake on our desire to read some kind of progressive political stance into Conrad's determination to write from an English point of view without being English. For instance, in *A Personal Record* (1912), Conrad's account of his life at sea and of the writing of *Almayer's Folly*, he noted that once he had begun work on this novel, he would hold "animated receptions of Malays, Arabs and half-castes in his imagination." He continues,

They did not clamor aloud for my attention. They came with silent and irresistible appeal – and the appeal, I affirm here, was not to my self-love or my vanity. It seems now to have had a moral character, for why should the memory of these beings...demand to express itself in the shape of a novel, except on the ground of that mysterious fellowship which unites in a community of hopes and fears all the dwellers on this earth?... After all these years...I can honestly say that it is a sentiment akin to piety which prompted me to render in words assembled with conscientious care the memory of things far distant and of men who had lived."[40]

Here Conrad puts forth a religious romanticization of novel writing intertwined with a celebration of the bonds of imperialism. This is a community of "men who had lived" and other men who bear witness. This *mysterious fellowship* is what makes novels necessary while simultaneously absolving novel writers of any political investments. For, as Conrad wrote in a critical essay entitled "A Glance at Two Books" –

He [the English novelist] does not go about building up his book with a precise intention and a steady mind. It never occurs to him that a book is a deed, that the writing of it is an enterprise as much as the conquest of a colony. He has no such clear concept of his craft.[41]

In these passages, Conrad provides a lucid reading of the political implications of his writing even as he suggests that such "enterprises" might function independent of authorial intent. And the comparison to colonial conquest is more than appropriate, especially if we are to contemplate the nature of Conrad's "animated" receptions with "silent" Malays, Arabs and half-castes. Conrad's discourse is that of the empire: what he presents with "conscientious care" is an alien land read against the idealization of England as Home and other races read against the category of whiteness. Englishness is whiteness at its whitest in this literature, so that race merges into nationality. Hence, the captains of industry on the Thames river, the "privileged reader," and the readers of *Blackwoods*, suggest *one* and perhaps the most immediate, imagined community that is constructed by Conrad's stories.[42]

Conrad's writing attempts to alert the English to the dangers that menace the home. Did he intend that his audience would further secure their home in the face of such dangers or was it his intention to force the readers to accept that their notion of "Home" was so far from the reality of things that it would be better abandoned?[43] I turn to Conrad's novels, primarily *Almayer's Folly*, *Lord Jim*, and *Heart of Darkness* for answers to these questions.

For, as Perry Anderson has said, "if texts are not to be criticized, on what grounds can societies?"[44]

ALMAYER'S FOLLY: RACE AND THE COMPANIONATE
MARRIAGE

The novel's title refers to the house that Almayer, an impoverished Dutch trader in one of the small river-side settlements in the Malay Archipelago, began to build in the vain hope that the British Borneo Company rather than the Dutch, would take over the area and that his trade would flourish again. When neither of these events takes place, Almayer abandons the building of his house. In its half-built stage, the tottering structure of the house pervades the novel as a mocking symbol of Almayer's failure in every sense – his trade, his marriage, his hopes for his daughter, his own self-esteem, and ultimately, his failure to be white.

The novel opens with Almayer on the veranda of his "new but already decaying house" dreaming up a "splendid future into the unpleasant realities of the present hour."[45] His hopes are high because he thinks that he has finally come close to possessing great wealth:

They would live in Europe, he and his daughter. They would be rich and respected. Nobody would think of her mixed blood in the presence of her great beauty and his immense wealth. Witnessing her triumphs he would grow young again, he would forget the twenty-five years of heart-breaking struggle on this coast where he felt like a prisoner. All this was nearly within his reach. *AF*, pp. 3–4)

Almayer himself has never been to Europe. He has only heard of it as a child from his mother, who, "from the depths of her long easy-chair" in their bungalow in Java, "bewailed the lost glories of Amsterdam, where she had been brought up" (*AF*, p. 5). And yet her evocation was powerful enough for him to imagine Amsterdam as "that earthly paradise of his dreams" where he would live like a "king amongst men" in his "fairy palace, the big mansion" (*AF*, p. 10).

It was in the hope of fulfilling this dream of relocating (geographically and in class terms) that Almayer agreed to marry a Malay heiress, the ward of a rich white trader. He thought that it would be "easy enough to dispose of a Malay woman," and yet, the woman (unnamed in the novel) cannot be disposed of and brings no lasting fortune with her (*AF*, pp. 10–11). The novel, which begins approximately seventeen years after this arranged marriage takes place, opens with the "shrill" voice of Mrs. Almayer startling Almayer out of reverie.

Almayer's adult life is the very antithesis of the Victorian ideal: his home is no secure haven. The "new" house is no more than a precarious structure where "stones, decaying planks, and half-sawn beams were piled up in inextricable confusion" (*AF*, p. 12). His "old house" where he lives, had once been a neat structure built by his wife's benefactor. But in subsequent years, his wife had burned the furniture and torn down the pretty curtains in periodic bouts of rage. Instead of the "companion in ideas and mental tastes" that Mill had so approvingly found in the Victorian wife, Almayer's wife has only scorn and resentment for him and for his political and speculative failures in the region. On his part, Almayer, "cowed by these outbursts of a savage nature [hers], meditated in silence on the best way of getting rid of her. He thought of everything; even planned murder in an undecided and feeble sort of way, but dared to do nothing..." (*AF*, p. 26).

Afraid of being poisoned by his wife, Almayer "built for her a riverside house where she dwelt in perfect seclusion." When Nina, their daughter, returns from a ten year stay at a convent in Singapore, she spends her time between the two dwellings. To Almayer's dismay, she doesn't reject her mother and, on what he calls her "bad days," she "used to visit her mother and remain long hours in the riverside hut, coming out inscrutable as ever, but with a contemptuous look and a short word ready to answer any of his speeches" (*AF*, p. 31). Nina, we are to understand, has been trained for a white future at the convent but is betrayed by her "bad" blood.

Nina falls in love with a Malay prince and leaves Sambir to be the queen in a kingdom in the interior of a jungle. Their love is presented as based on physical attraction and is shrouded in political intrigue. Before she leaves for the interior, Nina's mother advises her on how to keep her lover "enslaved" to her: another version of the marital advice a Victorian or Edwardian mother would give her daughter. The underlying "female stratagem" is apparently the same the world over: Nina is to ensure that she will always be the perfect *wife*, no matter what self-denial or other violence this project entails.

"There will be other women," she repeated firmly; "I tell you that because you are half white, and may forget that he is a great chief, and that such things must be. Hide your anger, and do not let him see on your face the pain that will eat your heart. Meet him with joy in your eyes and wisdom on your lips, for to you he shall turn in sadness or in doubt. As long as he looks upon many women your power will last, but should there be one, one only with whom he seems to forget you, then —"

"I could not live," exclaimed Nina, covering her face with both her hands. "Do not speak so, mother; it could not be."

"Then," went on Mrs. Almayer, steadily, "to that woman, Nina, show no mercy."...

"Are you crying?" she asked sternly of her daughter... "And remember, Nina, no mercy; and if you must strike, strike with a steady hand." (*AF*, pp. 153–4)

Conrad's representation of Mrs. Almayer touches several registers – she is the once docile Malay beauty, now given to "savage" fits, often the thwarted politician and diplomat. Here, we see her as the woman whose own desire for power and skill at handling intrigue gets exercise on the occasion of her daughter's impending departure. Mrs. Almayer is a "civilizing project" gone awry. She tells Nina to be joyful, wise and a source of strength for her prince – conventional Victorian motherly advice except that Nina is to kill or otherwise dispose of the occasional mistress with whom he might be seriously enchanted. When Almayer tries to stop Nina from abandoning him and the great "white" future that he would provide for her, it is partly because he cannot foresee a future as a "wife" for her with Dain:

Have you no pity for yourself? Do you know that you shall be at first his plaything and then a scorned slave, a drudge, and a servant of some new fancy of that man?... What made you give yourself up to that savage? For he is a savage. Between him and you there is a barrier that nothing can remove. I can see in your eyes the look of those who commit suicide when they are mad... Have you forgotten the teaching of so many years? (*AF*, pp. 177–8)

Here, Nina interrupts him, and uses the exact same racial equations to put herself and Dain, her Malay lover on the same side of the "barrier." She tells Almayer,

No...I remember it well. I remember how it ended also. Scorn for scorn, contempt for contempt, hate for hate. I am not of your race. Between your people and me there is also a barrier that nothing can remove. You ask why I want to go, and I ask you why I should stay?...I mean to live. I mean to follow him. I have been rejected with scorn by the white people, and now I am a Malay! He took me in his arms, he laid my life at his feet. He is brave; he will be powerful, and I hold his bravery and his strength in my hand, and I shall make him great. His name shall be remembered long after both our bodies are laid in the dust (*AF*, pp. 179–80)

Here Nina overturns Almayer's use of the term "savage" by declaring herself "Malay." This appropriation of a non-European national/racial subject position as a *preferable* option is unusual in colonial fiction. However, this provocative stance is quickly contained by the narrative; in the very next sentence, Nina's language "degenerates" into the mawkish declarations of feminized melodrama. Her declaration that she will henceforth be Malay becomes no more than another utterance in a chain of sentimental exaggerations that follow, "he took me in his arms..."

The language of these exchanges between Nina and Almayer supports two contradictory readings. First, the European notions of home, love and marriage are not universal in that they do not accommodate persons who do not meet the requirements of race, class and wealth. Nina realizes this; Almayer does not. Her use of language resembles her mother's more than it does her father's. The language of the popular romance that Nina uses is closer to her aspirations than Almayer's grandiose romance of a "white" future. The second reading would suggest that these notions of bourgeois domesticity are universal and what we witness in this novel is the alarming disintegration of these cherished values under the corrupt, violent and decadent influence of the foreign land and its people. Mrs. Almayer's characterization would justify such a reading. In this case, Almayer would be the hero who is weak, ineffectual and handicapped by his corrupt surroundings, but who valiantly holds onto the idea of Europe amidst the shambles of his life and fortunes. Which of these two interpretations did Conrad intend and which dominates the text as we have it? One needs to refer to other Conradian novels set outside Europe, before one can determine which of the two given interpretations would be better justified.

LORD JIM: THE PARSONAGE VERSUS PATUSAN

Critical readings of *Lord Jim* invariably draw comparisons between the Patna and Patusan.[46] The novel demonstrates quite ably that the Patna and Patusan are variations on the same theme; the real comparison to be drawn is that between the parsonage where Jim grew up and Patusan where we see him live out his last years. What Jim regrets most about the Patna debacle is not the shame of what he has done, but his inability to "go home" after the scandal is known to the world.[47] The question that we are left with at the end of the novel is not whether Jim redeems what he had lost with his jump from the Patna. The question is whether in offering himself up to one father (Doramin) for the loss of a son (Dain Waris), Jim can compensate his own father for his disappointment in his son.

Jim's father's world is represented as being much less complicated than Jim's. And yet the pastor believes that virtue is one all over the world...

It [the letter] was from his father, and from the date you can see he must have received it a few days before he joined the Patna...There are four pages of it, easy morality and family news...The old man goes on equably trusting Providence and the established order of the universe, but alive to its small dangers and its small mercies. One can almost see him, grey-haired and serene in the inviolable shelter of his book-lined, faded, and comfortable study, where for forty years he had conscientiously gone over and over again the round of his little thoughts about faith and virtue, about the conduct of life and the only proper way of dying; where he had written so many sermons, where he sits talking to his boy, over there, on the other side of the earth. *But what of the distance? Virtue is one all over the world,* and there is only one faith, one conceivable conduct of life, one manner of dying. He hopes his "dear James" will never forget that "who once gives way to temptation, in the very instant hazards his whole depravity and ever-lasting ruin. Therefore resolve fixedly never, through any possible motives, to do anything which you believe to be wrong." (*LJ*, p. 221, emphasis added)

Within this lengthy passage, in which Marlow paraphrases and quotes from Jim's father's last letter to his son, we have the code that Jim attempts to live by. Marlow's attitude is clear from the derisive tone he uses: the old pastor does not know how inadequate his "little thoughts" are in the context of the world of imperial trade and politics. But for Jim these words represent the code that he has failed to live by; "he had treasured it [the letter] all these years" (*LJ*, p. 221). The description of the parsonage on the very second page of the novel is written in language that is evocative of centuries of untroubled "easy morality." Marlow despises the bourgeois comfort that is drawn from religion. His sarcasm is inescapable, and yet there is a tinge of desire in the language used to paint this unchanging home:

Jim's father possessed such certain knowledge of the Unknowable as made for the righteousness of people in cottages without disturbing the ease of mind of those whom an unerring Providence enables to live in mansions. The little church on the hill had the mossy greyness of a rock seen through a ragged screen of leaves. It had stood there for centuries, but the trees around probably remembered the laying of the first stone. Below, the red front of the rectory gleamed with a warm tint in the midst of grass-plots, flower-beds, and fir-trees, with an orchard at the back, a paved stable-yard to the left, and the sloping glass of greenhouses tacked along a wall of bricks. The living had belonged to the family for generations; Jim was one of five sons... (*LJ*, p. 2)

It is the stress on continuity and the links with childhood (and beyond) that make this a description that invokes desire. Marlow, who has chosen to live outside these environs, is clearly aware of the lulling effects of social piety. And yet, as the fragments quoted above demonstrate, there is a *real* power in the sense of roots, religious binding and community, however *imagined* such feelings may be. Despite his worldly wise ways, Marlow too, understands the need to present a decent account of oneself at home. Musing on why he was so eager to see Jim settled in Patusan, he concludes that his main purpose was to "get him out of the way," and to do so before himself going home to England. Marlow elaborates:

I repeat, I was going home – to that home distant enough for all its hearth-stones to be like the hearthstone, by which the humblest of us has the right to sit. We wander in our thousands over the face of the earth, the illustrious and the obscure, earning beyond the seas our fame, our money, or only a crust of bread; but it seems to me that for each of us going home must be like going to render an account. We return to face our superiors, our kindred, our friends – those whom we obey, and those whom we love, but even they who have neither, the most free, lonely and irresponsible and bereft of ties, – even those for whom home holds no dear face, no familiar voice, – even they have to meet the spirit that dwells within the land, under its sky, in its air, in its valleys, and on its rises, in its fields, in its waters and its trees – a mute friend, judge, and inspirer. Say what you like, to get its joy, to breathe its peace, to face its truth, one must return with a clear consciousness. All this may seem to you sheer sentimentalism; and indeed very few of us have the will or the capacity to look consciously under the surface of familiar emotions. There are girls we love, the men we look up to, the tenderness, the friendships, the opportunities, the pleasures! But the fact remains that you must touch your reward with clean hands, lest it turn to dead leaves, to thorns, in your grasp. I think it is the lonely, without a fireside or an affection they may call their own, those who return not to a dwelling place but to the land itself, to meet its disembodied, eternal and unchanging spirit – it is those who understand best its severity, its saving power, the grace of its secular right to our fidelity, to our obedience. Yes! few of us understand, but we all feel it though, and I say *all* without exception, because those who do not feel do not count. (*LJ*, p. 143)

It is these ties that Jim sees himself as having broken because of his "jump." Here Marlow echoes the accepted equation of one's home (and of England in general) to copies of the divine estate.[48] For Jim, the figure of his father takes on the proportions of home, of country and of god:

"He has seen it in all the home papers by this time," said Jim. "I can never face the poor old chap...I could never explain. He wouldn't understand." (*LJ*, p. 50–51)

Yet after the Patna incident, when Jim tells Marlow that "there was not the thickness of a sheet of paper between the right and wrong of it," Marlow's reply is "How much more did you want?" (*LJ*, p. 83). By Marlow's seaman's code abandoning a ship full of passengers is a crime. Hence, what we can conclude is that, clearly, some crimes, like the abandoning of the Patna, are criminal from both the pastor's and Marlow's code. But does this make virtue "one all over the world?" And is "the distance" of any importance? For our purpose it seems vital that we answer these two questions. The point to be settled is *whose* definition of virtue do we follow? A man like Jim who has failed both codes struggles to discover another that is equally acceptable. And this is what makes him, in Marlow's book, "one of us." Belonging in this "gang of virtue" (a term taken from *Heart of Darkness*) requires a certain amount of wrestling with the ethics and morals of home and travel.

Lord Jim, since it is narrated by him, seems to favor Marlow's seaman's code. Jim's father lives in the sheltered world of bourgeois, Christian universality. For him, distances amount to nothing. There is only one way of living and dying. Marlow's code is more adaptable, more flexible, but only for the pragmatic reason of applicability to all the different colonial situations. His code is as deeply enmeshed in the ideology of colonial/capitalist exploitation as the Pastor's is in that of heaven and haven. Despite the distance that Marlow draws between the two codes, they are complementary: one for the pastors and citizens (especially the women) in the home country to live by and the other for the "real men" who venture out into the heart of darkness. And yet, at the heart of both codes lies an unchanging allegiance to an ideology of differentiating between "us" and, as Marlow puts it, "those who do not feel [and therefore] do not count" (*LJ*, p. 143).

HEART OF DARKNESS: "TWO GOOD ADDRESSES" VERSUS THE WILDERNESS

As in *Lord Jim*, a character called Marlow is the master-narrator of *Heart of Darkness* (1899).[49] The narrative role of this character is similar in both novels; he tells an audience of seafaring men about his encounter with a man who began his career in the world of colonial trade and shipping (as any other white man might have) and then carved out a separate and spectacular destiny for himself.

In *Heart of Darkness*, the two codes that are weighed against each other are, once again, a secure life in a European metropolis versus trials in the colonial world. At a crucial point in the telling of his story, Marlow bursts out with:

This is the worst of trying to tell...here you all are, each moored with two good addresses, like a hulk with two anchors, a butcher round one corner, a policeman round another, excellent appetites and temperatures normal – you hear – normal from year's end to year's end...

You can't understand. How could you? – with solid pavement under your feet, surrounded by kind neighbours to cheer you on or to fall on you,

stepping delicately between the butcher and the policeman, in the holy terror of scandal and gallows and lunatic asylums – how can you imagine what
particular region of the first ages a man's untrammeled feet may take him
into by way of solitude – utter silence, where no warning voice of a neighbour can be heard whispering of public opinion? These little things make all
the difference. When they are gone you must fall back on your own innate
strength, upon your own capacity for faithfulness. (*HD*, pp. 48–50)

According to Marlow, the skills required to deal with civilization are
easier and more circumscribed than those required to survive the
wilderness. Marlow believes that the wilderness strips away all the
shelter and security provided by civilization and the only thing that
can see one through is one's "innate strength or capacity for faithfulness" (*HD*, p. 3). This faithfulness is always to "the idea at the back of
it" – the idea that redeems the exploits of the British colonialists (*HD*,
p. 3). Sitting aboard the Nellie, on the Thames, near London – the
"biggest and greatest town on earth" – Marlow tells his English host
and friends: "What saves us is efficiency – the devotion to efficiency.
But these chaps were not much account, really. They were no colonialists" (*HD*, p. 6).

Marlow and Kurtz are both part of the "new gang – the gang of
virtue" when they enter the wilderness (*HD*, p. 26). And yet they are
not the ones who survive the jungle. Ironically, it is the ordinary,
commonplace trader who "inspired neither love nor fear, nor even
respect" who has been the manager in the interior for nine years. He
has "no learning and no intelligence"; his only qualification is that he
has never been ill: "because triumphant health in the general rout of
constitutions is a kind of power in itself" (*HD*, p. 22). Hence, Marlow's
code is no more a defense against destruction of the self in the wilderness than is the dominant bourgeois ideology back home. And this is
best illustrated in the case of Kurtz.

Kurtz's "virtue" is so flexible that he embraces the wilderness, and
"lacking all restraint," he goes native. "The wilderness had patted him
on the head...it caressed him, and – lo – he had withered" (*HD*, p. 49).
There seems to be a simple cause and effect relationship between the
"caress" of the wilderness (personified in the "Amazon") and the "with-
ering" (castration) of the white male. In *Heart of Darkness*, women and
the society they represent – Africa in the case of the "Amazon" and
Europe in the case of the "Intended" – are bestowed with a certain
power and control over the destiny of white men. Neither white women
nor the colonized (men and women) benefit from being placed on the

same side of this divide. The perceived inadequacies and anxieties of the colonizer's code are transferred onto everything that is seen as a danger to it: in this novel, the jungle and women. The "Amazon" conflates both to become "junglewoman," powerful and threatening:

there was something wanting in him – some small matter which, when the pressing need arose, could not be found under his magnificent eloquence. Whether he knew of this deficiency himself I can't say. I think the knowledge came to him at last – only at the very last. But the wilderness had found him out early, and had taken on him a terrible vengeance for the fantastic invasion. I think it had whispered to him things about himself which he did not know, things of which he had no conception till he took counsel with this great solitude – and the whisper had proved irresistibly fascinating, It echoed loudly within him because he was hollow to the core... (*HD*, pp. 58–9)

As presented by Marlow, there is nothing positive or admirable about this power of the "weak" over Kurtz. Instead, the urgent though covert message seems to be that "feminine" power is a perversion or a negation of the pure power of the white, male, explorer and the only way of overpowering this "dark," female power is by exterminating it. The power of the "weak" is variously represented: by the destruction of Kurtz, by Marlow's desperate need to lie to the Intended, and most tellingly by the kinship between the Intended and the "Amazon" that Marlow recognizes.

To Marlow, the "Amazon" is "like the wilderness itself: – a site where the female, the animal, the untamed earth with its natural wealth meet" (*HD*, p. 62). The Intended, by contrast, is presented as the personification of "civilization" at its greatest remove from the ability to cope with life in the business/colonial world of competition. She is presented as femininity entombed in her home in the sepulchral city of Brussels. Marlow sees safety in immuring the Intended so that, ignorant of the truth about male failure, she cannot slip into the role of the "Amazon." Marlow suggests that she has the potential to be this (sexually) powerful figure: "I shall see this eloquent phantom as long as I live, and I shall see her too...resembling in this gesture another one, tragic too and bedecked with powerless charms" (*HD*, p. 78).

Thus Marlow suggests that the only way of suppressing the "Amazon" in the white woman is to keep her drugged with a "ransom of pretty, shining lies." Earlier in the novel, Marlow had said to his all-male audience, "they – the women I mean – are out of it – should be out of it. We must help them stay in that beautiful world of their own, lest ours gets worse" (*HD*, p. 49). In the original manuscript, Conrad had made this passage even more explicit by adding: "That's a monster-truth with many maws to whom we've got to throw every year – or every day – no matter – no sacrifice is too great – a ransom of pretty shining lies" (*HD*, p. 49).

This brings us to a curious impasse in the novel's logic. Marlow feels trapped both in the houses of the civilized world, which are presided over by women, and by the wilderness, which is also female.[50] To Marlow, on one side, there is the world of "two good addresses" where he (like Jim in *Lord Jim*) cannot explain himself or feel at home after what he has experienced in the world, and, on the other side, there is colonialism – the "cause entrusted us by Europe" where a "singleness of purpose," "efficiency," "the idea behind it," are the only shields against the darkness (*HD*, pp. 3–6).

In this novel more than in any other, Conrad seems to reject outright the very ideological basis on which the popular idealizations of home stand. The world of marriage and domesticity seems very far away. Of course Kurtz had gone to the Congo to make himself financially worthy of marrying the Intended. And yet, he seems to have been more content with his home in the clearing at the heart of the river, with the "Amazon" as his partner and human heads as fence posts. In the early part of Marlow's stay in the headquarters, he is told how Kurtz once almost returned to the company of white men, only to go back at the last instant. Marlow imagines the scene:

I seemed to see Kurtz for the first time. It was a distinct glimpse: the dugout, four paddling savages, and the lone white man turning his back suddenly on the headquarters, on relief, on thoughts of home – perhaps; setting his face towards the depths of the wilderness, towards his empty and desolate station. (*HD*, pp. 32)

Later in the novel, Kurtz attempts to crawl back on his hands and feet to the Amazon. Kurtz may have gone "mad," but this aversion for civilization (*the lone white man turning his back suddenly on the headquarters*) is shared by Marlow who, as narrator, succeeds in making it look more justified. The masculine dilemma, as represented in this novel, is that men like Marlow and Kurtz have no destinations awaiting them where they can be wholly themselves. The domestic world from which the brutalities of empire are painstakingly erased and the rough public world where those with virtues and delicate constitutions cannot survive are the available options. The only other location is the ship and the sea.[51]

Conrad makes his reader (the male, white, educated reader of *Blackwood's*) aware of the menace facing him both at home and overseas. The menace is the inability to see the world for what it is − a rough and frightening place. To survive in it, one has both to learn to live without the "ransom of pretty, shining lies," and yet maintain this pretense for the "ladies" and for others who do not engage in the colonial enterprise, and also to outsmart the "common fellows," like the manager of the headquarters or the members of the "Eldorado Exploration team," whose wiles and lower-class sturdy health will otherwise enable them to reap/rape the colonies.

Given the historical period in which Conrad wrote these novels, it is not surprising that he thought that civilization was inadequately equipped to deal with the complexities of the modern world. In "Autocracy and War," an essay written on the occasion of the Japanese defeat of Russia in 1905, Conrad spells out his fears:

Civilization has done its little best by our sensibilities for whose growth it is responsible. It has managed to remove the sights and sounds of the battle-fields away from our doorsteps. But it cannot be expected to achieve the feat always and under every variety of circumstance. Some day it must fail, and we shall have then a wealth of appallingly unpleasant sensations brought home to us with painful intimacy.[52]

This passage could be mapped directly onto the plot of *The Secret Agent* written in 1907.[53] In this novel, despite their involvement in the "battlefield" of class insurrection and international spying, the Verlocs manage to "remove" its "sights and sounds" from their domestic haven until the death of Stevie brings the appalling fact of their complicity "home to [them] with painful intimacy."

The disasters that unfold in this novel do not, as in the earlier novels, concern exotic Patusan or the Malay or African interior. Set in London, *The Secret Agent* describes threats of anarchy that hover over such familiar and seemingly immutable features of the national landscape as Greenwich Park. The entire novel reads as a warning against the menace of the proletarian rabble; the menace that civilization and all its handmaids − religion, tradition, the class structure − have tried to contain over the years. The last paragraph of the novel screams out the threat and the foolishness of letting it go unchecked:

And the incorruptible Professor walked too, averting his eyes from the odious multitude of mankind. He had no future. He disdained it. He was a force. His thoughts caressed the images of ruin and destruction. He walked frail, insignificant, shabby, miserable − and terrible in the simplicity of his idea calling madness and despair to the regeneration of the world. Nobody looked at him. He passed on unsuspected and deadly, like a pest in the street full of men. (*SA*, p. 311)

Conrad's urgency is so strongly felt that his language collapses into incoherence – "He walked frail, ... of the world." The Professor with his rubber ball always handy, represents the antithesis of human endeavor and aspiration as prescribed by popular discourses. Each of the other anarchists displays some human weakness, some desire for social institutions such as "home," and this "corruptibility" renders them, ultimately, as vulnerable and harmless as the retarded child Stevie.[54]

If these lower-class "revolutionaries" are children, then the upper class would play the role of the kindly patriarch, a role that is significantly vacant in this novel. In *Under Western Eyes*, a novel written by Conrad four years later, explicit use is made of family metaphors to characterize the Russian political and social structure. In *Under Western Eyes*, the autocratic Russian government is the patriarch whose authoritative presence serves to quell all disruption and dissent. One can read in the absence of a kind patriarch in *The Secret Agent* an implied criticism of the "slackness" of authority under western capitalism. This novel, therefore, ends with the professor stalking the streets, waiting to explode.

Sixty years after *The Secret Agent* was written, Perry Anderson had the advantage of hindsight when he lamented the lack of a serious anti-establishment movement in England. However, for Conrad in 1907, anything was possible. As he wrote in "Autocracy and War," the "sights and sounds of the battle-field" seemed close enough to home for the alarm to be rung.

CONRAD AT THE CROSSROADS: NAIPAUL AND ISHIGURO

Texts are not finished objects. They are, as Raymond Williams once said, notations and cultural practices. And texts not only create their precedents as Borges said of Kafka, they also create their successors. The great imperial experience of the past two hundred years is global and universal, it has implicated every corner of the world, the colonizer and the colonized together.

Edward Said

Notions of home and travel have remained literary, political tropes long beyond Conrad's contributions to literature in English. Not surprisingly, Conrad remains as a pivotal figure, as one of the first western writers whose fiction forces this trope to confront its political implications in an international arena. In *London Calling: V. S. Naipaul,*

Postcolonial Mandarin, an outstanding reading of V. S. Naipaul's travel writing and his modes of self-authorization as the eternal exile, Rob Nixon cautions against "the common perception of Conrad as a trail-blazer" and against the "tendency to use Conrad as base camp" that can be occupied by writers who come after him.[55] Writing on the *Heart of Darkness* tradition, in the work of Graham Greene, Hannah Arendt, André Gide and Naipaul, Nixon demonstrates how: "Conrad has retained his usefulness for those who wish to situate Third World cultures outside the bounds of history" (p. 96). What Nixon wants to resist is the "pressure of Conrad's assumed priority as the 'natural' starting point for a Western understanding of Africa" (p. 104). I will argue that Conrad's fiction serves as an important starting point for a *non-western understanding of the west.* In the context of global literature in English, this becomes the more generative angle from which to view Conrad's work. It is not a "natural" starting point by any means, rather one which serves as such because of the specifics of Conrad's personal location and because of the terrain covered by his fiction. To read Conrad in the context provided by the epigraph to this section which is taken from Said's essay on third world intellectuals and met-ropolitan culture is to substantially alter Nixon's assessment.[56] Recognizing this role of Conrad requires acknowledgment of the complex allegiances held by global writers in the English language. In this arena, literary precedents and successors do not necessarily "bor-row" only from those earlier practitioners whose political stance they mean to mimic or keep alive.[57]

In *The Political Unconscious,* Fredric Jameson begins his chapter on Conrad by noting that the lack of "the windless closure of high natu-ralism" is what has kept these novels alive. He writes,

Perhaps, for that reason, even after eighty years, his place is still unstable, undecidable, and his work unclassifiable, spilling out of high literature into light reading and romance, reclaiming great areas of diversion and distrac-tion by the most demanding practice of style and *écriture* alike, floating uncer-tainly somewhere in between Proust and Robert Louis Stevenson. Conrad marks, indeed, a strategic fault line in the emergence of contemporary nar-rative, a place from which the structure of twentieth-century literary and cul-tural *institutions* becomes visible...In Conrad we can sense the emergence not merely of what will be contemporary modernism (itself now become a liter-ary institution), but also, still tangibly juxtaposed with it, of what will vari-ously be called popular culture or mass culture, the commercialized cultural discourse of what, in late capitalism, is often described as a media society.[58]

Jameson's argument remains circumscribed by the conventional terms of western art – high and low, modernist versus popular culture, etc. However, his astute analysis can be read in light of an equally tangible presence in twentieth-century fiction in English – the work of global writers.

I would argue that Conrad's novels are kept alive for the reasons that Jameson provides as well as because they now serve as the fictional originary for a whole genre of *international* twentieth-century writing in the English language. From this perspective, Conrad does serve as "a strategic fault line" – but a fault line that has since served for other outsiders as an *entrance* into the literary institution of "English Literature." Conrad's novels are "alive" in their "reincarnations," that is, in the novels that they have engendered.

It is Conrad's curious homelessness and the seeming ease with which he tackles what should be foreign to him – the ideology of the British Empire and its attendant idealizations of the domestic – that give him his stature in the arena of global writing in English. There is also the issue of Conrad's bilingualism that makes his work of special interest to non-western writers. For, despite the often quoted "fact" that Conrad did not speak a word of English before the age of twenty, his novels luxuriate in the language. Conrad brings to literary English an elaborate, extravagant usage whose aim is to get at a precise and truthful rendition of the event or emotion being described through the language of excess. In such an enterprise, his "foreignness" becomes a tool rather than a handicap.

This is not to suggest that Conrad is always held in high esteem or that his ambiguous political stance is universally acceptable. There is his evident seduction by the idealizations of the English discourses he was so fluent in – the ideologies of gender, domesticity, race, empire, efficiency and social order. This participation in the projects of western literary politics has placed him at the entrance to the "Great English Tradition," as the first of the "Great Names" with whom the outsider has to negotiate. Serving as the entrance to the house of English fiction, Conrad's novels have the benefit of both views – the "great books" that lie inside and the world that lies outside. This accounts for the ambiguous nature of his political stance: is he critic or collaborator? Rather than read Conrad as one of Perry Anderson's "white emigres," I choose to re-present him as the first of many colonial subjects – irrespective of color – who, rather than perform as "foreign practitioners" in English culture, will instead make English culture, and especially its literature, seem foreign. Hence Conrad is followed by G. V. Desani, Samuel Selvon, V. S. Naipaul, Jean "Binta" Breeze, Wilson Harris, Salman Rushdie and many others.

For the global writer of literature in English, Conrad is a body of work that one has to work through *if* one is interested in positioning one's own work in relation to the "Great English Tradition." The result is often outright rejection – as manifest in Chinua Achebe's declaration that Conrad was no more than "a bloody racist." Other writers of global English, such as Wilson Harris in *The Palace of the Peacock* and V. S. Naipaul in *A House for Mister Biswas*, have "revised" Conrad through their own fictions. Such revisions, I will insist go beyond the usual connotations of "influence" and "imitation." Hence, I will not defend my reading of Conrad through Naipaul against Paul Theroux's declaration that – "Wholly original, he [Naipaul] may be the only writer today in whom there are no echoes of influence."[59]

First published in 1961, Naipaul's *A House for Mister Biswas* is a partly autobiographical novel that is written with a wisdom and generosity that his later work lacks. Naipaul's novel necessarily alters our reading of *Almayer's Folly*. Biswas's predicament is precisely that of Almayer in Conrad's novel. Both see the worth of their lives as measured by the house that they build for themselves. Both characters fail to build anything but pitiful replications of the house and life they have dreamed of for themselves and their children. Both Almayer and Biswas are coerced into marriages that hold out the promise of lives of monied ease. Both are disappointed with what follows after marriage. Both chafe at the "trap" that they see themselves as having fallen into as a result of their marriage.

The narrative stance that the two writers adopt toward their main protagonist is central to the differences between the two texts. Naipaul's story of the troubles and setbacks that hound Mr. Biswas is narrated with constant empathy. Conrad's sympathy for Almayer wavers even at crucial points in the narrative such as when his daughter scorns his dreams of "white" success. Reading *A House for Mister Biswas* gives the reader of Conrad's novel the political context for understanding Almayer's predicament. Like Biswas, Almayer is a colonial subject for whom the strongest of desires are those that are, of necessity, unobtainable by one of his class, geographic location, and in other situations, color. The disenfranchisement of Almayer and Biswas does not prevent them from dreaming about an adequate house in which to install an adequate self. The great degree to which these notions of the idealized domestic are prescribed by dominant colonial ideologies is what marks them as desiring colonial subjects. For instance, in Naipaul's novel, Biswas has a very precise notion of what he wants in his dream house:

He had thought deeply about this house, and knew exactly what he wanted. He wanted, in the first place, a real house, made with real materials. He didn't want mud for walls, earth for floor, tree branches for rafters and grass for roof. He wanted wooden walls, all tongue-and-groove. He wanted a galvanized iron roof and a wooden ceiling. He would walk up concrete steps into a small verandah; through doors with coloured panes into a small dining room; from there into a small bedroom, then another small bedroom, then back into a small verandah. The house would stand on tall concrete pillars so that he would get two floors instead of one, and the way would be left open for future development. The kitchen would be a shed in the yard; a neat shed, connected to the house by a covered way. And his house would be painted. The roof would be red, the outside walls ochre with chocolate facings, and the windows white.[60]

Especially noteworthy is Biswas' understanding of "real materials" and of "a real house" which he holds in opposition to indigenous housing materials and building techniques. Biswas' category of "real" building materials and "real" houses could be read alongside Marlow's declaration in *Heart of Darkness* that "normal" temperatures are those of England's climate— concepts that have become *fact* thanks to the persuasive powers of the imperial ideology. When Biswas finally decides to build this dream house he is amazed that Mr. Maclean, the impoverished black builder he interviews for the job, is so conversant with the parameters of his desires. The exchange, which takes place in the yard of Maclean's "crumbling wooden house in a small Negro settlement" is as follows:

With a switch he [Maclean] flicked some fowl droppings from the yard into the thick dust under the floor of his own house. Then he drew two equal and adjacent squares on the ground."You want two bedrooms."

"And a drawing room."

Mr. Maclean added another square of the same size and said, "And a gallery."

"That's it. Nothing too fancy for me. Small and neat."

"You want a door from the gallery to the front bedroom. A wooden door. And you want another door to the drawing room. With coloured glass panes."

"Yes, yes."

"For the front bedroom you want glass windows, and if you get the money you going to paint them white. The back windows could be pure board. And you want a plain wood staircase at the back, with no banister or anything like that. The kitchen you going to build yourself, somewhere in the yard."

"Exactly."

"That's a nice little house you have there. A lot of people would like it..." (Emphasis added.[61])

Maclean is hired on the spot. Despite his claims of being extremely busy with other house constructions projects, Maclean arrives that very afternoon to look over the site chosen by Biswas. Naipaul is brutal in his use of the comic as a means of exposing what Larrain has called the "contradictions which have not been solved in practice," but his sympathy for Biswas is unflinching. In this novel Naipaul carefully delineates an issue that is central to several novels by Conrad, namely, masculine failure. In the fiction of the young Naipaul, masculine failure is endemic to the very colonial situation. It is not, as in Conrad's and other imperial romance novels, an outcome of the perennially hot weather of the generic "tropical land" nor is it simply ascribed to personal or moral weakness.

Reading *Almayer's Folly* through the discourse of postcolonialism that Naipaul's novel participates in, forces us to reassess Almayer's failure. Failure becomes a very interesting trope in most postcolonial literature in English because it serves as a direct commentary on the pressures of negotiating with the competing allegiances that are available at these historical junctures.[62] In Conrad's narrative, however, the responsibility for Almayer's failures falls directly on his own shoulders – he is no more than a pathetic disgrace to his gender and race – there is no larger explanation. The narrative creates a portrait of a European male who is slowly demolished by his own greed, his lack of generosity, his inclination to corruption and his lack of honest enterprise. It is possible to read *Almayer's Folly* in the contexts of the machinations of empire; Almayer is then as limited by the political history of his geographic location, by what he desires and by his class, as is Biswas.

It could be argued that there is much that is generative about Conrad's undeniable presence in today's cultural texts. And yet Rob Nixon argues that despite precedents for "counter-hegemonic co-option" such as the appropriation of Caliban as the "triumphant, resisting slave and hero of decolonization," his "sense is that *Heart of Darkness* has become so entrenched in metropolitan discourse about the globe's 'periphery' that [he is] pessimistic about the capacity of Third World writers to appropriate this insistent trope by reversing it" (p. 106). Holding this pessimism (and the very legitimate reasons for it) in view I turn to England, where Kazuo Ishiguro travels Conradian paths in *The Remains of the Day*, a much acclaimed novel written in 1989.[63] I wish to garner support for my reading of this novel from "The Fortunate Traveller" written by the Caribbean poet Derek

Walcott. The section of the poem that is most relevant in the context of my reading of Ishiguro's novel, is as follows:

> The heart of darkness is not Africa.
> The heart of darkness is the core of fire
> in the white center of the holocaust.
> The heart of darkness is the rubber claw
> selecting a scalpel in antiseptic light,
> the hills of children's shoes outside the chimneys[64]

Commenting on this passage, Nixon dismisses Walcott's effort to relocate the heart of darkness from Africa to Europe as "a thin straw in a very strong wind" (p. 105). Ishiguro's novel, I believe, operates beyond simple reversals and writing back as it recycles the dynamics of *Heart of Darkness*. *The Remains of the Day*, then, quietly stands by Walcott's impassioned judgment on Europe.

Ishiguro, like Conrad, catalogues England in terms of a series of idealizations taken from the immediate past. In Ishiguro's novel, such an examination of England is occasioned by a five-day touring trip around the English countryside taken by Mr. Stevens the narrator. Suggestively set in the 1950s, the period of initial decolonization, the novel is written in the form of a series of journal entries by Stevens, a butler at Darlington Hall, one of the last of the "great old houses" in England. Having rarely ventured more than a few miles away from the Hall in his entire life, Stevens sets forth on this trip with trepidation and excitement. The journey that Stevens narrates is similar to Marlow's wanderings in the outskirts of Empire. Both are compelled by their encounters with the unknown to evaluate their own view of the world. Both Marlow and Stevens avoid the personal crisis that should ensue when they are confronted with the hollowness of their lives by turning at this very juncture to work and to the notions of efficiency, restraint and order. Both refuse to acknowledge that the heart of darkness lies with the men (Kurtz, Lord Darlington) to whom they have given their allegiance.

As I have argued earlier in this chapter, in *Heart of Darkness* two codes are weighed against each other: a secure life style in a European metropolis versus the trials in the colonial world. Marlow laments that his English audience, "moored with two good addresses," with "normal temperatures" and "solid pavement under your feet," cannot understand that in the wilderness the only solid ground is provided by "one's innate strength," "restraint," and devotion to "efficiency." These, very *English*, codes are also those valorized in *The Remains of the Day*. In Stevens' imagination, Darlington Hall has taken on the proportion of both home and country – although technically it is neither. Stevens firmly believes that

crucial decisions [are] arrived at, in the privacy and calm of the great houses of this country. What occurs under the public gaze with so much pomp and ceremony is often the conclusion, or the mere ratification, of what has taken place over weeks or months within the walls of such houses. To us, then, the world was a wheel revolving with these great houses at the hub, their mighty decisions emanating out to all else, rich and poor, who revolved around them. It was the aspiration of all those of us with professional ambition to work our way as close to this hub as we were each of us capable. For we were, as I say, an idealistic generation for whom the question was not simply one of how well one practiced one's skills, but *to what end* one did so; each of us harboured the desire to make our own small contribution to the creation of a better world, and saw that, as professionals, the surest means of doing so would be to serve the great gentlemen of our times in whose hands civilization had been entrusted.

This faith in the rightness of the old ways is shaken by Stevens' interactions with his countrymen. Chance encounters make him question his idolatry of the late Lord Darlington who, as Stevens slowly reveals, was, perhaps unwittingly, a Nazi collaborator in the war and in the deliberations after the war. In coming to terms with this accusation from the past and other aspects of his master's politics, such as his flagrant anti-semitism in the war years, Stevens puts forth Marlow-like propositions on the codes that matter *and of the places that matter:*

Indeed, I have seen in encyclopedias and the *National Geographic Magazine* breathtaking photographs of sights from various corners of the globe; magnificent canyons and waterfalls, raggedly beautiful mountains. It has never, of course been my privilege to have seen such things at first hand, but I will nevertheless hazard this with some confidence: the English landscape at its finest – such as I saw this morning – possesses a quality that the landscapes of other nations, however more superficially dramatic, inevitably fail to possess. It is, I believe, a quality that will mark out the English landscape to any objective observer as the most deeply satisfying in the world, and this quality is probably best summed up by the term "greatness". For it is true, when I stood on that high ledge this morning and viewed the land before me, I distinctly felt that rare, yet unmistakable feeling – the feeling that one is in the presence of greatness. We call this land of ours *Great* Britain, and there may be those who believe this a somewhat immodest practice. Yet I would venture that the landscape of our country alone would justify the use of this lofty adjective.

And yet what precisely is this "greatness"? Just where, or in what, does it lie? I am quite aware it would take a far wiser head than mine to answer such a question, but if I were forced to hazard a guess, I would say that it is the very *lack* of obvious drama or spectacle that sets the beauty of our land apart. What is pertinent is the calmness of that beauty, its sense of restraint. It is as though the land knows of its own beauty, of its own greatness, and feels no need to shout it. In comparison, the sorts of sights offered in such places as Africa and America, though undoubtedly very exciting, would, I am sure, strike the objective viewer as inferior on account of their unseemly demonstrativeness.

This whole question is very akin to the question that has caused much debate in our profession over the years: what is a "great" butler?[65]

Stevens, like Marlow, belongs to the "gang of virtue": the colonists and butlers who aspire to greatness. While colonists and butlers do indeed occupy different class positions in their own and in the popular imagination, there are similarities in their self-representations as scripted by Conrad and Ishiguro. Both Marlow and Stevens are convinced of the rightness of the rule(s) of *their* land. The red places on the map where real work is done are necessarily English. The British colonies were marked in red on colonial maps and Marlow notes in *Heart of Darkness* that "there was a vast amount of red – good to see at any time, because one knows that some real work is done there."[66] In *The Remains of the Day*, Stevens insists that

butlers only truly exist in England. Other countries, whatever title is actually used, have only manservants...Continentals are incapable of the emotional restraint which only the English are capable of...In a word, "dignity" is beyond such persons. We English have an important advantage over foreigners in this respect and it is for this reason that when you think of a great butler, he is bound, almost by definition, to be an Englishman.[67]

The ironic tinge that shades so much of this novel operates here and elsewhere completely unknown to the narrator, Stevens. Like Stevens, Marlow does not think highly of his fellow workers (colonists such as those in the Eldorado Exploring Expedition) on the continent and of their endeavors. The "emotional restraint" that Stevens identifies as exclusively English is the very quality that Marlow sees Kurtz as lacking. As I have mentioned earlier, it is this lack of restraint that results in Kurtz's capitulation to the lures of "the jungle."

In the last of his encounters on the road, Stevens meets Miss Keaton, the one-time housekeeper at Darlington Hall with whom he has a relationship that approached romance. This meeting comes after a gap of twenty years which was when she left the Hall to get married. Miss Keaton serves the function that Kurtz does in *Heart of Darkness* even as she occupies the structural position that the Intended does in Conrad's novel. Like Marlow who sets out in search of Kurtz, Stevens sets out in search of Keaton. At the end Marlow has an interview with the

Intended as Stevens does with Miss Keaton. My interest in doing such a
parallel reading of the two texts is not so much to match details but to
highlight the ways in which echoes of Conrad still resonate in late twentieth century fiction. The desire and pleasure that marks Stevens' memories of the young Miss Keaton and of his beloved Lord Darlington,
infuses an eroticism to the bond between Kurtz and Marlow. Miss
Keaton tempts Stevens as Kurtz tempts Marlow with the prospect of
out-stepping boundaries, with transgressing the ruling work ethic, with
sexuality. And Stevens just about manages to resist her seduction as
Marlow does with Kurtz. In both novels, the bond between the two central characters is repressed, transposed and denied and yet it surges up
and engulfs the narrative. What holds recognition of this bond at bay is
Stevens' and Marlow's devotion to "work." As they part once again,
Stevens asks Miss Keaton about a particular phrase she had used in a
letter to him – "the rest of my life stretches out like an emptiness before
me." This utterance takes on the stature of Kurtz's final words – "the
horror, the horror." Miss Keaton (now Mrs. Benn) asks Stevens what the
future held for him at Darlington Hall. He replies:

Well, whatever awaits me, Mrs. Benn, I know I'm not awaited by emptiness.
If only I were. But oh no, there's work, work and more work.[68]

Both Marlow and Stevens refuse to share the horror of the emptiness.
They determinedly refuse any kinship with either Kurtz or with Miss
Keaton. Stevens like Marlow in *Heart of Darkness*, sees work, efficiency
and "the idea behind it" as the only things that matter. Stevens'
"restraint" is what keeps him from finding personal happiness with
Miss Keaton, but it is also what helps him accept this loss with equanimity. What lies ahead of him in Darlington Hall is truly just work,
work and more work – and that too with a reduced staff and for an
absentee master, the rich young American, Mr. Farraday. As for
Marlow, the boat, the "cannibals," and the "pilgrims" keep him
busy.[69] The only instance in which Marlow's "restraint" falters is
when he finds himself unable to bear the suffocating heterosexual
voraciousness of Kurtz's Intended as she delights in claiming every
part of Kurtz for herself.[70]

In an earlier quoted passage from *Lord Jim*, Marlow evokes the idealized notion of England as Home. Stevens would fit right into
Marlow's category of "the lonely without a fireside or an affection they
may call their own" but who "understand best its [England's] severity,
its saving power, the grace of its secular right to our fidelity, to our obe-

dience" (LJ, p. 143). "Yes!" Marlow continues, "few of us understand, but we all feel it though, and I say all without exception, because those who do not feel do not count." Under this rubric, Jim, Almayer, Stevens and *even* Biswas are amongst those who "count." Conrad may not have anticipated having to include Mr. Biswas (or for that matter, Mr. Naipaul) in this circle, but his novels open up the category.

Regardless of the details of time, nationality and geographic location, Marlow, Stevens, Almayer and Biswas are all subjects of European colonialism. As Edward Said has written in the passage that serves as an epigraph to this section of this chapter – "The great imperial experience of the past two hundred years is global and universal, it has implicated every corner of the world, the colonizer and the colonized together." Hence to read Almayer, Biswas, and Stevens alongside each other is not a dismissal of historical or geographic distance but an insistence on global implications of the English language and its literature. Again, in terms of literary genre, I would stress that despite the obvious differences, Conrad, Naipaul and Ishiguro have produced similar cultural products. Through representations such as Stevens' adoration of Lord Darlington, Jewel's love for Jim, Jim's view of himself, Biswas' dreams for himself, the Intended's view of Kurtz, and Nina's love for her Malay Prince, these novels examine the possibility of sustaining a masculine heroism taken from romance novels in fiction that intends to be realist.

At the end of the day the genre remains, yet it is radically altered. Literature written in English is no longer a site that serves an exclusive white, upper-class clientele as an imaginary home or resting place. The "strategic fault line" inscribed by Conrad's novels has become quite a writers' colony in itself. In retrospect then, Conrad best serves the genre of fiction in English not as a second-class modernist but as a site for global writers and readers to enter, experience and exit the western world. The terms of this travel are constantly being transformed and contested in the writing.

In the next chapter, I will examine the impetus to make oneself at home as well as the urge to place others in appropriate establishments through an analysis of first world assessments of "third world" literature. "Home," as I have tried to demonstrate in this and in the previous chapter, is imagined in literature as sites where the political contradictions and contestations are erased or at best, held under erasure. Literary theory enables its target audience to "feel at home" in a genre, and when such comfort is impossible, works on setting up friendly sign posts for readers who venture out onto alien literary terrains. Of the theoretical texts that attempt to chart routes for western readers to enter and understand the worlds of non-western literature, perhaps the most important is Fredric Jameson's "Third World Literature in the Era of Multinational Capitalism." Jameson, I will argue, attempts to provide his western readers of non-western fiction with a theoretical "Home" from which they can unproblematically evaluate the "alien" writing produced in the "Third World" in the age of multinational capitalism. Through elaborate and sophisticated theoretical maneuvering, Jameson identifies the place that "Third World Literature" occupies. Such an identification of place ultimately amounts to *a putting in place*, an insistence on "us" versus "them" even as the categories become anachronistic.

CHAPTER 4

Nostalgic theorizing: at home in "Third World" fictions

> How do we negotiate between my history and yours? How would
> it be possible for us to recover our commonality, not the ambigu-
> ous imperial-humanist myth of our shared human attributes
> which are supposed to distinguish us from animals, but more
> significantly, the imbrication of our various pasts and presents, the
> eluctable relationships of shared and contested meanings, values,
> material resources?...Could we, in other words, afford to have
> entirely different histories, to see ourselves as living – and having
> lived – in entirely heterogeneous and discrete spaces?
>
> S. P. Mohanty

Having argued that twentieth-century realist fiction in English problematizes the assumed distance between private and public politics
through the representation of "home," I now turn the focus once again
to literary theory and to its modes of domestication. Literary theory provides us with home bases from which to read as well as with objects of
analysis whom we can place (and displace) in accordance with our political priorities. The deployment of these very terms "us" and "we" (no
doubt useful rhetorical conveniences) gestures toward a discourse, participation in which is graciously extended by the writer to the implied
readers. And yet the term "we" implies the existence of a (never directly
named) "they." Problems arise when "they" who are the "objects of
analysis" also insert themselves into the category of readers and writers.
When the locations assigned by a text to "us" and the "not-us" are rendered problematic, the home that the text constructs is also violated.

bell hooks has defined the politics of location as a call to "those of
us who would participate in the formation of counter-hegemonic cultural practice to identify the spaces where we begin the process of
revision."[1] Of course, it does not always follow that recognizing one's
spatial privilege immediately produces "counter-hegemonic cultural
practices." Privilege can become a vantage point from which the

Otherness of those excluded can be mapped out in ways that once
again reinforce the hegemonic.[2]

In this chapter, my central focus will be on presenting Fredric
Jameson's 1986 essay, "Third World Literature in the Era of
Multinational Capitalism" as a text that sets out to enable its readers;
to make "us" at home in the alien territory of "Third World
Literature."[3] However, in doing this it also defines a "they" that operates in opposition to Jameson's "we." The reading practice that
Jameson offers "us" is grounded in what Johannes Fabian has termed
a "denial of coevalness."[4] Such denial is rendered problematic when
"they" begin to read, to speak, to write back and to refuse categorization *or* when those who could easily belong to the "we" group
refuse such comfortable quarters.[5] Aijaz Ahmad's strongly worded
response to Jameson's article, titled "Jameson's Rhetoric of Otherness,
and the 'National Allegory'" is written from the point of view of one
who sets out as reader and finds himself "the object of analysis" in
terms that do not allow him to join the comfortable "we" group.[6]
Ahmad's reaction is to refuse this inscription. His essay declares that
there is nothing called "Third World Literature" and it ends with the
refusal to see himself as Jameson's Other.

I will use this discussion of Jameson's article to further the examination of a fundamental question in the politics of location: how do "we"
read, understand or participate in resistive texts produced from locations other than our own? How do we recognize resistance produced
from elsewhere when there seems to be no translation required? What
do we do about counter-hegemonic meanings that entirely escape us –
distances to which we cannot travel even when we speak the language?

FIRST WORLD/THIRD WORLD: UNBEARABLE NEATNESS OF BEING

Today, in postcolonial literary criticism as practiced in the west,
Fredric Jameson's "Third-world Literature in the Era of
Multinational Capitalism" (*TWL*), which creates and then depends on
a controversial model of reading that assesses literary productions
from various parts of the globe in terms of their alleged relationship
with nationalism, is tacitly given the stature afforded to founding texts
in any discourse. Jameson's primary argument in this essay is that "all
third-world texts are necessarily...allegorical, and in a very specific
way: they are to be read as what I will call *national allegories*" (*TWL*, p.

69). He goes on to elaborate: "Third world texts, even those which are seemingly private and invested with a properly libidinal dynamic – necessarily project a political dimension in the form of national allegory: *the story of the private individual destiny is always an allegory of the embattled situation of the public third-world culture and society*" (*TWL*, p. 69). What is to be noted is that Jameson is not simply saying that all texts are political, but that all politics in these texts is national allegory. "Need I add," Jameson writes immediately after this underscored statement, "that it is precisely this very different ratio of the political to the personal which makes such texts alien to us at first approach, and consequently, resistant to our conventional western habits of reading."

This "alien" terrain is not one that urges us to consider the complicity of various global locations – what S. P. Mohanty has called "the imbrication of our various pasts and presents."[7] Nor does it urge us to consider the hegemonic arrangements that allow the west to requisition only those non-western literatures, music, or cuisines that do not require much effort to digest. "Detached from the site of their production," David Lloyd and Abdul JanMohamed have argued, "minority cultural forms become palatable."[8] Detached from their site of production, third world texts *become* minority cultural forms – always already "minor" in the first world. The "alienness" of these texts is simply an obstacle in the path of easy consumption. This then is the only resistance Jameson finds in third world texts – one that is decoded and defused in this announcement of national allegory. In reading the "alienness" of these texts as national allegory, Jameson allows us to continue with "our western habits of reading" both as students and as teachers – a reading experience that is never discomforting because we are never implicated in the politics of the literature. "We" remain in "the West" and "they" remain in "the Third World." Jameson's resolute placement of third world narratives outside the west, displays the untenable neatness of his world map: if what currently happens "there" does not happen "here," then comparisons between the two are easier to map. What is left out of the picture are the novels produced by minority writers in the west who often refer to their world and fiction as "third world."

What or where is this "Third World"? Several literary critics have put forward definitions and reasons to continue using the term as well as reasons to desist from using the economic division of the globe into first, and third worlds in the context of cultural practices. Trinh T. Minh-ha has suggested that "Third World" has both "negative *and* positive connotations" which depends mainly on "*who* uses it"[9] — a kind of politics of location. In an article that examines the way "Third World" writing is consumed in "the West," Kumkum Sangari succinctly elaborates on the burden carried by the two terms: Third World is "a term that both signifies and blurs the functioning of an economic, political, and imaginary geography able to unite vast and vastly differentiated areas of the world into a single 'underdeveloped' terrain." The West is, according to Sangari, "a term produced to opposite effect by the same procedures."[10]

Much of this discussion of the usefulness of terms like "Third World" and "the West" has been brought to the fore in debates around colonial and postcolonial literary production. While the terms are still in use, albeit with qualifications, Trinh T. Minh-ha's position seems to underlie the usage. There is a tangible difference in the way the term is used in Chandra Mohanty's *Third World Women and the Politics of Feminism* and in V. S. Naipaul's travel literature. Similarly there are distinctions to be made in the use of the term "nationalist literature" by critics who work on literary products and periods in specific national histories and as used by Jameson in this essay.

Today, nationalism has a currency in literary studies as practiced in western academia that is very closely linked to readings of literature from non-western parts of the globe.[11] This is taken to the extent where all and any politics in these diverse literatures are read as the politics of "Nation." Underlying this well-forged link between nationalism and literature are a few key texts. Amongst them the shortest, yet perhaps the most influential piece from *within* the western literary academy is Fredric Jameson's seminal essay entitled "Third World Literature in the Era of Multinational Capitalism." Since the publication of this article in a 1986 issue of *Social Text*, and Aijaz Ahmad's volatile rebuttal of Jameson's argument in a subsequent issue of the journal, this exchange has framed the writing about and the teaching of contemporary non-western fiction in the western academy. Other Euroamerica based critics like Gayatri Spivak and Homi Bhabha are clearly the names more closely associated with postcolonial criticism, but Jameson's article provided one of the earlier, theoretically grounded guides to those in the west who wanted to be informed on how to read this entity called "the Third World novel."[12]

If we examine recent studies such as *Nation and Narration*, a collection of essays edited by Homi Bhabha in 1990, or *Salman Rushdie and the Third World: Myths of the Nation* by Timothy Brennan, published in

1989, we find that Jameson's article enjoys a privileged status.[13] In *Nation and Narration*, nationalism has been re-presented as an "international" phenomenon that is available at various levels of discourse. In his article entitled "DissemiNation: Time, Narrative, and the Margins of the Modern Nation," Bhabha evokes Jameson's notion of national allegory to develop his own, related thesis on the "metaphoricity of the migrant."[14] Bhabha aligns his own reading of "nation" and "nationalism" alongside Edward Said's "wordliness," Jameson's invocation of "national allegory" and Kristeva's notions of "exile."[15] Brennan presents nations and nationalisms as "discursive formations," that are *not simply* allegory or imaginative vision, but goes on to state that these discursive formations are, *nevertheless*, "a gestative political structure which the third world artist is very often consciously building or suffering the lack of."

Then there is the strange silence of texts like *The Empire Writes Back* (1989) which repeatedly mentions Jameson in the context of postcolonial writing but never this essay by him.[16] In "Love and Country in Latin America: An Allegorical Speculation," Doris Sommers uses the notion of national allegory in order to make her argument but insists that her theorizing stems not from this essay by Jameson but from Benjamin's formulations.[17] Of Jameson's essay, she writes:

This reading lesson is a gratifying acknowledgement for some of us, and a welcome reminder for others, about the way many people still read and write, so that it will not do to dismiss the relationship between nation and allegory. But Jameson both affirms too much by it (since clearly some third world texts are not "national allegories") and too little (since "national allegories" are still written in the first world, by Pynchon and Grass, among others). I also wonder if his assumption that these allegories "reveal" truth in an apparently transparent way, rather than construct it with all the epistemological messiness that using language implies, doesn't already prepare him to distinguish too clearly between third- and first-world literatures. Even he strains at the borders by including Dostoevsky with Proust and Joyce as purveyors of first-world satisfactions. In any case, the texts that concern me here date from a period before that vexed ego-literary breakdown, before Jameson's guilt-ridden worry over our readerly disappointments with "under developed" literature.[18]

Sommers' critique validates the efforts of those like her who have been reading the right way all along. Her dismissal of Jameson's argument is more of a claim of its irrelevance to her purposes than a rejection of its stance. This brief cautionary statement about the excessive claims of both Jameson and of his critics, specifically Aijaz Ahmad whose article Sommers cites in a footnote, is perhaps all the attention that this article by Jameson (an otherwise acute reader of literature) requires. Sommers at least thinks so for she goes on to write about a specific manifestation of national allegory in Latin America.

Sara Suleri has noted that it is "the familiar and unresolved confrontations between the historical and the allegorical" that is "starkly represented in the paradigmatic exchange between Fredric Jameson and Aijaz Ahmad."[19] Her assessment commends and criticizes both positions as "necessary misreadings":

> Jameson's intuitive apprehension of the blurred lines of cultural demarcation between the idioms of *postcolonial* public and private discourse notwithstanding, his recourse to a rhetoric of "third-worldism" bespeaks a theoretical fear that has still to reconcile the uneasy distance between alterity and the problematic of national specificities. Aijaz Ahmad's very considered response to Jameson's reliance on a first- and third-world binarism, on the other hand, is perhaps too heavily invested in a reading of the "real" to provide an adequate theoretical alternative to the potentially alteritist allegory of Jameson's argument. (p. 13)

Does any more need to be said on this matter? Much depends on what is signified by the word "postcolonial" and "theoretical" in the above quotation. Does "postcolonial" in Jameson's article mean anything other than "Third World"? In which case is there no such blurring of public and private in western texts? Is Jameson let off the hook by the concession that his is *only* a "theoretical fear" even as Ahmad's reading is deemed not to provide an "adequate theoretical alternative"? The publication in 1992 of Aijaz Ahmad's collection of essays, *In Theory: Classes, Nations, Literatures* which includes a reprint of the above mentioned 1987 essay, has once again generated varying assessments of Jameson's article, and the value of critiquing it after this gap of almost a decade.

In Theory has initiated an extended debate in US and British academic journals, mainly around Ahmad's extremely critical assessment of Edward Said's work. In the process of doing a thorough job of refusing Ahmad's severe reading of Edward Said, several prominent reviewers of *In Theory* have also found it necessary to vindicate Fredric Jameson's *TWL* essay. Benita Parry suggests that when Ahmad's response to Jameson was published in 1987 "it was welcomed by critics – including those who do not share a millimeter of theoretical ground with him, and were perhaps gratified by the rebuke of Jameson – for its critique of 'Third-Worldist Theory' and the homogenizing notion of 'Third World Literature.'"[20] The suggestion is that Ahmad has overstayed his welcome, for now Parry finds his critique not that necessary nor accurate. She notes that Ahmad had failed to mention the several points in *TWL* where Jameson scrupulously problematizes his project. Citing such instances, Parry declares that, in her reading, "this does not amount to reducing the colonized or once-colonized worlds to the West's Others; rather it registers a stance that, mindful of the risk, concedes as does Christopher Miller, that the Western reader 'labors under the ethical imperative to be attentive to difference.'"[21]

In a 1993 special issue of *Public Culture* devoted to the debate generated by *In Theory*, several cultural critics have variously reassessed Jameson's *TWL* essay.[22] I would like to briefly present some of these references and note the ways in which they gloss over the impact and contents of the most egregious lapses in *TWL*. Once again, as a kind of preface to their defense of Edward Said's prodigious work, many of the contributors to this special issue have deemed it necessary to either minimize the impact of the *TWL* essay or to see it as not so problematic after all. In his spirited essay, Vivek Dhareshwar insists that it "would be hard to persuade oneself that Rushdie's *Shame* and Jameson's minor piece have been 'seminal' and 'defining' for literary theory."[23] Partha Chatterjee also finds it "hard to be persuaded that this casual and clearly peripheral piece can be a part of the corpus of Jameson's serious scholarly work."[24] This needs to be read against Jameson's final footnote in *TWL*, where he suggests that his essay, which "sketches a theory of the cognitive aesthetics of third-world literature," be read as "a pendant to the essay on postmodernism which describes the logic of the cultural imperialism of the first world and above all of the United States" (*TWL* p. 88). Rather than being peripheral or minor, then, *TWL* along with "Postmodernism, or The Cultural Logic of Late Capitalism" provides us with Jameson's world map.[25] I will return to the issue of "mapping" as intrinsic to the nexus of nation and novel in the conclusion to this chapter. Years after its initial publication, Jameson's argument has been reworked and modified, so that its weakest moments have been discarded. Selective reworkings of the broad strokes etched by his argument substantiate the hurried assessments of non-western fiction (as in undergraduate papers in "World Literature" classes) and often even the most sophisticated writing on postcolonial literary discourses.

I begin with a critique of Jameson's argument in *TWL* to demonstrate what is necessarily erased and necessarily highlighted because of his insistence on seeing nation and national allegory prefigured in every cultural text from the non-west. I will attempt to do this by locating Jameson's essay in several historicized frames: first, his own investment in the central themes of Western Marxism, a discourse that is gendered masculine; second, in terms of identified stages of non-European nationalisms as formulated by Partha Chatterjee and others; third and finally, I will comment briefly on fiction from the "third world" that cannot be read as national allegory and that is therefore in danger of not being read and sometimes in danger of not being published at all. I will use *The Dark Room* (1938), one of the noted Indian author R. K. Narayan's early novels, to articulate this last point.

The ambitious nature of this project will undoubtedly reveal the gaps in its logic. Rather than paper over these gaps and untidy loose ends, I have chosen to leave them in order to avoid replacing one constricting system with another. What follows then, is an attempt to enter the terrain of postcolonial literature from a point of view that insists on including the politics of location as a central contributor to any articulation of "us/they," "here/there," "now/then."

In *Imagined Communities: Reflections on the Origin and Spread of Nationalism*, Benedict Anderson insists that all texts that are read in a society are intertwined with the imagining of that community.[26] Following Anderson, it could be argued that print commodities, especially realist fiction that are read as mirroring the real, also help us visualize communities *other than our own*. In *TWL* for instance, Jameson uses specific novels to help him construct *his* "third world" and its literature. What Jameson does is to postulate a present "third world" and then place it as the past of the accompanying "first world" that his text also constructs. The chronology is familiar; we have encountered it in the texts that place contemporary non-western nationalism in the past of western nationalism.[27] In Jameson's essay, we are presented with a contemporary "third world" literature that is "already known" to his audience because they have apparently already encountered it in previous eras of western literatures.

Jameson's essay begins with a focusing of attention on nationalism, or, to be more precise, on "that old thing called 'nationalism,' long since liquidated here and rightly so" (*TWL*, p. 65). He goes on to explain why his essay will ponder this anachronistic phenomenon... "Yet a certain nationalism is fundamental in the third world (and also in the most vital areas of the second world), thus making it legitimate to ask whether it is all that bad in the end."[28] In some ways this statement takes us full circle from the classic western definitions of nationalism as espoused by Carlton Hayes, Leonard Doob, Elia Kedourie and others, which deny authentic nationalism to the non-western world.[29] Jameson, it seems, in this statement and in the course of his article, would like to convince us that nationalism is the *only* authentic cultural attribute of the non-western parts of the world. And even this "fundamental" attribute has already been experienced in the past of western literature. Hence, "third world" texts are "unmodern" and therefore:

as western readers whose tastes (and much else) have been formed by our own modernisms, a popular or socially realistic third-world novel tends to come before us, not immediately, but as though already-read. We sense, between ourselves *and this alien text*, the presence of another reader, of the Other reader, for whom the narrative, which strikes us as conventional or naive, has a freshness of information and a social interest that we cannot share. (*TWL*, p. 66)

What Jameson means to imply by the hyphenated "already-read" is less straightforward than it seems at first. There is of course, this "Other reader" whom Jameson envisions as getting to read the text before it reaches the western reader. And yet it is important to note the ease with which this reader who reads in the cultural/historical location from which the text is produced is labeled "Other." How did this "implied reader" get to become Othered?[30] However, given the organization of the international publishing industry, it is often the case that western readers are the first to read the "third world" text which is written in English. It is only with commercial success in the west that some of the non-western novelists see their work in English published or distributed in their own countries.[31] The same is true for avant-garde cinema, whose returns are not guaranteed and are therefore not picked up by local distributors until they have proved their commercial worth in the west. Big, multinational publishing houses do also have resources that can easily overcome competition from locally owned publishing outfits. Often censorship in the home-country, especially during times of national turmoil, results in a foreign publication preceding the domestic publication of a text. And yet, the less neutral meanings of Jameson's "already-read" have to be brought into play – according to him, the "third world" text is "already-read" by the western reader in the sense that its literary anachronism makes it appear "conventional and naive."

There is in Jameson's essay an equivocating swing between the urge to "compare" and the urge "not to compare" the two categories of literature which he alternately calls first/third world literature and canonical/non-canonical literature. Jameson's equivocation here is matched by his swinging in and out of the "we" category of conservative western readers that he sets up in the introductory section of his article. His hesitation to make comparisons stems from his conviction that his category assigned "third world literature" would fare poorly if such comparisons were permitted. And yet...

Nothing is to be gained from passing over in silence the radical difference of non-canonical texts. The third world novel will not offer the satisfactions of Proust or Joyce: what is more damaging than that, perhaps, is its tendency to remind us of outmoded stages of our own first world cultural development and to cause us to conclude that "they are still writing novels like Dreiser or Sherwood Anderson." A case could be built on this kind of discouragement, with its deep existential commitment to a rhythm of modernist innovation if not fashion-changes; but it would not be a moralizing one – a historicist one, rather, which challenges our imprisonment in the present of postmodernism and calls for a reinvention of the radical difference of *our own* cultural past and its now seemingly old-fashioned situations and novelties. But I would rather argue all this a different way, at least for now: these reactions to third world texts are at one and the same time perfectly natural, perfectly comprehensible, *and* terribly parochial. (*TWL*, pp. 65–6)

It is interesting to note how the "radical difference" in the first sentence quoted here slides intentionally into "its tendency to remind us of outmoded stages of our own first world cultural development" in the next sentence. Hence the crucial difference is not really "radical" nor "different"; it is merely that one literature *is read as* operating as the past of the other. So that to explore non-western literature is to "call for a reinvention of the radical difference of *our own* cultural past" *(emphasis in original)* – thus allowing for nostalgic reading experiences. Elsewhere in this essay, Jameson writes,

allegorical structures, are not so much absent from first-world cultural texts as they are *unconscious* and therefore they must be deciphered by interpretative mechanisms that necessarily entail a whole social and historical critique of our current first-world situation. The point here is that, in distinction to the unconscious allegories of our own cultural texts, third world national allegories are conscious and overt: they imply a radically different and objective relationship of politics to libidinal dynamics. (*TWL*, pp. 79–80)

The adjectives used in Jameson's article (fresh, conventional, overt, outmoded, socially realistic, old-fashioned, and so on) suggest a contradictory stance on "third world" literature. Halfway through this essay, Jameson declares that his essay has "praised and valorized positively" the "radical otherness of the culture in question."[32] He continues:

I don't see how a first-world intellectual can avoid this operation [of differentiation] without falling back into some general liberal and humanistic universalism: it seems to me that one of our basic political tasks lies precisely in the ceaseless effort to remind the American public of the radical difference of other national situations... (p. 77)

The setback comes in Jameson's refusal to see how differentiation is set into operation. This "ceaseless effort" should be directed toward examining our own methods and investments in defining difference.[33] What begins as an analysis of "third-world literature" ends on the last page of Jameson's essay as an assessment of a singular "third-world" individual and a singular "third-world" culture itself. In the logic of his argument, this is exactly where such analysis would culminate: because of "the allegorical nature of third-world culture...the telling of the individual story cannot but ultimately involve the whole laborious telling of the experience of the collectivity itself" (*TWL*, pp. 85–6). According to Michael Sprinker, it is this conclusion on collectivity, that rescues Jameson's argument. In his lead essay in the *Public Culture* special on *In Theory*, in which he presents Ahmad, Jameson and Said's work on "the national question," Sprinker concludes his summary and assessment of *TWL* by arguing that "underlying Jameson's often unsustainable views about the distinctions between First and Third Worlds lies a provocative hypothesis" – that of the collectivity of third world societies. Sprinker concludes: "In sum, is it not possible, as Jameson here maintains, that certain forms of collective life have until now persisted more powerfully outside the metropolitan countries? And if this be so, of what value are these, perhaps residual but still vital, forms of social practice?"[34]

This stress on the collective, is also integral to Deleuze and Guattari's "What is a Minor Literature?" an equally impactful essay published in 1986.[35] This valorized category named "minor literature" includes literatures that meet three requirements. First, it is a one which "a minority constructs within a major language" (p. 16). Second, "everything in them is political" and the third characteristic of minor literature is that "in it everything takes on a collective value"(p. 17). Deleuze and Guattari also add that "minor literature no longer designates specific literatures but the revolutionary conditions for every literature within the heart of what is called great (or established) literature" (p. 18). In formulating their theory of "Minority Discourse," Abdul JanMohamed and David Lloyd interrogate Deleuze and Guattari's "minor" literature through their category of "minority" literature. Lloyd and JanMohamed observe –

the collective nature of minority discourse is not due to the scarcity of talent, as Deleuze and Guattari claim, but due to other cultural and political factors. In those societies caught in the transition from oral, mythic, and collective cultures to the literate, "rational," and individualistic values and characteristics of Western cultures, the writer more often than not manifests the collective nature of social formation in forms such as the novel, thus transforming what were once efficacious vehicles for the representation of individually, atomistically oriented experiences into collective modes of articulation. However, more importantly, the collective nature of all minority discourse also derives from the fact that minority individuals are always treated and forced to experience themselves generically. Coerced into a negative, generic subject-position, the oppressed individual responds by transforming that experience into a positive, collective one.[36]

Several points need to be made here. Lloyd and JanMohamed's nuanced reading of "collective" once again justifies Trinh T. Minh-ha's rule of thumb – much depends on how a disputed term is used. Second, "minority discourse" in this passage refers primarily to that produced by minorities within the West. For Deleuze and Guattari, Kafka provides the foremost example of the deterritorialized producer of "minor" literature. For them, the issue is as simple as refusing citizenship within language – "absolute deterritorialization" calls for the writer to be "a sort of stranger *within* his own language" (p. 26). The details of this plan for linguistic revolution are indeed problematic, for what is finally advocated is a search for "linguistic Third World zones by which a language can escape" its own oppressive qualities. Thus, while JanMohamed and Lloyd use this project of "becoming minor" to further their formulations on "minority discourse," they do stress the correctives that are necessary:

But where the point of departure of poststructuralism lies within the Western tradition and tries to deconstruct its identity formations "from within," the critical difference is that minorities, by virtue of their social being, must begin from a position of objective nonidentity that is rooted in their economic and cultural marginalization vis-a-vis the "West." The nonidentity that the critical Western intellectual seeks to (re)produce discursively is for minorities a given of their social existence.

Here we need to recall JanMohamed and Lloyd's powerful suggestion that the collectivity that is read onto/into minority subjects and their cultural productions derives from the genericism they are subject to. A corollary to this genericism of the "them" group is the assumption that the "we" group's highly theoretical forays into the unknown are *unmarked* by membership in distinct communities or collectives, and are indeed individualistic, even idiosyncratic musings. Jameson's "point of departure" in the *TWL* essay, I will now demonstrate, is provided by his membership in a community of literary critics who are guided by, and in turn formulate, the central precepts of Western Marxism.

THEORETIC NOSTALGIA

Jameson's *TWL* establishes for what is called "third-world literature" a place in the western literary canon that is at the same time a site of nostalgia for the early days of theorizing on the novel as it was practiced by Western Marxists of the stature of Lukács and Benjamin. In "third world" literature, Jameson locates an object of inquiry that can be read in relation to contemporary western fiction *as* taking the place that the epic does in relation to the novel in Lukács' *The Theory of the Novel* or that wisdom does in relation to information in Benjamin's "The Storyteller."[37]

The nostalgia and yearning for totality that mark Lukács' and Benjamin's writing are central concerns of Western Marxism as well as of western culture itself. In his examination of Western Marxism's investment in this concept, Martin Jay writes:

"Totality" has indeed enjoyed a privileged place in the discourse of Western culture. Resonating with affirmative connotations, it has generally been associated with other positively charged words, such as coherence, order, fulfillment, harmony, plenitude, meaningfulness, consensus and community. And concomitantly, it has been contrasted with such negatively valanced concepts as alienation, fragmentation, disorder, conflict, contradiction, serialization, atomization, and estrangement.[38]

I want to suggest that Jameson's reading of "third-world" literature as being in opposition to "first-world" literature can be read entirely through the parameters of this central dynamic of western culture.

In his critique of *TWL*, Aijaz Ahmad notes that the distinction that Jameson makes in this article, between "first" and "third" world, corresponds directly to the differences that an earlier text by him posed between the preindustrial and industrialized eras in society.[39] One could take Ahmad's criticism of Jameson further by noting the similarities between Jameson's thesis on "first" and "third" world literature and Lukács' theorizing in the 1920s when he differentiated the era of the novel from that of the epic.

For Lukács, the epic era evoked the sense of wholeness, of an organic totality best expressed in the sense of "being at home in the world." In contrast, Lukács presents the era of the novel as one of "homesickness," of fragmentation, of a lack of wholeness that is manifest in the deliberate constructions of totality that the era undertakes. In the lyrical words of the young Lukács:

The epic gives form to a totality of life that is rounded from within: the novel seeks, by giving form, to uncover and construct the concealed totality of life. (*TN*, p. 60)

Lukács locates his epic era in Greek civilization and the era of the novel in the nineteenth and early twentieth-century bourgeois culture. According to Lukács, the epic and the novel "differ from one another *not* by their authors' fundamental intentions but by the given historico-philosophical realities with which the authors were confronted" (*TN*, p. 59). Despite his fascination with this time and place, Lukács' repeated insistence that the Greek mind and world is "essentially different from ours," is echoed in Jameson's reading of "third world" literature as "radically different." Of the epic world, Lukács writes: "It is a homogeneous world and even the separation between man and world, between 'I' and 'you,' cannot disturb its homogeneity" (*TN*, p. 32).

The masculine romanticism of form and content explicit in Lukács' reading of Greek civilization as an era where *man*, community and nature are one, is implicit in readings that locate similar virtues in "third" world texts. Hence the following statements, culled from Lukács' passages on the epic, appear, albeit refashioned, in Jameson's writing on "third world-literature":

The epic hero is, strictly speaking, never an individual...its [the epic's] theme is not a personal destiny but the destiny of a community...the epic cosmos creates a whole which is too organic for any part of it to become so enclosed within itself, so dependent on itself, as to find an interiority – i.e. to become an individual. (*TN*, p. 66)

Jameson's essay, it can be argued, relocates Lukács' epic era to the contemporary cultural productions of the "third world" and updates the Lukácsian era of the novel to apply its strictures to the contemporary western world.

In "The Storyteller," Walter Benjamin writes of the difference between the age of the story, of wisdom and the age of the novel, of information, in terms similar to Lukács'. The loss of the era of the story and the storyteller is deeply lamented by Benjamin for it is the loss of wisdom, of collectivity and of art that has social use-value. This is replaced in the era of the novel by information, isolation and the individual. The story and the storyteller, Benjamin argues in the closing lines of this essay, are auratic. "Third world" literature is equally auratic for Jameson — its investment in national allegory gives it the social use-value as well as the attributes of collectivity and community that Benjamin writes of in this essay.⁴⁰ Hence perhaps Jameson's confident claim that his examination praises and positively valorizes *the* Other culture.

In *Marxism and Form*, Jameson discusses the salient point of Benjamin's writing in a section entitled "Walter Benjamin; Or, Nostalgia." The terms of Jameson's assessment of Benjamin's work can be mapped onto his own essay on "third world" literature — as a corroboration of his stance. Jameson begins this section with a discussion of allegory in Benjamin's work. He reads Benjamin as "the theorist of allegory" — one whose writing embodies an unending search for auratic works of art and times.⁴¹ Hence, "Benjamin's work seems to me to be marked by a painful straining toward a psychic wholeness or unity of experience which the historical situation threatens to shatter at every turn."⁴²

"Aura," Jameson quotes Benjamin as writing in *Schriftren*, is "the single, unrepeatable experience of distance."⁴³ He extrapolates from this quotation that "aura is thus in a sense the opposite of allegorical perception, in that in it a mysterious wholeness of objects becomes visible."⁴⁴ This opposition of aura and allegory is blurred in *TWL* where an auratic "unity of experience" is theorized as "conscious and overt" allegory. It is in first world literatures, where the aura is past or broken, that allegory comes into cultural practice as an "unconscious," post-auratic, modern phenomenon.

In urging a comparison between Benjamin's and Sartre's analyses of story versus novel, Jameson spells out the distinction I see him as making in *TWL* between "first" and "third world" literature:

It is instructive to compare Benjamin's analysis of the tale (and of its implied distinction from the novel) with that of Sartre, so similar in some ways, and yet so different in its ultimate emphasis. For both, the two forms are opposed not only in their social origins (the tale springing from collective life, the novel from middle-class solitude) and in their raw materials (the tale using what everyone can recognize as common experience, the novel that which is uncommon and highly individualistic).⁴⁵

In *TWL*, the two forms of literature are opposed in precisely these terms: the "third world" literature of national allegory also springs from "the collective life and from common experience," just as Jameson's "first world" fiction is that of isolation and solitude as well as "uncommon and highly individualistic." In Lukács', Benjamin's and Sartre's distinctions, there is a clear progression from one stage to the next and return is impossible except through nostalgic indulgences in things past. While Lukács and Benjamin write of two stages in the history of a heterogeneous "western culture," Jameson ends up sacrificing another entire history (of the heterogeneous "third world") by his nonchalant placement of its cultural effects as the past of western culture.

Despite his romantic idealization of the Greeks, Lukács is unambiguously clear on the progression of the two eras: "The novel is the artform of virile maturity, in contrast to the normative childlikeness of the epic" (*TN*, p. 71).[46] The use of the trope of masculine potency leaves no doubt as to the gendering of this entire project. Like Lukács, Benjamin aligns the earlier age with that of an untarnished positive childhood and the age of the novel with the advent of sexual knowledge or corrupt maturity. Hence, this logic leads him to suggest that this is why the fairy tale is popular with children even today – for it "teaches children to this day," the wisdom it "taught mankind in olden times." Hence,

"And they lived happily after," says the fairy tale. The fairy tale, which to this day is the first tutor of children because it was once the first tutor of mankind, secretly lives on in the story...The liberating magic which the fairy tale has at its disposal does not bring nature into play in a mythical way, but points to its complicity with liberated man. A mature man feels this complicity only occasionally, that is, when he is happy: but the child first meets it in fairy tales, and it makes him happy. (*ST*, p. 102)

In both Lukács' *The Theory of the Novel* and in Benjamin's "The Storyteller," it is clear that the art of the epic and of story telling has come to an end, except in a few isolated instances: fairy tales, the writing of Dostoevsky for Lukács, of Nikolai Leskov for Benjamin. Such an era is located in the past and is described as "remote," as "distant" and as "innocent." Jameson, who in his other writing is well aware of the pull of nostalgia, finds in the "third world" literature a manifestation of the epic and of storytellers who are once again – remote, distant, alien and somewhat simple, *yet contemporaneous to the western novel*. His insistence that nationalism is "an anachronism" that has been "long outdated" in the west and his accompanying insistence that allegory is "a form long discredited in the west," allows him paradoxically to place the present third world in the past culture of the west.

What Jameson "finds" in his "third world" is not so much "unmodern texts" (to use his term) as much as texts that can be made subject to "unmodern" literary theories. Postcolonial literatures must not become the new ground that can be nostalgically tilled with the old-fashioned yet charming tools of early twentieth-century western literary theories.

NEGOTIATING CATEGORIES

In *Nationalist Thought and the Colonial World*, Chatterjee identifies three stages in passive revolution or in the general form of transition from colonial to postcolonial states in the twentieth century. Using the geographically and historically specific case of the Indian Nationalist movement to critique state nationalism, Partha Chatterjee identifies these three distinct stages as a) the moment of departure, b) the moment of maneuver, and c) the moment of arrival.[47] The moment of departure is marked by the awareness and acceptance of essential cultural differences between "the East" and "the West" which leads to an effort to combine the best of both, as manifest in the writing produced by Bankimchandra Chattopadhyay. The moment of maneuver is ushered in by the mobilization of masses in the cause of an anticolonial struggle that decries the modern or the imported and offers in place a homespun ideology of the people. Chatterjee identifies this strategy in M. K. Gandhi's discourse. When nationalist thought attains its fullest development and is articulated in a single, consistent voice that glosses over contradictions and difference, the moment of arrival has been reached. Manifest in the Indian case in the writings of the first prime minister of independent India, Jawaharlal Nehru, this "moment of arrival" as Chatterjee calls it, is when a nationalist discourse utters its own life history. It is at this period of time, in the literary productions of the society, that one finds even the most banal event to be overdetermined by the dominant politics of nationalism. Jameson's argument can, in some instances, be read as an accurate assessment of the literature produced in this third stage of a nationalist discourse – the moment of arrival. But history, literature and even nationalisms move *beyond* this third moment.

One could further complicate such schema by noting that within the so-called "nationalist literature" there are different and distinct literary stances toward the nation, and to national politics. Hence, Salman Rushdie's *Midnight's Children* with its pack of wonder-children born on the stroke of midnight, 15th August 1947, precisely when India gains independence, could be categorized as a prime example of the nationalist literature of, what I will call, "utopian plotting." Such literature, I believe, puts the nation on the literary map by

drawing attention to the specificities of its particular history. Also to
be included in this category are Mulk Raj Anand's *Untouchable*, and
Chinua Achebe's *Things Fall Apart*. *Shame*, which laments a corrupt,
post-independence (thinly disguised) Pakistan, is a clear manifestation
of another category of nationalist literature – that written in "the
mourning after" independence from direct colonial rule.[48]

I would also place Ayi Kwei Armah's *The Beautyful Ones Are Not Yet
Born* and *Petals of Blood* by Ngugi Wa Thiong'o in this category. *The
Satanic Verses*, a novel about immigrants in England, can be seen as
redefining the very concept of nation. This third type of nationalist fiction, that which redefines nation and national belonging, is also manifest
in Beryl Gilroy's *Boy-Sandwich* and Jessica Hagerdorn's *Dogeaters*.

The novels that I have included in these three stages of Nationalist
literature are grouped in accordance with national events in the locations from which they were produced as well as according to an idiosyncratic notion of their literary themes.[49] Counter-categorizations can
be readily spun. For instance, *Untouchable* and *The Beautyful Ones Are Not
Yet Born* both demonstrate the anger, confusion and helplessness felt by
some writers when they return to their home-country after a long
sojourn abroad. Such novels are often marked by a scatological narrative that serves as a register of both dismay and disgust at how much
needs to be done to make independence meaningful. My attempt to
schematize "nationalist literatures" into three categories only makes a
minimal improvement on Jameson's scheme. Even with the aid of
Partha Chatterjee's three stages of Gramscian "Passive Revolution," it
is truly impossible to process through *one* equation all literatures called
"Third World" that closely follow national events. Besides which, the
location in which these texts are consumed also necessarily alters their
resonances. One can imagine the diverse ways in which a novel like
Chinua Achebe's *Things Fall Apart* would be read in the following scenarios in the US: in a high school class room, in a college freshman
survey of world literature, in a graduate seminar in postcolonial literary theory and literature, in a Peace Corps orientation class, in a
Foreign Service course on African culture. In each of these scenarios,
one or more of the following reading strategies may be applied – orient-
alizing interpretations, sociological readings, reading for national
allegory, or reading fiction as documents of resistance.

Needless to say, there are times, places and texts in the non-west
that are not related to nationalism – directly or *even* allegorically. Yet
nationalism gives the texts that Jameson calls "alien" a focus that ren-

ders them recognizable. In the absence of "subjects" that "Third World" literatures apparently lack, nationalism becomes the subject of the text. Without this subject, the problem becomes one of attempting to read and teach a literature whose other preoccupations cannot be recognized and which therefore remain alien.

The pressures on "Third World" writers to produce novels that can be easily fitted into the established framework of the western academy and western publishing houses are tremendous. "In a world in which everything was equal," Ama Ata Aidoo notes, "writers would not represent anything other than themselves. But in 1991 everything is far from equal, and those inequalities are particularly heightened in the African world. Most Africans are not in the position to write or speak of their lives, and we few writers who do have the chance become representative."[50] Agnes Sam, a South African writer writes of the difficulty of getting her experimental novel *What Passing Bells* published in the west:[51]

The original draft was impressionistic, its form suggestive of a fractured society, of people in an apartheid system isolated from each other. It combined poetry with prose. Its purpose was to frustrate the reader's need for continuity because this is precisely how we are frustrated in our understanding of the South African situation. I've seen other works published which are experimental and this reinforces my view that it isn't simply that publishers determine what is acceptable for some prescribed market, but they have a stereotype of how one should write if belonging to a specific group. One publisher's representative asserted very firmly that Black women write autobiographically. A black woman experimenting with language and form has no business writing. In the new Commonwealth, those writers who do not conform to these stereotypes are said to have been influenced by Western tradition, to have had an "English" as opposed to a "Bantu" or "Third World" education, or they are said not to be writing for the "people"...But the crunch comes when we disregard Western tradition and publishers' stereotypes, and attempt to experiment – this isn't tolerated.[52]

Similarly, Aidoo has noted that when it comes to publication in today's global market, "[s]omeone can declare that your manuscript doesn't read like a manuscript from a third world person."[53] What we do get from these excerpts is a sense of the ways in which Jameson's theory on "Third World Literature" complies so harmoniously with the publishing priorities of its time and place.

An important article, called "Redefining Relevance" written by Njabulo Ndebele, the South African writer and critic, draws attention to an impasse in contemporary South African literary writing that provides us with a succinct analysis of a situation similar to the one I tackle in this chapter.[54] Arguing that today, in South Africa, "Protest literature" may have run its course, Ndebele finds that much of the literature written after 1976 *still* reproduces the Protest tradition with very little modification, despite the fact that the genre has "lost its objective basis" (p. 49).

What one is attempting to do here is to hint at its [the moral position espoused in Protest Literature] possible limitations. This task is essential when a particular way of viewing reality gathers its own momentum over a period of time and becomes a predominant mode of perception even when conditions justifying its existence have passed. At this point the mode of perception, by failing to transcend its own limitations can become part of the oppression it sought to understand and undermine. It does not do so intentionally, of course: it simply becomes trapped. Such entrapment may even lead to the development of a dangerous predisposition to reform rather than to radical change. (p. 43)

Ndebele's essay urges a reconsideration of the tasks of socially committed writers in contemporary South Africa. In broad terms, this criticism could be mapped onto hegemonic readings of "third world" literature that result in the kind of literary straitjacket that Agnes Sam and Aidoo describe.

My concern is with the reception of this and other such literature in the "first world." Reading (as much as writing) in a *politically committed* fashion amounts to more than locating metaphors of national or state politics. There are other issues which may be more circumscribed, banal, everyday concerns but that provide every society with a wealth of fictional and political material. In the prologue to her most recent novel, *Changes*, Ama Ata Aidoo writes:

Several years ago, when I was a little older than I am now, I said in a published interview that I could never write about lovers in Accra. Because in our environment, there are more important things to write about...[55]

Aidoo is aware that her concern in this novel – "what happens to a woman who wants to have a career, who also wants to have love," – is not "an issue that is being confronted by most Ghanian or African women." However, it is, she insists, "an issue of our times for women."[56] Why does a well-established writer have to justify her literary focus in this elaborate fashion?

As Ndebele argues, the exclusion of any aspect of the social conditions limits "the possibilities of any literary revolution" – through both writing and reading. Reading non-western fiction in the west, outside the location from which it was produced, requires an equally alert and up to date reading practice – one that is willing and able to look for political subjects in every location.

READING *THE DARK ROOM*

In this section of the chapter, I intend to do a "close reading" of R. K. Narayan's novel, *The Dark Room*, first, as national allegory and, then, for what is left out in such a limited reading of literary politics.[57] While the text does support a very substantial reading as national allegory, I will argue that this is the kind of reading one does when one cannot read the "alien" dynamics of the text. Using a novel by R. K. Narayan for these purposes is especially challenging because his work is known for its transparency, straightforward realist style and his precise use of an Indianized Queen's English.

First published in 1938, *The Dark Room* was the second full-length novel written by Narayan. The novel opens with a quarrel between an upper middle class, middle-aged married couple, Ramani and Savitri. She retreats, as is apparently her usual habit after a fight with her husband, into the "dark room" in their house to "sulk." She is reminded of her wifely duties by an older female friend, Janamma, and comes out after a day spent in the dark. Ramani's patriarchal sway over the household (Savitri, their three children and the servants) continues and all is well in this prosperous brahmin household. Ramani then falls in love with Shanta Bai, a newly recruited insurance officer whom he hires in his capacity as Head of the Malgudi Branch of the Englandia Insurance Company. When Savitri learns of this infatuation that soon blossoms into an affair, she quarrels with her husband and leaves the house. She attempts suicide and is saved by Mari, a low-caste petty thief and handyman. Mari and his wife help Savitri find suitable employment at a local temple. Despite wanting to live and sleep in the temple courtyard, in the open air, she is compelled by the temple priest to inhabit a dark, enclosed shack. Alone in this confined space, a second "dark room," Savitri misses her children and her comfortable home. She returns to her husband and children the very next morning. Ramani is relieved to have her back but he does not break off his relationship with Shanta Bai. Savitri goes back to being the good traditional wife. She believes that her rebellion was futile.

Though the novel was published nine years before Indian independence was won in 1947, nationalist fervor was rife in the subcontinent in the 1930s. There is much in this novel that can be read as allegorical or otherwise indirect references to this burgeoning nationalism and its many attendant valorizations of Indian traditions. In Indian cinema of the period the usual practice of criticizing British rule – not directly for that would invite censorship – but indirectly was through the criticism of a westernized Indian: the adulterous husband, the frock-wearing vamp, the wife who loves socializing, or the heartless landlord who has no sense of kinship with those he oppresses.[58] The seduction of educated upper class/caste Indians by western lures was viewed with alarm in nationalistic recastings of Indian culture.[59] Westernized Indians (those who smoked cigars, pipes and cigarettes, danced in the western styles, drank "scotch," lapsed into English or wore western clothes) in Indian films and other cultural texts in the 1930s were usually the object of much ridicule.[60] Shanta Bai and Ramani are subject to similar criticism.

Shanta Bai is the "rootless" modern woman: the self-proclaimed drifter. The contrast in Savitri and Shanta Bai's attitudes to life is repeatedly dramatized and can be read as an indication of their respective commitment to (Hindu) nationalism. When Ramani takes Savitri to see an Indian theological film, it is for her, a religious, self-affirming event:

The hall became dark and the show began. Savitri, like the majority of those in the hall, knew the story, had heard it a number of times since infancy, the old story from the epics, of Krishna and his old classmate Kuchela, who was too busy with his daily prayers and meditation to work and earn, and hence left to his wife the task of finding food for their twenty-seven children...

Savitri sympathised intensely with the unfortunate woman, Kuchela's wife. "The poor girl!" she muttered to her husband.

"Note how patient she is, and how uncomplaining," Ramani remarked...

The picture carried Savitri with it, and when in the end Kuchela stood in his "pooja" room and lit camphor and incense before the image of god, Savitri brought her palms together and prayed. (*DR*, pp. 21–3).

When Ramani and Shanta Bai go to the movies, the theater is showing another theological film. The event is described as follows:

When they reached the theatre, she looked at the posters and exclaimed, "A wretched Indian film! I'd have given my life to see a Garbo or a Dietrich now." "What shall we do?" "Anything is better than nothing." She sat in the dark hall besides him, whispering criticisms of the picture before her: a stirring episode from the "Ramayana," in which the giant monkey god set fire to Lanka. "What rubbish the whole thing is!" she said. "Our people can't produce a decent film. Bad photography, awful acting, ugly faces. Till our film producers give up mythological nonsense there is no salvation for our films. Let's go out. I can't stand this anymore." (*DR*, p. 68)

In Narayan's novels, criticism of Hindu traditions is always couched in such a comical, overdramatized manner that its impact is immediately dissipated. Here, Shanta Bai's derision of the mythological themes is an indication of her lack of an Indian identity. This is specifically indicated through her absolute lack of identification with the silent, suffering and therefore much venerated women from this mythology. Her "philosophy of life" is gained not from the ancient texts or from lessons learned through childhood stories, but from western films and from Omar Khayyam: "'I will laugh and dance. That is my philosophy of life. Laugh, clown, laugh – it was a film I saw years ago. Laugh, clown, laugh, though your heart be torn,' she said, unable to quote the exact words of the film" (*DR*, p. 67). Shanta Bai loves to dramatize her own life. When it comes to expressing emotions, she is a consummate actress: "She compressed her lips and jerked her head in the perfect Garbo manner: the temperamental heroine and impending doom" (*DR*, p. 66). Shanta Bai is portrayed in this novel as a manifestation of the poverty of the self-identity that colonialism offers those who reject their "Indianness." Indianness is, in this discourse as elsewhere, completely subsumed by the precepts of Hindu ideology.

Narayan's Malgudi, the fictitious small town where this and all his other novels are set, can be read as a microcosmic representation of Utopian present and future India sketched from the point of view of an upper class/caste intellectual.[61] It is the Utopia of a benevolent Hinduism. The order and pattern that Narayan maintains in his novels constructs a conservative nationalism in its confidence that Hindu India survives assaults of outsiders – be they Muslim or Christian from the nearby big city of Madras, from North India or from England.[62] Hence, all the "loose" (i.e., immoral, Westernized) women and men in Narayan's novels are outsiders; they do not belong to Malgudi. After they have upset the quiet rhythm of Malgudi, the outsiders are cast out into the big anonymous city of Madras. Their future is of no consequence. And though each of these outsiders may make attempts to belong to the community, there is no place for them in Malgudi.[63]

What Narayan establishes in his fiction is a society that does not change under outside pressure. Over the sixty odd years that he has been writing about Malgudi, the town and its inhabitants have remained essentially the same. Factories and new houses have sprung up in Malgudi, but everything new and prosperous is looked at with suspicion. Within the brahmin family that Narayan describes, the men are always sensitive, quiet and mildly irritated with ceremonies and the niceties of the caste system. Yet none of them dares do more than complain mildly. The brahmin women are models of virtue and are steeped in the ancient traditions. There are old grand-mothers who tell stories from the ancient texts, the silently suffering but beautiful wives and the pure, radiant virgins who are adored from afar. All these "types" live a sheltered existence within the four walls of a home. For the traditional, caste-minding Hindu who has been alarmed by the social, religious (especially on the issue of caste) and political upheaval in India over the present century, Narayan's reiteration of the importance of a traditionally ordered society serves to consolidate the solace offered by Hindu nationalism in 1938, as in 1995.

However, it would be a travesty to stop with such a reading of *The Dark Room*. Narayan's novel will not feature in scholarship that discuss politics in "third world" literatures on the basis of their links with nationalism. The central focus of the narrative is on religious and social duty in the everyday context of domesticity. Like most of Narayan's other fictions, *The Dark Room* has a religious ideological framework that controls and directs the novel to a predetermined closure. I will now read this novel in terms of this framework – an exercise that is equally if not more compelling than searching for national allegory.

The particular philosophical ideas that form the core of Hinduism and of Narayan's fiction are the fundamental principles of *Karma* and *Varnasramadharma*. The principle of *Karma* is best explained as a relationship between deeds and their consequences. This relationship is worked out both in this life and in successive births until the spirit is released from the cycle of birth – death – rebirth. The principle of *Karma* is ruled by a hierarchy of values generally classified as *dharma* or the right action, *artha* or worldly interest, and *kama* or love. The better one's *dharma* is, the sooner one is released from the cycle of rebirth. The longer and more deeply one is caught in *artha* and/or *kama* the slower the release from cyclically ordered time.

The principle of *Varnasramadharma*. divides the human life into four idealized stages. These stages are always represented as applying first and foremost to men and then in a secondary fashion to women. Women's duties lie in playing the role required of them to facilitate their fathers, husbands and sons as the men go through the four stages. According to traditional prescription, for women all stages of the cycle and all salvation lies in serving her household and her household gods, prime amongst whom is her husband.[64] The first stage in a man's life is the condition of being a student, a youth intent on learning. The second stage is that of a householder; in this period of his life, a man marries and gives his entire attention to family responsibilities. The next stage is one of withdrawal and contemplation during which a man tries to detach himself from his family and other worldly interests. Living the life of a hermit, he prepares himself for the fourth and most difficult stage in his life. This final stage is that of being a *sanyasi* or a man who has renounced the world. A *sanyasi* leaves his family and his worldly possessions and tries to exist without being affected by the lures of the world. Once the "sanyasi" has learned to completely renounce the world, he is free of its *mayajal* (the nets or traps of *illusionary* pleasures and material wealth to be gained in the world). He is now ready, both physically and mentally for death. If his *sanyas* has been pure, his death will free him from the cycle of rebirth.

Narayan's novels are situated in the conjunction of the two philosophical principles of *Karma* and *Varnasramadharma* – firmly anchored in a society organized by caste hierarchies. In the novels, this religious ideology is never questioned. What is questioned and – more often than not – ridiculed and even punished is the individual's attempt to break with these religious principles. Narayan's major fiction repeatedly follows a pattern that is a variation on the following sequence of events: an individual starts out as an integrated part of a traditional society (s/he is in the student or householder stage of life). Then, because of a momentary disillusion or entrapment in the *mayajal* of *artha* (material wealth) or of *kama* (love), the individual abandons his/her traditionally prescribed role. For a short period of time, it seems as if the individual has broken free from the rigidity of traditional thought. But at the closure of the novel, the "erring" character is brought back to the realization that following the principles of *karma* and *varnasramadharma* is the only path one can take. The individual then questions and rejects his/her own deviation from these principles. Narayan sees this self-chastisement as "self-knowledge." The resolution, then, comes with the protagonist's return to his/her "true identity"; an identity that is written over by the requirements of a traditional society.[65] Hence, in Narayan's novels, this social norm is reproduced through its violations and then at the end of each novel with the restoration of the norm, readers who are conversant with these societal mores are sutured back into narrative.

In *The Dark Room*, Savitri is bound by her upbringing, her traditional beliefs and by her very name, to be the silent suffering wife. In the Hindu imagination, the ideal image for the devoted wife is supplied by a mythological story about a woman called Savitri. The mythological Savitri is revered (and sometimes derided) in popular culture because she outwitted Yama, the god of death, by wresting her husband's life back from him through her clever manipulation of the idea of wifely purity.[66] Narayan's Savitri is also the epitome of wifely virtue. However oppressive that role may be, like Kuchela's wife in the film, it is her duty (her *karma*) to play the part. So when Savitri leaves her home, husband and children, it is, in terms of *varnasramadharma*, an attempt to escape a prescribed stage in her life cycle. In Narayan's narratives, such escape is always illusionary.

When Savitri leaves her husband, she is very clear about why she has to leave him. She has decided that she would rather "starve and die in the open, under the sky, a roof for which we need to be obliged to no man" (*DR*, p. 84).[67] She does not take her children or her jewelry because: "What possessions can a woman call her own except her body? Everything else that she has is her father's, her husband's or her son's" (*DR*, p. 84). This is a feminist rebellion against a Hindu prescription of the role of women as inscribed in the *Manusmriti*, one of the many Hindu scriptures written in the last few centuries B.C. "The Code of Manu" prescribed that a woman was to be under the authority of men all through life: first of her father, then of her husband and, in her old age, of her son.[68] Savitri defies this authority in her words and actions; the Code of Manu sets the very terms of her rebellion. But it is not a rebellion against religious prescriptions so much as against its patriarchal manifestations in her personal life – she finds a job in a temple. For a brief while she confronts her fear of life, of her husband and of living without male protection.

And yet she returns home. Narayan's narration of this sudden turnabout is not wholly convincing. It is only when one has read a number of his novels and has become accustomed to the pattern of sudden reversals to the path of tradition that Savitri's behavior seems convincing. Savitri returns home, the novel tells us, because she misses her comfortable bed and her children (*DR*, pp. 142–3).

Savitri's brief rebellion does not dramatically change her domestic situation. When Ramani comes home from work that day, she serves him his meal as she usually does. She even attempts to laugh at his jokes and to respond to his flirtatious remarks. Outwardly, she lives up to the image that her name connotes. And yet, she reflects: "A part of me is dead" (*DR*, p. 156).[69] When she hears Mari, her rescuer, shouting his services outside her home, she curbs her impulse to run out and greet him: "Why should I call him here? What have I?" (*DR*, p. 157).

Savitri's character is contrasted with Shanta Bai's. The latter's name suggests that she is not a south Indian, nor a Tamilian brahmin. Separated from her husband, Shanta Bai has no traditional role to play. In terms of *varnasramadharma*, her husband-less status makes her an outcast. In certain parts of India, the name "Shanta Bai" would be perfectly respectable, with "Bai" referring to no more than a honorific term for woman. And yet, in the popular culture "Bai" has the connotations that "Madame" has in English – of brothel manager or even prostitute.

A strong case can be made for reading this novel for its stance on love, marriage, female desirability, and the politics of domestic power. In such a reading, religion and domesticity, rather than nationalism, would serve as the ruling ideologies. This is not to insist on the domestic as a private space that is unmarked by "larger" politics, but to note that domestic relations restructure public alliances. One could argue that the dynamics of (Hindu) nationalism in this novel's narrative are extensions of domestic issues at the center of the text rather than the other way around. Savitri's domestic crisis and its unsettling resolution, Ramani's blustering confusion between tradition and temptation, and Shanta Bai's precarious existence do not need to be allegorically interpreted in order to be of significance. Nor does reading the novel in terms of home-making automatically cancel its political charge.

In the attempt to explain his partiality for Narayan's fiction, Graham Greene wrote:

There are writers – Tolstoy and Henry James to name two – whom we hold in awe, writers – Turgenev and Chekhov – for whom we feel a personal affection, other writers whom we respect – Conrad for example – but who hold us at arm's length with their "courtly foreign grace." Narayan (whom I don't hesitate to name in such a context) more than any of them wakes in me a spring of gratitude, for he has offered me a second home. Without him I could never have known what it is like to be Indian.[70]

Is Graham Greene's "we" the same as Jameson's "we"? Narayan offers Greene a second home – what would the status of Greene, the white critic and writer, be in Narayan's Malgudi? This naive and romantic notion would be quickly dispelled if Greene were to try and *live* in his "second home." As an outsider in Narayan's Malgudi, he simply cannot belong, a fact that is emphasized repeatedly through the fate of every stranger who enters this fictional city. For all his empathy with the Narayan Hero, Greene would perhaps be seen as no more than the "red faced, beef eating" British official in *Mr. Sampath* or the alien, white college principal in *The Bachelor of Arts*.[71] Every kind of change or alteration is ferociously resisted in Malgudi. Hybridity is not a possibility here.

Jameson insists that national allegory is consciously plotted by the "third world" writer.[72] In *The Dark Room*, Narayan's Hindu nationalism never solidifies into conscious authorial intent. An exclusionary brahmin nationalism is perceived only when one reads against the grain of the narrative. Up front we have the semblance of a pure, peaceful, orderly community where even Graham Greene feels at home.

CONCLUSIONS

In her brilliant critique of Western feminism's readings of women's issues in the non-west, Chandra Mohanty poses a crucial question: "What is it about cultural Others that makes it so easy to analytically formulate them into homogeneous groupings with little regard for historical specificities?"[73] "What makes it easy, according to Mohanty, is the unproblematized practice of "discursive colonialism" which she defines in terms of the specific focus of her article:

What I wish to analyze is specifically the production of the "Third World Woman" as a singular monolithic subject in some recent (Western) feminist texts. The definition of colonization I want to evoke here is a predominantly discursive one, focusing on a certain mode of appropriation and codification of "scholarship" and "knowledge" about women in the third world by particular analytic categories employed in specific writings on the subject which take as their referent feminist interests as they have been articulated in the US and western Europe.[74]

Jameson himself provides the most comprehensive critique of "total system[s] of logic" in an earlier article entitled "Postmodernism, or The Cultural Logic of late Capitalism," which he suggests we read in conjunction with *TWL*.[75] In the context of the postmodern west, Jameson objects to periodization and its "possible obliteration of heterogeneity" of contemporary society.[76] He writes:

What happens is that the more powerful the vision of some increasingly total system or logic – the Foucault of the prison book is the obvious example – the more powerless the reader comes to feel. Insofar as the theorist wins, therefore by constructing an increasingly closed and terrifying machine, to that very degree he loses, since the critical capacity of his work is thereby paralyzed, and the impulses of negation and revolt, not to speak of those of social transformation, are increasingly perceived as vain and trivial in the face of the model itself.

Having written this, what allows Jameson to design a totalizing dynamic for what is called "third world" literature? Contrary to what he writes in the passage quoted above, totalizing systems do not necessarily render the reader powerless when what is totalized is the cultural practices of Others. In his final footnote to *TWL*, Jameson writes that part of the philosophical underpinnings for this article comes from Lukács' notion of "mapping" as formulated in *History and Class Consciousness*. "Mapping" is in Jameson's words, "the grasping of the social totality [that] is structurally available to the dominated rather than the dominating classes...what is here called 'national allegory' is clearly a form of just such mapping of totality."[77] Hence, for the western reader of *TWL*, Jameson's "map" provides an effortless means of entering and assigning meaning to cultural productions that are outside their domain. It serves ultimately, to make the western intellectual comfortable, at home everywhere.[78] In these two essays by Jameson there is an undeniable hesitation to theorize the self in the terms in which one is ready to theorize others.

The primary concern that has fueled my analysis in this chapter is the problematic question of how one reads and teaches global literature in ways that pay due attention to the politics of location: "ours" as well as "theirs." How can our reading of contemporary non-western literatures do something other than provide one more avenue for reinforcing the existing western hegemony and neo-colonialism in other aspects of global relations? How do we read so that texts produced by other cultures remain both resistant and resonant? How do we do this without going to the extreme that Jamaica Kincaid does in *A Small Place* when she declares in anguish over the present-day Antigua that the only good (western) tourists are the ones who stay at home? How does one avoid the stance that would see the only good western reader of non-western texts as s/he who does not presume to read these texts at all? How does one work toward reading internationally and thinking globally without the aid of universalisms? There are no easy answers. What we need to guard against is allowing ourselves to take up the position of the disinterested, unimplicated "first world" reader whose global responsibilities can be theoretically elided.

In the chapter that follows, I examine the politics of one genre of "Third World Literature" in the "era of multinational capitalism": specifically, the fiction produced in English by elite Indian women

writers in and around the 1980s. The impact of national politics is
more diversely inscribed in these novels than can be traced through
locating national allegories. The more challenging issue that confronts
the reader of these novels can be briefly intimated as follows: what is
to be done with a common literary plot that presents women protagonists who have every comfort of home (domestic comforts, social status, leisure, language,) and yet find themselves unsatisfied with their
privileges, unable to articulate this angst and unable to alter their
lives? In an earlier chapter I examined the rhetoric of home in the
writing of/on the English memsahib in India, to argue that it was
their racial privilege and their own investment in colonial ideologies
that led to the confirmation of "unified and autonomous" subjecthood
to their Englishwoman protagonists. The elite plot that upper-class
Indian women are trapped in is found to be equally problematic even
as it represents women who long for a unified and autonomous subjecthood that would put an end to their fragmented sense of self. But
what complicates a dismissal of this fictional genre is evidence that
these writers (through their protagonists) vigorously protest and often
reject the privileges that accrue to women in their position in postcolonial societies. Earlier chapters have examined various instances of
leaving homes of comfort; the stance adopted by the feminists discussed in chapter 1, by Englishwomen outside England in chapter 2.
Leaving home becomes a very different project in the case of the
Indian woman who is privileged by class. The literary means that
could provide ways out of such entrapment are too heavily invested in
colonial/nationalist, Romantic projects to be able to help in the construction of alternative and adequate locations.

CHAPTER 5

Elite plotting, domestic postcoloniality

Her husband shut her
In every morning; locked her in a room of books
With a streak of sunshine lying near the door, like
A yellow cat, to keep her company, but soon,
Winter came and one day while locking her in, he
Noticed that the cat of sunshine was only a
Line, a hair-thin line, and in the evening when
He returned to take her out, she was a cold and
Half-dead woman, now of no use at all to men.

from "The Sunshine Cat," Kamala Das

Not long ago a woman who spoke about herself
was considered a loose woman.

Anees Jung

In a richly textured introduction to *Third World Women and the Politics of Feminism*, Chandra Mohanty stresses the need to move beyond the notion that "simply being a woman, or being poor or black or Latino, is sufficient ground to assume a politicized oppositional identity."[1] While Mohanty draws our attention to the fact that "not all feminist struggles can be understood within the framework of 'organized' movements," she also notes that she does "challenge the notion 'I am, therefore I resist'" (p. 35). In this chapter I want to challenge the notion "I write, therefore I resist" through an examination of novels written by Indian women in English in roughly the last quarter of the twentieth century.

Novels like Shashi Deshpande's *That Long Silence*, Nayantara Sahgal's *The Day in the Shadow* and Anita Desai's *Where Shall We Go This Summer?* construct the figure of a contemporary, upper-class, urban, Indian female subject who is unsatisfied and unhappy, yet lacks the means to change the world or the subject positions she finds herself trapped in.[2]

In these and several other novels in English by contemporary Indian

131

women, a paradigmatic feminine self is constructed through the narration of a central domestic crisis.[3] What is striking about this fiction by women writers such as Deshpande, Desai and Sahgal is its repeated use of essentially the same plot: the novel or short story begins on the eve of a domestic crisis for the young or middle-aged female protagonist – a husband's loss of job, a divorce, an extramarital affair, an unpleasant encounter with suffering, a cross-class confrontation. Often this event may be no more than a ripple on the placid waters of her everyday life. Whatever its scale, the event develops into the central event or crisis of the narrative, whose reverberations force the protagonist to confront the parameters of herself, her life and her worth. This period of self-examination is followed by a return (often with relief) to her life of domestic boredom, which she may have earlier found stultifying, *or* by a rejection of the entire enterprise of domesticity. The suspense lies in the reader's involvement in guessing the path taken by the female protagonist after this momentous turn in events.

A short story titled "Portrait of a Childhood" by Shama Futehally and published in 1992 provides a useful introduction to this literary plotting and to the subjects such narratives create.[4] This story adopts the literary technique of looking back to an "elite" (economically defined) childhood to focus on events that taught the female protagonist her class privilege and served to render "normal" the vast inequalities in India. This is accomplished through several cross-class confrontations in which the young protagonist learns that her beautiful, glowing world is carved out of the misery and hard labor of servants and other working-class persons. At the end of the story we are left with the product of such lessons in entitlement: a literary representation of a young postcolonial Indian woman who expects life to be seamlessly beauty-filled, whose escapes to the swing at the bottom of her lovely garden increase in frequency, and who is left, the last sentence of the story tells the reader, "feeling unmistakably dead, as I was to do for many years to come."

Toward the end of *Where Shall We Go This Summer?* Sita, the heroine recalls the general dissatisfaction which led to her leaving home earlier in the novel as she tries to decide whether she should return home with her husband:

Again and again the wave repeated its rush forward, its rush backward. Watching it, she saw again that point in time when she had realized what a farce marriage was, *all* human relationships were. It was the day she had admitted, out of a passion of boredom she could no longer contain and that burst, swamping her, that she was bored, bored, bored. "Bored?" he had exclaimed, in genuine surprise. "Why? How? With what?" and looked so puzzled, so pained. Then it was her turn to be puzzled and pained – she could not believe that he had really believed that all was well, not known that she was bored, dull, unhappy, frantic. She could hardly believe that although they lived so close together, he did not even know this basic fact of her existence.[5]

How do we understand the intricacies of this "passion of boredom"? How do we place this boredom within the many international and local studies that show that women in India and elsewhere perform more than two-thirds of the work hours in the world?[6] I use the term *elite Indian women* in order to bring to the fore the complex sense of entitlement that accrues to upper-class Indian women and their counterparts elsewhere in the geographic third world. This entitlement is more than class privilege – it is an assurance that comes (or should come) with wealth, education, and the possession of the powers allotted to domesticated womanhood in patriarchal societies.

And yet, time and again in this fiction, the heroine is just a step away from a complete breakdown. These fictional women crave for meaning and purpose yet find that their needs have lowest priority in every avenue that provides redress. Jaya, the married, middle-aged heroine of Shashi Deshpande's *That Long Silence* describes herself in a moment of painful self-deprecation as: "Middle class. Bourgeois. Upper caste. Distanced from real life. Scared of writing. Scared of failure. Oh God, I had thought, I can't take it anymore. Even a worm has a hole it can crawl into. I had mine – as Mohan's wife, as Rahul's and Rati's mother."[7] In the context of a developing country, where poverty is considered the greatest social and economic problem, to have material comforts is to have everything. And yet in the above quoted passage there is none of the confident contentment that leisured women are supposed to radiate.

What these women protagonists desire remains undefined and elusive in the novels.[8] And yet one can gather from reading various novels that it is a desire for something more than mere material comforts. It is a desire for an imagined self and setting that allows escape from the mundane domestic routine of everyday life *and* from the usual alternative that a more public life, (as working woman or as a socially committed public figure), would provide. It is a desire for a feminine/feminist self that will be a viable *counter* position to the gendered roles of daughter, mother and wife. It is also a desire for a place of feminine creativity where beauty, art and unfragmented universalisms can flourish unhampered by material realities and social relations. As such, it is a desire to evolve into a female subject that is "free" from the many representations of ideal womanhood that are abundantly produced in various cultural texts and yet the contours of this desired self remain defined by these representations. In keeping with the patriarchal ideologies current in the society, folk wisdom maintains that women are meant to be fluid and accommodating. Like water, they must be able to take the shape of whatever vessel (read as husband) they are poured into. Outside the vessel water has no shape. Hence, folklore logic maintains, the need for containing women – for their own good. The fictional narratives I examine here attempt to construct women who struggle to "hold their shape" outside of the vessels or containers provided by society. Hence, in a move that contradicts current feminist theory's close association of women of color and the celebration of multiple subjectivities and fluid selfhood, the longed for ideal self in these narratives is a unified, solid entity which will not be splintered into fragments by the multiple demands made on these women. Women writers such as Desai, Deshpande and Saghal try to bring this self-sufficient woman into existence in their fiction, working with and against the resources available: a Romantic rhetoric and female role models constructed by religious, nationalist and feminist lore about *stree-shakti* (women's power). Ultimately the search for satisfying selfhood that these female protagonists undertake is frustratingly unspecific, invariably incomplete, and yet, always an unstaunchable desire.

An examination of these novels disrupts our expectations of "post-colonial women's writing" and of "Third World Feminism." Frequently, the protagonist in these novels is an educated woman who is also a writer of varied success. Writing the first person narrative becomes for these female protagonists, a means of questioning the order of their lives and then a way of reordering it. Writing fiction, in this context, is not *always* the radical, resistive move, that we have come to automatically associate with the very term "postcolonial." Often it becomes an act of recuperation and reconciliation – at worst a means of dispelling the boredom of immured domesticity. If we expect this ennui, which leads in *That Long Silence, The Day in the Shadow* or even in a popular novel like *Socialite Evenings* by Shobha Dé to the production of written texts, to evolve into a radical political declaration, we will be disappointed. Such action is, I will argue, beyond the scope of this writing because the players (authors, protagonists and implied readers) are often those left out of the political and linguistic scenarios in which resistance, as understood in the literary context, is formulated.[9] Perhaps, James C. Scott's analysis in *Weapons of the Weak: Everyday Forms of Peasant Resistance* could be adapted to illuminate this genre's different encoding of resistance.[10] Scott begins with a consideration of what the peasantry does "between revolts" to defend its interests as best it can (p. 29). He contrasts this "everyday resistance" which disavows "public and symbolic goals" with the "open defiance" that marks peasant revolts that get documented as resistance. Scott's analysis of everyday resistance could be also extended to explicate the texture of the feminism in play in these novels. What circulates in these texts is a disdain for organized feminism that is matched by deeply feminist preoccupations and musings. "Everyday forms of resistance," Scott writes, "make no headlines" (p. 36). These institutionally invisible protests are what mark our heroine until the moment when the central domestic crisis leads her into open defiance. And yet, it is difficult to decide whether sulking, weeping, boredom and running away are the very features of elite entitlement or a protest of the same.[11]

Locating the dynamics that govern a specific fiction genre (in this case the novels of elite Indian women writers) forces an acknowledgment of the containment effected by the category of the "postcolonial" and "third world." For instance, it is common practice in today's academic publishing and literary instruction to allocate to some texts the *privilege* of representing a region on the map. Hence anthologies of world literature or of literary criticism on global literatures organize literary products according to the nationality and gender of the writer. A few short stories and poems metonymically represent an entire (national) body of work. The case of the Indian woman writer points squarely to the inadequacy, and even dangers, of such organizing principles. Desai, Deshpande and Saghal's fictions are not representative of Indian women writers, nor of Indian women. These writers are members of an English speaking, upper-class/caste Hindu elite that may hold political power but are not therefore automatically or metonymically representative of the rest of India.

Does the very act of writing and reading further the isolation of the woman of privilege? Kamala Das's "The Sunshine Cat" suggests that the writing produced is "only a/Line, a hair-thin line," of sunshine that cannot substantially nourish this woman writer.[12] More often than not, writing becomes yet another domestic appliance, to which the housewife "applies" herself. Is this isolation in which these narra-

tives of self-production are woven, a continuation of earlier practices
of seclusion? The self that is born of this writing in the language and
diction of privilege, while it is meant to serve as an embellishment to
the bourgeois subject that the protagonist embodies, instead makes
her painfully aware of her "uselessness." This is the realization about
her self and situation that the female protagonist in novel after novel
reaches and tries to alter. More often than not the protagonist accepts
her limited life and returns to her old situation after a period of struggle, for it is after all the only place they know as home.

What follows then, in this chapter, is an attempt to arrive at explanations for this present plot/pattern in the writing of elite Indian
women writers through an examination of the novels and of related
non-literary histories. I use this common plot rather than the specific
details of the writers' class and/or caste position to determine "elite-
ness." I am aware of the many differences in the lifestyles and backgrounds of even the three writers whose novels serve as the ground for
this discussion. Sahgal's connections to the Nehru family, for instance,
or Anita Desai's German background do not enter into the discussion.
Instead, it is in the plot formation that appears over and over again in
these narratives that I locate the "elite" subject. I account for this common "plot" by briefly examining the ways in which the related Indian
histories of nationalism, of the "Hindu way of life," of English-lan-
guage Indian literature, and of Indian women's movements have
worked in unison to establish the unenviable situation that the elite
Indian woman finds herself in: she has all the material benefits of
home, of consumerism, of leisure and yet finds herself deeply unful-
filled and completely alienated from the roles available to her.

In reading the narratives of postcolonial struggles for gendered self-
identity there is the temptation to locate such struggles in the past of
contemporary Western culture. Hence, it would be possible to read
the novels that are under discussion in this chapter as no more than
an anachronistic replaying of the crisis of white middle-class
American housewives in the 1960s à la Betty Friedan's diagnosis in
The Feminine Mystique. The literary phenomenon that I study in this
chapter, is set in a specific historical location (the 1970s and 1980s in
post-independence, urban India) and has a specific cultural/politi-
cal/linguistic trajectory leading to and from it. However, this is not to
imply that this literature is wholly unmarked by western mainstream
feminism as scripted by Friedan, Gloria Steinem, Germaine Greer
and others. This writing by Indian women demonstrates that the fic-

tions produced from a colonial education and culture may be stymied by its very reliance on the notions of liberty, freedom, feminist equality; notions that are received as universally applicable but which reveal their "locality" when the idioms are brought to bear on a different locale. What is acted out in these novels are struggles to make feminist idiom fit experience. As such, this plot does have the potential for possible formulations of oppositional or resistive ideologies.

What motivates my examination of this elite plot is the suspicion that when *all* the sufferings of *all* Indian women are stilled and remedied, "selfhood" may still be deemed an unnecessary accessory – as unnecessary and "imported" as it would be to a well-fed, well looked after cow. If women whose every material need has been met have to automatically and necessarily efface their personal desires, then clearly the only desires of women considered worth meeting are the basic trio: food, shelter and clothing. An earlier chapter in this book demonstrated how English women in the Indian empire were led to believe that their liberation was a completed project even before they won the right to vote. This stance which served the purposes of British imperialism as well as it did British patriarchy, was accomplished by the women's own insistence on seeing themselves and their lives as vastly superior to that of their "Eastern sisters." A similar though not identical operation takes place through the class and caste divisions among women in post-independence India. Upper-class Indian women insist on seeing their lot as vastly superior to that of women of the lower classes – which it is in material and economic terms.[13]

And yet, imperialism, nationalism and women's movements have collaborated in hollowing out all specificity from Indian women. They have been used as symbols of nation, of tradition, of modernity, of suffering, of strength (as Durga), of love and self-sacrifice (as Mother India), of destruction (as Kali) *but never as important in themselves*. As a gendered person, this elite Indian woman does not merit notice – unless she suffers (which immediately makes her "woman") or unless she is symbolic of national values (which immediately makes her "Indian"). Her crises are never important enough to merit attention because there are always scores of women (and less privileged men) whose needs are more urgent. Even as our heroine sets out on her search for an adequate feminine (if not feminist) self, their project is represented – even in first person fictional accounts – as self-serving, self-absorbed narrative. The "failure" of these expeditions in search of the self present us with a situation in which we have to acknowledge

the limited usefulness of literary texts as political tools for social transformation.

THE ROMANTIC IDIOM: POLITICAL IMPLEMENT AND IMPEDIMENT

Characteristic of this fiction which struggles to establish adequate selfhood for its female protagonists is the use of a poetic rhetoric drawn
primarily from the language of nineteenth-century British Romantic
poets. This rhetoric is commonly used in some of the poetry and in
most realist fiction written in Indian English and has only recently been
discarded by young and upcoming writers. In 1957, K. R. Srinivasa
Iyengar, the most prolific and authoritative of Indian critics of Indian
literature in English, dubbed "Indo-Anglian" writing "Janus-faced"
because its investment in India was matched by its reliance on Indian
literary traditions.[14] Of the first group of Indian writers in the English
language (those writing between 1870 and 1900), Iyengar writes:

These were the pioneers, but the mere imitators, the practitioners who tried
in vain to effect a marriage of Indian modes of thought or feeling and
English forms or formulae of expression, were many. The English Romantics
– the poets and novelists of the early nineteenth century – fatally attracted
them, but the Indo-Anglian experiments were more often than not mere tin-
sel. Presently however, the time-spirit threw up a number of extraordinary
men and women who demonstrated over and over again that they could
achieve triumphant self-expression through the medium of English.[15]

This language of the Romantic poets continued to serve as a model for
self-expression and creative writing long after independence was won
in 1947. Gauri Viswanathan's *Masks of Conquest* provides a brilliant
analysis of the impact of literary curricula in British India on the shape
and content of canonical English literature. In doing so, she demonstrates how and why English literature came to be the primary literature taught in India in the nineteenth century and offers explanations
for "the more rapid institutionalization of the discipline in the Indian
colony than in the country where it originated."[16] However, given "the
fact that English continues to be taught and studied in today's India,"
Viswanathan cautions against "reading the history of nineteenth-century English studies as continuous with contemporary educational
practice in India."[17] Without claiming a continuation of the same, for
obviously *some* things did change with the take over of power by
Indians in 1947, I will assert that the models of literary excellence

remained, for the most part, unchallenged *long after independence from the British was gained.*[18] English literature had so successfully been established by the British imperialists as the best in the world and as universally resonant, that Indians, especially of the generations after independence, did not (and do not) directly associate this "universal" literature with the other institutions of British imperialism. Hence the cultural imperialism that prevailed long after the British left India has to be understood not as a blind veneration of the oppressor's culture but as the heartfelt appreciation of "universal" literature.

The colonial educational system that is the norm *continues* to reinforce the anthologized Wordsworth, Keats, Shelley and Coleridge as the ultimate poets and the ultimate purveyors of feeling. The poems that celebrate an allegiance to nature, to spontaneous outbursts of emotion, to liberty, freedom and beauty, have become institutionalized as the zenith of expressive writing. Even Mrs. Indira Gandhi, as quoted in Anees Jung's sociological study on population and Indian women, expressed herself in this Romantic idiom: "It [the quality of life] does not lie in what an individual has but what he or she is. It can only be measured in that person's capacity to achieve harmony and resonance with her fellow beings and with nature; to perceive the meaning of thought and experience the beauty of action. In short to find joy in life."[19] The language of Gandhi's statement is positively Wordsworthian in its lyricism, and yet apparently an acceptable analysis of "quality of life" in a context where more than half the population lives below the poverty line.

The titles of Indian novels in English with the preponderance of references to light, silence, dawn, beauty and shadows, as well as the many epigraphs drawn from nineteenth and early twentieth-century English poets, underlines this reliance on the Romantic poetic turn of phrase.[20] T. S. Eliot's poetry and prose serve as a treasure trove for titles and epigraphs as evinced in Attia Hussain's novel *Sunlight on a Broken Column.*[21] These phrases from Eliot's poetry and prose are used alongside those provided by the Romantic poets in a harmonious manner that stresses the continuations between the Romantics and High Modernists often denied in literary criticism.

In the novels in English by Indian women writers, these titles evolve out of the central female character's experience of crisis and of the "re-birth" that often follows. This process is symbolically patterned through the references to light, dawn and shadows, and so on. And yet, like much else in this fiction, these titles are often read as symbolic of concerns larger than those with which the woman protagonist grapples in the narrative. In her analysis of *The Time of Morning*, by Nayantara Sahgal, Ramesh Chadha mentions in passing that the title "obviously suggests the 'Morning of National Freedom'."[22] Why is this *obvious*? Clearly, Sahgal's writing, more than the writing of any other woman writer discussed in this chapter, is consistently concerned with weaving together events in her female protagonists' life with events in national politics. However, the story of Rashmi who desires a new start, (for marriage has reduced her to "a moth trapped in cement") can just as readily be inferred in this title.

Why does the metaphoric "morning of the new day" in the life of the female protagonist follow from national independence and only then, in a secondary fashion, from the changes she brings about in the domestic narrative that is central to the text? I will argue that such relegation of the elite woman herself, and of the projects intimate to her, to secondary or peripheral places is an unquestioned feature of both conservative and progressive discourses in twentieth-century India. It is a devaluation of female selfhood that is reinforced by all dominant and resistive ideologies that even these women subscribe to.

In *The Woman in Indian Fiction in English*, Shanta Krishnaswamy documents the "one basic fact" that emerges from her study of women in the writing of six novelists:

The woman, by occupying frequently the dominant or most significant role in the plot, proves to be a potent vehicle for an author who wishes to express himself forcefully and has the talent to do so. An author's interest in the woman leads to his involvement with the problems of human development within Indian society as he conceives them. Passive or assertive, traditional or modern, she reflects his own insecurity, isolation, fear, bewilderment and emotional vulnerability. Even when the author chooses to withdraw from Indian society and seeks escape abroad, as is seen in the case of Jhabvala, even in a negative approach, the woman becomes a mirror image of the author's own predicament. The general shift in contemporary Indian literature from larger national and philosophical issues to emphasis on introspection and individualism comes in handy for the author who transforms the female protagonist in his novel into an agent in his own quest for psychological insight and awareness.[23]

Krishnaswamy's use of the masculine pronoun for "the author" is meant to cover both sexes, for she examines the novels of Raja Rao, Bhabani Bhattacharya, R. K. Narayan, Kamala Markandaya, Anita Desai and Ruth Prawer Jhabvala. Her analysis records one more instance of the ways in which the Indian woman is represented as an empty signifier waiting to be infused with symbolic meaning. I will proceed with an examination of the processes by which the interests of elite Indian women are side-stepped in Indian nationalism ⸱⸱ Indian feminism.

NATIONALISM: THE ELITE INDIAN WOMAN AS SYMBOL

In an article entitled "Tracing Savitri's Pedigree: Victorian Racism and the Image of Women in Indo-Anglian Literature," Susie Tharu examines early twentieth-century literature written in English by Indian women for what it reveals of "the psycho-social economy that gives rise to a text, and in turn, the limits of the imaginative self images we inherit."[24] Tharu argues that this writing by Indian women and about Indian women in the pre-independence period used "Woman" as a symbol of "Indianness" – a symbol that could strategically represent *both* the Indian potential for progress (Westernization) and the nationalist revival of tradition (Sanskritization) as any given rhetorical occasion might demand.[25] Tharu writes:

No doubt partly in response to the British focus on women, the movement [emergent nationalism] chose to create an image of the Indian woman who was not socially victimized, but who voluntarily *chose* the path of suffering and death in order to save her people. Indeed, she became a heraldic device...

The burden of saving the nation: politically (Gandhi), spiritually (Aurobindo) and aesthetically/metaphysically (Raja Rao) is not just on women, but on the feminine.[26]

Reading the poetry of Toru Dutt (1856–1877) and of Sarojini Naidu (1879–1949), Tharu argues that this nationalism placed,

an enormous burden on the women who came within its defining scope. It was the women, their commitment, their purity, their sacrifice, who were to ensure the moral, even spiritual power of the nation and hold it together. But even as we point this out, we must not forget that this phase also made for a positive evaluation of femininity that did allow for a limited growth.[27]

Caught in this bind that Tharu refers to, India's elite women win some ground and yet lose a lot more by being elevated to the status of "national symbol." The most crucial loss is that of knowledge of an adequate self that can be imaginatively constructed *independent of* the larger than life, symbolic delineations of "womanhood" that nationalist fervor instituted in place of the ordinary mortal.[28]

Having productively traced "the history of woman as an imaginative construct in the literature of emerging nationalism" Tharu assesses the situation for Indian women today: "If we were the heralds of a vision yesterday, today we are the betrayers, for the dream has failed...Both

the hatred and the inevitable disgust is projected onto women who surprisingly often still symbolize the land."²⁹ Hence, both as dreamer and
betrayer of the dream, Indian women are evoked in projects that offer
them no context for agency that is not turned outward, beyond themselves. Tharu urges contemporary Indian women to be aware of "the
designs literature has on us, of the way it forms and controls our imaginative self images and of the regeneration of a critical voice."³⁰

Reading fiction in English produced by Indian women beyond the
period that Tharu covers in this article, one finds that in independent
India there are new and urgent factors that once again require that
the educated woman pay attention to issues *outside* herself.

FEMINISM AS SOCIAL WORK

Both progressive and conservative projects collaborate to erase "self-
centered" narratives initiated by elite Indian woman. Both urge her
to efface herself in light of other more urgent concerns. For the mate-
rially comfortable upper-class woman to assert her own needs or to
assert her dissatisfaction with the limitations placed on her is to have
a tantrum. It is in this context that Anees Jung's statement that serves
as an epigraph to this chapter must be read.³¹

The "self" that is independent of or that overarches the many
roles prescribed for Indian women is a luxury, an indulgence, an
unnecessary (illusionary) pleasure. Personal happiness is self-indulgence from the point of view of nationalist *and* mainstream feminist
causes, as well as in the dominant religious ideology of Hinduism.
Hence, writing in 1991 about Kamala Markandaya's *Some Inner Fury*,
and specifically of the heroine Mira's decision to leave her British
lover for the Indian nationalist cause, Rama Jha notes:

In light of the Gandhian thought that pervaded the 1940s, Mira's painful
decision constitutes a sacrificial gesture, *befitting a woman of her strength who is
free of self-indulgence.* By showing Mira accepting her fate with equanimity,
Markandaya highlights the image of an Indian woman who may choose
suffering over her own selfish desire for happiness.³² (emphasis added)

This short passage clearly reveals Jha's understanding of the prioritizing
expected from Mira as an Indian woman of her time and place. Elite
women, if they do not suffer bodily deprivation (for a patriotic cause in
this instance), can at least suffer emotionally. To qualify for the status of
"Indian Woman" one needs to go beyond the self (preferably through
suffering), in order to facilitate the transmogrification into a symbol.

Mainstream Indian feminism is not organized around the needs of elite women. Their only role is to aid in fighting for the rights of less privileged women. This is not to undermine the goals of feminism in India, but rather to underline the very distinct focus of feminist practices in post-independence India.[33] Assessing the work of the "women's liberation" organizations in India in 1985, Vibhuti Patel writes:

Over the last decade and a half, women's organizations there [in India] have concentrated on a number of demands, many of which are probably alien to women in the west. We have taken up the cause of maid-servants, fought against temple-prostitution, denounced superstition and witch-hunting, opposed deforestation and the exploitation of Dalit and tribal women. The problems of women living in slums and the socio-economic oppression of working-class and peasant women have always been to the forefront. This is hardly surprising, as the overwhelming majority of women in India live in conditions of extreme poverty and deprivation. At the same time, rape, wife-beating, economically motivated killings and other atrocities against women show no sign of declining. The tasks confronting the women's movement in India are formidable indeed.[34]

This passage makes obvious the reasons why the development of subjecthood for women of privilege was not a priority even within the women's movement. In her brief history of "contemporary Indian feminism" Radha Kumar notes that feminist events and women's organizations in India came into being as offshoots of larger political parties and movements.[35] Women's activism in the sixties and seventies, Kumar tells us, was part of several radical movements that "spanned a political spectrum from Gandhian-socialist (that is nonviolent protest, based in explicitly moral values, over specific working or living conditions) to the far left, in particular the Maoists."[36] Political activism by women in this period was linked to trade unionism, consumer action groups, anti-corruption movements and anti-casteism agitations. Kumar notes that neither the activists nor others "looked upon these movements as feminist, nor did they advance any theories of women's oppression."[37]

In the late seventies, following Indira Gandhi's imposition of a state of Emergency on India in 1975, there was state repression of most kinds of political activism. This imposition led, as Kumar points out, to a change of focus from activism to discussion of issues. In 1977 when the Emergency was lifted, several women's groups emerged from former underground discussion groups. These groups were based in the major cities (Bombay, Delhi, Madras, Pune, Patna, Bangalore, Hyderabad, Ahmedabad). Kumar writes of the philosophy and composition of these groups:

Though there was no particular uniformity between them, their members were largely drawn from the urban educated middle class and this was an important reason for their feeling that their own needs were minor, and different from the needs of the large, and poor, majority of Indian women.[38]

Hence, from the very start of this post-independence women's activism several distinctive features were established. First, urban, educated, upper and middle class women had a vital role to play in the direction that "Indian feminism" took. However, a central aspect of playing this role was the necessary effacement of their own needs, desires and aspirations. As the citations from Patel and Kumar demonstrate, issues concerning the general populace and ensuring survival for the vast majority of women have always been at the forefront of women's movements in India.[39] For an upper-class woman to prove her worth was to leave behind her self and to step forward to serve others – as in nationalism, in Hindu orthodoxy, so too in "feminism."

In light of this appropriation of the body, labor and intellect of the elite Indian woman by projects other than the development of herself, how do we locate the fiction produced in English by Desai, Deshpande and Sahgal? What contribution does this fiction make to Indian women's struggles to bring about (gendered) equality for all Indians?[40] In their spectacular and suggestive introduction to *Women Writing in India: The Twentieth Century, Volume II*, Susie Tharu and K. Lalitha note that "neither the women's texts that emerged in the middle of the twentieth century, nor those of their male contemporaries, bear marks of those political encounters [between the self and colonial or state authorities]." Tharu and Lalitha go on to discuss post-independence literary production in terms that provide one of the many frames I use for the argument made here. They write:

The rigours of colonialism are peeled off like prison uniforms, and writers seem only too ready to forget them. The truths of the nation seem to have displaced the myths of empire and *to have made the land and its waters available once more as free and neutral ground on which artists, who are curiously historyless and universal but at the same time essentially Indian, might once more pursue eternal verities.* The sense in the literature is of ground so well and truly consolidated that to go over it would be tiresome, of questions so totally resolved that even the memory of struggle can be set aside and the real human business of living and standing up to mortality – which, the implication is, is finally also the real business of art – can be resumed...The writer who had earlier staunchly refused to accept the housing offered by a colonial authority, in the fifties and the sixties slips only too smoothly back into the "human" family. For the solitary heroine (or hero) in search of herself, the outside world fuses with the one inside. [emphasis added]

Locating fiction in English by Indian women within this matrix, will bear out and complicate Tharu and Lalitha's reading of the larger picture. Given the large canvas Tharu and Lalitha cover in their two volumes (women's writing from 600 BC to the present), a decision was made not to include the work of Indian women who write in English in the second half of the twentieth century.[41] Even so, Tharu and Lalitha's nuanced reading of what is believed to be "the real business of art" provides a context in which these novels can be read as sharing some of the preoccupations of Indian literature of the time.

CLIMBING UP THE WALL: BOREDOM OR REBELLION?

The reader of *Where Shall We Go This Summer?*, *That Long Silence* and *The Day in Shadow* is immediately assailed by the broken, tentative, ellipses filled, articulations of the central female characters as they try to find satisfactory explanations for their overwhelming grief. Copious extracts from the novels are necessary to convey the slight nuances and general abstractions through which grief and despair are represented in these narratives. I will discuss Deshpande's novel first and in detail, because it best demonstrates as well as challenges some assertions I have made.[42]

Published in 1988, *That Long Silence* is Shashi Deshpande's fourth novel. The central character and the narrative voice is that of a middle-aged woman called Jaya. She is married (to Mohan), is the mother of two teenage children and a writer of a weekly "women's column" called "Seeta" in *Women's World*, a popular women's magazine. Jaya sees herself as a failed writer and her life as a series of compromises that she has enacted through the various "roles" she has dutifully played over the years.

The narrative begins with a domestic crisis: Mohan, a successful engineer is accused (and rightly so) of being part of a corrupt group of high ranking officials. Fearing the eruption of a major scandal and an official investigation, Mohan decides to "lie low" for a while. The children are away on holiday with family friends and the couple move back to an old flat in the unfashionable suburb of Bombay that they lived in before their prosperous days. This is how Jaya sees her immediate acquiescence with her husband's plans:

Sita followed her husband into exile, Savitri dogging Death to reclaim her husband, Draupadi stoically sharing her husband's travails...
No, what have I to do with these mythical women? I can't fool myself. The

truth is simpler. Two bullocks yoked together...it is more comfortable for them to move in the same direction. To go in different directions would be painful and what animal would voluntarily choose pain? (*LS*, pp. 11–12)

Despite this cynicism, the first person narrative reveals the extent to which Jaya is energized by this threat of impending doom:

> The illusion of happiness – yes, I had to let it go...I had to admit the truth to myself – that I had often found family life unendurable. Worse than anything else had been the boredom of the unchanging patter, the unending monotony. I remember now how often I had sighed for a catastrophe, a disaster, no, not a personal one, but anything to shake us out of our dull grooves. (The eight-planet configuration, which they had said presaged a disaster, had roused my hopes once.) Why was it, I had often wondered, that wars always took place in other countries, tidal waves and earthquakes occurred in far-off places, unknown places, that murder, adultery and heroism had their places in other people's lives, never in ours? The very words *disaster, wrongdoing, retribution* seemed wholly irrelevant to our lives. Like the Chorus of Greek drama, we were distanced from suffering, one foot in front of another, one foot in front of another, until death came to us in a natural form.
>
> But finally it came to me after all, my own special disaster; it came like a prize packet, neatly tied with coloured ribbons, a gift to me from my husband. And I was at such a loss. I did not know what I was to do with such a gift. It seemed to me, impossible. Mohan had to be wrong. Life would go on for us as before, punctuated by dreary quarrels, the children's successes and failures, their estrangements from each other, from us, our resentment and bitterness, old age for us, perhaps widowhood for me – this was our future. Nothing else was possible for people like us. (*LS*, pp. 4–5)

Jaya's boredom is so intensely felt that any interruption of her life – even one with potentially disastrous consequences – provides a welcome break from the monotony of the life allowed her as a middle-aged mother and wife. And yet, the narrative that shifts between past and present soon reveals that Jaya, despite her protests against "the boredom of the unchanging pattern," is haunted by two recent deaths. The death that undermines her strength is that of Kamat, her friend, neighbor and confidante – the only man with whom she has intellectual conversations about herself and her work. This relationship that borders on adultery is abruptly put to an end by Kamat's death. It is a death she cannot openly mourn because to do so would be to acknowledge the intensity of their relationship.

The second death is that of her cousin and poor relative, Kusum, who has a nervous break-down and subsequently commits suicide. Jaya is informed of Kusum's death in a letter from her mother who writes, "it was a good thing in a way. She was of no use to anyone after she went crazy, nobody needed her." Echoes of Kamala Das's "of no use at all to men" resonate through these novels. And indeed, it is the phrase *"of no use to anybody"* that frightens and upsets Jaya for she has always seen herself as inexplicably linked to Kusum –

The day I heard she was sick I felt relief...with Kusum's madness I became aware of my own blessed sanity. Thank God, Kusum, you're nuts, I had thought; because you are that, I know I'm balanced, normal and sane.

Suddenly it occurs to me – as long as Kusum was there, I had known clearly who I was; it had been Kusum who had shown me out to be who I was. I was not-Kusum. Now, with Kusum dead..? (*LS*, p. 126)

Jaya's sense of her self is demarcated by her distance from her "mad" cousin, her impoverished servants, her poised daughter, her stern mother and finally from Suhasini, the new first name her husband had chosen for her – as is customary in some orthodox Hindu communities – at marriage. Jaya transfers the burdens of her various roles as mother and wife onto this "Suhasini" persona:

And I was Jaya. But I had been Suhasini as well. I can see her now, the Suhasini who was distinct from Jaya, a soft, smiling, placid, motherly woman. A woman who lovingly nurtured her family. A woman who coped. When I think of her in this way, I know who it is that Suhasini reminds me of. She's like the sparrow in the story of the crow and the sparrow which we were told as soon as we got into the "tell me a story" phase...There's the foolish, improvident, irresponsible, gullible crow; and the cautious, self-centered, worldly-wise, dutiful, shrewd sparrow. The survivor is the sparrow, the sparrow who keeps the crow waiting for hours, and finally, in the guise of providing sympathy and shelter, kills the crow...the victim, the crow is a male, and the victorious sparrow a female!

I have a feeling that even if little boys forget this story, little girls never will...eventually they will become that damnably, insufferable priggish sparrow looking after their homes, their babies...and to hell with the rest of the world. Stay at home, look after your babies, keep out of the rest of the world, and you're safe. That poor idiotic woman Suhasini believed in this. I know better now. I know that safety is always unattainable. You are never safe. (*LS*, pp. 15–17)

Suhasini becomes Seeta, the woman in the weekly column that Jaya publishes in *Women's World* – a column which she describes as "light, humourous pieces about the travails of a middle-class housewife" (*LS*, p. 149). Her own troubles, *as Jaya*, are no more than the travails of a middle-class housewife, but as the passage quoted above displays, she has nothing but contempt for such a life and for such persons. A woman can lose herself in these roles. She is supposed to find fulfillment in inhabiting these roles. Jaya however, cannot find in these prescribed roles of Suhasini or Seeta, one that is large enough to inhabit full-time. She finds herself fragmented, harassed and distressed by the many roles she is supposed to joyfully take on.

The narrative in this novel is made of Jaya's recollections of her childhood, of her college days, of the early years of marriage, of her frustrations at her success as the writer of the "Seeta" stories that she holds in contempt. Interspersed with this recollection of the past is the narrative of the present in which Jaya and Mohan's marriage falls apart. In a crucial scene, Jaya accuses Mohan of all the things *he* caused her to forfeit. Yet even as she voices her complaints, she cannot help but note the formulaic nature of her recitation:

> The job I wanted to take, the baby I had wanted to adopt, the anti-price campaign I'd wanted to take part in...But even as I listed these to myself, it came to me that perhaps it had nothing to do with Mohan, the fact that I had not done these things, that I had left them alone. Perhaps I had not really cared enough about these things myself. Instead I said, and my voice sounded sullen even to me, "I've done everything you wanted me to."
>
> And now, I thought I must add: "I've sacrificed my life for you and the children." But real bitterness clawed its way through this self-mockery, and I was conscious of having been chained to his dream, the dream that had begun for him when he was a boy, he had seen a gleaming vision of three women in a dingy corridor. It seemed to me that I'd carried those three women of his through all the years of our marriage. (*LS*, p. 120)

Mohan responds with a deluge of angry accusations, the specifics of which go unmentioned:

> "My wife..." the words ran like a refrain through his outburst. And I could see her, the woman I had seen in the mirror the day of our wedding – a woman who had not seemed to be me, who had taken the burden of wifehood off me. A humourless, obsessive person. But Mohan's eyes, as he spoke of her, were agonised, the eyes of a man who'd lost a dear one. (*LS*, p. 121)

Jaya steps out of this figure of "the wife" when she distances herself from Suhasini but even without the mantle of this sanctioned role she finds that she had "finally to bear it myself, the burden of wifehood" (p. 121). Mohan continues to mourn the loss of his illusion:

> "If ever I'd been irresponsible and callous," Mohan was saying..."but I've never been that. I've always put you and the children first, I've been patient with all your whims, I've grudged you nothing. But the truth is that you despise me because I've failed. As long as I had my job and position, it was alright; as long as I could give you all the comforts, it was alright. But now, because I'm likely to lose it all..." (p. 121)

An angry Mohan leaves the house and does not return for several days. Jaya has convinced herself that he will not come back to her when he cables that "all is well" and that he will be back soon. Presumably, he has "fixed" the corruption allegation.

At the end of the novel, Jaya starts collecting the scraps of paper on which she has been scribbling the narratives that make up this novel and asks herself,

What have I achieved by this writing? ... The panic has gone. I'm Mohan's wife, I had thought and cut off the bits of me that had refused to be Mohan's wife. Now I know that kind of fragmentation is not possible (p. 191).

The fragmentation that Jaya refers to in this passage is her refusal to lose herself completely in the figure of Suhasini or Seeta. She knows Mohan will be back. She hopes that he might have changed. She hopes that his "all is well" means "something more than going back to where we were" (p. 193). At the end of this novel, it seems as if Jaya is sobered by the possibility of being rejected by her husband and decides to "pull herself together." How difficult such a pulling together is going to be is evident in the struggles between Jaya and Suhasini. The specter of Kusum stands as the only available alternative in this narrative.

Anita Desai's 1982 novel *Where Shall We Go This Summer?* records the anguish of Sita, a woman who suffers trauma similar to Jaya's in *That Long Silence*. A series of "small incidents" lead her to leave her comfortable house in Bombay for a now abandoned island cottage where she spent her childhood and youth. These "small incidents," as Sita's husband Raman calls them, are: an unwanted (fifth) pregnancy, Sita's unsuccessful attempt to save a wounded eagle from being eaten alive by a pack of crows, a violent fight between a group of urban maid servants including her own, a fight between her two young sons whose aggression is styled in a manner learned from watching films, her daughter Menaka's random decision to tear up her own paintings. Sita's fastidiousness and her disdain of popular culture extends to a general distaste for "ugliness." When Sita informs Raman of her decision to leave he is amazed: "But you're not leaving for such small incidents, Sita? They occur in everyone's life, all the time. If you are an adult you know how to cope with them – they are only *small* incidents" (*WSW*, p. 37). Sita's constant dissatisfaction, which she interprets as boredom, is epitomized in the hours she spends on her balcony, watching the sea:

"Are you waiting for someone?" she was occasionally asked by one of the children dashing past or by her husband, as she sat out on the balcony, smoking, not reading the book on her lap, looking at and then looking away from the

sea. Sometimes she answered with a nod for it was true, she was always waiting. Physically so resigned, she could not inwardly accept that this was all there
was to life, that life would continue thus, inside this small enclosed area, with
these few characters churning around and then past her, leaving her always in
this grey, dull-lit empty shell. I am waiting, she agreed – although for what she
could not tell...But till she came to it, she would live on, smothered by this
endlessly damp, soft grey sand, and it seemed that these years of her life were
dyed, coloured through and through, with the colour of waiting. It was not a
pure colour – it was tinged at times with anxiety, at others with resignation. Or
with frenzy, patience, grimness, fear. But whatever its tint, its tone, it had
seeped through her, flowed along every smallest capillary till she herself was
turned to the colour of waiting, was turned into a living monument to Waiting.
When there was a fifth baby to wait for, she rebelled. She would not wait for
it to come, for anything to happen. She...willed only that it would not be
born and that nothing would happen. It became unthinkable that anything
should happen – for happenings were always violent. (*WSW*, pp. 54⁻5)

Sita's "rebellion" is doomed to be futile: she is going to "will" the
baby not to be born. She cannot bear to bring a child into such a
"violent" world, but the very mention of an abortion by her husband
displays the distance between the two of them as well as the precarious state of her grasp on reality:

"What do you mean – abortion?" she gasped, her eyes burning.
"I suppose that's what you mean – you want one."
"Mad!" she gasped."You're quite mad. *Kill* the baby? It's all I want. I want
to *keep* it, don't you understand."
"No," he shouted in exasperation, feeling himself made a fool that she
spun round and round on her finger till he was sick and giddy. "You just said
you don't want it. Now you say you do want it. What's up? What's up?"
"I mean I want to *keep* it – I don't want it to be born."
"Mad," he breathed in relief, understanding all in a stumbling access of clarity.
(*WSW*, p. 35)

This determination not to give birth leads Sita to Manori, the island
where her father, a Gandhian figure and independence leader in his own
right, tended to the villagers with an artful blend of modern science, seduction, faith healing and charisma. The narrative suggests that Sita's idealism springs from an unconventional childhood spent on this island. It was
a childhood haven where seemingly miraculous "cures" were wrought by
her father. Raman mocks her desire to work her own miracle, what he
derisively calls her "immaculate conception in reverse" (p. 36).

Of course, once she is on the island such a reversal of pregnancy
does not take place. However, Sita succeeds in introducing the two
children that she brings with her (the oldest daughter and the youngest

son) to the beauties of sea, shells and plants. Yet the simple island pleasures she offers the children cannot compete with the comforts and entertainments of their father's home. The daughter writes to her father and has him come to the island and take them back to Bombay. Her action is not so much a betrayal of her mother as an assertion of her own desire. Menaka, the daughter, who wants to be a doctor, needs to return to Bombay in order to take the Medical College entrance exam. Her mother would rather she become a painter:

"Oh Menaka," Sita sighed..."I wish I had your talent. I would nurse it so carefully – like a plant – make it grow, grow. I used to think – after I left this island and had to think about what I would do next – that if only I could paint, or sing or play the *sitar* well, really well, I should have grown into a sensible woman. Instead of being what I am," she said with stinging bitterness..."I should have known how to channel my thoughts and feelings, how to put them to use. I should have given my life some shape then, some meaning. At least it would have had some for me – even if no one else had cared." (*WSW*, p. 117)

Menaka does not change her mind; she is determined to become a doctor. Unable to convince Menaka, Sita reacts in outrage: "It's [science, numbers] a mask, a shroud, nothing else. It leads to a dead-end. There are no dead-ends, now, in art. That is something spontaneous, Menaka, and alive and creative..." (*WSW*, p. 116). Sita's reading of art here and elsewhere is drawn directly from the popular understanding of the artistic credo of the Romantic poets. This credo becomes by extension the rightful function of art. Art is born of an innate "talent" – it is not a skill acquired through training. Art is aligned with nature; it is not "production," it is not science. Sita's lament is that unlike her sister, an untrained but gifted singer and unlike Menaka, she is without talents, hence without any source of self-sustenance. The irony is that it is Sita who, because of her investment in this philosophy, is caught at a "dead-end." When Raman comes to the island, Sita returns with her children to Bombay and to her life of "waiting."

Here, the use of the Romantic idiom fits seamlessly into the ideological requirements of other Indian cultural projects such as an understanding of "female creativity" as rejuvenative and life-bringing as well as a long-standing popular Indian interpretation of all art as expressive, spontaneous and ecstatic. In his contribution to a collection of essays titled *A Common Poetics For Indian Literatures*, K. Krishnamoorty attempts to use components of the poetic theory propounded by Bharata in the *Natyasastra* (300 BC) in reading contemporary Indian literatures.[43] Working with concepts

such as *rasa, guna, dhwani,* Krishnamoorty sees the task of the literary critic
as explaining "the beauty-core of poetry...supplemented by an equally profound philosophy of emotive meaning." Bharata's theorizing, according to
Krishnamoorty, "propounds a semantic approach which highlights the
inmost core of *rasadi* or emotive content as *sui generis* and unique: as something revealed in a flash to a responsive mind."[44] Krishnamoorthy's text
attempts to place art within the matrix envisaged by Bharata, but as
expressed in English his discussion is more immediately evocative of the
widely anthologized artistic philosophy propounded by the Romantic
poets. The critic, according to Krishnamoorty, "values the poem for its
immediate delight rather than its indirect message"– this is precisely how
art functions for Sita and for other Romantics.[45]

   C. D. Narasimhaiah and C. N. Srinath, two well-established Indian
literary critics and the editors of *A Common Poetics For Indian Literatures,*
a collection that attempts to formulate this "common poetics," make
the argument quite differently. In an appendix to the book, they
write:

> In the Indian tradition, Literature has an immediate and an ultimate use:
> immediately there is in the presence of a work a *prayojana,* usefulness, such as
> sensitizing the mind, likened to cleansing of the dust-covered mirror and
> awakening, or unfolding, of the lotus of man's inner being; the ultimate use,
> *purushartha* is the nature of value which consists in cultivating an attitude so
> aptly described by Matthew Arnold as the Indian virtue of detachment. [46]

The editors are quite clear in their judgment of literary experiences
that stop at immediate delight – these are essentially incomplete. The
Romantics, Narasimhaiah notes in an early aside, "in their pre-occu-
pation with their own agony and ecstasy, are in the nature of an aberration."[47] Art must transcend such "personal emotion" – it is in possessing this attribute that "art has been said to be the layman's *yoga.*"[48]
Unlike in Krishnamoorty's theory of poetics, in Narasimhaiah and
Srinath's article, the immediate use-value of art is less important than
its ultimate goal which is to inculcate detachment, to move the reader
out of "personal emotion." Despite the contradictory poetics that are
formulated in these two essays, the commonality lies in the assumption
of two levels of affect – the immediate and the indirect. Art is conceived as operating within these two registers and at its best elevating
the participant out of material realities and into the solace, detachment and refreshment provided by yogic postures. It is this sublime
position that is tentatively elaborated upon by Sita in *Where Shall We
Go This Summer.*

At the end of the novel, before they leave for Bombay, Sita and her husband go for a walk on the beach. Here she tells him of the one moment in their life together when she had "seen that life had meaning." She then describes a couple in a park – an old man and a young sickly looking girl who she had seen sharing a togetherness that was "tender, loving, yes – but *inhumanly* so." At this point in the novel we are familiar enough with Sita's vocabulary to read into the stressed word "inhuman," the terms: sublime, ethereal and poetic. She notes wistfully that the couple appeared to her to be "like a work of art" – a pale, ill yet smiling woman in the arms of an older man. This woman is rendered exotic and erotic through a description of her attire – a full-length *burkha* worn by Muslim women and when she lifts her veil, her "very, very pale and beautiful" face is framed "in those black folds like a Persian lily...Fatally anaemic – or fatally tubercular." For Sita then, meaning and happiness comes from this vision of a living (yet barely alive) exoticized work of art. Raman's response to this confession that Sita wrenches out of herself is as follows:

"And *that* was the only happy moment in your life?...Any woman – *any* one would think you inhuman. You have four children. You have lived comfortably, always, in my house. You've had no worries. Yet your happiest memory is not of your children or your home but of strangers, seen for a moment, some lovers in a park. Not even of your own children." (*WSW*, p. 147)

Sita's rebellion is ultimately an aesthetic one. Raman's astonishment at his wife's chronic unhappiness and boredom is exactly like Mohan's in *That Long Silence* and, as we will see, like Som's in *The Day in Shadow*. At the end of this exchange, Sita thinks she has found the explanation for her grief – in a poem by D. H. Lawrence whose entirety had till then teasingly escaped her memory.[49] She is about to shout the lines of this poem to Raman, to tell him that "Lawrence clarified it all for her," and that "the great gap between them would be newly and securely bridged," when Raman speaks to her of ordinary everyday things. He has apparently forgotten her anguished confession as well as his anger. The narrator writes,

She laughed too, gulping down the words of explanation, the poem, in painful swallows. She thought how nice he really was, how much the nicest man she knew. She allowed him then to have his triumph, not to try and cap it with her verse. He deserved that triumph, purely by being so unconscious of it, so oblivious. (*WSW*, p. 151)

Like Jaya, Sita falls back into the role of the supportive wife and the strain shows immediately. Raman and she walk back to the cottage

and Sita packs to leave for Bombay. She has been allowed her
tantrum, her whimsical holiday and is now graciously taken back
home by her husband. She cannot decide if her life in Bombay was
her "real life" and her time on the island was "the life of pretense and
performance" *or* if her "escape back to the past, back to the island,
had been the one sincere and truthful act of her life, the only one not
false and staged" (*WSW*, p. 153). Except for her love of the poetic
idiom, Sita does not have the analytical tools that would help her
answer this question that is crucial to her search for personal happiness. Ultimately, her poems and her appreciation of art and nature,
can only provide answers in their own rhetoric:

> She shook her head angrily at the confusion, the muddle of it all. Neither sea
> nor sky were separate or contained – they rushed into each other in a rush
> of light and shade, impossible to disentangle. (*WSW*, p. 153)

Less abstract rhetoric may have better expressed the lessons that Sita
may (or may not) have learned about herself on the island. The
reader may long for the heroines of these fictions to articulate solutions, to chart new courses...But for Sita as for Simrit, in Nayantara
Sahgal's *The Day in Shadow*, the answer lies not in striving for material
solutions but in seeking solace through art and nature.

The Day in Shadow, published in 1971, is Nayantara Sahgal's fourth
novel. Like Jaya in *That Long Silence*, Simrit, the heroine of this novel
is also a writer. She has written one book, is planning another and in
the meantime works as a freelance writer. The mother of four children, Simrit has just been divorced from Som at the beginning of the
novel. The "consent terms" of the divorce, drawn up by Som and
signed by a naive Simrit, have completely impoverished her and call
for a greatly reduced standard of living for her and her children.
Adjusting to life in a small flat without a phone and the other comforts that she and her children have become accustomed to, Simrit is
wearied by the everyday difficulties of establishing a home in urban
India. She is helped in coming to terms with her new life by Raj, the
young idealist politician who is at first a friend and soon her lover.
When Simrit complains of the daily tensions in her life, Raj consoles
her:

> "Be patient, Simrit. It's how we'll have to live in this country for years yet, in
> a bit of a mess, with things not in their places, and not nearly enough of them
> to go around. And we'll have to learn to love the process, to get something out
> of it and go on giving something to it. There are no magic formulas. We can't
> make coaches out of pumpkins except by our sweat, and that takes time."

It was all very well for the country, she thought tiredly, but what about *her* life? A small wail started in her whenever she thought of *that*, she who loved order and beauty excessively and not because she had been born to them. They were her trade. She could never understand the theory that writers and artists were untidy people glorying in chaos. How could she whose working hours were spent struggling to give fine structure to the unformed, putting ideas into clear language, chiseling precise sentences and paragraphs from a welter of feeling, not be disciplined? Not that it mattered now when the chaos was inside her. She couldn't order it by putting chairs and tables, or even painfully ground sentences into place – though it helped. Somehow, obscurely, it helped.[50]

Simrit displays the same fastidiousness, the same concerns about beauty and order that Sita does in Desai's novel. For the first time in her life Simrit is beleaguered by financial troubles and has to acknowledge the importance of that aspect of life. However, the central domestic crisis in Simrit's life predates her divorce. The novel is framed by the divorce and the changes it imposes on Simrit's life but a large part of the novel recounts events from Simrit's marriage with Som.

While still married, Simrit's general and unnameable dissatisfaction with her life takes a turn for the worse when Som successfully negotiates an international arms deal that promises windfall profits. Simrit cannot ignore the violence that irradiates their personal life when Som proudly boasts of his arms deal:

"Stop crying Simrit. What on earth is there to cry about? I'm a damned good husband to you, aren't I? What have you got to complain about? We're having a wonderful life and it's going to get better and better."

He got up, hands thrust in his pockets, and talked vehemently, suppressed laughter in his voice.

"Think of it, we can go abroad any time we want, any bloody time, buy anything we want. We can aircondition this whole place, furnish it all over again, and Rudy's right. You ought to have something to mark the occasion. What would you like? You didn't say."

I want a world whose texture is kindly, she thought. Surely there is such a world. After all, people once believed it was flat and it turned out otherwise. If its shape could turn out different, so can its texture.

She began, "Som, the world is so full of violence."

"Yes, of course it is. It has always been. Don't tell me that's what you are crying about."

She drew her hand across her eyes.

"I don't mean war – that's far away. I mean people with each other. And look at the arid way we live, without friends."

"What are you talking about? Of course we've got friends. And what's got into you? You've never found anything wrong with the way we've lived all these years." (*DS*, p. 89)

Simrit's dissatisfaction is a combination of shock at Som's uncaring attitude toward the product he will make his profits from and disgust at his inability to appreciate the finer pleasures in life. Her aesthetic refinement and her distaste for violence and for the seamy side of life is very much like Sita's in *Where Shall We Go This Summer?* Baffled by her inarticulate unhappiness, Som tells his German friend and business partner, Rudy Vetter—

"She doesn't need me to spend more time with her – she's very complete with the children and her writing and the rest of it – she wants me to spend more time with *myself.* You know sit and contemplate about goals and so on...Think with a capital T, and about matters not connected with what I have to do from morning till night. Tell her she's got more to give the children because of the business and the life I lead – more money, more extras – and it's just so much water off a duck's back, she just doesn't care." (*DS*, pp. 77–8)

After her divorce, Simrit is at first oblivious of the monetary implications of the "consent terms" of her divorce. When he first reads the terms of this agreement, Raj is exasperated at her impracticality and passivity:

She could get lyrical about a river and a godown filled with her children's junk but there wasn't even a spark to spare for anything that affected or even threatened her future. He wished that he could jolt her into some response about practical matters. He had thought the divorce settlement dictated by her husband was the ultimate in outrage, inflicted on an unresisting, unsuspecting victim. But every layer of her past uncovered something equally shocking. The Hindu race! – mute, acquiescent, letting things happen to it, from a country to the mind and body of a woman. An educated woman at that. One who prized her learning and had a profession. (*DS*, pp. 37–8)

Cast as the progressive Christian, Raj is irritated as well as attracted to Simrit's unworldly disinterest in her own financial situation. He associates her lyricism with something deeper than her affinity with a certain school of English poetry – her membership in the Hindu race. Simrit's own reading of her particular situation and the state of the world is equally revealing and completely different:

Living according to him [Raj] was acquaintance with things in the raw...with human beings at all levels – the cook or the postman as much as your husband or grandmother. Her own ideas about life were quite different. The human element was there, of course. There were the children – the concrete, demanding details of their upbringing, and all that she gave them otherwise of herself. But there her concern with her fellow men ended. Her own replenishment came from another source, from untouched unspoilt non-human things. Explaining it all to Raj she quoted a passage she had memorized as a child: "The feeling of almost physical delight in the touch of the mother-soil, of the winds that blow from Indian seas, of the rivers that stream from Indian hills..."

"Aurobindo wrote that," she told Raj.

He was not impressed. "A writer," he insisted, "has to be concerned with people."

"I'm not that kind of writer. And I hate this century – except for the freedom it's brought for countries and people, especially for women. But it is barbaric otherwise, full of rotten, elastic standards and the worship of money. I hate the whole mess of human affairs. The only clean clear things left are the hills and rivers and the shape of a leaf, things like that."

...She had been planning a book about India in terms of the look and texture of earth and sky – and in between all the nuances of its seasons. People wrote historical romances, but here was romantic geography, almost too much for one country's share. (*DS*, pp. 34–5)

Simrit is an apolitical artist: for her culture is a corruption of "the clean clear things." Her propensity to quote from Indian writers of the Romantic school and from English translations of the Hindu scriptures is shared by other heroines like Jaya in Deshpande's novel and Sita in Desai's *Where Shall We Go This Summer?* This drawing of sustenance from various literatures serves unproblematically (for Simrit, Jaya and Sita, to whom these are no more than the appropriate quotations that express a sentiment better than they can) to knit a philosophy that has of necessity to avoid material facts (consent terms, money, abortions, violence, corruption charges) if it is cohere. Such a philosophy flounders when it is expected to explicate real life, material effects like consent terms and hegemonic religious practices. Hence Eliot, Keats, the Upanishads, Lawrence, Aurobindo Ghose and Robert Burns, all mesh together to form an aesthetic credo that is necessarily an abstraction. In articulating her domestic crisis, Simrit does not move outside abstractions. She matches Som's patriarchal demands on her as "wife" with her own Romantic demands of him as "husband and protector." She glides out of one marriage and toward another (with Raj, her new protector) in a kind of daze that is fueled by elusive poetic longings that simply cannot be fulfilled except within a poetic idiom.

DISPLACEMENTS AND THE PLACE OF LITERATURE

In a searching essay on "the almost unbearable tension between a culturally sanctioned femininity and female imaginative power" in the context of pre-independence Indian women writers, Meena Alexander formulates a crucial question:

What does it mean for a woman to gain self-knowledge or display what Tagore has called "the true self." Or even more to the point how is a woman and a colonized being at that, to reach the measure of self-knowledge essential to creativity? And how can language help in the process when it bears the imprint of colonial domination, the very unreality imagination must struggle through?[51]

Is self-knowledge essential to creativity as Alexander insists it is? In the three novels just considered, Desai, Deshpande and Sahgal make the pursuit of acceptable feminine selves the object of their creativity. Alexander's concerns in this essay evolve out of her reading of Toru Dutt (1856–1877), the much acclaimed Indian woman writer whose colonial education and travels "alienate[d] her from any possible world in which she might have been at home."[52] Alexander reads Dutt's letters to her European women friends to great effect, to suggest that these letters were attempts to search out through feminine others something of the real substances of her alienated life, herself as she was, cut loose from the marginality forced upon her in part by her own colonized gaze.[53]

Alexander fleshes out the usual complaint that Indian literary writing in English was (and is) "unauthentic" by demonstrating Dutt's complete alienation from her everyday life in Calcutta and even from her writing style.[54] Calcutta, for instance, in Dutt's writing becomes the Lake District so dear to the English Romantic poets. Indians in her letters are referred to as "natives." Alexander then goes on to contrast Dutt's predicament with that of two women writers, Lalithaambika Antharjanam and Balamaniamma: both were born in the first decade of the twentieth century and both wrote in their mother-tongue, Malayalam. Female identity in Antharjanam's writing is, according to Alexander, born out of the tensions between "culturally sanctioned femininity and female imaginative power" in a way that is impossible in Toru Dutt's poetry in English, despite Dutt's use in her later poems of Indian mythological figures such as Savitri. Thus Alexander contrasts the richness of the writing in Malayalam with the imitative pallor of Dutt's work in English. What must however, be taken into consideration is the fact that Toru Dutt was a sickly, sheltered child and young adult who, like her sister and poetic collaborator, died before she was twenty-one years old.

Alexander contrasts the "full-fledged maturity" of the Malayali writers' work, especially manifest in their representations of maternity as a "virile" and nationalist force, with the confused and feeble attempts at self-representation in Dutt's work. Alexander defines the project of women writers struggling with the self and forms of writing sanctioned by colonialism as follows:

Such a writer *if she has grown to full maturity* finds herself creating a work that does not necessarily hold together in the requirements of the established aesthetic. Or she is conscious of working with materials that have no previously sanctioned place, either in her own traditional society, or in the formalities of a borrowed aesthetic. The female effort at decolonization then, struggles, with a radical problem of situation. For the woman writer, if she is from a traditional, hierarchal society like India, must come to terms with varieties of displacement, some more violent than others, as well as the poise of a ritualized order. [emphasis added][55]

Alexander's essay suggests that in a colonial situation the language "chosen" for creative expression *in itself* determines the feminine self that will be created. However, as many commentators have noted, the language that colonial and postcolonial writers use is not always a matter of choice. Indeed, it is often determined by the place, time and class that the writers inhabit. Hence for Desai, Deshpande and Sahgal, being educated in urban India in the period just before and just after independence and being part of an educated upper class, all combine to determine that they will write in the English language.

In "Feminism and Decolonization," Gayatri Spivak briefly sketches the complex relationship between "vernacular" and Indo-Anglian writing:

The relationship between the writer of "vernacular" and Indo-Anglian literatures is a site of class-cultural struggle. This struggle is not reflected in personal confrontations. Indeed, the spheres of Indo-Anglian writing and vernacular writing are not in serious contact. By "class-cultural struggle" is meant a struggle in the production of cultural or cultural-political identity. If literature is indeed a vehicle of cultural self-representation, the "Indian cultural identity" projected by Indo-Anglian fiction, and more obliquely, poetry, can give little more than a hint of the many "Indias" fragmentarily represented in the many Indian literatures.[56]

A similar and continuous argument can be made about the relationship between the projects of the women writers whose work I examine in this chapter and the writing of Indian women writers in the "vernacular" languages, such as Mahashweta Devi (Bengali), Ismat Chugtai (Urdu), Amrita Pritam (Punjabi), Mahadevi Verma (Hindi), Ambai [C. S. Lakshmi] (Tamil).[57] Even a casual perusal of the stories by women writers that are translated into English from other languages in recent anthologies will immediately reveal that different female subjects are represented in these multifarious fictions. The feminine selves represented in the writing of Desai, Deshpande and Sahgal need to be read in the context of these other fictions and other literary feminisms.[58]

English is still the only linguistic currency for negotiating any kind of success in upper-class urban India today. Since the passing of the 1963 "Official Languages Act" whereby English was adopted as the

associate official language of India (without a specified time limit)
this language has been legislated into the national educational policy.[59] In the late twentieth century, English appears to be the most
politically neutral language for common use in India. And yet, literature in English in India is hardly where "the revolution" or more
modestly, social change, will come from. In a country with only a
36.23 per cent overall literacy rate (1981 census report) where only 3
per cent of the population (about 20 million) is listed as English-speaking bilingual (1983) it would be foolish to expect that significant social
changes can be wrought single-handedly by written texts in this language.[60] Until the late 1980s, no more than two to three thousand
copies were printed in the Indian first editions of the novels by the
best-known Indian women writers.[61] Hence, it is futile to give these
women writers and literature (specially in English) the kind of reach
and scope that it would have in a culture of literacy. Gayatri Spivak
gestures toward this position when she states in "Feminism and
Decolonization" that: "To think of the Indo-Anglian novel, even in its
aggressively post-colonial manifestations as 'popular,' is to think of
Sons and Lovers as a novel of the international working class."[62]

In *The Day in Shadow*, Raj, the energetic young builder of modern
India, wonders why he invests so much in trying to wean Simrit
"away from [her] abstractions into some kind – any kind – of life."

Why? he wondered. Why did it matter how one particular person reacted –
except that in a compelling way, if this nation were ever to come to life, the
educated and privileged like her must make the most, not the least, of what
they had. They must magnify and expand their gifts. He was utterly convinced of that. (*DS*, pp. 36–7)

Should we assume that women in the upper echelons of the Indian
class structure, fluent in international currencies (English, western
feminisms) are necessarily the ones from whose acts and whose writing, feminism and other progressive ideas will emanate? What preparation do these women have – outside their investment in the
Romantic idiom – that will awaken them to "their gifts"?

In *Masks of Conquest*, Gauri Viswanathan forcefully argues that it
is erroneous to accept that because England and India shared common educational histories, "the functions of education remain constant regardless of context."[63] It is also erroneous to accept that
because a common language is used in global literature in English in
the late twentieth century, that the functions of this literature remain
constant regardless of context, content and location. To give Indian

literature in English the resonance that say the novel in nineteenth-century England had is to impose an "unnatural" literary burden onto such writing at the cost of ignoring its own ideological struggles.

To extend the argument I draw attention here to the many "Indian women" who lie outside representation in both English and "vernacular" languages. In the Indian context, perhaps the medium to look at for both heterogeneous and stereotypic representations of Indian women would be film. Not because Indian film makers are disenfranchised or subaltern but because the audience that is catered to is wider than the literary audience. India has the largest film industry in the world. More than seven hundred films are produced annually in Hindi alone. In a situation where illiteracy is the norm, film is a very profitable industry. These films are produced and managed by Indian financiers, though of late an increasing proportion of the financial investments comes from NRIs (Non-Resident Indians). It is important to note that in the forty-five years since independence not even a handful of Indian feature films have been made in the English language. Lola Chatterji notes that only approximately 2 per cent of state-controlled TV and radio time is given to English language programs.[64] The movie industry has kept a finger on the pulse of ruling and resistant ideologies even in its most "commercial" moments.[65]

It would be interesting to see how Indian films of the period reproduce these domestic fictions. I will now briefly examine the way in which *Subhah* (Morning) (1982) a Hindi film based on *Beghar* (Homeless) a novel by Shanta Nisal, depicts a woman going through much of the same trauma that our literary heroines wrestle with.[66] The film opens early one morning with the shot of Savitri, a bored young housewife stretched out in a rattan chair in a large lush garden while her busy household whirls about her.[67] Her mother-in-law, a social worker and politician, sails out in her chauffeur-driven car. Savitri's husband, a lawyer, rushes out to work as does her brother-in-law, a doctor. Her sister-in-law who is childless and dotes on Savitri's pampered young daughter Rani, bustles about with the servants getting organized to cook some special dish for her niece. Savitri's dissatisfaction with her life is quickly sketched in these first few scenes. We learn that she has just completed a degree program in social work and is encouraged by her husband, Suresh and her mother-in-law to take up some work – preferably alongside the latter as a kind of assistant to this imperious old lady. Suresh, who offers to take her on a vacation as yet another possible solution, exclaims, in English – "you are just rotting here, sitting at home."

We have here the classic situation that the domestic fiction discussed in this chapter has made familiar. And yet there are a few differences. Savitri is quite articulate from the start and her husband is quite responsive to her aspirations. He balks at first at her insistence on taking up a job as the supervisor of a women's reform home about three hundred miles away from where this joint family lives. After a family council during which the matriarch makes known her disapproval – daughters-in-law may work outside the home she notes, but she cannot approve of leaving the home for a job – Savitri is permitted to leave. The objections raised are put to rest by Suresh who announces that his wife has his permission to go. The sister-in-law has already taken over the job of mothering Rani.

As supervisor, Savitri must deal with the corruption, sexism, classism and general apathy of the governing body of the reform home. She also has to acknowledge her helplessness in the face of social customs that lead to the ostracism of lesbians, of unwed mothers, of widows, and prostitutes. Her own attempts to enforce decorum, order, art (group singing, group prayer, film shows) and middle-class morality within this system fail at all points. She is fired from her job when several inmates commit suicide and murder to escape the clutches of the institution she represents. Savitri returns home.

Savitri finds that she has not really been missed. Her daughter does not seem to need her. Her mother-in-law is coldly civil. Suresh is happy to have her back but he informs her that he has acquired a mistress whom he does not intend to give up. He notes that since he was so understanding of her needs, he expects the same from her. The next morning as Savitri begins to pack a suitcase in preparation to leave him once again, Suresh tells her not to set out on another "adventure" (the English word is used in a Hindi sentence in the film) from which she will only have to return once again. He goes down to join the family for breakfast in the garden. We are left with Savitri looking down from her bedroom window at this happy familial scene, clearly torn by a desire to stay and a desire to leave. We are also familiar with this decisive moment in the domestic crisis. At this point, Rani recites a little poem in English to her adoring audience in the garden. The camera presents the scene from Savitri's vantage point. The poem, a simple English nursery rhyme, needs to be reproduced here as its message is self-evident:

> What does little birdie say
> In her nest at peep of day?

"Let me fly," says little birdie,
"Mother, let me fly away."

"Birdie rest a little longer,
till the little wings are stronger."
So she rests a little longer
then she flies away.

The reverse shot is of Savitri looking out of a train window. She has left home. Where is Savitri off to? We do not know. But for the first time in the film she looks calm and joyous. The credits roll up across her face.

Subhah substantially alters the terms of this familiar domestic plot even as it uses almost every device identified earlier in this chapter. Hence, Savitri will not join her mother-in-law's benevolent, even feminist, activism nor her wheelings and dealings in the name of social reform. Savitri may have spent much of her life waiting, but when she has a chance to fashion a different life, she does so. She may be idealistic and deeply invested in neatness and order, but when the reform home experience exposes her to corruption and a class-based gender oppression, she does learn hard lessons about the world she and the other women inhabit. Yet in the context of this elite plot, the most radical step that Savitri takes is to read in her daughter's recitation of an English poem an incitement to personal political action. *Subhah* demonstrates that political agency can be instigated by even the most flimsy poetic moment.

CONCLUSION

Today the "Indo-Anglian" literary scene has begun moving away from patterns set more than a hundred years ago. Specifically, since the mid 1980s, fictional writing in English in India has undergone spectacular changes. An entire new school of writers have written novels that use English in ways unknown to an earlier generation of Indian writers. The old guard will find in their younger compatriots' work some justification of their own effort to keep alive the Indian novel in English in a period when the entire enterprise was suspect. In 1990, Khushwant Singh, a prominent writer and journalist wrote: "Most of us of the old generation really felt that English was a dying language and that there would not be much coming out in the way of creative fiction but just the reverse has happened."[68]

Shashi Tharoor, a young writer who confidently titled his own first work, *The Great Indian Novel* states: "The most distinguishing feature of

Indian writing in English is that it has acquired a certain self-confidence as a genre because there is a whole generation for whom there is no need to feel self-conscious about the use of this language or the kind of stories we tell in it."[69]

Hence, for better or for worse, R. K. Narayan, Mulk Raj Anand, Santha Rama Rau, Nayantara Sahgal, Kamala Markandaya, Dom Moraes, Khushwant Singh, Kamala Das, Attia Hussain and Raja Rao, have quietly been ousted by younger writers like Salman Rushdie, Amitava Ghosh, Shashi Tharoor, Zai Whitaker, Shama Futehally, Githa Hariharan and Vikram Seth – all born into independent India. Anita Desai and Shashi Deshpande fall chronologically between the older and younger writers listed above. There is a continuation of some of the thematic concerns in these novels. The poised, intelligent, idealistic young heroine of novels such as *Some Inner Fury* (Markandaya, 1956) and *Remember the House* (Rama Rau, 1956) has grown into the middle-aged, married, disillusioned and yet still idealistic woman in the novels I have discussed. The dynamics of the genre of Indian women's writing in English has been set by these established writers. While the novels examined in this chapter were written in the 1970s and 1980s, more recent novels like *The Thousand Faces of Night* (1992) by Githa Hariharan and *Up The Ghat* (1993) by Zai Whitaker once again spin the very same story – the young bored wife, a crisis, a moment of no return, a reconciliation. There are of course some changes. For instance, Whitaker's novel is remarkable in its very effective use of humor and Hariharan's heroine Devi shares the spotlight with her widowed mother Sita, and less substantially with an elderly maid servant, Mayamma. However, to see the terms of this dynamic significantly reworked, we need to examine the writing of new literary voices like that of Rohini and the entirely different angle presented by a writer like Shobha Dé.

Shobha Dé's novels are an offshoot of this "elite" domestic plot which is then grafted onto an Indian English narrative genre that has been perfected in popular film magazines. Since 1989, Dé has written five spectacularly successful novels set mainly among the "filmi" crowd of Bombay. *Socialite Evenings* (1989), *Starry Nights* (1990), *Sisters* (1991), *Obsession* (1992) and *Sultry Days* (1994) all construct a vision of a fast-paced, elite lifestyle in Bombay that is mainly sketched out through copious references to foreign brand-name perfumes, western designers, western cities, restaurants around the globe, and cuisines from everywhere. The truly elite, in Dé's world, are equally at ease with these citations that mark them as part of an international jet-set as they are with the Indian "ethnic" scene. Dé, founder and editor of popular film and high society glossy magazines (*Stardust, Society, Celebrity*) creates heroines who manipulate and are manipulated by men, dally with Bombay underworld dons, swill in lust, adultery, lesbianism, ambition, greed and jealousy even as they work on "finding themselves" or at least finding the perfect (rich, handsome, dangerous, rough, powerful) mate. Her work, although published by the very respectable Penguin Press and despite being the best-selling Indian fiction in English, always garners derisive attention in popular magazines and in academic journals.[70]

Socialite Evenings opens with a woman, middle-aged, married and separated from her husband, sitting at the computer in order to begin writing her own life history. The domestic crises have passed: what we have is a narrative that begins with Karuna's middle-class childhood, her social ascent through marriage to an unimaginative man, the break-up of their marriage and her evolution (without training, capital or much effort) into a successful film maker (with many suitors all of whom she disdains) writing her memoirs. This is not one of our confused, dazed heroines who can barely articulate her desires and her dissatisfactions. Though Dé's Karuna is not very forthcoming on *why* she acts as she does, she is forever making changes, moving on, improving herself. At the end of the novel, we see her through the eyes of a young American (of Indian origin) reporter with *The Washington Times* who wants to make a documentary that would serve as "an update on the status of urban Indian women, using you, babykins, as the central figure" (p. 305). Karuna, however, decides that she can document her life story without his help – the novel is presented as her *own* rendition of her self-transformation. An excerpt from the reporter's enthusiastic sketch of this biography as he envisions it, provides a fairly representative example of the literary and social terrain that Dé covers as well as the language in which she sails forth:

Your first love and jam sessions at Bistro's. Learning the Peppermint Twist and jiving to Chubby Checker. Conforming to parental expectations, toeing the line of authority. Forays into modelling – the Anjali character is a sure-fire winner, the "safe" marriage – do you think hubby dearest will agree to an interview? Or the Old Bird – is she still alive? Breaking out of the holy bonds of matrimony, finding your feet in a career you happened to drift into. The success story that followed – hey, how did she do it? Did she sleep around, compromise herself? Work her way to the top on her back? I just love this part.
Anyway – cut to you as you are now – disgustingly self-assured and revolt-

ingly self-sufficient. Baby – you'll give one of those padded-shouldered Wall Street American broads a run for their money. This is going to be a terrific project. I can see it – maybe we can throw in an Indira Gandhi angle, link it up with the *desi* lib movement (p. 305).

The English that Dé uses is that pioneered in her film magazine *Stardust*: an aggressive, florid blend of Bombay Hindi, Marathi and English in syntactical arrangements that are peculiar to Indian English.[71]

The success of Shobha Dé's novels can be attributed to her diligent efforts to provide Indian readers with the vicarious pleasures of living it up in a hyper-real Bombay that has been crafted over the years in Hindi commercial cinema, Dé's own magazines, and other cultural texts. However, the popularity of these novels might be traced to the calculatedly irreverent manner in which Dé jettisons the burdens that lie on the shoulders of elite Indian women in the contemporary Indian cultural context. Her delineation of Indian womanhood champions consumerism, pleasure, indulgence, and female sexuality that is not bounded by heterosexual, monogamous marriage. Thus Dé sanctions and shapes a growing middle-class' curiosity about the lives of women who work their way up into the world of the "rich and famous." For Dé's heroines, the burden of being a representative or symbol of a singular (and strangulating) "rich Indian culture and tradition" is no more than an exoticized wearing and shedding of their "Indianness" *at will*. Feminism, patriotism, marriage, and religion are no more than clothes in the closet that Dé's heroine rifles through as she decides on her "look" for the moment.[72]

These heroines can miraculously rebuild lost fortunes, lose weight, gain lovers, toss out husbands, survive deadly rumors, travel – in short they end up "disgustingly self-assured and revoltingly self-sufficient."

I would like to conclude this chapter with an examination of the new directions for Indian writing in English that are charted in *To Do Something Beautiful* (1990), a novel by an unknown writer called Rohini.[73] After Markandaya's sentimental *Nectar in a Sieve* (1954), this is probably the only novel in English that attempts a sustained examination of female selfhood in the context of Indian women outside the upper and middle classes.[74] *To Do Something Beautiful* sets out deliberately to change the dimensions of the self as defined through writing in English by Indian women. By linking the search for adequate selfhood with the Romantic appreciation of "beauty" so central to these texts, *To Do Something Beautiful* echoes Desai's, Deshpande's and Sahgal's novels. But Rohini does more than map the isolation and boredom of the privileged Indian woman. She attempts to cover a wide social spectrum of life in contemporary Bombay. The novel weaves together the lives of a dozen women from different classes, castes and religions. This is an unusual text– part activist's handbook, part narrative about feminist bonding of women across difference, and part romance fiction. The purely literary context for Rohini's novel is yet to come into writing in Indian English.

To Do Something Beautiful fictionalizes the activities of women's organizations in Bombay over the last two decades. The novel depicts women's activism on issues of rape, wife beating, child-care, safe urban transportation, "eve teasing" and sexual discrimination as well as documents the starting of community kitchens, of lunch delivery services and of unionization, which have been central concerns of women's organizations in Bombay.[75] Interwoven with these issues is the story of Kavita, the bored housewife who is disenchanted with her husband and with her life's limited scope. Kavita's domestic crisis is read in the perspective offered by the lives of other women, and yet, her grief is not considered unimportant. She is rejuvenated by her entry into women's organizational work not because she proves to be of some use to others as much as because she begins to value herself. She finds solutions to everyday setbacks in her own and other women's daily battles at home and in the workplace. This narrative is interlaced with the narratives of others, such as men who struggle to build trade unions and other coalitions, for women and men are partners in activism in this novel. It is not always an equal partnership but power, territories and responsibilities are constantly under negotiation.

To Do Something Beautiful begins with the following sentences: "Free at Last! Renu stood on the balcony gazing out vacantly and feeling that all life, all energy, all hope had been drained out of her."[76] The reader of novels by Desai, Deshpande and Sahgal will immediately identify in Renu, yet another bored, unhappy, upper-class Bombay housewife, waiting on the balcony like Sita in *Where Shall We Go This Summer?* for her life to be infused with meaning. In Rohini's novel, however, Renu, the female character in the opening passage, is a full-time maid servant to a household of twelve in urban Bombay. Unlike the vacancy and loss of energy that brings Sita to her balcony, Renu is there on a Sunday evening because she is too exhausted by hard manual labor to do more than this on her one weekly free evening. Her isolation is also very different from Sita's. Having left her village to take up this job, she is new to the city and knows hardly anyone in Bombay. While Renu stands on the balcony, a woman appears on the balcony of the adjacent flat. She is the mistress of that household. We are introduced to Kavita through Renu's eyes:

On the next balcony a tall, rather thin woman stood, looking as tired and despondent as Renu felt. But within a few minutes came the sound of a baby crying and she hurried inside. Renu had seen her several times before, always wearing attractive saris, had even met her once or twice on the stairs or at the shops. On these occasions she had smiled in a friendly way, but when she wasn't smiling her face looked sad. What could women like that look sad about, Renu wondered? They lived in their own homes, good apartments; they had husbands who earned plenty and could support them and their children in comfort; they didn't go out and work, or if they did, had interesting jobs, not like this endless, soul-destroying drudgery.[77]

That our introduction to Kavita is framed through Renu's narrative inverts the usual representation of servants through the eyes of the mem-sahib. This introduction also puts Kavita's unhappiness and exhaustion in the perspective offered by the hard physical labor done by women of other classes. Kavita is the subject of the next chapter. Her life is more like the ones we are familiar with through our reading of other novels in English by Indian women writers. She is a housewife who has just had a third child and has just been told by her husband who is a university professor of his recently concluded affair with a woman from his "study circle." Despite Kavita's education and upper-class background, her story is given no more and no less attention than that of the other women whose lives make up the mosaic of stories in this novel.

To Do Something Beautiful draws its organizing principles not from the literary model established by earlier Indian women's fiction in English but from following the daily struggles and triumphs of several women characters as they go through the day. The narrative follows the plotting of the labor strikes and political organizing that the women are involved with instead of relying on a more "literary" pacing of events. The most important difference from the novels we have examined in this chapter is the fact that there is no single central protagonist, no single domestic crisis. Instead there is a multitude of such crises that criss-cross, sometimes blow up and sometimes continue to simmer. Romance is presented as one more site where women have to be alive to the political power negotiations involved. The central characters, both female and male, are activists fighting for better living conditions for themselves and others. The novel concludes not with the resolution of personal and group projects but with the multiple plots of activism and struggle continuing *beyond* the last page. In terms of literary form, this novel could have ended fifty pages earlier or could chronicle fifty more pages on the intertwining lives of these different (in terms of age, religion, class, caste, geographic home) women whose lives intersect in the cosmopolitan urban sprawl of Bombay. New solidarities are formed and old ones change in an episodic fashion that is in keeping with the contemporary TV serials on social issues produced in countries such as Mexico, India and Pakistan.

In a crucial scene in the novel, Kavita's nine year old daughter, Asha, makes a poster for an International Women's Day exhibition. In her description of this poster, Rohini presents the reader with a *visual* account of her mosaic-like feminist project:

> From a distance Kavita got the impression of an intricate design of brilliant colours. But when she came closer she saw that it consisted of countless women and girls engaged in all manner of activities. They were dancing and singing and playing the guitar; working in factories, fields, hospitals and kitchens; writing, drawing and teaching; two women were playing with three small children; there was Preeti perhaps, a little larger than some of the others, with something which looked like a carved panel, and another woman with some tremendously complicated-looking equipment; girls playing cricket and football and two of them simply holding hands; and many many more. Above the picture was written in an arc: "IF IT'S SOMETHING BEAUTIFUL" – and below, in bigger letters, "LET HER DO IT!"[78]

Asha's name is carefully chosen, for its meaning falls between "hope," "aspiration" and "desire" in Hindi. The reader can trace some of the characters in this novel such as Miriam, Kavita, Preeti, Nirmala, Mangal and Asha herself in this description of the women in the poster. There are also some representations in the poster that cannot readily be identified with characters in the novel. These women and the "many many more" that the narrator mentions lie outside the confines of novels, of films and academic studies. Most importantly, there are no "dead-ends" in this picture – neither in art nor in science, neither in work nor in play, nor in women's writing.

Rohini's novel reworks what I had earlier called the frustratingly unspecified, invariably incomplete, and yet unstaunchable desire for a more viable female subjecthood into specific material goals that spring from present conditions and that can be (and are) fulfilled in the present and the future. This could make Rohini's novel the most politically naive of the fictions I have analyzed here. Her vision (as depicted in Asha's poster) brings back the romantic veneration of beauty. Yet "something beautiful" is radically altered in what it signifies: searching for this something is not a purely aesthetic pursuit but a political act.

In writing this chapter, my intention has been to revise the easy association of an adequate home (domestic or national) with an adequate sense of self. Citizenship in a postcolonial nation and the citizen's satisfaction with herself as full subject may have no positive correlation even for the most privileged of postcolonial subjects. For the elite Indian women in this chapter, belonging to – indeed being the showpiece of – a newly independent nation and a privileged home, holds no guarantees. The dynamics of gender, religion, education, as well as a host of other ideologies complicate the relationship between the home and the self. This cultural and political baggage can strangulate and sabotage the project of imagining anew in a much too familiar landscape and language.

In the chapter that follows I examine the fiction of immigration produced in the context of being between homes and between (or beyond) national affiliations. Immigration makes one self-conscious of the cultural baggage carried over to the new land. In a situation where home needs to be reimagined, much of what the subject carries over is refashioned to facilitate a sense of belonging. And yet, the fiction produced from such locations pays close attention to the absence of home (and home-countries) and more often than not finds them quite dispensable and/or replaceable. This next chapter then challenges some of the assessments made about immigritude, postcoloniality and the very concept of marginality. I read *The Gunny Sack*, a novel by M. G. Vassanji, and other fictional and non-fictional texts written in global English in order to further my project of presenting "the self", "nation," "homelessness," "belonging" and " (post)colonial subjects" as dynamic, multi-faceted constructs – at best, fictions that we employ to feel at home.

CHAPTER 6

"Traveling light": home and the immigrant genre

And no anthems on their lips, they travel great distances.
"The Previous Occupant" Agha Shahid Ali

Got no bag and baggage to slow me down
I'm a travelling so fast my feet ain't touching the ground
travelling light, travelling light.
"Travelling Light" Cliff Richard

Following Barbara Harlow's practice of naming literary genre by
political and ideological contents rather than by formal attributes, it
could be argued that the contemporary literary writing in which the
politics and experience of location (or rather of "dislocation") are the
central narratives should be called the "Immigrant Genre."[1] Distinct
from other postcolonial literary writing and even from the literature
of exile, it is closely related to the two.[2] For the immigrant genre, like
the social phenomenon from which it takes its name, is born of a history of global colonialism and is therefore a participant in decolonizing
discourses. Like the distance that exile imposes on a writing subject,
writers of the immigrant genre also view the present in terms of its
distance from the past and future. This genre, I will argue, is marked
by a disregard for national schemes, the use of a multigenerational
cast of characters and a narrative tendency toward repetitions and
echoes – a feature that is often displayed through plots that cover several generations. Most importantly, the immigrant genre is marked by
a curiously detached reading of the experience of "homelessness"
which is compensated for by an excessive use of the metaphor of luggage, both spiritual and material.

I argue for a distinct genre because such a move lessens to some
degree the burdens and constraints that contemporary criticism has
placed on the category known as "postcolonial literature." In the west
today, the literature that is recognized as postcolonial is that produced
by authors with a "Third World" affiliation. It is read as being chiefly

concerned with issues of nationalism and/or national allegory as well as with articulating a critique of colonialism. Though written primarily in English, Spanish and French it is expected to *and does*, constantly "translate" itself by dexterously and continuously explaining the local allusions and cultural practices that are incorporated into the narrative. Thus, although often located in the non-west, this fiction's ultimate literary destination is taken to be the western metropoles.

It can be said that in the postcolonial era, all locations, all writers, all subjects are postcolonial, in that the history of colonialism is shared by the globe albeit with different impact on different locations and peoples. The immigrant is only *one* of the many manifestations of this common global history. Hence, while colonization is part of the historical (and even current) *baggage* of all nations involved, the onus of what is called "postcolonial discourse" is borne by writers and academic practitioners whose personal histories include birth, childhood and possibly an early education in one of the former colonies, but whose work is published and received by western publishing houses and academic (as well as other) readers. It is this writing that primarily qualifies for the category of the "immigrant genre" as I envision it.3

For readers in the west, as well as for readers in the once-colonized parts of the world, there is as much familiar landscape as there is foreignness in this genre. Given that immigrant fictions are often concerned with the experience of immigration to western nations and are written in global languages, these fictions seem to straddle the geographic world. As a result this literature travels well. It is therefore not surprising that when we in the west talk of postcolonial fiction our reference is usually specifically to the immigrant genre. Similarly, the recent focus on internationalism or cosmopolitanism as exhibited in literature is read on the body of texts generated by the processes of immigration, migration and exile.4

In the last four decades, numerous novels have taken the issues of immigration as their central narrative: to name a few examples – *ByeBye BlackBird* by Anita Desai (1970); *Wife* by Bharati Mukherjee (1975); *Second Class Citizen* by Buchi Emecheta (1974); *The Satanic Verses* by Salman Rushdie (1989); *Meatless Days* by Sara Suleri (1989); *Boy-Sandwich* by Beryl Gilroy (1989).5 As early as in 1956, Sam Selvon published *The Lonely Londoners*, a novel on West Indian immigrants in England.6 In 1972, A. Sivanandan, editor of *Race and Class* drew attention to the literary and economic continuations that mandated reading the practice of immigration as well as the discourses it produced as *directly* linked to the history of imperialism.[7] More recently in "DissemiNation: Time, Narrative, and the Margins of the Modern Nation," Homi Bhabha puts forth a detailed and theoretically nuanced reading of the writing that inscribes the nation from its margins.[8]

Assessing the work of immigrant writers in Canada, Jurgen Hesse has argued that the "cultural burdens" that these writers carry "will be of little or no value to them."[9] Their cultural knapsack, he writes "is less of a movable asset; it becomes a hindrance within the bewildering cultural landscape which they are entering."[10] Immigrant novels themselves suggest that traveling light or arriving with luggage are both serviceable ways of entering the new location. Immigrants have to come to terms with the spiritual, material and even linguistic luggage they carry or inherit. Do such belongings impede or facilitate belonging? Over and over again, in the literature of immigration and exile, there are scenes that (either lovingly, as a matter of fact or in despair) catalogue the varied luggage that immigrants carry over. Salman Rushdie's novel, *Shame*, explores the nature of this luggage:

When individuals come unstuck from their native land, they are called migrants. When nations do the same thing (Bangladesh), the act is called secession. What is the best thing about migrant peoples and seceded nations? I think it is their hopefulness. Look into the eyes of such folk in old photographs. Hope blazes undimmed through fading sepia tints. And what's the worst thing? It is the emptiness of one's luggage. I'm speaking of invisible suitcases, not the physical, perhaps cardboard, variety containing a few meaning-drained mementos: we have come unstuck from more than land. We have floated upwards from history, from memory, from Time.[11]

Some fictional immigrants, like Annie John, the seventeen-year old protagonist of Jamaica Kincaid's novel, determinedly leave their native lands without baggage.[12] *Annie John* is an Antiguan *Bildungsroman* which ends with Annie's immigration to England. On the morning of her departure from Antigua for England where she will train as a nurse, Annie resolves never to return and never to remember:

Everything I would do that morning until I got on the ship that would take me to England I would be doing for the last time, for I had made up my mind that, come what may, the road for me now went only in one direction: away from my home, away from my mother, away from my father, away from the everlasting hot sun, away from people who said to me, "This happened during the time your mother was carrying you."... The things I never wanted to see or hear or do again now made up at least three weeks' worth of grocery lists. I placed a mark against obeah women, jewelry, and white underwear.[13]

Annie John's anger stems from feeling betrayed by an ambitious and adoring mother who wants the best that a colonial education can offer her daughter. This "best," as I argue later in this chapter, necessarily includes separation, distance and finally leaving Antigua. But Annie, for whom mother and country are often conflated, reads such motherly encouragement to make the best of one's opportunities as wholesale rejection:

Why I wonder, didn't I see the hypocrite in my mother when, over the years, she said that she loved me and could hardly live without me, while at the same time proposing and arranging separation after separation, including this one, which, unbeknownst to her, *I* have arranged to be permanent?[14]

Following the trajectory of a successful colonial education means leaving Antigua. And loving mothers arrange separation after separation to ease the pain of the inevitable leave taking. If we attempt to imagine Annie John beyond the contours of the novel, as an Antiguan nurse trainee in England, a potential immigrant, these declarations with which the novel ends are only the first stage in a political awakening. The irony that coats this seventeen year old's emphatic utterances stems from the wisdom of the narrator who is an older Annie John, writing from outside Antigua with a clearer understanding of the ways in which a future abroad (preferably in England, the Mother country) had always been the focus of her colonial childhood.[15]

Exile, though very different from immigration, is the other instance in which one carries the baggage of the past along wherever one wanders. In *After the Last Sky: Palestinian Lives*, an evocative narrative on the lives of present day Palestinians, Edward Said writes of the ways in which Palestinians living in exile handle such baggage:[16]

When A. Z.'s father was dying, he called his children, one of whom is married to my sister, into his room for a last family gathering. A frail, very old man from Haifa, he had spent his last thirty-four years in Beirut in a state of agitated disbelief at the loss of his house and property. Now he murmured to his children the final faltering words of a penniless, helpless patriarch. "Hold on to the keys and the deed," he told them, pointing to a battered suitcase near his bed, the repository of the family estate salvaged from Palestine when Haifa's Arabs were expelled. These intimate mementos of a past irrevocably lost circulate among us, like the genealogies and fables of a wandering singer of tales. Photographs, dresses, objects severed from their original locale, the rituals of speech and custom: much reproduced, enlarged, thematized, embroidered, and passed around, they are strands in the webs of affiliations we Palestinians use to tie ourselves to our identity and to each other.

Sometimes these objects, heavy with memory – albums, rosary beads, shawls, little boxes – seem to me like encumbrances. We carry them about, hang them up on every new set of walls we shelter in, reflect lovingly on them. Then we do not notice the bitterness, but it continues and grows nonetheless. Nor do we acknowledge the frozen immobility of our attitudes. In the end the past owns us. My father spent his life trying to escape these objects, "Jerusalem" chief among them – the actual places as much as its reproduced and manufactured self. Born in Jerusalem, as were his parents, grandparents and all his family back in time to a distant vanishing point, he was a child of the Old City who traded with tourists in bits of the true cross and crowns of thorn. Yet he hated the place; for him, he often said, it meant death. Little of it remained with him except a fragmentary story or two, an odd coin or medal, one photograph of his father on horseback, and two small rugs. I never even saw a picture of my grandmother's face. But as he grew older, he reverted to old Jerusalemite expressions that I did not understand, never having heard them during the years of my youth.[17]

The vicious, debilitating injustice of exile that coats the narrative here is missing in the immigrant novel. The immigrant genre is often marked by a detached and unsentimental reading of the experience of "homelessness" – which has (as in the case of *Annie John*) often been read as indicative of the apolitical stance adopted by immigrants.[18]

The sentiment accompanying the absence of home – homesickness – can cut two ways: it could be a yearning for the authentic home (situated in the past or in the future) or it could be the recognition of the inauthenticity or the created aura of all homes. In the context of the immigrant novel it is the latter that usually prevails. For instance, *The Lonely Londoners* begins on a bitterly cold winter afternoon at Waterloo station, where Moses, an immigrant from Trinidad, waits to pick up a new immigrant from Jamaica. When Henry Oliver saunters off the train "as if he in an exhibition hall on a pleasant summer evening," Moses is shocked to see that he is wearing a light summer suit. Having ascertained that Oliver is not sick, Moses proceeds to ask him about his luggage:

"Where your luggage?"
"What luggage? I ain't have any. I figure is no sense to load up myself with a set of things. When I start work I will buy some things."
Now Moses is a veteran, who living in this country for a long time, and he meet all sorts of people and do all sorts of things, but he never thought the day would come when a fellar would land up from the sunny tropics on a powerful winter evening wearing a tropical suit and saying that he ain't have no luggage.[19]

The tone adopted by immigrating subjects in novels like *The Lonely Londoners* or *ByeBye BlackBird*, is one of cocky defiance, fear, awe, nervousness and always an underlying excitement. "Floating upwards," to use Rushdie's term, the immigrant reconstructs a series of oxymorons: new histories, new memories, new time. Ultimately then, it is from the cardboard boxes with their "few meaning-drained mementos" that invisible luggage is created, and repeatedly created, as an empowering bag of tricks that tells the textured tale of who the immigrant is and where s/he belongs.

This chapter will base its formulation of the genre of immigrant fiction primarily on a novel called *The Gunny Sack* written by M. G. Vassanji, an East African writer of Indian origin, and published in 1989 in the Heinemann African Writers Series.[20] This novel fabricates an elaborate reading of wandering that spans several continents and an entire century. While it is not representative of all novels of immigration, and while the motivations of its immigrant characters cannot be mapped onto every immigrating subject in and out of fiction, it serves as a useful text through which to read "this immigrant business" as Rushdie calls it in *Shame*.[21]

The Gunny Sack offers a historical narrative of cross-continental immigration from India to East Africa to North America over the lifetime of four generations of the Govindji family. Vassanji's novel begins with the word "Memory" and then goes on to create a multi-generational saga of an Indian family of traders and shopkeepers on the East African coast. From the arrival of the patriarch Dhanji Govindji in Zanzibar in 1885 to his great grandson Salim Juma's departure to the US in the mid 1970s, the novel narrates the lives and fortunes of various family members. The opening event, set in the 1970s in an unnamed metropole in North America, is the funeral of Ji Bai, who was the daughter-in-law of Dhanji Govindji. After the funeral, the primary narrator of this text, Salim Juma (also called Kala), Ji Bai's grand-nephew, inherits the gunny sack that she carried with her through the last years of her life.[22]

This gunny-sack, the prototype of the humble traveler's suitcase, is filled with a lifetime of mementos secreted away by Ji Bai; these objects activate the narratives that make up this novel. The opening paragraph demonstrates the uncontainable slippage between the two categories that Rushdie has called the "invisible" and "cardboard variety" of luggage:

Memory, Ji Bai would say, is this old sack here, this poor dear that nobody has any use for any more. Stroking the sagging brown shape with affection she would drag it closer, to sit at her feet like a favorite child. In would plunge her hand through the gaping hole of a mouth, and she would rummage inside. Now you feel this thing here, you fondle that one, you bring out this naughty little nut and everything else in it rearranges itself. Out would come from the dusty depths some knick-knack of yesteryear: a bead necklace shorn of its polish; a rolled-up photograph; a cowrie shell; a brass incense holder, a Swahili cap so softened by age that it folded neatly into a small square; a broken rosary tied up crudely to save the remaining beads: a blood stained muslin shirt: a little book. There were three books in that old gunny that never left her bedside, four-by-six-inch, green, tablet-like, the front cover folding over into a flap fastened with a tiny padlock! On the cover of each, neatly carved, two faded inscriptions in gold, wriggling in opposite directions: one in an Arabic-looking hand, the other indecipherable, supposedly in a secret script. "He who opens it will suffer the consequences," she, who did not read, would gravely pronounce to her awed listener. (*GS*, p. 3)

The gunny sack brings a familial history of wandering into the present of the fourth generation characters. Its contents both material and spiritual, bring to the basement apartment in the western metropole, memories of a wandering life as "trading immigrant peoples" that had a corresponding identity prior to the limited "marginal" sense of self that immigration imposes on the contemporary immigrant. Over the course of the novel we are repeatedly confronted with the complex issue of whether Shehrazade, Shehrbanoo or Sheru (as Kala variously calls the sack) falls into *both* the Rushdie category of "invisible luggage," as well as in his accompanying category of the unevocative "physical, perhaps cardboard, variety." For Kala, the gunny is the repository of a family history that is embodied in "some knick-knack of yesteryear." For other family members like Aziz, (another of Ji Bai's grand nephews who is also her traveling companion for the last few years of her life), the gunny sack is an encumbrance that should be left behind in the past. As he delivers it to Kala, he says:

"If my family had had their way they would have burnt it long ago. It's brought nothing but bad luck, they say. They want you to burn it, once and for all to bury the past."
"And you – do you want me to burn it?"
"Look at it first – it's what she wanted, after all. Then, maybe burn it. To tell you the truth, I almost burnt it instead of bringing it here." (*GS*, p. 5)

When Kala first opens it, a ball of Kapok (cotton lint) floats out of Ji Bai's gunny sack, and with this lint, the sack, a "Shehrazade postponing her eventual demise spins out yarns, telling tales that have no beginning or end, keeping me awake night after night, imprisoned in this basement to which I thought I had escaped." (*GS*, p. 5). It is interesting that Kala here refers to the sack as "a Shehrazade postponing her eventual demise."

What does the rather offhand mention here of her "eventual demise" indicate? And how does the basement in the western metropole serve as an *escape* that would paradoxically be compromised, if the gunny sack of memories were let loose in it? Forgetting the past, burning or burying it, creates the illusion of providing an escape route into the present that looks ahead rather than behind. Having discarded the luggage of the past, one can desire inclusion into the modern nation. But immigrants and others on the margins do not automatically or necessarily desire a (national) subject status that is identical to the mainstream citizen's.

In coming to terms with the gunny sack and its shifting status as albatross or sustenance, Vassanji's novel productively engages with several of the issues central both to the literature and to the theorizing on the discourse of immigration. It does this, first, by the narrative use of repetitions and echoes to construct meaning from the time-space frames of the immigrant; second, by the thematics of multiple generations; and third, by displaying immigration as a challenge to national projects.

GENERATIONS OF WANDERERS

While this is a multi-generational saga that begins with the figure of the patriarch and ends with his great-grandson, it is significant that the family history does not lie in the three padlocked books of Dhanji's that Kala finds in Ji Bai's gunny sack and which he and his brother, Sona fight over. Similarly, it can be argued that the family tree sketched out at the beginning of the novel is not useful in helping the reader understand the affiliations that different family members hold dear. Family histories cannot be traced through account books like Dhanji's or via family trees alone. Vassanji resolutely refuses to sentimentalize either home or family just as his text is always skeptical of the comforts provided by a sense of communal and/or national belonging.

Vassanji's use of the multi-generational saga is a crucial manifestation of the immigrant genre's continuous project of straddling several times, spaces and languages at every point in the narrative. As the narrative maps the lives and travels of several generations, it also marks the changing political map of the world in which these generations live. Hence, one could compare Dhanji's travels in search of his son, unrestricted by passports and visas, with the second, third and fourth generation's travels which are marked by secrecy, forged passports and immigration interviews. Of course, lest we indulge in nostalgia for the ease with which Dhanji crossed lands, we are told that he did so with money stolen from the funds entrusted with him for safe keeping by his sect. And, as the narrative suggests, the consequences of this theft can (and do) erupt on the surface of the present.

The "Shamsi" sect that Dhanji Govindji's family belongs to, though invented by Vassanji, is similar to existing religious organizations. The sect has a world-wide network that serves as a support system for immigrants and other wanderers who need to be made at home in an unfamiliar place.[23] Thus there are *Mukhis* or religious heads, wherever Shamsis live... "in London, in Singapore, in Toronto" (*GS*, 10).

You could land in Singapore and call up the local mukhi. "Mukhi Saheb," you say, "I am new here and I need a little help." "Where are you staying?" the mukhi would ask. He doesn't let you finish. "No, no, no, that simply won't do. *Aréy*, listen to me, you come here first, then we'll see." Which is exactly what young Dhanji Govindji did. (*GS*, p. 10)

And nearly two hundred pages and nearly a hundred years later in the story, when Kala is sent to a remote camp as part of his National Service duties, he does what his great grand-father had done before him: he inquires about the local *mukhi*.

We might be tempted to see in the existence of this semi-religious sect a form of community that provides the benefits of both family and nation, but Vassanji once again refuses us such a resting place. The Shamsi community is beset with its own deceptions: first, the stealing of community funds by Dhanji; second, his violent death, allegedly at the hands of sect members. In Kala's case, there is the attempt by an Indian family of fake Shamsis to seduce Kala into marrying their daughter by showering him with hospitality when he is far from his home.

The Gunny Sack chronicles the ways in which immigrants articulate a sense of home amidst homelessness by building on familial and communal ties. These ties invade the individual's sense of independence and self-interest in ways that only "family" is allowed to do. Hence, during the British crackdown on the Mau Mau movement, Juma refuses to risk his family's safety in order to hide the son of Mary, the Kikuyu woman who had been like a surrogate mother to him. The narrator, Kala, who is Juma's son, remembers this incident from his childhood as "one more bad memory" that "the gunny would like to throw out."

"The police would have found him anyway," said my father. We never saw Mary again. Perhaps she too was taken away, to be screened, detained even. Was she a Mau Mau sympathizer? What did we know of her – a friend from another world who came periodically and then once at night in an hour of need – whose memory we now carry branded forever in our conscience...(p. 78)

The terms in which this "bad memory" is recalled are marked by syntactical ambivalence and incompleteness: Mary is, after all, from "another world" and yet, there is the guilt of having failed her in her hour of need. In a moment of crisis, the shelter offered by "home" and "family" becomes exclusive.

And yet, what determines "family" is not always evident. For instance, Huseni is stepson in his father's (Dhanji Govindji's) house because he is born of Dhanji's union with Bibi Taratibu, the African slave woman. Ousted by Dhanji's marriage to Fatima, the narrator tells us "Gentle Bibi Taratibu, *of course*, had to go. She moved to a house *at the further end* of the village, *bordering* the forest" (p. 13, emphasis added). She is pushed to the margins, and, as the novel tells us repeatedly in its descriptions of the geographical layout of several colonial urban and rural settlements, the location of Bibi Taratibu's house at the border of the forest, throws her back into the African section of the village. Replaced by the legally and racially legitimate wife Fatima, Taratibu is no longer "family." Thus the immigrant community constructs its own marginal places and persons.

Perhaps it is co-residence rather than blood that determines family. Thus Kulsum's sister's children, Mehroon and Yasmin, as well as her brother's three daughters, Shamin, Shiraz and Salma, live with her at various times as cared-for and caring members of her family. And yet, Juma who lived as a child and young man with his aunt's family, was made painfully aware of his status as an inferior outsider. Clearly, for Juma and for his father, Huseni before him, it is their "mixed" blood, the result of the union between Indian male and African woman that serves to mark them as different. In the next generation, Salim Juma who inherits his father's dark skin, is nicknamed "Kala" – the word for "black" in several North Indian languages and he is the one person in his generation who falls in love with an African.

But the desires of different generations of immigrants differ: this is what makes the interaction between generations such a vital feature of the immigrant novel and experience.[24] Would the story be different if the Dhanji Govindjis had stayed with the Bibi Taratibus and if together they had had Africa's children? Early in the novel Vassanji's narrator considers this alternate history that did not take place: "Tell me, Shehrbanoo, would the world be different if that trend had continued, if there had been more Husenis, if these chocolate Husenis with curly hair had grown up unhindered, playing barefoot in kanzus and kofias, clutching Arabic readers..." (*GS*, p. 11). What is wistfully contemplated here is a knitting together of different racial communities through marriage and procreation.

In the opening address at the "Nationalisms and Sexualities" conference held at Harvard University in the summer of 1989, Benedict Anderson put forth a theory that examined the proximity of politics and sexuality in nationalist novels. Working primarily with Indonesian nationalist novels Anderson claimed that "love" in nationalist novels leaps across politically unbridgeable chasms, such as caste, class and race. Given the difficulty of the task, such "impossible loves" (as in inter-caste, inter-class and inter-race marriages and sexual unions) are doomed to fail. Anderson noted, that this strategy of the nationalist novel serves, however, to eroticize the nation by making its narrative one of love and passion.[25]

Here, in *The Gunny Sack*, Dhanji and Taratibu and later Amina, a young African woman, and Kala enter into relationships that leap over political and social chasms, but do not succeed in bringing together different communities. Taratibu in the novel represents the old Africa of slavery and exploitation. Amina is used by the narrative as an eroticized symbol of young Africa. The danger of one union revealing itself as the double of the other is always present, for Amina and Kala, as much as for the reader. Hence there is, despite the evident regret, very little surprise worked into the narration of the failure of these relationships. Musing on the difficulties of conducting unorthodox relationships, Kala writes in broken sentences that display his inability to reach conclusions on such speculations. Or perhaps language can only inconclusively map the experience described here:

To have met in the jungle and fallen in love there, among people we did not know, on the banks of a stream, under a tree, how easy it was. No sooner were we back in the city than we started carrying the burdens of our races...For me, it was simply to be doing the unthinkable; to be the subject of discussion for anyone in the community, from precocious ten-year-olds to the senile: *the children, religion, the differences, it's not easy, nothing to do with racism, of course*...And what words did Dar say to her...to have fallen in love with one of the exploiter class, a dukawallah, mere agents of the British, these oily slimy cowardly Asians, what future did they have...the world had so much to offer a bright young African girl. (*GS*, p. 228)

To get back to Dhanji Govindji. Did he know love...Did he tell Bibi Taratibu before he sent her away, This won't work, our worlds are too far apart, they won't let us? And Bibi Taratibu, the Gentle One who later ran a tea shop at the end of the village, watching her half-caste son grow up into a loafer, did she love, or did she simply put up with the pawing of this lonely Indian? And my grandfather Huseni escaped from this intolerant world but left behind a pining woman...did he also love and control, as Edward would have it?...There was Uncle Goa, who in another scenario would have run away with my mother and now, as Amina told me, Edward...unrequited loves, because we catch the world unprepared for us. (*GS*, pp. 229–30)

It is the language in which such romances are re-presented that determines whether these are "impossible loves" that implicate the national in the personal or mere instances of failed endeavor or desire. In other words, are these *always* impossible speculations insofar as one can never know if this alternate history (familial and national) could exist precisely because it did not exist? Or is this no more than another instance of the narrator's inability to move beyond an ambivalent language and confront his own intolerance?

What is the "scenario" that is required for these "unrequited loves" to be returned, to be successful? Kala's use of the language seems to work against his desire for Amina, so that he finds not just the "world," but also the "word" unprepared for such loves.[26] Written in a language which has the potential to serve as a linguistic bridge between Africans and Indians, Vassanji's narrative lapses instead into the English language's historic failing to present the different as equal.[27] However, it is not just the language that fails Kala. For in this case, as in the ambivalent language used to describe the guilt at his multiple betrayals of Taratibu, Mary, and of African aspirations several times, the narrator presents himself as fully constructed by the community to which he belongs. Hence, for instance, the narrator repeatedly describes African cities in terms of feminized wombs awaiting the entry of the masculine outsider, Indian, Arab or European. And ultimately, the narrator does not quite succeed in convincing the reader, in the passage quoted above or in other passages, that his love for Amina is any different than the sexually exploitative relationship Dhanji had with Taratibu. The pattern of repetition is so forcefully suggested that neither the characters nor the reader can quite shake it off. Kala is subject to the same myths as the rest of his community, so that when it comes to loving and living with an African woman he cannot imagine doing so other than in ways that would violate the pattern of relationships that have his community's sanction. Thus history repeats itself and Kala, like the men and women in earlier generations, follows the well trodden path of having racially legitimate wives chosen for them.

REPETITION AND IMMIGRANT NARRATIVES

On reading *The Gunny Sack*, we may ask as Homi Bhabha does in "DissemiNation": "But what kind of 'present' is this if it is a consistent process of surmounting the ghostly time of repetition?" (*D*, p. 295). The narrative present in this novel, which is mainly available in the first and last chapters, is set in an unnamed western metropole. The events that gain the significance and recognition that we habitually assign to "plot" and "story-line" are those that are relevant to this narrative frame.

At the end of the first chapter, the narrator writes: "Sona and Kala: Our nicknames. Gold and black. The colours of Africa" (*GS*, p. 12). Here, "Africa" is the continent, the nation, that is ambiguously left behind. There is nostalgia for it. The word activates memory and stories, but even as it pervades the present, *it is the past*.[28] Yet nowhere in this text do we see a 'present' that is unmarked by the past. No place is significant except insofar as it is like or unlike other places. A spectacular example of this phenomenon of immigrant novels is set forth in Anita Desai's *ByeBye BlackBird* when Dev, the young immigrant protagonist who has just arrived in London from India, first walks down the High Street:

His mood of carelessness, so easy and so fluid, of familiarity and ease, changed quickly out on the High Street where he was a stranger again and all was strange to him. Yet not – he paused and faltered, bumping into a passerby or two – so strange after all. Somehow recognizable too, faintly, surrealistically, for strolling lopsidedly down the High Street, it seemed to him he was strolling down the Mall of a Himalayan hill station, the Mall of Simla or Mussoorie or Darjeeling or any one of the little towns that the heat-maddened, homesick British colonists had created in the incongruous Himalayas, created in the shape and memory of little English country towns and little English suburbia, left oceans behind...Now, recognizing in the High Street those echoes of the Indian hill station Malls, he realized that the holiday retreats of his childhood had not been the originals he had taken them to be but copies...Too dazed to retain any haughty poise, he exclaimed, "But this is the Mall!" [29]

In this context, for the colonial subject Dev to enter the world of the colonizer is to have his past instantly compromised or otherwise radically altered – for he now sees the frame of reference that guided the architecture of his past world. A nice reversal of this incident is offered in the opening passage of *First Light* by Leena Dhingra where the "frame of reference" that guides an eleven year old recently immigrated young girl through London streets is her memory of the

Monopoly game board: "Eleven years old and walking down Piccadilly on my own, I felt quite safe. It was my first time in London, but I felt quite safe. 'I'm in Piccadilly now so I can't go to jail because the lowest the double dice can turn is two!'"³⁰ No journey in *The Gunny Sack* is recorded except in terms of its difference or similarity to earlier journeys. No event, no relationship, the list is endless... with the result that the narrative cannot describe Ji Bai's funeral except in terms of other funerals that it is not. As a result, the entire narrative in this first chapter is split by bracketed asides – and other asides that should be in brackets. The ostensibly bracketed asides, such as: "A sob stifled, a wail choked (practiced wailers some of these), the coffin was closed" (*GS*, p. 4) train us to recognize the unbracketed but potentially bracket-able asides that bring past and future into the syntax of the present: "I could see the body shrink under icy pressure, the skin dry and peel off and fly away like a kite, the skeleton rattle and fold and rearrange itself to form a neat square heap like the firewood that was once sold outside her store in Dar." (pp. 4–5) In this sentence, as elsewhere, one could claim that it is the present that is bracketed or even erased out of the narrative...except for the "neat square heap" that echoes the Swahili cap "so softened by age that it folded neatly into a small square" in the gunny sack. The present serves primarily as a frame that the narrative throws around a multi-layered recollection of the event being described.

The distraction and/or comfort offered by these memories of other times and places makes the immigrant more multi-faceted a figure than does the equation that delivers a subject who is marginal and therefore yearns for assimilation into the mainstream. While the desire for assimilation into the mainstream is popularly read as the trademark of the immigrant experience, "feeling at home" may or may not require assimilation. At the same time, the process of making oneself at home is a project that may not be completed even by several successive generations.

The wandering never stops nor is the past completely left behind. This pattern of repetition continues through the novel – the ball of kapok glides out and sails away like Ji Bai's skin, like a kite, like Sheru's yarns, like Dhanji Govindji's travels, like Yasmin's going to England to train as a nurse, like Begum going off to England with Mr. Harris the Physics teacher, like Sona going to Cambridge, Massachusetts, like Kala who follows him there...the list is endless. When Juma tries to stow away on a steamer that sails from East Africa to India, he is apprehended as he tries to disembark in Bombay. Thus, for this Indian, all he ever sees of India is a brief glimpse of the city of Bombay from the porthole of the cabin he was locked up in. Attempting to run away to a "past," he is thrown back into the present.

Musing on Juma's ejection into the present, Kala with the aid of the gunny sack, tentatively formulates a theory that once again poses the central question in immigrant literature: the issue of wandering. I quote this passage in its entirety:

Running away. Wanderlust. Having come to this theme yet once again, memory plays a trick on me. From her corner Shehru throws a wink at me...and do I imagine that the gaping mouth with its sisal moustache has a silent laugh on its thin old lips...

The question that comes to mind is: in coming here, have I followed a destiny? Satisfied a wanderlust that runs in the blood? Or do I seek in genes merely an excuse for weakness that's in the blood: can you distinguish such weakness from wanderlust? When does a situation become impossible enough to justify escape?

I too have run away, absconded. And reaching this grim basement, I stopped to examine the collective memory – this spongy, disconnected, often incoherent accretion of stories over generations. Like the karma a soul acquires, over many incarnations, the sins and merits, until in its final stages it lumbers along top-heavy with its accumulations, desperately seeking absolution.

I, like my forefathers before me, have run away. But what a price they paid. Dhanji Govindji, his self-respect and his sanity. His son, the joys of family life, the security of community life. My father Juma, I don't know what price he paid for running away – it was Hassam Pirbhai who paid the cash price – but he did pay a price for coming back. He joined his tormenters. And in joining them he lost his compassion for those of whom he was also a part – if only a quarter.

Perhaps I judge too harshly. (*GS*, pp. 65–6)

Earlier in this chapter, while commenting on the ambivalence of the language used by the narrator to describe the "impossible loves," I tried to reach an assessment on whether the fault lay with the narrator, i.e., at the level of "purely" personal failure of desire or if the inability to conduct difficult loves was an inescapable aspect of attempting to bridge racial or national chasms through literary prose. Here the narrator reveals himself to be well aware of his own "weakness" and yet questions whether it stems from his "genes" or a series of "impossible situations." The reader may choose to read national implications or the shortcomings of the English language into this reference to "impossible situations." But does the text allow for this reading? In the last line, Kala defers judgment, and compels us to follow likewise.

CHALLENGING NATIONAL PROJECTS

In "DissemiNation," Homi K. Bhabha argues that today the modern nation is written at its margins by those who occupy these spaces. According to Bhabha, a great number of persons occupy the margins: "the colonized," "women," as well as "the migrant" and "the immigrant." Moreover, the difference of those at the margins from the mainstream citizen *in itself* refuses the harmony imposed by readers who suggest that nations are born of peoples sharing an imagined community. Bhabha's intention is, in part, to force a rethinking of Benedict Anderson's *Imagined Communities*, which argues that nations come into being when diverse people imagine a sense of shared community.[31] According to Bhabha's corrective, those at the margins of modern nations "disturb the ideological manoeuvres through which 'imagined communities' are given essentialist identities" (*D*, p. 300). The discourse produced at the margins, then, serves as a "supplement" to "the dominant discourse," and as such, it "antagonizes the implicit power to generalize, to produce the sociological solidarity" (*D*, p. 306). Immigrants and other wanderers are, according to Bhabha, "themselves the marks of a shifting boundary" of a modern nation (*D*, p. 315). And this shifting boundary writes a doubleness, splitting or ambivalence into the narratives produced at the margins. Ultimately, Bhabha claims that it is "through this process of splitting that the conceptual ambivalence of modern society becomes the site of *writing the nation*" (*D*, p. 297).

One could argue that "the nation" is precisely that which is not inscribed by the writing that is produced at the margins. Perhaps the location sought in these instances ought not to be read in terms of national subjectivity and/or national space. Immigration, one could argue, *unwrites* nation and national projects because it flagrantly displays a rejection of one national space for another more desirable location, albeit with some luggage carried over.

We could alternatively examine this issue by attempting to assign a national allegiance to Vassanji's novel. While the book is published in Heinemann's African Writers Series, it could just as easily be part of the "ethnic" literature of Canada, which is where Vassanji lives, writes and works as a teacher. His text would then, fall into the category of "South Asian Canadian Literature" the title of an article written by Vassanji and published in an Indian literary journal.[32] Vassanji is the editor and founder of *The Toronto South Asian Review*. The acknowledgments for this novel include mention of "assistance" from the Ontario Arts Council and Multiculturalism Directorate. And lastly, India could of course stretch the limits of her literary field and claim Vassanji as one of her own far-flung writers.

Vassanji's text at its boundaries – the beginning and the end – disturbs the national calculations of the western nation (Massachusetts, USA or Canada) and all through the text the saga of this family disturbs the national calculations of first German then British imperialism and then independent Tanzania's *Ujamaa* socialist project. For Bhabha, when the supplements are taken into account, "the language of national collectiveness and cohesiveness is [what is] now at stake" (*D*, p. 304). And what this living at the edge, in basements or at the margins calls for is a doubleness (variously present as repetitions, as a sense of déjà vu,) in the discourse that such experience engenders. Yet, Bhabha's theory of "DissemiNation" or of "double writing" from the margins is "not simply" he claims, "a theoretical exercise in the internal contradictions of the modern liberal nation" (*D*, p. 299). Rather, Bhabha insists:

The postcolonial space is now "supplementary" to the metropolitan centre; it stands in a subaltern, adjunct relation that doesn't aggrandise the *presence* of the west but redraws its frontiers in the menacing, antagonistic boundary of cultural difference that never quite adds up, always less than one nation and double. From this splitting of time and narrative emerges a strange, empowering knowledge for the migrant that is at once schizoid and subversive. (*D*, p. 318–19)

Here Bhabha seems to equate the postcolonial with the migrant and the migrant with the subaltern. In "Women in Difference," Gayatri Spivak argues, like Bhabha, that the modern nation is (ready or not) being written over by those at the margins. Commenting on a short story by Mahasweta Devi entitled "Doulati the Bountiful," Spivak draws attention to those left out of the "relay race between Empire and Nation, between imperialism and independence."[33] Here, the reference is to the specific Indian aboriginal communities about which Mahasweta Devi writes. These aboriginals or "adivasis" as they are called in India, occupy, in Spivak's words – the "space that cannot share in the energy of this reversal [from colony to independent nation]." Spivak uses the conclusion to Mahasweta's story to further her argument with great impact. Doulati, an adivasi woman sold into prostitution, is found on the morning of independence day to be lying dead on a clay map of India drawn by a patriotic village school master in the school yard for the day's celebrations. The presence of her putrid and diseased body on the map makes it physically impossible to stage any kind of flag-day ceremony. Spivak comments: "The space *displaced* from the Empire-Nation negotiation now comes to inhabit and appropriate the national map, and makes the agenda of nationalism impossible." Spivak correctly describes this space as "the habitat of the subproletariat or the subaltern." And Mahasweta's stories amply demonstrate how these communities are erased out of national calculations or, worse still, included in national projects through violent schemes.

However, the immigrant who often opts out of national projects such as liberation day euphoria is not always subaltern. Especially not the immigrant who speaks her story through collections of luggage – spiritual, material, linguistic: written or oral. If *The Gunny Sack* does possess the kind of "empowering knowledge" that Bhabha claims for narratives from and of the margins, then, in the last instance, the novel subverts Bhabha's project by its consistent rejections of any national identity for its protagonists and by repeatedly revealing that hegemonic national discourses do not take kindly to those who inhabit marginal spaces.

The novel's focus on members of the Indian community in East Africa, requires that we attempt to map Bhabha's theory to non-western nations and to instances of immigration to these nations. The Indian communities in Africa, while they are on the margins and supplementary to the modern nations imagined there, are *not* automatically or necessarily subaltern. Entering the African continent as traders from as early as the sixteenth century, and later brought in by British imperialists to build the railway that was to link all of British Africa, the Indians have often occupied a privileged position when compared to Africans in Africa. A similar position was occupied by the Greek and the Lebanese communities in West Africa. Outside Africa, the Syrian community in Antigua provides another example of a minority group that has established itself in a position of privilege. The local antagonism against these communities, was, and is, also quite similar. In *A Small Place*, Kincaid's strongly worded assessment of Antigua today, the Syrian community is introduced in the course of a description of their palatial house:

The people who live in this house are a merchant family who came to Antigua from the Middle East less than twenty years ago. When this family first came to Antigua, they sold dry goods door to door from suitcases they carried on their backs. Now they own a lot of Antigua; they regularly lend money to the government, they build enormous (for Antigua), ugly (for Antigua), concrete buildings in Antigua's capital, St. John's., which the government then rents for huge sums of money; a member of their family is the Antiguan Ambassador to Syria; Antiguans hate them. Not far from this mansion is another mansion, the home of a drug smuggler...[34]

The antagonism in the above passage cannot be smoothed over. Antigua is too small a place with too few resources to allow one Syrian family, albeit a powerful one, to set up home here. As in *The Gunny Sack*, the links between trade and colonial (and neocolonial) exploitation are too close to be ignored by the indigenous population or at least by parts of it. The suitcases carried on the backs of immigrants are in this instance not so much scraps from a faraway reverently remembered home but tools of the trade, the means of livelihood.

As *The Gunny Sack* and other documents demonstrate, under colonialism (British and German) the Indians were used as a buffer class and race that further distanced the Europeans from the Africans. It was a buffer status that was adopted and adapted by the Indians as they strove to maintain their identity as outsiders. Consider this "theory of creation" that is attributed to Kulsum, the narrator's mother, a pivotal figure in the text:

Kulsum's theory of creation.

When God was well and ready after all his exertions finally to create mankind, he sat himself beside a red-hot oven with a plate of dough. From this he fashioned three identical dolls. He put the first doll into the oven to finish it, but, alas, brought it out too soon: it came out white and undone. In this way was born the white race. With this lesson learnt, the almighty put the second doll into the oven, but this time he kept it in for too long. It came out burnt and black. Thus the black race. Finally the One and Only put the last doll inside the oven, and brought it out at just the right time. It came out golden brown, the Asian, simply perfect. (*GS*, p. 73)

This passage brings to light a very important aspect of "immigritude." This myth-making that Kulsum passes on to her children, suggests that those at the margins may read their marginality as a positive, even superior stance from which to experience the modern nation.[35] Perhaps this is an instance of the "strange empowering knowledge" that Bhabha attributes to the immigrant. And yet, there may be absolutely no desire on the part of immigrants to write themselves into a national discourse *except* as aliens.[36]

The problems arising from this immigrant stance of maintaining their distance from the mainstream comes to a head when the center refuses to include this (alien) margin as a part of the whole and decides instead to evict it. As amply illustrated by the fate of Indians expelled in 1972 from Idi Amin's Uganda, the "adjunct" or, following Bhabha, "supplementary" position occupied by these Indian communities in East Africa was and is indeed precarious. But a community that has sat on the fence (or rather that has a history of being used as the fence that divided colonizer from the colonized) is endangered when a unifying national discourse, as in a post-independence era, requires it to pick allegiances. The immigrants in Vassanji's text have always already renounced such allegiances. Writing on the implications (for the Indian communities) of the British and German conflict as it extended to their respective colonies in East Africa during the period of the First World War, Vassanji states:

> Among the trading immigrant peoples, loyalty to a land or a government, always loudly professed, is a trait one can normally look for in vain. Governments may come and go, but the immigrants' only concern is the security of their families, their trade and savings. Deviants to the code come to be regarded and dismissed as not altogether sound of mind. Of the ten store-owning families in Rukanga, seven were Indian; six packed up and were ready to leave by dawn. Again, the gunnies stuffed with one-rupee notes, the jewelry tied around their waists; once more the promises of returning... (*GS*, p. 52)

This passage challenges Bhabha's assertion that it is the "nation" that is written or rewritten at these marginal sites. For the immigrant characters in this novel, having left one national space, leaving another and yet another, are given facts of the wandering life.[37] Bhabha writes:

> The scraps, patches and rags of daily life must be repeatedly turned into the signs of a national culture, while the very act of the narrative performance interpellates a growing circle of national subjects. (*D*, p. 297)

This argument holds only for immigrants who actively desire for themselves an integration into a national culture as national subjects. In *The Gunny Sack*, the "scraps, patches and rags of daily life" are "repeatedly turned into the signs of" *a family history that is of little value to most family members*. This history replaces rather than replicates a "national culture." It is what the immigrant *may choose* as a compensation for the lack of other filiations, rather than as a microcosmic or allegorical version of the nation.

Vassanji's text repeatedly displays the nitty gritty details of living at the margins of a constantly changing center. Over the century that the novel covers, there are several changes of power at the centers of the colonial and then national spaces in East Africa. The repercussions on the margins are different in each instance, and the immigrant has to make sure that s/he is not too deeply implicated in any political allegiance if s/he is to survive the new order. The narrative displays the political flexibility that is necessary for the immigrant's survival. Toward the end of the First World War, sensing that a German defeat is imminent, the Indian community prepares to leave German Rukanga:

> Once more the promises of returning, the hiring of men to watch over what was left behind. But in the mukhi the Germans had a friend; he had supplied the boma [colonial, administrative office] when it was in use and it turned out that he had supplied its former inhabitant the captain in the bush. The mukhi stayed; and so did Ghulam's brother Abdulla, who had learnt German in Bibi Wasi's classroom in Matamu and became Germany's lifelong friend.
>
> The road to Dar es Salaam was uneventful. They stayed close to the railway line and after some time saw a train. They also saw motor vehicles and troops moving west and hailed, "Biritish, Zindabad! Rani Victoria, Zindabad!" (*GS*, pp. 52–3)

The decision to stay or leave is purely pragmatic and "loyalties" change over the course of a paragraph. This passage suggests that in this context the politics of the profession, rather than those of national affiliation or disaffiliation, rule the day. Here, a livelihood made from trading between borders requires that one have a foothold on either side of the fence. Hence, the move from being subjects of Deutsch Ost Afrika to British subjects is marked through shouts of "long live Queen Victoria" – a comic hailing because she is long dead, but politically astute because she is a metonym for the British empire. This declares to those in the trains and motor vehicles (the entering British troops) that the Indians are already compliant with the new order. There is apparently no need for forced conversions here.[38]

SCENES OF LEAVE-TAKING

Scenes of leave-taking mark the boundaries of these texts in ways that display the ease with which narrative escapes the confines that (national) border controls try to impose on immigrants. Sara Suleri's autobiographical novel *Meatless Days* begins with the following passage:

> Leaving Pakistan was, of course, tantamount to giving up the company of women. I can tell this only to someone like Anita, in all faith that she will understand, as we go perambulating through the grimness of New Haven and feed on the pleasures of our conversational way. Dale who lives in Boston, would also understand. She will one day write a book about the stern and secretive life of breast feeding and is partial to fantasies that cul-

minate in an abundance of resolution. And Fawzi, with a grimace of recognition, knows because she knows the impulse to forget. (p. 1)

In the very first passage then, this novel lays bare the marks of the immigrant genre: the easy movement between past, present and future, and between Pakistan, New Haven and Boston, as well as the juxtaposition of recognition and the impulse to forget. As is typical of this genre, the narrative does not "leave" Pakistan. And yet the novel is set going by this act of leave-taking.

The frequency of scenes of leave-taking in the novels on immigration poses the question: is the postcolonial world no more than places that one tries desperately to leave and places that one tries desperately to get entry into? In Jamaica Kincaid's novel, Annie John thinks of herself as she walks to the boat jetty that will take her away from Antigua to England:

My mother and my father − I was leaving them forever. My home on an island − I was leaving it forever. What to make of everything? I felt a familiar hollow space inside. I felt I was being held down against my will. I felt I was burning up from head to toe. I felt that someone was tearing me up into little pieces and soon I would be able to see all the little pieces as they floated out into nothing in the deep blue sea.[39]

Try as she might, Annie cannot gather together a self-identity that is more substantial than "a familiar hollow space inside." Attempting to suture together her past and future, she feels herself torn into little pieces. All she can muster together is a name: "'My name is Annie John.' These were the first words that came into my mind as I woke up on the morning of the last day I spent in Antigua, and they stayed up there, lined up one behind the other, marching up and down, for I don't know how long."[40] Following the trajectory of a successful colonial education means leaving Antigua. The "best" colonial education nurtures in the colonial subject a rejection of the home-country as a necessary step in a "proper" education. This rejection is fueled by Annie's school lessons in literature, geography, history, art and economics which teach that England is the ultimate destination. Hence those who learn their lessons best are those who immigrate to the mother-country. Annie John has already left Antigua before she takes the ship out.

For Sona, in *The Gunny Sack*, leaving Tanzania occasions an understanding of himself as a colonial subject, one of Britannia's stepchildren. This mirror is held up to him at London airport where he stops en route to the US. In his first letter from London, he describes waiting in line to get immigration clearance, at London airport:

And how does Britannia treat her offspring who come from all over the world to pay their respects? At the Airport, lines, long lines: coloured, white, coloured, white... A coincidence? Hardly. First class and second class British subjects. You look at the others in your line, and you wonder, Am I one of these? Why do they look so strange ... and dark? You ask yourself, Why do these Indian women always travel with bedding, for God's sake? You want to move away from them and then you check yourself. It could be your mother. You smile. (*GS*, p. 236)

He reports his conversation with the women in his line, *"Kidhar se atey ho? Amritsar. Aap? Tanzania."* [Where are you coming from? Amritsar. And You? Tanzania.] While the Hindi word *"kidhar"* translates most accurately as "where" or "whether," the sentence that would best convey the sense of "where do you belong" would use the word *"kaha"* instead. Yet *"kidhar"* is appropriate here because it better suggests the temporary nature of "belonging" and "leaving" that becomes quite everyday in the context of immigration. What is equally significant is that neither of the two say "India" or "I'm Indian" in reply to the queries but that is the basis of striking up this conversation and of confidently conducting it in Hindi. Does this recognition convey the existence of a flexible identity of "Indian" that survives transportation? In this case, the ability to exchange a few sentences in a common language, makes one's country of origin a mere circumstance.

For the immigrant in this novel, identity is linked to a specific location (here India) only hypothetically. There is no urgent desire to return to the place on the map called India. Elsewhere as in Said's *After the Last Sky* for example, Palestinian identity without a Palestine is marked with the anguish of homelessness that is absent in Sona's letter. Said writes of the condition of exile:

No Palestinian census exists. There is no line that can be drawn from one Palestinian to another that does not seem to interfere with the political designs of one or another state. While all of us live among "normal" people, people with complete lives, they seem to us hopelessly out of reach, with their countries, their familial continuity, their societies intact. How does a Palestinian father tell his son and daughter that Lebanon (Egypt, Syria, Jordan, New York) is where we are, but not where we are *from*? [41]

The centrality of "nationhood" and the importance of "state designs" in the context of exile is defused in the immigrant novel. The urgency with which Said's narrative awaits a viable Palestine is in sharp contrast to the exuberance with which Sona looks forward to the move to the US. On his way to Harvard, Sona has done better for himself than other offspring of Britannia including the suspicious immigration official who interrogates him at London airport. He writes in his letter of this interrogation session:

"You've completed school."
"Yes, that's why I'm going to university."
"You don't want a job in London, for instance?"
"Why would I want a job here when I've got a scholarship to study in America?"
"This scholarship. They just gave it to you?" (Is he jealous?)
"Yes."
"Anyone can apply?" (Not you, if you're so dense.)
Finally, after several hours, he let me through... (*GS*, p. 237)

"Travelling Light," Cliff Richard's 1959 hit love song that was popular all over the English speaking globe in the 1960s and 1970s could well have been the tune on Sona's lips as he jauntily boards the plane. Like his traveling ancestors, Sona is able and willing to move to the most desirable location available to him – in this case, Harvard University, Cambridge, Massachusetts.

The final section of the novel deals with the coming of age of the fourth generation, that of Kala and Sona. Set in the 1960s and early 70s, the political events in this section revolve around Tanzanian independence.[42] The novel examines the impact of Julius Nyerere's "Ujamaa" socialist project, and the status of Indians in this newly defined national "family."[43] What this section demonstrates is that while immigrants disturb the easy interpellation of national subjects by a hegemonic national discourse, the very formulation of national projects such as "Ujamaa" challenges, disturbs and threatens the immigrants' project of "being immigrants," of remaining marginal, on the fence.

Consider the silence in the Indian section of Dar es Salaam during the Independence Day celebration. In a passage that begins with "Independence was painless," a phrase that is repeatedly used, Vassanji reveals the pain that exists for the Indian – the pain of not knowing whether in Tanzania one is the enemy: "Independence was painless. A Man's colour is no sin in Tanganyika, said Nyerere... Tanganyika is not Congo, where nuns were raped and hundreds murdered and shops looted..." (*GS*, p. 156).

It is not clear if the "wide, stocky pipes left in the center of the road" for the purpose of supporting street decorations on independence day, will be used as anti-Indian riot weapons as is rumored to have happened elsewhere in newly independent Africa.[44] But the Indian community decides to play it safe – they stay indoors.

Independence was painless. Prince Philip came to give the country away, but in Kichwele we stayed home and followed the events in the newspapers and on the radio. And on independence day, at midnight, zero hour, while the decorated street below was empty of man or motor vehicle, sitting silent, neglected, like a bride not picked up on the fateful day: upstairs, sitting quietly around the ancient Phillips oracle, we saw in our mind's eye the lights turn off at the National stadium, the Union Jack quietly come down and the lights turn on again to reveal the new green and black and gold national flag flying; we heard the thunderous applause in our sitting room, carried by radio waves, and again, we all swore, far away at the National stadium, carried this time by the wind. (*GS*, pp. 156–7)

This scene is familiar to readers of postcolonial African fiction: the joyous celebration at the changing of flags that marks independence, a new national beginning.[45] Yet this time around, the fictional apparatus speaks from the margin of this national event. It is as with a wedding where the best seats are taken by family members. The narrator cannot give a first-hand account because he does not have first-hand experience of this crucial moment in Tanzanian national history. Hence, in one of the key instances in which a people imagine themselves as a nation, the immigrant prudently keeps a safe distance. Prince Philip comes to play "father-of-the-bride" and "give the country away." But the Indian part of town is "like a bride not picked up on the fateful day." This scene, more than any other in the novel, makes this an African, or more specifically, a Tanzanian novel.[46] Who is to say that the Indians do not participate in this crucial moment of national history in the making? They "hear" and cheer if only from their living rooms.

Are nations and discourses deemed national large enough to accommodate the supplements? To argue, as I would like to do with the assistance of Vassanji's text, that the terms "nation" and/or "national subject" are *not* "large enough," is perhaps, to construct the nation as a solid cohesive entity as Bhabha accuses Ben Anderson of doing.[47] And how do we tell the old (monolithic) nation and its discourses apart from the modern nation whose potential, according to Bhabha, lies in its bursting and splitting seams? Especially when both discourses speak at the same time, and when in most instances it is the discourse at the center which determines whether what is spoken at the margins will be heard.[48] In *The Gunny Sack*, the lack of acceptance of even fourth generation Indians as *integral* to Tanzanian nationalism, very forcefully suggests that the terms nation and national writer are not large enough to include all. What grants membership into "Families"? Who are the outsiders? *The Gunny Sack* explores the different constructions of "family," "home" and "nation" as ideological and physical structures that can engender the self. Nevertheless, the reader is compelled to acknowledge that every assertion of "belonging" is systematically undercut by the narrative.

To the question "where is the immigrant at home?", this novel poses another question "what is not a foreign place for immigrants?" In the following passage, in the exchange between Aziz and Kala, when the former hands over Ji Bai's sack to the latter, the use of "here" and "there" may confuse the reader but the referents are apparently clear to the speakers themselves:

"Come, come...what if she had died there? Would you have posted it?"
"But she died here."
... She had said that she would travel, and Aziz accompanied her, first to India and then here. Wherever she went the gunny went with her. Did she know she would die in this foreign place, then? (*GS*, p. 5)

Here, Vassanji suggests that one *can* be at home in foreign places. For some immigrants, home is traveling with gunny sacks, always postponing Shehrazade's "eventual demise." For others like Aziz's family, feeling at home requires the burning, the forgetting of the gunny sack and of memory. In keeping with the novel's repetitive narrative style the issue is reframed in another context when Kala goes on his National Service camp trip and is urged by his relatives to take along a big black truck filled with Indian snacks and other "essentials" for surviving life in the camp. Once he gets there, Kala is punished by his supervisors for bringing along excess baggage; his punishment is to run up and down a hill with his trunk on his head. A few weeks after this grueling experience, Kala writes in a letter to a friend:

We Indians have barged into Africa with our big black trunk, and every time it comes in our way. *Do we need it?* I should have come with a small bag, a rucksack. Instead I came with ladoos, jelebis, chevdo. Toilet paper. A woolen suit. And I carried it on my head like a fool. (*GS*, p. 204, emphasis added)

"Do we need it?" Does the immigrant need the "invisible luggage"? At the end of this novel, Kala attempts to liberate himself from the "baggage of paraphernalia" that is his past (*GS*, p. 268). Releasing the gunny sack's narratives is a first step toward this "disposition of the past." Kala yearns to "embrace the banal present," but such banality comes only at the cost of great violence. The last image we have of the gunny sack is as follows: "She lies on the floor, crumpled, her throat cut, guts spilled, blood on the floor" (*GS*, p. 268). For Annie

John, there is no compensation for the eviction from "Home," and the anger and frustration of this novel seeps into Kincaid's 1990 "sequel" *Lucy*. At the end of *Lucy*, however, the young woman protagonist begins to come to terms with her "homelessness" through the act of writing. Like Kala, Lucy writes in order to be reconciled with her past and thus to lighten her immigrant luggage or at least to rearrange the items so that it makes an easier load.

Belonging in any one place requires a judicious balancing of remembrance and forgetting. Writing on the discourses that inscribe the modern nation, Bhabha states: "it is this forgetting – a minus in the origin – that constitutes the *beginning* of the nation's narrative" (*D*, p. 310). He goes on to add: "It is through this syntax of forgetting – or being obliged to forget – that the problematic identification of a national people becomes visible." (*D*, p. 310). To this *The Gunny Sack* responds: Which "nation"? India? East Africa? Tanzania? Britain? USA? Canada? And which "national people"? Here, there are only generations of wanderers who travel great distances with no anthems on their lips.[49]

CONCLUSIONS

What happens to the category of "postcolonial literature" after this sub-category of the immigrant genre is carved out of it? Rather than shrinking, the category of "postcolonial literature" would *expand* to include all twentieth-century literature produced from any location that is informed by the dynamics of colonialism. Under this rubric, all literary texts that unsentimentally interrogate the seductive pleasures of "feeling at home" in homes, genders, a specific race or class, in communities and nations, could be read as "immigrant" fictions. By expanding the parameters of the "postcolonial" one recognizes that no single formulation, however elastic, can do justice to this vast terrain. Locating literature within global English is only one project among the many possible discussions on postcoloniality.

Epilogue. All homesickness is fiction

To be rooted is perhaps the most important and least recognized
need of the human soul.

Simone Weil

we pretend that we are trees and speak of roots. Look under
your feet. You will not find gnarled growths sprouting through
the soles. Roots, I sometimes think, are a conservative myth,
designed to keep us in our places.

Salman Rushdie

If "roots" are a conservative myth, then all homesickness is fiction.
Should we then look for ways to move beyond "home," to resist and
unlearn the seductive pleasures of belonging? And is such a move
possible?

The first chapter of this book concerned itself with an examination
of the encoding, elaborations and subsequent revisions made in the
many discussions on homes. "Home" was read as a concept that
could be recycled in progressive ways and yet the best of the theorizing stopped "en route." Where would a deconstruction of "home"
and of the subject-home equation take us? Could change ultimately
return us to the same location? The second chapter served to check a
certain feminist optimism about change, especially about change
wrought by women. English women in British India soon found
themselves completely at home in their new empire, with the idealizations of the domestic and of femininity refurbished rather than
rejected by the dramatically changed locale. In their everyday life
they replicated the machinations of Empire and their writing constructed and consolidated imperial power. Englishwomen, in this discourse of imperial romance, were empowered colonial subjects.

Working the same sentimental idealizations of the "Home," Joseph
Conrad undercuts the literary representation of the self-confident colonizer. His novels begin a steady literary erosion of the most deeply

199

ingrained understanding of the home as foil to the world, of empire
as distinct from nation, of races as bearers of separate destinies.
Writers in his wake, such as V. S. Naipaul and Kazuo Ishiguro, continue, albeit in a more ironic mode, to revise and rework the literary
plot that elaborates on the theme that is basic to most Conradian sto-
rylines – the desire for sutured, secure (masculine) self-identity in a
world where sure knowledge and fixities are always compromised.

The urge to domesticate the foreign, to understand and categorize
marks the theoretical reading of "Third World Literature" today. But
literature always surprises us. Read in the context of global English, literary texts do not always perform as expected. Conrad is still Achebe's
"bloody racist," but his novels have generated some of the subtlest
examinations of race issues. Much work needs to be done on the complicated writerly allegiances that are in play at specific sites of literary
production in global English. In the writing of Indian women working
in English we find postcolonial citizens who have all the comforts of
home and are yet completely "disenfranchised" in the various (gendered) roles available to them. In *this* instance, women's writing does
not consolidate feminist victories, nor does it serve to securely knit
women's issues into other progressive political projects. Here, literature
only offers solace; it cannot envision solutions or inscribe agency.

Immigration and the fictions it engenders teach a certain detachment about "home." In these texts identity is linked only hypothetically (and through hyphenation) to a specific geographical place on
the map. And yet, wandering at the margins of another's culture does
not necessarily mean that one is marginal. Home in the immigrant
genre is a fiction that one can move beyond or recreate at will. The
association between an adequate self and a place to call home is held
up to scrutiny and then let go. As postmodern and postcolonial subjects, we surprise ourselves with our detachment to the things we were
taught to be attached to.

Perhaps the stance to take, while writing and reading fiction as
much as in living, is to acknowledge the seductive pleasure of belonging in homes and in communities and in nations – while working
toward changing the governing principles of exclusions and inclusions.
In a special issue on patriotism in *The Nation*, Edward Said writes:

Which country? I've never felt that I belonged exclusively to one country,
nor have I been able to identify "patriotically" with any other than losing
causes. Patriotism is best thought of as an obscure dead language, learned
prehistorically but almost forgotten and almost unused since. Nearly every-

thing normally associated with it – wars, rituals of nationalistic loyalty, sentimentalized (or invented) traditions, parades, flags, etc. – is quite dreadful and full of appalling claims of superiority and pre-eminence. But perhaps those are all the results of applied patriotism. Is theoretical patriotism really that much better? Thinking affectionately about home is all I'll go along with. (July 15/22, 1991, p. 116)

"Thinking affectionately about home" is all that Said will allow himself as a conscious political decision. This book is an attempt to think affectionately *and* critically about the politics of home.

Notes

PROLOGUE. ALL FICTION IS HOMESICKNESS

1 It is worth speculating that changes in the realist form and contents are the genre's way of addressing the changes in the ideology of home in circulation in a specific location. Hence, Ama Ata Aidoo's experimental novel, *Our Sister Killjoy; or, Reflections from a Black-eyed Squint* (New York: NOK Press), published in 1977 but written much earlier, is about a protagonist whose story cannot be presented as unproblematically situated within the strictures of the usual realist narrative. The heroine of this novel has to rethink the entire notion of home and self from a foreign country at the moment when her own home-country is undergoing rapid reformulation. The plot of *No Telephone to Heaven* (New York: Vintage Books, 1987) by Michelle Cliff also dictates a similar disruption of the usual sequencing of realist fiction. The reader can "make sense" of Clara Savage and her "return home" only by sifting through several seemingly unrelated events and peripheral characters. These novels suggest that in negotiating the places between real and idealized homes that the characters grapple with, the very norms of realist fiction get revised.

2 See p. 115 in James Clifford, "Traveling Cultures," in Greenberg, Nelson and Treichler, eds., *Cultural Studies* (New York: Routledge, 1992), pp. 96–116.

3 "Location is about vulnerability," writes Donna Haraway in *Simians, Cyborgs and Women: the Reinvention of Nature* (London: Free Association Press, 1991), p. 196. Chandra Talpade Mohanty defines the "politics of location" as "the historical, geographical, cultural, psychic and imaginative boundaries which provide the ground for political definition and self-definition for contemporary US feminists." See "Feminist Encounters: Locating the Politics of Experience," in Michele Barrett and Anne Phillips, eds., *Destabilizing Theory: Contemporary Feminist Debates* (California: Stanford University Press, 1992), p. 74.

4 Of course in the 1990s, global English is as much a manifestation of American cultural imperialism as it is a hangover of British colonialism.

5 Benedict Anderson, *Imagined Communities: Reflections on the Origin and Spread of Nationalism* (London: Verso, 1983).

6 See Nancy Armstrong, *Desire and Domestic Fiction: A Political History of the Novel* (England: Oxford University Press, 1987); Minnie Bruce Pratt, Elly

203

Bulkin and Barbara Smith, *Yours In Struggle: Three Feminist Perspectives on Anti-Semitism and Racism* (New York: Long Haul Press, 1984); Biddy Martin and Chandra Talpade Mohanty, "Feminist Politics: What's Home Got to Do With It?" in Theresa de Lauretis, ed., *Feminist Studies/Critical Studies* (Bloomington: Indiana University Press, 1986), pp. 191–212; Caren Kaplan, "Deterritorializations: The Rewriting of Home and Exile in Western Feminist Discourse," *Cultural Critique* 6 (Spring 1987), pp. 187–98; Maria Mies, *Patriarchy and Accumulation on a World Scale* (London: Zed Books, 1986); Barbara Smith, ed., *Home Girls: A Black Feminist Anthology* (New York: Kitchen Table Press, 1983); Evelyn Torton Beck, ed., *Nice Jewish Girls*, (1982, repr. Boston: Beacon Press, 1989); Adrian Forty, *Objects of Desire: Design and Society from Wedgewood to IBM* (New York: Pantheon, 1986); Gillian Rose, *Feminism and Geography: The Limits of Geographical Knowledge* (London: Blackwell, Polity, 1993); Jennifer Wolch and Michael Dean, eds., *The Power of Geography: How Territory Shapes Social Life* (Boston: Unwin, Hyman, 1989); Anthony King, *The Bungalow: The Production of a Global Culture* (London: Routledge, 1989); Kumkum Sangari and Sudesh Vaid, eds., *Recasting Women: Essays in Colonial History* (New Delhi: Kali for Women, 1989); Anthony Vidler, *The Architectural Uncanny: Essays on the Modern Unhomely* (Cambridge, MA: MIT Press, 1992); Ann Cvetkovich and Avery Gordon, "Not in Our Names: Women, War, AIDS," in Michael Ryan and Avery Gordon, eds., *Body Politics: Disease, Desire, and the Family* (Boulder, CO: Westview Press, 1994), pp. 32–44.

7   Such theorizing usually follows from Foucault's definition of the almost mutually exclusive categories of "subject to someone else by control and dependence" and "tied to his own identity by a conscience or self-knowledge" (see chapter 1 for a more detailed assessment of these categories). Another (Foucaultian) text, Edward Said's *Orientalism* (New York, Pantheon Press, 1978), buttresses much of the current theorizing on "the colonial subject." For instance, in *Siting Translation: History, Post-Structuralism, and the Colonial Context* (Berkeley: University of California Press, 1992), Tejaswini Niranjana develops the notion of "the colonial subject" as follows: "The colonial subject is constituted through a process of 'Othering' that involves a teleological notion of history, which views the knowledge and ways of life in the colony as distorted or immature versions of what can be found in 'normal' or Western society" (p. 11). Here and elsewhere in her book, the term refers exclusively to those of the colonized races who are constructed through the violence of colonialism. See pp. 1, 2, 28, 31–2. Also see Gauri Viswanathan, *Masks of Conquest: Literary Study and British Rule in India* (New York: Columbia University Press, 1989). In a very persuasive discussion of her decision to limit her study to the colonizers, Gauri Viswanathan defines the colonial subject as "a construct emanating from the colonizer's head...real only to the extent that it provides the rationale for his [the colonizer's] actions" (p. 12).

8   Perry Anderson, "Components of the National Culture," *New Left Review* 50 (July/August 1968), pp. 3–58.
9   Fredric Jameson, "Third World Literature in the Era of Multinational Capitalism," *Social Text* 17 (Fall 1986), pp. 65–88.
10 Reading literary texts forces us to rethink the political assessments made in different disciplines or at earlier moments in cultural analysis. For instance, in justifying her use of the term "post-colonial" rather than the often favored "neo-colonial," Tejaswini Niranjana rightly points out the need to distinguish between the definitions reached by economic theorists from those reached by cultural theorists. "This is not" she writes, "to posit two separate realms of analysis, but merely to suggest that a term appropriate at one level may not be as accurate at another" (*Siting Translation* fn. 10, pp. 7–8).
11 One has only to consider instances where the concept of community has fulfilled its potential as a safe home for *some* to resist the temptation of working toward such safety. Consider for instance, the ugly ring that the words "communal" and "community" have taken in the daily, violent confrontations between the Hindu community and Muslim community in contemporary urban India.

1 HOME-COUNTRIES: NARRATIVES ACROSS DISCIPLINES

1   In the epilogue to *Desire and Domestic Fiction* (Oxford University Press, 1987), Nancy Armstrong notes that the "most powerful household is the one we carry around in our heads" (p. 251). This is equally true for an understanding of what constitutes home; so much so that most persons can list the ingredients that make "a good home" in his/her culture.
2   The following books are representative of the great volume of scholarly texts written in the twentieth century on the topic of nationalism. Hans Kohn, *Nationalism: Its Meaning and History* (Princeton, NJ: D. Van Nostrand, 1955); Anthony D. Smith, *Nationalism in the Twentieth Century* (New York University Press, 1979); Carlton J. H. Hayes, *Nationalism: A Religion* (New York: Macmillan, 1960); Leonard W. Doob, *Patriotism and Nationalism: Their Psychological Foundations* (New Haven, CT: Yale University Press, 1964).

A quick survey of the contents page from Carlton Hayes' *Nationalism: A Religion* reveals the direction that his scholarship follows. Third world nationalism is the focus in the penultimate chapter entitled "Contemporary World-Wide Nationalism." The subheadings in this chapter are as follows: "1. Nationalist Imperialism of Communist Russia, 2. Native Nationalism versus Western Nationalism, 3. Ambiguous Character of Nationalism in Asia and Africa, 4. Nationalism and Tribalism in Africa." The Eurocentrism of the study as evinced in these section headings continues to be apparent all through the text. "Native nationalism" serves as an umbrella term for all nationalism that is non-western. Definitions offered in the very first chapter, "What Nationalism is" set the frame within which one can process the terms "ambiguous" and "tribalism." The first chapter ends with the following assertion: "We shall note, as we go, that in its original form nationalism was simply an expression of tribalism, that then it declined and was displaced by broader loyalties, that its resurrection occurred in modern times and among traditional Christian peoples, that its full flowering in the West and its implanting elsewhere have been relatively recent" (pp. 18–19).

Hence, we are told from the very first that tribalism as an expression of nationalism has "declined" and yet, the section on African nationalism reinforces rather than questions this assertion – "tribalism is itself a type of nationalism, however primitive and on however small a scale" (p. 161). *Nationalism: a Religion* is typical of the studies on Nationalism written after the Second World War and at the beginning of the decade of African national independence. Metaphoric references to nationalism that emerges in every non-western instance as "imported seed" are common in all traditional studies on nationalism (p. 154). What such a reading of nationalism does to and for African and Asian nationalisms is to keep them in the place defined by words such as "ambiguous," "borrowed," and "transplanted" – that is, always doomed to be seen as alien from the very instances that root their existence.

3   See Partha Chatterjee, *National Thought and the Colonial World: A Derivative Discourse?* (London: Zed, 1986).

4   *Ibid.*, p. 11.

5   J. Douglas Porteous, "Home: The Territorial Core," *Geographical Review* 66, 4 (October 1976), pp. 383–90.

6   See Mary Layoun, "Telling Spaces: Palestinian women and the Engendering of National Narratives," in Andrew Parker et al., eds., *Nationalisms and Sexualities* (New York: Routledge, 1992), pp. 407–23.

7   Sara Suleri, *Rhetoric of English India* (Illinois: University of Chicago Press, 1992), p. 9.

8   However, as Tejeshwini Niranjana has so ably demonstrated, translation does not always require the acknowledgment of a difference which is recognized as positive and equal to that which it differs from. See *Siting Translations: History, Post-Structuralism, and the Colonial Context* (Berkeley: University of California Press, 1992).

9   Of course recent work in subaltern studies and on events that take place alongside national movements suggest that even the dominant narratives of nationalism are much more complex and variegated than my use of "common ground" would suggest.

10   Ngugi Wa Thiong'o, "The Writer in a Changing Society," *Homecoming* (London: Heinemann, 1972), p. 48.

11   Edward Said, *The World, The Text and The Critic* (Cambridge, MA: Harvard University Press, 1983), p. 8.

12   See Barbara Harlow, "The theoretical-historical context," *Resistance*

Literature (New York: Methuen Books, 1987), pp. 1–30. Here Ha[adapts Said's distinction between "filiation" and "affiliation" to fur her own examination of resistance literature. Like Said, Harlow locates and approves of the "social and political transformation from a geneal-ogy of 'filiation' based on ties of kinship, ethnicity, race, or religion to an 'affiliative' secular order" (p. 22).

13 Said, *The World*, p. 20.

14 In *Nationalism: A Religion*, Carlton Hayes in an analysis of patriotism, pro-vides a schema that is similar to Said's. Hayes draws on the distinction made in French between "patrie" (one's whole nation or fatherland) and "pays" (one's immediate homeland):

> Everybody, besides having a "patrie," has a "pays." My own "pays" is New York...This pays is for me a primary and most natural stimulus of patriotic senti-ment and loyalty. Yet I have been taught – and am expected – to extend this sen-timent and loyalty to such unfamiliar places as Alaska, North Dakota, Oklahoma and Utah, and at the same time to withhold them from Canada and Mexico.
> Similarly, loyalty to familiar persons – family, friends and neighbors – is natural and usual. But special civic training is required to make a man loyal to a sum total of persons, familiar and unfamiliar, who constitute his whole nationality.

Both Hayes and Said are bound by the vast space their theorizing maps to mistakenly define one set of affiliations as "natural and usual" and another as "learned or taught."

15 Jomo Kenyatta, *Facing Mt Kenya: The Tribal Life of the Gikuyu* (1st ed., 1938, New York: Random House, 1965), p. 305.

16 *Ibid.*. Such usurpation of land is more keenly felt when the economy is mainly agricultural – as was the case for the Gikuyu.

17 See Chandra Mohanty, "Introduction: Cartographies of Struggle," in Mohanty, Russo and Torres, eds., *Third World Women and the Politics of Feminism* (New York: Routledge, 1992), pp. 1–47. Also see Masao Miyoshi, "A Borderless World? From Colonialism to Transnationalism and the Decline of the Nation-State," *Critical Inquiry* 19 (Summer 1993), pp. 726–51.

18 Carl G. Jung, *Memories, Dreams and Reflections* (London: Collins, 1969), p. 253. See Clare Cooper, "The House as Symbol of the Self" in J. Lang et al, eds., *Designing for Human Behavior* (Philadelphia: Dowden, Hutchinson and Ross, 1974), pp. 130–46, for a Jungian approach to reading the "house."

19 Jung, *Memories*, p. 184.

20 *Ibid.*, p. 250.

21 See Gaston Bachelard, *The Poetics of Space* (Boston: Beacon Press, 1969); Clara Cooper, "The House as Symbol of the Self"; Adrian Forty, *Objects of Desire: Design and Society from Wedgwood to IBM* (New York: Pantheon, 1986); J. Douglas Porteous, "Home: The Territorial Core"; Witold Rybczynski, *Home: A Short History of an Idea*; E. Relph, *Places and*

Placelessness (London: Pion, 1976); David Sopher, "The Landscape of Home: Myth, Experience, Social Meaning," in D. W. Meinig, ed., *The Interpretations of Ordinary Landscapes: Geographical Essays* (England: Oxford University Press, 1979), pp. 129–49; Yi-Fu Tuan, *Space and Place: The Perspective of Experience* (Minneapolis: University of Minnesota Press, 1977).

22 See Gillian Rose, *Feminism and Geography: The Limits of Geographical Knowledge* (London: Blackwell, Polity, 1993), p. 47.

23 Porteous, *Home: The Territorial Core*, p. 383.

24 Sopher, "Landscape of Home", p. 147.

25 Yi-Fu Tuan, *Topophilia: A Study of Environment, Perception, Attitudes and Values* (New Jersey: Prentice-Hall, 1974).

26 See Vidler, *The Architectural Uncanny: Essays on the Modern Unhomely* (Cambridge MA: MIT Press, 1992), p. 55.

27 See Elsie De Wolfe, *The House in Good Taste* (New York, 1913) and Emily Post, *The Personality of A House* (New York, 1930). For brilliant approaches to the complex intertwinings of gender and space in colonial India, see Kumkum Sangari and Sudesh Vaid, eds., *Recasting Women: Essays in Colonial History* (New Delhi: Kali for Women, 1989). Also see Dipesh Chakrabarty, "The Difference-Deferral of (a) Colonial Modernity: Public Debates on Domesticity in British Bengal," *History Workshop*, 36 (Autumn 1993), pp. 1–34.

28 Hobsbawm notes that distinctions between the two worlds were not the simple divisions between industrialized and agricultural societies. He writes:

> The "second world" contained cities more ancient than and/or as enormous as the first: Peking, Constantinople. The nineteenth-century capitalist world market generated, within it, disproportionately large urban centers through which the flow of their economic relations was channeled: Melbourne, Buenos Aires, Calcutta, all had about half a million inhabitants each in the 1880s, which was larger than Amsterdam, Milan, Birmingham or Munich, while the three-quarters of a million of Bombay was larger than all but half-a-dozen cities in Europe. (p. 20)

Eric J. Hobsbawm, *The Age of Empire 1875–1914* (New York: Vintage, 1987).

29 E. M. Forster, *A Passage to India* (1924, New York: Harcourt, Brace, Jovanovich, 1984), p. 7.

30 Norma Evenson, *The Indian Metropolis: A View toward the West* (New Haven, CT: Yale University Press, 1989), p. 1.

31 See Bill Ashcroft, Gareth Griffiths, and Helen Tiffin, eds., *The Empire Writes Back: Theory and Practice in Postcolonial Literature* (London: Routledge, 1989). The editors identify the construction and demolition of houses as one of several recurrent themes in postcolonial fiction (p. 28). R. K. Narayan's first novel, *Swami and Friends* (1935 repr. East Lansing: Michigan State College Press, 1954), is an evocation of pastoral innocence and the unshakably solid notions of family and community within

which young Swaminathan lives. It would be interesting to compare this representation of childhood with later representations of the precocious, maladjusted child on whose body, mind and psyche the rigors of colonialism leaves its scars (in the work of postcolonial writers such as Rushdie, Ngugi Wa Thiong'o, Jamaica Kincaid, Tahir Ben-Jalud, Buchi Emecheta, Joan Riley and Amitava Ghosh).

32 For an incisive assessment of home-making in Southern California, see Mike Davis, "Fortress L. A.," *City of Quartz* (New York: Vintage, 1992), pp. 223–63. Clara Cooper in "The House as Symbol of the Self" briefly dwells on the consequences of the equation of home and self in US culture: "The frontier image of man clearing the land and building a cabin for himself and his family is not far behind us. To a culture inbred with this image, the house-self identity is particularly strong. In some barely conscious way, society has decided to penalize those who, through no fault of their own cannot build, buy or rent their own housing. They are not self-made men" (p. 133). According to Cooper, it is these factors that account for the general resistance to subsidized housing in the US.

33 Michel Foucault, "The Subject and Power," in Hubert L. Dreyfus and Paul Rabinow, eds., *Michel Foucault: Beyond Structuralism and Hermeneutics* (Illinois: University of Chicago Press, 1982), p. 212. The quotation is taken from the section entitled "Why Study Power: The Question of the Subject" which was written in English by Foucault.

34 And yet, in the early novels of two established women writers from India, Santha Rama Rau (*Home to India* [1945, repr. New York: Harper Brothers 1956], and *Remember this House* [New York: Harper Brothers 1954]) and Kamala Markandaya (*Some Inner Fury* [New York: J. Day & Co., 1956]), there is a firmly and proudly presented assertion that for a certain (wealthy, educated, upper-caste) "cultured" Indian there is a secure and full-fledged "self." This colonial subject is at home in Indian and English settings and very aware of being culturally on a par with the English colonials she encounters. While the class-attributes of the postcolonial novel in English need to be acknowledged it is never as simple as reading class (and in this case, caste) into the script. Bessie Head's *Maru* (1971) provides a good example of the many inflections within such novels. The character of Dikeledi is similar to that of the beautiful, idealistic, self-possessed, upper-class young women in the novels by these Indian women. Yet, Head's portrayal of Dikeledi as the ideal modern young African woman is undercut by her representation of Maru who has the same credentials except for the crucial one of race purity and is therefore unsuccessful in her struggle for subjecthood.

35 For a nuanced discussion of "the return of the subject" in postcolonial scenarios, see Homi K. Bhabha, "Postcolonial Criticism" in Stephen Greenblatt and Giles Gunn, eds., *Redrawing the Boundaries* (New York: MLA, 1992), pp. 437–65.

36 See p. 191, Biddy Martin and Chandra Talpade Mohanty, "Feminist

Politics: What's Home Got to Do with It?" in Theresa de Lauretis, ed., *Feminist Studies/Critical Studies* (Bloomington: Indiana University Press, 1986), pp. 191–212.

37 In "The Subject and Power" Foucault notes that his own work examines: "the way a human being turns him– or herself into a subject ... I have chosen the domain of sexuality – how men have learned to recognize themselves as subjects of "sexuality" (p. 208).

38 Minnie Bruce Pratt, "Identity: Skin Blood Heart" in Minnie Bruce Pratt, Elly Bulkin and Barbara Smith, *Yours in Struggle: Three Feminist Perspectives on Anti-Semitism and Racism* (New York: Long Haul Press, 1984), pp. 11–63.

39 Martin and Mohanty, "Feminist Politics," p. 191.

40 *Ibid.*, p. 196.

41 *Ibid.*, p. 197.

42 *Ibid.*, p. 47.

43 See Witold Rybezynski, *Home: A Short History of an Idea*. In his preface, Rybezynski declares that his aim in writing this book was to further his own education on the importance of comfort – an aspect of design that was ignored in the architectural training he received. Rybezynski goes on to examine what his chapter headings ("Intimacy and Privacy," "Domesticity," "Ease," "Efficiency" etc.) suggest – all, apparently, basic, indisputable attributes of "home."

44 Caren Kaplan, "Deterritorializations: The Rewriting of Home and Exile in Western Feminist Discourse," *Cultural Critique* 6 (Spring 1987), pp. 187–98. Kaplan explains that "'Deterritorialization' is one term for the displacement of identities, persons, and meanings that is endemic to the postmodern world system. Deleuze and Guattari use the term 'deterritorialization' to locate this moment of alienation and exile in language and literature...This defamiliarization enables imagination, even as it produces alienation" (p. 188).

45 Michelle Cliff, *Claiming an Identity They Taught Me to Despise* (Watertown, MA: Persephone Press, 1980); Gilles Deleuze and Felix Guattari, "What is a Minor Literature?" in *Kafka: Toward a Minor Literature*, Dana Polan, trans. (Minneapolis: University of Minnesota Press, 1986). This formulation of "Minor Literature" is further examined in later chapters of this book.

46 Kaplan, "Deterritorializations," p. 191.

47 *Ibid.*, p. 189. Here Kaplan uses the terms and theory of Immanuel Wallerstein as formulated in *The Modern World System* (New York: Academic Press, 1974). Very briefly, Wallerstein's "world systems theory" proposes that different countries, rather than operating in a dynamic of dependency, are all equally implicated in a global economic relationship that has central and marginal positions. As Kaplan's use of this economic theory demonstrates, it has the potential to serve as a model for cultural dynamics between margin and center. Crucial to Wallerstein's theory is

the assertion that those at the margins are not passive recipients in this relationship.

48 Kaplan, "Deterritorializations", p. 191.

49 I return to this topic of cultural baggage in chapter 6. While the focus in that chapter is on counter readings of nation and home through immigrant literature, it should be evident that what is also resisted is the use of "the minor" and of minority status as a place that unilaterally confers redemption.

50 Kaplan, "Deterritorializations", p. 194.

51 *Ibid.*, pp. 189–90.

52 Michele Cliff, *Claiming an Identity*, p. 52.

53 Kaplan, "Deterritorializations," pp. 197–8. One needs to note that both Cliff and Pratt's texts are autobiographical. The theorizing that is present in both texts are born of location adjustments Cliff and Pratt make in their own lives as they record their respective personal agendas of claiming and rejecting identity. If one pays attention to the politics of location how can we expect Woolf to speak from the borderlands? Demanding "a room of one's own" was, from Woolf's location, a radical manifesto.

54 See p. 87, Mohanty, "Feminist Encounters: Locating the Politics of Experience," in Michele Barrett and Anne Phillips, eds., *Destabilizing Theory: Contemporary Feminist Debates* (Stanford University Press, 1992), pp. 74–92.

55 See p. 15, "Choosing the Margin as a Space of Radical Openness," bell hooks, *Framework* 36 (Special Issue, "Third Scenario: Theory and The Politics of Location", 1989, pp. 15–24.

56 Rose, *Feminism and Geography*, pp. 158–9.

57 Bernice Johnson Reagon, "Coalition Politics: Turning the Century," in Barbara Smith, ed., *Home Girls: A Black Feminist Anthology* (New York: Kitchen Table, Press, 1983), pp. 356–68.

58 "Feminist Criticism, 'The Yellow Wallpaper and the Politics of Color in America," Susan S. Lanser, *Feminist Studies* 15, 3, Fall 1989, pp. 415–41. Further references to this article will be made by the page number in the text.

59 I use the term "safe-home" to deliberately complicate matters by using the term employed by some volunteer women's organizations to refer to their practice of offering women who wish to escape domestic violence an alternative, *safe* house to live in until they can decide on their future. Can one question the safety offered by such safe-houses or question the exclusion of the spouse who inflicted the domestic abuse from such safe-houses? I think not.

2. THE AUTHORITATIVE ENGLISHWOMAN

1 Crowther et al, eds., "Facts for Visitors: Women Travelers," *Lonely Planet Travel Survival Kit: India* (New York: Lonely Planet, 1990), p. 71. Elizabeth Fox-Genovese, "Placing Women's History in History," *New Left Review* 133 (May/June 1982), p. 29.

2 Kaplan's essay is an exceptionally nuanced example of recent feminist criticism that tries to formulate ways of rectifying the flaws of 70s and 80s white feminism by advocating that white women move outside the comfort zone of their relative privilege. While this stance does enhance one's understanding of what and who was left out of earlier decades of feminist theorizing and praxis, my contention is that such travel has a prior parallel in the advent of benevolent imperial women on the colonies. I will argue that this prior moment of travel had as far reaching implications for feminism at that time as our contemporary, feminist "nomads" might have on the future of western feminism. See chapter 1 for a more sustained discussion of this article. Caren Kaplan, "Deterritorializations: The Rewriting of Home and Exile in Western Feminist Discourse," *Cultural Critique* 6 (Spring 1987), pp. 187–98. For more recent work on the topic by Kaplan and collaborators, see Inderpal Grewal and Caren Kaplan, eds., *Scattered Hegemonies: Postmodernity and Transnational Feminist Practices* (Minneapolis: Minnesota University Press, 1994).

3 Kaplan, "Deterritorializations," p. 197. See Gilles Deleuze and Felix Guattari, "What is a Minor Literature?" in *Kafka: Towards a Minor Literature*, Dana Polan, trans. (Minneapolis: University of Minnesota Press, 1986), p. 17.

4 Kaplan, "Deterritorializations," pp. 194–5.

5 The "Indian sub-continent" includes contemporary Pakistan, India, Bangladesh, parts of Afghanistan and smaller nations such as Myanmar and Nepal. The East India Company was in the area from as early as the sixteenth century. With the mutiny/revolt of 1857, control of the area passed from the company to the British crown. In 1947, colonial India was partitioned into two independent countries – Pakistan and India. In 1972, East Pakistan declared its independence and became Bangladesh after warring with West Pakistan.

6 Fox-Genovese, "Placing Women's History," p. 26.

7 For an astute and nuanced analysis of the various, conflicting representations of memsahibs, see Jenny Sharpe, "The Rise of Memsahibs in an Age of Empire: *On the Face of the Waters*," in *Allegories of Empire: The Figure of Woman in the Colonial Text* (Minneapolis: University of Minnesota Press, 1993), pp. 85–112.

8 See Janaki Nair's "Uncovering the *Zenana*: Visions of Indian Womanhood in Englishwomen's writings, 1813–1840," in Cheryl Johnson-Odim and Margaret Strobel, eds., *Expanding the Boundaries of Women's History: Essays on Women in the Third World* (Bloomington: Indiana University Press, 1992), pp. 26–50, for a useful discussion of how and why the only Indian women represented in Englishwomen's texts were those whose communities practiced a gendered separation of domestic space. *Zenana* women then were read as representative of all Indian women (p. 29).

9 Nancy Armstrong, *Desire and Domestic Fiction: A Political History of the Novel* (England: Oxford University Press, 1987), p. 66.

10 Ellen Carol DuBois, "Woman Suffrage and the Left: An International Socialist-Feminist Perspective," *New Left Review* 186 (March/April 1991), p. 24. Here DuBois argues against the accepted reading of woman's suffrage movements as conservative Faustian bargains made at the cost of other political freedoms for all women. She maintains that in the period from 1890 to 1920, women's suffrage was a "left" or "militant" demand that "reflected the existence and vigor of both the socialist and feminist movements" (p. 23). See, also by DuBois, "The Radicalism of the Woman Suffrage Movement: Notes Toward the Reconstruction of Nineteenth-Century Feminism," in Anne Phillips, ed., *Feminism and Equality* (New York: New York University Press, 1987).

11 Anna Davin, "Imperialism and Motherhood," *History Workshop* 5 (1978), p. 26.

12 J. E. Gemmell, "Presidential Address, North of England Obstetrical and Gynaecological Society," *Journal of Obstetrics and Gynaecology of the British Empire* (December 1903), p. 590, quoted in Davin, "Imperialism and Motherhood," p. 21.

13 "There is, as we have repeatedly learned, no fluent trajectory from feminism to a truly sexually democratic humanism; there is no easy passage from 'women' to 'humanity'." Denise Riley, *"Am I that Name?" Feminism and the Category of "Women" in History* (Minneapolis: University of Minnesota, 1988), p. 17.

14 For instance, despite focusing on the issue of English women's authority (in the period between 1890 and 1920) in the context of women's rights, the vote, the debate on public and private spheres etc., Ellen DuBois does not mention imperialism or the establishment of homes in the colonies. Carole Pateman's otherwise comprehensive study of the public/private debate, is also silent on the issue of imperialism. See Carole Pateman, "Critiques of the Public/Private Dichotomy" in *Feminism and Equality*, pp. 103–26. The exceptions invariably focus directly on imperialism as is the case with the earlier cited article by Anna Davin entitled "Imperialism and Motherhood." Antoinette Burton's "The White Woman's Burden: British Feminism and 'The Indian Women,'" in Nipur Chaudhuri and Margaret Strobel, eds., *Western Women and Imperialism: Complicity and Resistance* (Bloomington: Indiana University Press, 1992), pp. 137–57, maps the "influence of imperial culture on late nineteenth-century feminist ideology" through an examination of Josephine Butler and other English feminists' efforts to bring about female educational and medical reforms in India in this period (p. 137). Burton painstakingly demonstrates how the Indian empire and Indian women were seen as the logical wider field of operation open to committed English feminists. Vron Ware's "Britannia's Other Daughters: Feminism in the Age of Imperialism," in *Beyond the Pale: White Women, Racism and History* (New York: Verso, 1992), pp. 119–66, also insists that "feminist ideology and practice were shaped by the social, economic and political forces of imperialism to a far greater extent than has

been acknowledged" (p. 119). Burton and Ware's arguments differ substantially from each other and from my overarching argument in this chapter. Burton concludes her essay by noting that "British feminists of the period were trapped within an imperial discourse *they did not create* and perhaps which they could not escape. That they collaborated in the ideological work of empire implicates them and the legacy of Western feminism we have inherited from them" (p. 152; emphasis added). In this chapter I demonstrate the ways in which English women did actively create these feminist/imperial discourses of women's self-worth and their national value. Ware examines the potential in English women to participate in "the political emancipation of the colonies" in the course of their feminist activism for and alongside Indian women. My concern is with how the colonies (and their women) participated in the political emancipation of English women. Jenny Sharpe's *Allegories of Empire* is also centrally concerned with the proximity of gender and imperial ideologies.

15 See Margaret Strobel, *European Women and the Second British Empire* (Bloomington: Indiana University Press, 1991). Here the white woman's authority is measured against white-male authority and not seen in terms of the entire hierarchy of power that girded the colonial world. Strobel argues: "If European women found opportunity in the second British Empire, they also continuously experienced, sometimes challenged, and sometimes reinforced the economic, political, and ideological subordination of women" (pp. xi–xii). Later in this study, Strobel notes that European women travelers in the empire "couched their interest in terms of service, not self-actualization" (p. 61). Again and again, in the contemporary feminist scholarship on gender, there is an unwillingness to examine both race and gender dimensions of power in *the same utterance*.

16 See 176–7, Gayatri Chakravorty Spivak, "Three Women's Texts and A Critique of Imperialism," in Catherine Belsey and Jane Moore, eds., *The Feminist Reader: Essays in Gender and the Politics of Literary Criticism* (London: Blackwell, 1989), pp. 175–96 and pp. 237–40.

17 In the seventeenth and eighteenth century women were sent by the shipload in what was called "fishing fleets," to search for husbands in India. Such arrangements were made by the East India Company for whom these men worked. Margaret MacMillan writes: "The cargo, divided into 'gentlewomen' and 'others', were given one set of clothes each and were supported for a year – quite long enough, it was thought, for them to find themselves husbands", *Women of the Raj* (London: Thames and Hudson, 1988), p. 17. The journey took as long as six months. The invention of steam power and the opening of the Suez Canal in 1869 helped shorten the trip to about four weeks. This, as well as the establishment of large administrative and military institutions that accompanied all colonial governments, increased the number of English women who traveled to India in the capacity of wife, sister, fiancée, daughter and missionary. Yet, throughout the British rule in India,

European men outnumbered European women three to one. In 1881 when the first India-wide census was taken, there were 145,000 Europeans out of a total population of 250,000,000. In 1921 there were 165,000 Europeans. Half of these Europeans lived in the cities and larger towns; specially in Calcutta and Bombay. When the British capital was moved from Calcutta to Delhi in 1911, the English population in that city mushroomed. Karachi (in present-day Pakistan) and Madras were other cities with sizable white populations in the early decades of this century (p. 42). Also see: Pat Barr, *The Memsahibs: In Praise of the Women of Victorian India* (London: Century Press, 1976); Marian Fowler, *Below the Peacock Fan: First Ladies of the Raj* (London: Penguin, 1987).

18 Maud Diver, *The Englishwoman in India* (London: Blackwood, 1909). Hereafter cited in the text as *EI*. This epigraph which appears on the unnumbered first page is attributed to Count Jon Konigsmark, *Die Englanders in Indien*. Benita Parry's biographical note on Maud Diver tells us that she was born in 1867 in India. The daughter of a Colonel in the Indian Army, she married Lieutenant-Colonel Diver when he was a sub-altern in the Indian Army. At twenty-nine, she settled in England and began writing her many novels on the British in India. See Parry's *Delusions and Discoveries: Studies on India in the British Imagination* (Berkeley: University of California Press, 1979) p. 79.

19 Riley, *"Am I that Name,"* p. 51.

20 *Ibid.*, p. 49.

21 Gayatri Spivak, "Three Women's Texts and a Critique of Imperialism," p. 185.

22 DuBois, "The Radicalism of the Woman Suffrage Movement," p. 128.

23 DuBois, "Woman Suffrage and the Left," p. 37.

24 See Carole Pateman, "Feminist Critiques of the Private/Public Dichotomy," for a comprehensive summary of the different feminist and liberal positions on the public/private debate since the publication of Locke's *Second Treatise* which, according to Pateman, set the theoretical basis for the liberal separation of the public and private.

25 Fox-Genovese, "Placing Women's History in History," p. 22.

26 *Ibid.*, p. 26.

27 Suzanne Howe, *Novels of Empire* (New York: Columbia University Press, 1949).

28 *Ibid.*, p. 32.

29 *Ibid.*, p. 35.

30 *Ibid.*, p. 34.

31 Parry uses the term Anglo-Indian to refer to the English who worked in and set up house in the Indian sub-continent. After Independence, in India, the term signifies those Indians who claim some proportion of English, Portuguese or other European blood.

32 See Robin Jared Lewis, "The Literature of the Raj" in *Asia in Western Fiction*, ed. Robin W. Winks and James R. Rush (Honolulu: University of

Hawaii, 1990) pp. 53–70. Lewis divides British writing about India into three periods: the era of romance (1800–57), the era of orthodoxy (1857–1914) and the era of doubt and disillusionment (1919–47). Lewis constructs a history of Raj Literature that is almost exclusively masculine in its authors, readership, desires, impact and even in the attention paid to female characters in the fiction. Except for stray references to unnamed women writers there is no sustained evaluation of the contribution of women writers to this literary genre. Lewis notes that the "novel of mixed marriage" which belong to the second period and were very popular, "were didactic tracts masquerading as imaginative fiction" and were written primarily by women. As with Parry's assessment, the suggestion here is that the texts by the many male writers that Lewis discusses were less didactic and "more imaginative." The reading list he provides at the end of the article does however include five women writers: Ruth Prawer Jhabvala, Mary Kaye, Alice Perrin, Flora Anne Steel, Mary Sherwood. The logic of including Jhabvala's and Kaye's work is hard to locate given that their novels were written in the 1960s and 1970s.

33 Parry, *Delusions and Discoveries*, p. 6.

34 Perhaps the difference between Parry's entry into this arena and mine can be simply attributed to the fact that her book was published before Said's influential *Orientalism* and mine comes after *Orientalism* and its critique.

35 Maud Diver, *Captain Desmond V.C.* (New York: Grosset and Dunlap, 1914), p. 6. In 1914, Diver published this revised version of her novel *Captain Desmond V.C.* which was to become the first in her series of novels set on the northwest border region of the Indian empire. The novel will be cited hereafter in the text as *CD*.

36 In the British Empire, the threat of violence enacted by the "black" male on the "white" female was constructed via prohibitory laws and restrictions on both parties. In the discourse of empire, this violence was always represented as sexual and illegitimate unlike the representation of relationships between white men and colonized women which was coded in terms of love and marriage between a subordinate wife and a masterful husband. Not surprisingly, the enterprise of imperialism was often similarly represented – see Theresa Hubel, "'The Bride of his Country': Love, Marriage, and the Imperialist Paradox in the Indian Fiction of Sara Jeanette Duncan and Rudyard Kipling," *Ariel: A Review of International English Literature*, 21: 1 (January 1990), pp. 3–19. The protest campaign mounted by English women against the introduction of the Ilbert Bill in British India in 1883, was partly on the grounds that this Bill (which was to allow Indian magistrates to judge criminal cases involving Europeans in rural areas) would increase the (natives') temptation to rape white women and in any case would violate their privacy. See Mrinalini Sinha's "'Chathams, Pitts, and Gladstones in Petticoats': The Politics of Gender and Race in the Ilbert Bill Controversy, 1883–1884" in Chaudhuri and Strobel, eds., *Western Women and Imperialism*, pp. 98–116. Also see Sharpe, *Allegories of Empire*, pp. 89–91.

Laws such as the White Woman's Protection Ordinance (Papua, New Guinea 1926) brought into legislation the death penalty for rape and attempted rape of white women At the time of its passage, Strobel writes, no white women had been raped in Papua, (*European Women and the Second British Empire*, pp. 5–6), and yet such a harsh law was considered quite necessary. Desmond's brutal "punitive expeditions" operate on the same logic of setting up the punishment and administering it before the crime can be committed.

37 Maud Diver, *Unconquered: A Romance* (London: G. P. Putnam's Sons, 1917). Hereafter cited in the text as *UR*.

38 It is interesting to note that the title and contents of Bel's speech "Women and War" echo very closely the concerns of the well-known feminist, pacifist, and public speaker, Vera Brittain.

39 "Hill-Station" is a term that was used in British India (and continues to be in usage) to refer to holiday resort towns that were constructed in mountain locales with moderate temperatures during the hottest months of the year.

40 Maud Diver, *EI.*

41 The contrasts are also illustrative for the ways in which Diver replaces the prevailing stereotype of the Kipling variety of "memsahib" with her own more positive ones. Evelyn, like the memsahibs disparaged by Kipling and others, "does not like natives" and admits to being frightened of them. She does not inspire respect or fear in her servants, nor does she care enough to rectify the situation. She does not know how to and does not want to economize on household and personal expenditure. She gets into debt and, despite her husband's many cautionary speeches, secretly borrows money from an undesirable (i.e., "half-breed") admirer. She flirts with men in her husband's regiment. She chafes at being stationed at the frontier with limited social events, and she is happiest on holiday away from home where she is willing to be flattered into the impropriety of an "affair." She is easily bored, unenterprising and not entertained by intellectual pursuits such as reading or playing chess. She is squeamish and unable to nurse her wounded husband competently.

Honor in contrast, silently loves her man and is always his friend and confidante. She is the perfect, unflappable house-keeper, shooting rabid dogs and preparing laundry lists with equanimity. She lives within her allowance and thus has a kind of financial independence that she prides herself on. Hence, she can step in and save her friend Evelyn much disgrace by paying off her debts. Honor is physically strong, she is a good rider who shoots well and has nerves of steel. She plays the piano and chess and thus can entertain herself and Desmond. She is "sympathetic to natives" and hence wins the respect of Evelyn's servants. Honor is honored by all; Desmond's servants approvingly foretell that she will one day be a "burra Memsahib" – for even they recognize and admire "star" memsahib material when they see it (*CD*, pp. 68–9). She gains the approval of the men in Desmond's regiment because unlike Evelyn she does not begrudge the claims that the regiment has on Desmond. She loves the India that belongs to Desmond and her.

42 F. A. Steel and G. Gardiner, *The Complete Indian Housekeeper and Cook: Giving the Duties of Mistress and Servants, the General Management of the House and Practical Recipes for Cooking in all its Branches* (London: Heinemann, 1917 edn.). This work will hereafter be cited in the text as *CIH*. It is interesting to read quite a different assessment of Flora Anne Steel and of this text as represented in Strobel's study: "A famous and indefatigable British woman from the late nineteenth century, Flora Anne Steel, coauthored the indispensable *Complete Indian Housekeeper and Cook*. Married at twenty to an officer in the Indian Civil Service, she took advantage of the relative isolation of his posting to learn several vernacular languages and dialects and accompany him on his inspection tours. In addition to compiling the hints that comprise her book, she designed the town hall where she lived, wrote on the oppression of small landowners by usurers, served as a semi-official school inspector in the Punjab, and worked for Indian women's education" (*European Women and the Second British Empire*, p. 8). To Strobel, Steel represents a positive and therefore "heartening" figure but one who is, "unfortunately," an exceptional aberration on all counts. I argue that Steel helped to construct the exemplar figure of the competent memsahib both through her written exhortations and through her personal self-fashioning.

43 Other writers in the discourse of empire reiterate this point. For instance, George Newman, author of *Infant Mortality* (1906) and the first Chief Medical Officer of Health to the Board of Education (appointed 1907) believed that homes were the vital core of a nation and that the British Empire depended "not upon dominions and territory alone, but upon men, not markets alone, but upon homes." Quoted in Davin, "Imperialism and Motherhood," p. 31.

44 The sentence in "Kitchen Hindi" exhibits the usual distortions of tense, gender and syntax. What is especially noteworthy is that the writers present this sentence as a direct quotation from the speech of Indian servants who are in the process represented as not having mastery over their own language. One could also read this casual insertion of "the native language" as an authorial demonstration of cultural and linguistic familiarity – an ease that is quite oblivious of linguistic errors.

45 Contemporary feminist scholars who write on the English women in the empire usually stress the many ways in which the class division in England was carried over and even inflated in its purchase over daily life. Hence Strobel, Fowler, MacMillan and Barr spend much effort in understanding and explaining the details of the rules of precedence that governed the social interactions of the British in the colonies. They list the many seemingly insignificant markers that made clear the class and rank hierarchy within any assembled group of British citizens. To break precedence or

"dastur" (a favorite Hindi word among colonists) as in ignoring rank while seating one's guests at dinner was to violently shake the established order of imperial hierarchy. Yet the overwhelming superiority of the Englishwoman on the lowest rung of the precedence ladder to any and all Indian men and women is not brought into *this* analysis. Not that this very obvious fact of the life of the female colonist is ignored by contemporary scholars but that such issues of white women's authority over the colonized are dealt with as if it were an entirely different and unrelated concern.

46 Timothy Mitchell, *Colonizing Egypt* (England: Cambridge University Press, 1988), p. 35.

47 What is to be noted here is that there were sustained debates about domesticity and varying assessments of the value of adopting European modes that were produced within specific Indian narratives of this period. See Dipesh Chakrabarty, "The Difference–Deferral of (a) Colonial Modernity: Public Debates on Domesticity in British Bengal" *History Workshop* 36 (Autumn 1993), pp. 1–34, for an in-depth analysis of the discourses that constructed middle-class domesticity (and thereby, Bengali Modernity) in colonial Bengal. Chakrabarty demonstrates the means by which this specific Indian domesticity is fashioned from the *gri-halakshmi* and memsahib articulations of public and private space. Also see Partha Chatterjee, "The Nationalist Resolution of the Women's Question," in Kumkum Sangari and Sudesh Vaid, eds., *Recasting Women: Essays in Colonial History* (New Delhi: Kali For Women, 1989) pp. 233–53, for discussion on the representation of memsahibs and the category of "mem-sahib like behavior" that was produced in the nineteenth and early twentieth-century discourses on educational, domestic and other social reform in Bengal.

48 Hilda Wernher, *My Indian Family: A Story of East and West within an Indian Home* (New York: John Day, 1945 edn.). Cited hereafter in the text as *MIF*.

49 This metaphor of letting English light into dark Indian homes is popular with several writers of colonial texts. Writing about the Lady Dufferin medical aid scheme (the details about which are available later in this paper) Maud Diver writes: "its ultimate aim is to roll away the stones from before the darkened doors; to flood the dim, cobwebbed corners of India's homes with the life-giving light of healing truth and love" (*EI*, p. 102).

50 For more information on the activities of prominent Indian women in the political and social spheres see Kumari Jayawardena, *Feminism and Nationalism in the Third World* (Zed Books, 1986), especially the sections called "Agitation by Women" and "Women in Political Action" in the chapter entitled "Women, Social Reform and Nationalism in India," pp. 73–109. Maud Diver's *The Englishwoman In India* contains a second, shorter section that follows the one entitled "The Englishwoman in India." This second section, entitled "Pioneer Women of India," contains short chapters on Pundita Ramabai, Dr. Anandabai Joshee, Maharani of Kuch

Behar and Cornelia Sarabji, all of whom had broken out of the conventional role prescribed to Indian women. While Diver praises these women, she repeatedly stresses that they were exceptions and, she concludes, albeit regretfully, that most of their lives and efforts were futile. The early deaths and chronic illnesses of these women are taken by Diver as proof of the fact that Indian women could not bear the mental and physical strain that leading a public life would demand from them.

51 bell hooks, *"Ain't I a Woman?" Black Women and Feminism* (Boston: Southend Press, 1981), p. 3.

52 See Gayatri Chakravorty Spivak, "French Feminism in an International Frame," *In Other Worlds: Essays in Cultural Politics* (Routledge: New York, 1988), pp. 134–53. Spivak writes, "in order to learn enough about Third World women and to develop a different readership, the immense heterogeneity of the field must be appreciated, and the First World feminist must learn to stop feeling privileged as a *woman*" (p. 136). In the conclusion to the same essay, Spivak writes that her emphasis on heterogeneity, discontinuity and topology may not "necessarily escape the inbuilt colonialism of First World feminism toward the third. It might, one hopes, promote a sense of our common yet history-specific lot" (p. 153). This passage from *My Indian Family* demonstrates that wanting "to learn enough" or even having this knowledge about third world women does not necessarily challenge this inbuilt colonialism. The European woman imperialist very often possessed a minute knowledge of her racial Others and of the "immense heterogeneity of the field." The narrator of Wernher's novel proudly and repeatedly displayed her easy understanding of the cultural differences between Indians from various parts of India, of different religions, castes, class backgrounds etc. Yet it is this very knowledge that supports her overarching knowledge of her superiority as a white woman.

53 During the recent Gulf war, in western commentaries on the status of Saudi women, the assessments were always defined by two factors: the veil and the prohibition to drive. The American woman soldier stationed in the desert was in contrast a manifestation of gender equality heaven that is the US and her emancipation was measured in her all-but equal opportunity to kill and die for her government.

54 I would like to draw attention to the statement on celibacy. The oddity of this particular comment arises from the fact that it is inserted in a text on household management. The premise of the household is based on marriage and procreation – the very opposite of celibacy. Yet, I don't think there is any ironic or unconscious aligning of "Christian" alongside "Hindu and Mohommadan" when celibacy is at issue. Do we read irony in the very next statement which begins "by means of this patriarchal system"? Again I do not think that Diver means to suggest that we read the English household arrangement as implicated in the term "this patriarchal system." If there is so much as the slightest doubt that there is, in this passage, some acknowledgment of commonalities between the

English domestic arrangements and those of the "patriarchal system" of "the Hindu and Mohommadan" then the use of the word "chance" in the last sentence should lay such suspicions to rest.

55 The Marchioness of Dufferin, wife of the British Viceroy (highest government official) in India in the 1880s, started the Female Medical Aid Fund, also called the Dufferin Fund to provide medical tuition for women in India (English and Indian) and thereby provide women and children in India with medical care that was administered solely by women.

56 Nancy Rose Hunt, "Domesticity and Colonialism in Belgian Africa: Usumbura's Foyer Social, 1946–1960," *Signs: Journal of Women in Culture and Society* 15, 3 (1990), pp. 447–74.

57 From the duties for four lady health visitors appointed by Birmington County Council in 1899, published in *Public Health* (August 1899), p. 721. Quoted by Anna Davin in "Imperialism and Motherhood," p. 37. See Davin's article for an in depth analysis of the ramifications of empire on the domestic life of the Englishwoman in England in the late nineteenth and early twentieth centuries. See Antoinette Burton's "White Women's Burden" for detailed discussion on the links between social reform in England and in the empire.

58 Janaki Nair's "Uncovering the *Zenana*" is exceptionally insightful on this issue.

59 Chatterjee, "The Nationalist Resolution of the Women's Question" p. 249. Cited hereafter in the text by page number.

60 Mitchell, *Colonizing Egypt*, p. 60.

61 See Penelope Dell, *Nettie and Sissie: The Biography of Ethel M. Dell and Ella* (London: Hamish Hamilton, 1977), pp. 69, 97. Clearly, Ethel Dell did not believe that a visit to India would enhance the quality of her novels set there – what she needed to know, she picked up from guidebooks, novels and from *Illustrated London News*. When her husband Lieutenant Colonel Gerald Savage was commissioned to go to India in the early 1920s, Dell insisted that he refuse the order. To refuse a commission was to give up one's career and Savage's military career was henceforth limited to serving as a reserve officer in England.

62 Mary N. Layoun, "Deserts of Memory," *Travels of a Genre: The Modern Novel and Ideology* (Princeton University Press, 1990), pp. 177–208.

63 *Ibid.*, p. 203.

64 See Edward Said's remarkable "Reflections on Exile" in Russell Ferguson, Martha Gever, Trinh T. Minh-ha, and Cornel West, eds., *Out There: Marginalization and Contemporary Cultures* (Cambridge, MA: M. I. T. Press, 1990), pp. 357–66. Here Said urges us to understand exile not through Joyce and Nabokov, but instead "to think of the uncountable masses for whom UN agencies have been created" (p. 359).

65 Rebecca Saunders, "Gender, Colonialism and Exile: Flora Anne Steele and Sara Jeanette Duncan in India," in Mary Lynn Broe and Angela Ingram, eds., *Women's Writing in Exile* (Chapel Hill, NC: University of

North Carolina Press, 1989), pp. 304–24. Maud Diver (in 1909) among others refers to the English women in India as exiles (*EI*, p. 33), Suzanne Howe (in 1949) calls them "ladies in exile" (*Novels of Empire*, p. 43).

66 In 1987, Helen Callaway published an ethnographic study of colonial women, *Gender, Culture and Empire: European Women in Colonial Nigeria* (Chicago: University of Illinois Press, 1987) in which her self-proclaimed agenda was to reverse the negative representation (in literary and other texts) of these women. Despite being "doubly alien" in the colonies, these women Callaway feels, were made to unfairly bear the blame for the excesses of empire. Perhaps the vast literature on Isabelle Eberhardt (1877–1904), the woman from Geneva who fashioned herself as a nomad and/or exile and who adopted Algeria as her homeland, provides the best examples of this use of the term "exile."

67 Thus, in *Captain Desmond*, the Kresneys' lack of the correct English accent is metonymic of their "taint of mixed blood." The following passage from the novel is illustrative: "Miss Kresney's insistence on the consonants and the final vowels was more marked than her brother's; for although three-fourths of the blood in her veins was English, very few of her intimate associates could make so proud a boast without perjuring their souls: and there are few things more infectious than tricks of speech" (*CD*, p. 84).

68 For a detailed discussion of the vexed status of white English women as national citizens under the law, see the excellent 1985 study by WING (Women for Immigration and Nationality Group). Jacqueline Bhabha et al, *Worlds Apart: Women under Immigration and Nationality Law* (London: Pluto Press, 1985).

69 The fear – of the working classes, of public lives for women as well as of their power over the domestic, of masses that could not be contained and disciplined, of competition from other colonial powers, of change, of the brown and black masses – all these features of British culture find voice in his novels. While other high modernists' texts refer obliquely to these cultural pathologies, none make them central foci as they are in the Conradian text.

3 THE GREAT ENGLISH TRADITION: CONRAD WRITES HOME

1 Salman Rushdie, *The Satanic Verses* (New York: Viking Press, 1988), p. 337. The first epigraph is taken from Conrad's "A Glance at Two Books," quoted by Ian Watt, *Conrad in the Nineteenth Century* (Berkeley, CA: University of California Press, 1979), p. 48.

2 See by Terry Eagleton, *Exiles and Emigres* (New York: Schocken Books, 1970); Eagleton, "Form, Ideology and *The Secret Agent*," in *Against the Grain: Essays 1975–1985* (London: Verso, 1986), pp. 23–32; Eagleton, "Ideology and Literary Form," in *Criticism and Ideology: A Study in Marxist Literary Theory* (London: Verso, 1976), pp. 102–61. Also see Fredric Jameson,

"Romance and Reification," in *The Political Unconscious: Narrative as a Socially Symbolic Act* (Ithaca, NY: Cornell University Press, 1981), pp. 206–81; Jameson, "Modernism and Imperialism," in Seamus Deane, ed., *Nationalism, Colonialism, and Literature* (Minneapolis: University of Minnesota Press/Field Day Company, 1990), pp. 43–68. Terry Collits offers an interesting assessment of Eagleton and Jameson's reading of Conrad's fiction in "Imperialism, Marxism, Conrad: A Political Reading of *Victory*," *Textual Practice* 3 (Winter, 1989), pp. 303–22. Collits' purpose in critiquing Eagleton and Jameson is to demonstrate that changing Marxist assessments of imperialism over the twentieth century have resulted in corresponding changes in the Marxist readings of politics in Conradian texts. There is vast scholarship on Conrad's fiction although very little discussion of his ambiguous ideological position as an insider/outsider, his representations of the domestic or his impact on fiction produced in the postcolonial period. In this chapter, I cite specific scholarship where relevant.

3 Perry Anderson, "Components of the National Culture" *New Left Review* 50 (July/August 1968), pp. 3–58. Also, see his "A Culture in Contraflow – I," *New Left Review* 180 (March/April 1990), pp. 41–78; and "A Culture in Contraflow – II," *New Left Review* 182 (July/August 1990), pp. 85–137. Anderson's two part article published in 1990 is more of an update than a revision of his earlier reading of British culture. His new analysis covers British culture from the late 1960s to the late 1980s. In the late 1980s, Anderson finds it impossible to talk of "*a* British culture" with the ease with which he did so in his earlier essay. He acknowledges that Britain itself is a conglomerate of conflicting nations and that its cultural borders with the US have become blurred over the last two decades. He now finds a flourishing sociology and a Marxist intellectualism whose seeds, Anderson admits may have been sown prior to 1968. Anderson points to over-simplification and a disregard of popular manifestations of British culture as the two major drawbacks of his earlier analysis. Anderson does not explicitly cite literature as one of these popular manifestations of culture though he does assess the work of literary and cultural theorists. On the whole, the 1990 essays do not invalidate Anderson's earlier argument. On the contrary the "revision" enriches our understanding of the pre-1968 period by providing a contrasting reading of the historical period that followed. Anderson's assessment in 1990 of the operations of feminism in British academic culture are particularly insightful and enabling in the context of this chapter.

4 Anderson, "Components of the National Culture," p. 56.

5 *Ibid.* Interestingly, Anderson leaves the natural sciences and aesthetic productions out of this 1968 consideration of British culture. His justification for this exemption is that the articulations within these two arenas are "more mediated" in their relationships with the social structure than are disciplines like political theory, literary criticism, anthropology, history or philosophy.

6 *Ibid.*, p. 17.
7 *Ibid.*, p. 19.
8 *Ibid.*
9 Eagleton, "Introduction" *Exiles and Emigres*, p. 9. Also see fn. 1, p. 9.
10 *Ibid.*, p. 10.
11 See pp. 9–19.
12 Jameson, "Modernism and Imperialism" pp. 50–1.
13 Eagleton, *Criticism and Ideology*, p. 137.
14 The theoretical ground on which I rest this reading of the feminine comes in part from Luce Irigaray's "Any Theory of the 'Subject' Has Always Been Appropriated by the 'Masculine'," *Speculum of the Other Woman*, Gillian C. Gill, trans. (Ithaca, NY: Cornell University Press, 1985), pp. 133–46. Over the course of this chapter, I will amend Irigaray's statement to suggest that any theory of the subject is masculine and white. However, such subjecthood can be wrested away, transformed or rejected outright by Others.
15 *Ibid.*, p. 135.
16 Ian Watt, *Conrad in the Nineteenth Century*, p. 48.
17 See Jameson, *The Political Unconscious*, p. 206. Also see Collits, "Imperialism, Marxism, Conrad," pp. 306–7.
18 Frances Armstrong, *Dickens and the Concept of Home* (Ann Arbor, MI: UMI Research Press, 1990), p. 2. Also see Walter E. Houghton, *The Victorian Frame of Mind* (New Haven, CT: Yale University Press, 1957), for an overview of the representation of Home in Victorian England. Like Armstrong, Houghton stresses the importance of the childhood memory of home in Walter Pater's writing as in James Froude's essay on homesickness entitled *The Nemesis of Faith*, pp. 341–72.
19 Armstrong, *Dickens*, p. 21.
20 See Randolph Trumbach, *The Rise of the Egalitarian Family* (New York: Academic Books, 1978), Philippe Aries, *Centuries of Childhood: A Social History of Family Life*, Robert Baldock, trans. (New York: Knopf, 1962).
21 Julia McNair Wright, *The Complete Home: An Encyclopaedia of Domestic Life and Affairs: The Household, in its Foundation, Order, Economy, Beauty, Healthfulness, Emergencies, Methods, Children, Literature, Amusements, Religion, Friendships, Manners, Hospitality, Servants, Industry, Money and History. A Volume of Practical Experiences Popularly Illustrated* (1870, repr., Philadelphia: Bradley, Garretson, 1883), p. iii., quoted by Armstrong, *Dickens*, p. 2.
22 Jorge Larrain, *Marxism and Ideology* (London: Macmillan Press, 1983), p. 28.
23 William M. Thackeray, *Vanity Fair* (1847–8, London: Penguin Classics, 1985), p. 794.
24 John Ruskin, "Of Queen's Garden," *Sesame and Lilies*, ed. Agnes Spofford Cook (New York: Silver, Burdett and Co., 1900), p. 84.
25 This ideology of the domestic holds sway over later texts such as the children's book *The Little Princess*, written in 1912 by Frances Hodgson Burnett. In this imperial romance for children, Sara (orphaned servant girl but also

heiress-to-be) stands shivering in the London winter and stares longingly into the cosy, warm living room of the "Large Family." Their domestic arrangements are faithful to the letter and spirit of this prescription by Ruskin. See Burnett, *The Little Princess* (New York: Lippincott, 1985 edn.), pp. 116–18.

26 John S. Mill, *The Subjection of Women* (London: World Classics, 1912), p. 540.

27 There were of course social conflicts that Anderson does not mention – for example, the London dock strike of 1889, the demands of the Home Rule for Ireland Party, etc. Nor does he mention the formation of the openly socialist, Independent Labour Party in 1893 (which had twenty-nine members in parliament by 1906). What Anderson notes in "Components of the National Culture" is that by 1900, "the harmony between the hegemonic class and its intellectuals was virtually complete," p. 15.

28 Roy Harrod, *The Life of John Maynard Keynes* (London, 1951), pp. 2–3, quoted by Anderson in "Components of the National Culture," p. 16.

29 Raymond Williams, *The Country and the City* (Oxford University Press, 1973), p. 280.

30 *Ibid.*, p. 281.

31 Thomas Carlyle, quoted by Walter Houghton, *The Victorian Frame of Mind*, p. 346.

32 In "Modernism and Imperialism," Jameson suggests that we view 1884 as an "emblematic break" which marks the inauguration of "a whole range of literary and artistic events." "The choice of such emblematic breaks" Jameson adds, "is not an empirically verifiable matter but a historiographic decision..." (p. 45).

33 Eagleton, "Form, Ideology and *The Secret Agent*," p. 31.

34 For an interesting reading of the sea as "both a strategy of containment and a place of real business" in *Lord Jim*, see Jameson, *The Political Unconscious*, p. 210.

35 Ian Watt, *Conrad in the Nineteenth Century*, p. 23.

36 The reference here is to Althusser's definition of ideology as "a 'Representation' of the Imaginary Relationship of Individuals to their Real Conditions of Existence." *Lenin and Philosophy* (New York: Monthly Review Press, 1971), p. 162.

37 Conrad, quoted by Watt, *Conrad in the Nineteenth Century*, p. 24.

38 I use the term "sentence" following Homi Bhabha, in "Postcolonial Criticism" in Stephen Greenblatt and Giles Gunn, eds., *Redrawing the Boundaries: The Transformation of English and American Studies* (New York, Modern Language Association of America, 1992). Working with Roland Barthes's notion of the cultural space "outside the sentence," Bhabha weaves together a nuanced articulation of the hybrid, supplementary, problematic space that postcolonial criticism bears witness to. Bhabha writes of wanting "to preserve at all times that menacing sense in which the nonsentence is contiguous with the sentence, near but different, not simply its anarchic disruption" (p. 448). It is in their

inability to participate in the productive menace that lies outside the sentence, that Naipaul's protagonists are subject to the sentence of colonialism, a sentence that appears self-inflicted because of the practice of mimicry.

39 See p. 128. Bhabha, "Of Mimicry and Man: The Ambivalence of Colonial Discourse," *October* 28 (Spring 1984), pp. 125–33.

40 Conrad, *A Personal Record* (Vermont: Marlboro Press, 1982) pp. 26–7.

41 Conrad, quoted by Watt, *Conrad in the Nineteenth Century*, p. 48.

42 The usage of Benedict Anderson's term "imagined communities" to demarcate a white, male readership for Conrad's fiction is not quite accurate here because clearly his extended readership includes non-white readers and writers of the English language. I return to this problematic issue later in this chapter.

43 In chapter 6 I return to this question in the context of M. G. Vassanji's novel about "homelessness" entitled *The Gunny Sack*. The gap between ideal and real homes is an issue that is as dynamic in this 1989 novel as it is in Conrad's fiction.

44 Perry Anderson, "A Culture in Contraflow – II," p. 88.

45 Joseph Conrad, *Almayer's Folly* (New York: Doubleday, Malay Edn, 1928), p. 3. Cited hereafter in the text as *AF*.

46 For recent critical readings that compare the Patna incident and the Patusan episode, see J. Hillis Miller, "Repetition as Subversive of Organic Form," in Harold Bloom, ed., *Joseph Conrad* (New York: Chelesa House, 1986), pp. 165–79. Also, see Martin Price, "The Limits of Irony: *Lord Jim* and *Nostromo*," in Harold Bloom, ed., *Joseph Conrad*, pp. 181–204.

47 Joseph Conrad, *Lord Jim* (1900, New York: Bantam, 1971), p. 144. This novel will be cited hereafter in the text as *LJ*.

48 See the earlier quoted passage from Julia McNair Wright. Also see J. Hillis Miller's *The Disappearance of God: Five Nineteenth-Century Writers* (Cambridge, MA: Belknap, 1963) which studies the various ways in which Victorians compensated for the "disappearance" of a God figure in their culture.

49 Joseph Conrad, *Heart of Darkness* (*Blackwoods* magazine, 1899, New York: Norton, 1963). Cited hereafter in the text as *HD*.

50 This argument could be extended by reading veiled references to engulfing female genitalia and masculine inadequacy in the descriptions of (male) colonizers' entry into the civilized world and into the wilderness. For example, Marlow begins describing his visit to the director's office with the following passage:

A narrow and deserted street in deep shadow, high houses, innumerable windows with venetian blinds, a dead silence, grass sprouting between the stones, imposing carriage archways right and left, immense double doors standing ponderously ajar. I slipped through one of these cracks, went up a swept and ungarnished staircase, as arid as a desert, and opened the first door I came to. Two women, one fat and one slim, sat...(p. 10).

Later in the novel, Marlow describes the progress of the steamboat up the river in similar terms:

Trees, trees, millions of trees, massive, immense running up high; and at their foot, hugging the bank against the stream, crept the little begrimed steamboat, like a sluggish beetle crawling on the floor of a lofty portico. It makes you feel very small, very lost, and yet it was not altogether depressing, that feeling. After all, if you were small, the grimy beetle crawled on – which was just what you wanted it to do...we crawled very slow. The reaches opened before us and closely behind, as if the forest had stepped leisurely across the water to bar the way for our return. We penetrated deeper and deeper into the heart of darkness. It was very quiet there. (p. 34)

51 Note that Marlow narrates the story of Kurtz to a group of men on board the "Nellie," a steamer on the Thames.

52 Joseph Conrad, "Autocracy and War," *Notes on Life and Letters* (New York: Doubleday, 1922), p. 110.

53 Joseph Conrad, *The Secret Agent: A Simple Tale* (1907, New York: Doubleday, 1928). Cited hereafter in the text as *SA*.

54 The political and domestic themes meet in the repeated use of the child as motif of both innocence and the lack of reasoned maturity. Almost all the male characters are referred to, in some instance or the other, as children. Michaelis' prison stay has deprived him of all power of logical or consecutive thinking. Stevie's stay with him in the country further accentuates the link between them, as does the fact that Stevie's crime is mistaken for Michaelis'. The Professor is almost childlike with his stunted frame and eggshell ears. Verloc himself competes with Stevie for affection and emotional comfort from Winnie.

In keeping with the representation of the male characters as children, the female characters serve in the role of mothers. Winnie Verloc is the prototypical "mother" who protects her retarded brother from the wrath of their father and rejects a marriage based on love (the romance with the young butcher) for the sterile but safe home that Verloc will provide for her brother. And when Verloc causes the death of Stevie, Winnie kills him. Her mother, who admits herself to a home for the aged so that Verloc will never feel resentful toward his wife's remaining relative (Stevie), is also a self-sacrificing woman. And then there is the Lady Patroness, who is simply described as a "fierce bodyguard," whose maternal instincts are gratified by Michaelis. At the bottom of this group of outstanding mothers is Mrs. Neale, the cleaning woman who is "devoured" and "oppressed" by her many children.

55 See p. 107, Rob Nixon, *London Calling: V. S. Naipaul, Postcolonial Mandarin* (England: Oxford University Press, 1992). Future references will be marked by page number in the text.

56 See p. 49, "Third World Intellectuals and Metropolitan Culture," Edward Said (*Raritan* ix:3, Winter 1990), pp. 27–50.

57 I return to this issue of the problematic allegiances of global literatures in

English in the next chapter on the politics of reading "Third World" literature in the west and then in chapter 5 where I examine the use of the rhetoric of the English Romantic poets in the writing of elite Indian women writers.

58 Jameson, "Romance and Reification: Plot Construction and Ideological Closure in Joseph Conrad," *The Political Unconscious*, p. 206. Jameson argues that this "emergence" of the popular in Conrad is most notable in the tangible "break" in narrative style between the telling of the Patna episode and the sojourn in Patusan.

59 Paul Theroux, *V. S. Naipaul: An Introduction to His Work* (London: Andre Deutsch, 1972), p. 7.

60 V. S. Naipaul, *A House for Mister Biswas* (1961, London: Penguin, 1978), pp. 210–11.

61 *Ibid.*, pp. 239–40.

62 See chapter 5 for further discussion of "failure" in another postcolonial literary context, namely, the work produced by "elite" Indian women writing in English in the late twentieth century.

63 Kazuo Ishiguro, *The Remains of the Day* (New York: Random House, 1989). Interestingly, this novel was published in Random House's "Vintage International" series, despite the fact that Ishiguro has lived in England since age six. If Conrad were writing today would he fall into this category?

64 Derek Walcott, *The Fortunate Traveller* (New York: Farrar, Straus, Giroux, 1981), pp. 193–4.

65 *Ibid.*, pp. 28–9.

66 Conrad, *Heart of Darkness*, p. 10.

67 Ishiguro, *The Remains of the Day*, p. 43.

68 *Ibid.*, p. 237.

69 For example, a reflective passage that begins with Marlow considering the nature of the "remote kinship" between him and the Africans on the shore that his boat passes, ends abruptly with: "Fine sentiments be hanged! I had no time. I had to mess about with white-lead and strips of woollen blanket helping to put bandages on those leaky steam-pipes – I tell you. I had to watch the steering, and circumvent those snags, and get the tin-pot along by hook or by crook. There was surface-truth enough in these things to save a wiser man" (p. 37).

70 See p. 79. Marlow tells the Intended that Kurtz died with her name on his lips. He is horrified by his lie, but more so by her "exulting and terrible cry, by the cry of inconceivable triumph and of unspeakable pain." Marlow's "heart stood still" and "it seemed" to him that "the house would collapse before I could escape, that the heavens would fall upon my death."

4 NOSTALGIC THEORIZING: AT HOME IN "THIRD WORLD" FICTIONS

1 See bell hooks, "Choosing the Margin as a Space of Radical Openness," *Framework* 36, 1989, p. 15.
2 See chapter 2 where this idea is explored through analysis of the literary self-representation of English women in the Indian Empire in the early twentieth century.
3 This essay by Jameson was published in *Social Text* 15 (Fall 1986), pp. 65–88. This essay will hereafter be cited in the text as *TWL*.
4 Johannes Fabian, *Time and the Other: How Anthropology Makes its Object* (New York: Columbia University Press, 1983), p. 31.
5 "Identity: Skin Blood Heart" by Minnie Bruce Pratt is an outstanding example of a narrative about a subject who rejects her right as a white American woman to automatic membership in a "we" (Southern, White, Christian woman) category. See Minnie Bruce Pratt, Elly Bulkin, Barbara Smith, *Yours in Struggle: Three Feminist Perspectives on Anti-Semitism and Racism* (New York: Long Haul Press, 1984), pp. 11–63. See chapter 1, especially the section titled "Homesick with nowhere to go," for a detailed discussion of Pratt's essay and other feminist theorizing on the need to reject the comforts of homes of privilege. Also see "Not in Our Names: Women, War, AIDS," by Ann Cvetkovich and Avery Gordon, in Michael Ryan and Avery Gordon, eds., *Body Politics: Disease, Desire and the Family* (Boulder, CO: Westview Press, 1994), pp. 32–44.
6 Aijaz Ahmad's response to "Third World Literature in the Era of Multinational Capitalism" published in *Social Text* 17 (Fall 1987), pp. 3–25, entitled "Jameson's Rhetoric of Otherness, and the 'National Allegory'" has established itself as the corrective companion piece to Jameson's essay. Ahmad explodes Jameson's theories by pointing to their dependency on binary oppositions, in this case nationalism/postmodernism.
7 See p. 13, S. P. Mohanty, "Us and Them: On the Philosophical Bases of Political Criticism" *Yale Journal of Criticism* 2, 2 (Spring 1989), pp. 1–31.
8 See p. 5, Abdul R. JanMohamed and David Lloyd, "Introduction: Toward a Theory of Minority Discourse: What Is To Be Done?" in JanMohamed and Lloyd, eds., *The Nature and Context of Minority Discourse* (England: Oxford University Press, 1990), pp. 1–16.
9 See p. 98, Trinh T. Minh-ha, *Woman, Native, Other: Writing Postcoloniality and Feminism* (Bloomington: Indiana University Press, 1989).
10 See p. 217, Kumkum Sangari, "The Politics of the Possible," in JanMohamed and Lloyd, eds., *The Nature and Context of Minority Discourse*, pp. 216–45.
11 The term "western academia" is used in this chapter to refer to established institutions of teaching and publishing primarily in the United States as well as in western Europe. I am aware of the lurking dangers of

lapsing into totalizations (or even totalitarianism) in using the word "western" to signify diverse geographic and discursive locations. For useful definitions of "Western" and "west," see Ruth Frankenburg, *White Woman, Race Matters: The Social Construction of Whiteness* (Minneapolis: University of Minnesota Press, 1993), p. 265.

12 In recent years, work by Homi K. Bhabha and Gayatri Spivak have become foundational texts for the field of postcolonial studies in western academia. Articles such as Bhabha's "Signs taken for Wonders: Questions of Ambivalence and Authority under a Tree Outside Delhi, May 1817" in Henry Louis Gates, Jr., ed., *"Race," Writing, and Difference* (Illinois: University of Chicago Press, 1986), pp. 163–84, and Spivak's "Can the Subaltern Speak?" in Cary Nelson and Lawrence Grossberg, eds., *Marxism and the Interpretation of Culture* (Chicago: University of Illinois Press, 1888), pp. 271–313, are clearly more often and more overtly acknowledged in recent writing than is this essay by Jameson.

13 Homi K. Bhabha, ed., *Nation and Narration* (London: Routledge, 1990); Timothy Brennan, *Salman Rushdie and the Third World: Myths of the Nation* (New York: St. Martin's Press, 1989).

14 This essay by Homi Bhabha is discussed in greater detail in chapter 6 of this book.

15 Bhabha, "DissemiNation", p. 292. In this passage, Bhabha goes on to list the many novels that use "the Nation as Metaphor" – a phrase whose debt to *TWL* is all pervasive in the essay.

16 Bill Ashcroft, Gareth Griffiths, Helen Tiffin, eds., *The Empire Writes Back: Theory and Practice in Post-Colonial Literatures* (London: Routledge, 1989), pp. 169–72. Allegory is mentioned early in this study but not *this* essay by Jameson. Ashcroft et al write: "Similarities across the different post-colonial literatures are not restricted to thematic parallels. As recent critics have noted they extend to assertions that certain features such as a distinctive use of allegory (Slemon 1986; 1987b), irony (New 1975), magic realism (Dash 1973; Slemon 1988a), and discontinuous narratives are characteristic of post-colonial writing"(p. 28). The bibliography in this book includes two other texts by Jameson but not this essay. There are other critical essays that I cannot catalog individually, that do read novels produced in contemporary Africa and the Indian-subcontinent as national allegories without citing their debt to Jameson. See for instance, Elleke Boehmer, "Transfiguring: Colonial Body into Postcolonial Narrative," *NOVEL* 26, 3 (Spring 1993), pp. 286–78.

17 Doris Sommers, "Love and Country in Latin America: An Allegorical Speculation," *Cultural Critique* (Fall 1990), pp. 109–28. In the next section of this chapter I argue that Jameson's argument in *TWL* is framed by the writing of Benjamin and other Western Marxists.

18 *Ibid.*, pp. 109–10.

19 See p. 13, Sara Suleri, *The Rhetoric of Indian English* (Illinois: University of Chicago, 1992).

20 See p. 129, Benita Parry, "A Critique Mishandled," *Social Text* 1992, pp. 121–33.
21 *Ibid.*, pp. 130–1.
22 *Public Culture* 6, 1 (Fall 1993). This issue contains ten spirited essays on *In Theory* and a response from Aijaz Ahmad, pp. 3–194. Essays cited will be footnoted individually.
23 See p. 45, Vivek Dhareshwar, "Marxism, Location Politics, and the Possibility of Critique," *Public Culture* 6, 1, pp. 41–54.
24 See p. 57, Partha Chatterjee, "The Need to Dissemble," in *Public Culture* 6, 1, pp. 55–64.
25 Jameson, "Postmodernism, or the Cultural Logic of Late Capitalism," *New Left Review* 146 (1984).
26 Benedict Anderson, *Imagined Communities: Reflections on the Origin and Spread of Nationalism* (London: Verso, 1983), p. 41.
27 A great volume of scholarly texts written between the 1950s and the 1970s on the issue of nationalism suggested that non-European nationalisms were and are little more than events "borrowed" from the past of European countries. See chapter 1 for further commentary on this issue.
28 Jameson does not specify what he means by "a certain nationalism," which he claims is identical in the "second" and third worlds. What are (or were) "the most vital areas" of the "second" world? And what are the common features of this nationalism?
29 See chapter 1 for further references to these classic texts on nationalism. For a truly comprehensive critique, see Partha Chatterjee, "Nationalism as a Problem in the History of Political Ideas," *National Thought and the Colonial World: A Derivative Discourse?* (London: Zed, 1986), pp. 1–35.
30 I use the term "implied reader" as articulated by Gayatri Chakravorty Spivak in "The Burden of English," in Rajeshwari Sunder Rajan, ed., *The Lie of the Land: English Literary Studies in India* (New Delhi: Oxford University Press, 1992), pp. 275–99. Spivak goes on to elaborate with her usual elegance on the possible implications of this term, but her initial proposition is that – "[t]he figure of the implied reader is constructed within a consolidated system of cultural representation. The appropriate culture in this context is the one supposedly indigenous to the literature under consideration" (p. 276).
31 For example, *Amritvela* by Leena Dhingra was first published by The Women's Press in London in 1988 and then as *First Light* by Rupa Press, New Delhi in 1991. *In My Own Name* by Sharan-Jeet Shan was first published by The Women's Press in 1986 and by Rupa Press in India in 1991. It is also more likely, given the legacy of the colonial educational system, that these "third world" novels are more likely to be taught first in the western academy and only then in once colonized countries.
32 The entire sentence is much more explicit than the phrases quoted in the text suggests. Writing on the impossibility of the "first world" critic to avoid

the differentiations that Said has called "Orientalism," Jameson adds: "It does not matter much that the radical otherness of the culture in question is praised or valorized positively, as in the preceding pages: the essential operation is that of differentiation, and once that has been accomplished, the mechanism Said denounced has been set in place" (*TWL*, p. 77).

33 As with his use of the "Other reader" to signify the implied reader of these texts, Jameson's use of the category "non-canonical" for literatures produced within literary trajectories other than the western canon, is also problematic. The method of differentiation employed here produces its own hierarchy of literary products and consumers. Very often these very same "third world" texts that are non-canonical in a western canon are securely canonized in their country of origin. R. K. Narayan whose writing is discussed later in this chapter provides a good example of a writer who occupies a high and central seat within the literary hierarchy in his home country yet whose novels enter the Euroamerican academic context as always already non-canonical, minority, Third World productions.

34 See pp. 7–8, Michael Sprinker, "The National Question: Said, Ahmad, Jameson," *Public Culture* 6, 1, pp. 3–31.

35 This essay is discussed in the context of theories of "deterritorialization" in the first and second chapters. This essay will hereafter be cited in the text by page number.

36 See pp. 9–10, Abdul JanMohamed and David Lloyd, "Introduction: Toward a Theory of Minority Discourse: What Is To Be Done?"

37 Georg Lukács, *The Theory Of the Novel* (1920) Anna Bostock trans. (Cambridge, MA: MIT Press, 1971). Cited hereafter as *TN*. Walter Benjamin, "The Storyteller" *Illuminations: Essays and Reflections*, ed. Hannah Arendt, Harry Zohn, trans. (New York: Schocken Press, 1968), pp. 83–109. Cited hereafter as *ST*.

38 Martin Jay, *Marxism and Totality: the Adventures of a Concept from Lukács to Habermas* (Berkeley, CA: University of California Press, 1984), p. 21.

39 Aijaz Ahmad, p. 14. The text by Jameson in question is *Marxism and Form* (Princeton University Press, 1971), pp. 165–7.

40 Jameson's article also echoes in its title as well as in its content many of the issues dealt with in Benjamin's "The Work of Art in the Age of Mechanical Reproduction" in *Illuminations*, pp. 217–51.

41 Jameson, *Marxism and Form*, p. 60.

42 *Ibid.*, p. 61.

43 Benjamin, *Schriften I*, p. 461, quoted by Jameson, *Marxism and Form*, p. 77.

44 *Ibid.*

45 *Ibid.*, p. 78.

46 In *Marxism and Totality* Martin Jay notes that although Lukács uses the metaphor that assigns the epic to the childhood of man and the novel to the age of virile maturity, he did not have a preference for "maturation" (p. 95).

47 See Chatterjee, *Nationalist Thought and the Colonial World*, pp. 51 and 131–66.

48 This evocative phrase is borrowed from Neil Lazarus' "Great Expectations and the Mourning After: Decolonization and African Intellectuals," *Resistance and Post-Colonial African Fiction* (New Haven, CT: Yale University Press, 1990), pp. 1–26 and pp. 235–42.

49 For periodizations of national literatures in the Indian context, see *Contemporary Indian Literature* (New Delhi: Sahitya Akademi, 1959). This publication under the auspices of the "Sahitya Akademi" (cultural academy) was the official cultural mouthpiece of the then newly independent country. This collection comprised of sixteen essays, each periodizing a regional literature in one of the sixteen official languages in India. There were some parallels, mainly offered by events in the national political history, but the other shaping influences were different for each literature.

50 See p. 299, Rosemary Marangoly George and Helen Scott, "A New Tail to an Old Tale: An Interview with Ama Ata Aidoo," *NOVEL: A Forum For Fiction* 26, 3 (Spring 1993), pp. 297–308. For a similar argument see "'Commonwealth Literature' Does Not Exist" written by Salman Rushdie in 1983 and reprinted in *Imaginary Homelands: Essays and Criticism 1981–1991* (New York: Viking and Granta, 1991) pp. 61–73. Here Rushdie argues against the straitjacket imposed on writers across the globe by the term "Commonwealth Literature" and the literary preoccupations that are seen as requisite to this fiction.

51 Agnes Sam, "South Africa: Guest of Honor Amongst the Uninvited Newcomers to England's Great Tradition," in Kirsten Holst Petersen and Anna Rutherford, eds., *A Double Colonization: Colonization and Post-Colonial Women's Writing* (Denmark: Dangaroo Press, 1986), pp. 92-6.

52 *Ibid.*, pp. 94–5. Ama Ata Aidoo's experimental novel, *Our Sister Killjoy: or, Reflections from a Black-eyed Squint* serves as a good example of the difficulty "third world" women have in publishing work that is not realist fiction based on personal experience. Though written in 1966, the novel was published only in 1977.

53 See George and Scott, "New Tail to an Old Tale," p. 305.

54 Njabulo Ndebele, "Redefining Relevance," *Pretexts: Studies in Literature and Culture* 1, 1 (Winter 1989), pp. 40–52. Further references will be marked by page number in the text.

55 Ama Ata Aidoo, *Changes* (London: The Women's Press, 1991), unnumbered first page.

56 George and Scott, "A New Tail to an Old Tale," p. 302.

57 R. K. Narayan, *The Dark Room* (1938) (Chicago: University of Chicago Press, 1986). Hereafter cited in the text as *DR*.

58 See Erik Barnouw and S. Krishnaswamy, *Indian Film* (England: Oxford University Press, 1980). For a similar criticism of westernization from another colonial location see *Song of Lawino: Song of Ocol* written in

1966 by the East African (Ugandan) poet, Okot p'Bitek (London: Heinemann, 1984).

59 See Gobinda Prasad Sarma, *Nationalism in Indo-Anglian Fiction* (New Delhi: Sterling Publishers, 1978).

60 A perfect example of a film from this era that mocked westernized Indians was the 1934 hit *Indira MA*. Barnouw and Krishnaswamy describe the plot of this film as follows: "Its central character was a highly Westernized Indian girl [Indira], complete with Masters of Art Degree, who forsakes the fine young man she was engaged to marry and weds a Westernized wastrel, with unhappy results" (p. 108). The moral is self-evident.

61 William Walsh chooses to read Malgudi as a metaphor of India and, by extension, of the world. Walsh sees Narayan's novels as "universal" texts. Caste does not figure in Walsh's assessment. See William Walsh, "R. K. Narayan," *Writers and Their Works* no 224 (London: Longman Group, 1971), p. 6.

62 See Shanta Krishnaswamy, "R. K. Narayan: Nightmare Comedy and the Ideology of Acceptance," *The Woman in Indian Fiction (1950–1980)* (New Delhi: Ashis Publishers, 1984), pp. 83-159. In the section entitled "India will go on," Krishnaswamy argues that Malgudi is remarkable "because it projects successfully the author's sense of the continuing spiritual coherence of India. No foreigner could succeed in breaking up the special bond between the Indian, his land and his gods" (p. 92). India here is synonymous with Hinduism and perhaps even specifically with brahminism. In this discourse, the generic Indian is gendered masculine. I will insist that in Malgudi, the term "foreigner" applies to those who attempt to break the orderly caste hierarchy – such actions are as "foreign" as the imposition of British rule.

63 At the end of this novel, though Ramani has not broken off his relationship with Shanta Bai, the reader knows that she will have to leave Malgudi in a matter of months because she has not brought in the requisite number of women clients for the Englandia Insurance Company. Though he is the Branch Manager, Ramani has no say in the decision to keep her on after the probation period.

64 See Ganganath Jha, ed., *Manusmriti*, 2 vols. (Calcutta: The Asiatic Society of Bengal, 1939).

65 In the next chapter I read similar plots in the novels written by mid twentieth-century Indian women writers of the novel in English. In these novels, however, the main protagonist's transgressions are presented within a secular, even feminist, discourse of selfhood.

66 This mythological association is deeply entrenched in popular culture in twentieth-century India. By 1938, which was when *The Dark Room* was published, six different sound films in four different languages (including the 1937 Hindi superhit *Savitri*) had been based on this story from the *Mahabharata*. The following Indian literary works in English have central female characters called Savitri or Savithri whose very name conjures an

image of the dutiful wife: Toru Dutt's lyric poem "Savitri" in *A Sheaf Gleaned in French Fields* (Bhowanipur, Calcutta: B. M. Bose, 1876); Aurobindo Ghose's epic poem *Savitri: A Legend and Symbol* (Pondicherry, India: Sri Aurobindo Ashram, 1950–1), Raja Rao's *The Serpent and the Rope* (London: John Murray, 1960).

67 The Punjabi poet Amrita Pritam echoes *and rewrites* Savitri's declaration in her own terms. Pritam writes: "one kind of love [is] like that of the sky. Another is like the roof over one's head. A woman seeks both – she first finds the roof and then opens a window to the sky." Quoted by Anees Jung, *Unveiling India: A Woman's Journey* (London: Penguin, 1987), p. 66. Savitri sets out to search for the open sky and finds instead that all she achieves is the exchange of one dark room for another.

68 For a detailed discussion of the social and economic position of women as scripted in Hindu theology, see Prabhati Mukherjee, *Hindu Women: Narrative Models* (1978, Calcutta: Longman Orient, repr. 1994).

69 It is tempting to read this reflection in a manner that has very little support in the text: the "part" of her that she says is "dead" is the obedient, grateful, devoted "Savitri" persona. She may have returned home to her husband and children, she may continue to service them with a smile, but she has no illusions about the precariousness of her position inside as much as outside her home in this patriarchal social arrangement.

70 Graham Greene, "Introduction," in R. K. Narayan, *The Bachelor of Arts* (Illinois: University of Chicago, 1984), p. v.

71 See R. K. Narayan, *Mr. Sampath: The Printer of Malgudi* (Illinois: University of Chicago Press, 1981), p. 106.

72 See Jameson, *TWL*, pp. 79–80.

73 Chandra Talpade Mohanty, "Under Western Eyes: Feminist Scholarship and Colonial Discourses," in Mohanty, Russo and Torres, eds., *Third World Women and the Politics of Feminism* (New York: Routledge, 1992), p. 340.

74 *Ibid.*, p. 333.

75 Fredric Jameson, "Postmodernism, or The Cultural Logic of Late Capitalism," *New Left Review* 146 (July/August 1984), p. 57.

76 Jameson, "Postmodernism," p. 57.

77 See Jameson, *TWL*, n. 26, pp. 87–8.

78 It is useful at this point to consider Perry Anderson's deft analysis of the ease with which British culture in the early part of this century exported its totalizations via academic theories on other cultures. As a result, Anderson argues, in place of a sociology of itself, British academic culture had a flourishing anthropology in which totalizing theories of other cultures were elaborated. See Perry Anderson, "Components of the National Culture." This article is discussed in further detail in chapter 3 in the context of Conrad's writing on location.

5 ELITE PLOTTING, DOMESTIC POSTCOLONIALITY

1 See p. 33, Chandra Mohanty, "Cartographies of Struggle," in Mohanty, Russo and Torres, eds., *Third World Women and the Politics of Feminism* (Bloomington: Indiana University Press, 1991), pp. 1–47. In this introduction Mohanty provides the reader with a comprehensive survey of the fundamental issues around the subject indicated by the book title. Cited hereafter by page number in the text.

2 Shashi Deshpande, *That Long Silence* (London: Virago Press, 1988); Nayantara Sahgal, *The Day in Shadow* (1971, New Delhi: Penguin, 1991); Anita Desai, *Where Shall We Go This Summer?* (1982, New Delhi: Orient, 1988).

3 See Indu K. Mallah, *Shadows in Dream-Time* (New Delhi: Affiliated East-West Press, 1991); Shobha Dé, *Socialite Evenings* (New Delhi: Penguin, 1989); Shakuntala Narasimhan, "Will You Step Into My Parlour," *Lucky Days* (Calcutta: Writers Workshop, 1989), pp. 14–18; Anuradha Mahindra, "Full Circle," *The Indian PEN*, 51, 4–6 (April/June 1990), pp. 1–9.

4 Shama Futehally, "Portrait of a Childhood," *In Other Words* (New Delhi: Kali for Women, 1992), a collection of short stories by Indian women.

5 Desai, *Where Shall We Go This Summer?*, p. 144. Hereafter cited as *WSW* in the text.

6 See Madhu Kiswar, "The Struggle of Indian Women" (New York: Women's International Resource Exchange, 1988), pp. 1–17.

7 Deshpande, *That Long Silence*, p. 146. Hereafter cited in the text as *LS*.

8 On the difficulties of breaking the silence and addressing urgent issues on domestic violence amongst East Indian immigrants, see Annaya Bhattacharjee "The Habit of Ex-Nomination" *Public Culture* 5, 1 (Fall 1992), pp. 19–44. Bhattacharjee attributes this refusal to acknowledge violence against women as characteristic of the (in this case, Indian) bourgeois determination to remain ideologically un-named, even when relocated in the US. Bhattacharjee borrows this concept of "ex-nomination" from Roland Barthes' *Mythologies* where he defines "the bourgeoisie as the class which does not want to be named, indeed needs no name as it postulates itself as the universal. It needs no name because it names everything" ([Paris, Seuil, 1957] p. 21). In this context, for the bourgeois woman to attempt to name her Self, to define her desires, is an uphill task especially given the impediments to articulation that this chapter goes on to specify.

9 See Barbara Harlow, *Resistance Literature* (New York: Methuen Books, 1987).

10 James C. Scott, "Normal Exploitation, Normal Resistance," in *Weapons of the Weak: Everyday Forms of Peasant Resistance* (New Haven, CT: Yale University Press, 1985), pp. 28–47.

11 It could of course be both. Writing of religious suffering, Karl Marx

noted that "it was at the same time an *expression* of real suffering and a *protest* against real suffering." See T. B. Bottomore, trans. and ed., *Early Writings* (London: Watts, 1963), p. 43.

12 Kamala Das, "The Sunshine Cat," in R. Parthasarathy, ed., *Ten Twentieth-Century Indian Poets* (New Delhi: Oxford University Press, 1976).

13 Maria Mies urges us to consider the privileges of Indian middle-class women and housewives not as privileges but as "disaster." She writes: "The 'privileges' of middle-class women are not only that they are domesticated, isolated, dependent on a man, emotionally fettered and weakened, and tied down to an ideology that totally objectifies them" (p. 207). See Maria Mies, *Patriarchy and Accumulation on a World Scale* (London: Zed, 1986), pp. 206–7. It is interesting that even an acute reader like Mies is almost always silent about Indian women who inhabit the class above the middle class. I have taken the liberty of reading her category of "third world" middle class as inclusive of upper-class women who are subject to the same "disasters" that Mies catalogs.

14 K. R. Srinivasa Iyengar, "English Literature," *Contemporary Indian Literature* (New Delhi: Sahitya Akademi, 1959), pp. 35–58. Srinivasa locates the source of the term "Indo-Anglian" to the publication of a book entitled *Indo-Anglian Literature* in Calcutta in 1883. Srinivasa writes: "More recently, especially during the past 25 years, the term 'Indo-Anglian' has acquired considerable currency. It has no racial or religious significance. It is reasonably descriptive, and it can be conveniently used both to label the writer and to describe the literature. No wonder the name has 'come to stay'" (p. 36).

15 *Ibid.*, p. 39.

16 Gauri Viswanathan, *Masks of Conquest: Literary Study and British Rule in India* (New York: Columbia University Press, 1989), p. 7.

17 *Ibid.*, p. 168.

18 From about the late 1980s, there has been a new approach to the entire field of English literary studies in India, which is best categorized under the term "English Studies." Working with and beyond Edward Said's theorizing on Orientalism, this new field has produced some outstanding books, articles and volumes of critical essays. See especially, founding texts like *Masks of Conquest* by Gauri Viswanathan; Rajeshwari Sunder Rajan, ed., *The Lie of the Land: English Literary Studies in India* (New Delhi: Oxford University Press, 1992); Zakia Pathak et al, "The Prisonhouse of Orientalism," *Textual Practice* 5, 2 (Summer 1991); Lola Chatterji, ed., *Women Image Text: Feminist Readings of Literary Texts* (Delhi: Trianka, 1986); Svati Joshi, ed., *Rethinking English: Essays in Literature, Language, History* (Delhi: Trianka, 1991).

19 Anees Jung, *Unveiling India: A Woman's Journey* (London: Penguin, 1987), p. 21.

20 Consider the titles of the following novels: Leena Dhingra, *First Light* (New Delhi: Rupa Press, 1991); Indu K. Mallah, *Shadows in Dream-Time*. Her novel

about an upper-class housewife who is suddenly widowed begins with an excerpt from T. S. Eliot's *The Family Reunion*. Also consider the following titles: Nayantara Sahgal's *The Time of Morning* (London: Gollancz, 1965) as well as *The Day in Shadow* (London: Gollancz, 1965); Shashi Deshpande's *Roots and Shadows* (Bombay: Sangam, 1983); Veena Paintal's *Spring Returns* (New Delhi: Hind Pocket Books, 1977); Sarala Barnabas' *The Promise of Spring* (Aurangabad, India: Parimal Prakashan, 1989). Anita Desai's *Clear Light of Day* (London: Penguin, 1980) begins with a line from an Emily Dickinson poem and a stanza of T. S. Eliot's verse.

21 Attia Hussain's *Sunlight on a Broken Column* was first published in 1961 in London by Chatto and Windus, and in 1988 it was republished by Virago Press with a new introduction written by Anita Desai. Hussain's novel begins with the stanza from T. S Eliot's "The Hollow Men" from which she takes the title of her novel. Salman Rushdie's first novel, *Grimus*, published in 1975, begins with the following line from Eliot : "human kind/ cannot bear much reality." This reliance – at least for titles and epigraphs – on Eliot and others in the tradition of the Romantic poets can be seen elsewhere in the fiction in English produced from once colonized parts of the world. For instance Chinua Achebe's *Things Fall Apart* takes its title from Yeats' "The Second Coming" and his novel *No Longer at Ease* takes its title from Eliot.

22 Ramesh Chadha, "Nayantara Sahgal: Politics and Personal Relationships," in Robert L. Ross, ed., *International Literature in English: Essays on Major Writers* (New York: Garland Publishing, 1991), p. 263.

23 Shanta Krishnaswamy, *The Woman in Indian Fiction in English* (New Delhi: Ashis Publishers, 1984), pp. 340–1.

24 Susie Tharu, "Tracing Savitri's Pedigree: Victorian Racism and the Image of Women in Indo-Anglian Literature," in Kumkum Sangari and Sudesh Vaid, eds., *Recasting Women: Essays in Colonial History* (New Delhi: Kali for Women, 1989), pp. 256–7.

25 I have adapted the use of the terms "Westernization" and "Sanskritization" from Joanna Liddle and Rama Joshi, *Daughters of Independence: Gender, Caste and Class in India* (New Delhi: Kali for Women and Zed, 1986), p. 6. Liddle and Joshi in turn get this terminology from Mysore N. Srinivas, "The Changing Position of Indian Women," *Man* 12 (1977), pp. 229–31.

26 Tharu, "Tracing Savitri's Pedigree," pp. 262–3.

27 *Ibid.*, p. 263.

28 This representation of women as symbols of "the Indian Woman" slips very easily into a religious representation when "Indian" is replaced by "Hindu." Such slippage occurs incessantly in popular discourses such as film where despite the sentimental representations of a secular India in general, when the spotlight is specifically on "the Indian woman," she is always virtuous according to the precepts of popular Hinduism.

29 Tharu, "Tracing Savitri's Pedigree," p. 264. See earlier cited works by Dipesh

Chakrabarty and Partha Chatterjee on issues of nationalism, the women's question and domesticity in the context of late nineteenth-century Bengal.

30 *Ibid.*, p. 265.

31 Jung, *Unveiling India*, p. 108.

32 Rama Jha, "Kamala Markandaya: The Woman's World" in Robert L. Ross, ed., *International Literature in English: Essays on Major Writers*, pp. 254–5.

33 Shanta Krishnaswamy writes in *The Woman in Indian Fiction in English*: "In western countries, the women's issue is mostly one of identity, job equality and sexual roles. In India, for the majority, it is a question of stark survival"(p. 5). I will provisionally make do with this blunt differentiation between Indian and "western" feminisms.

34 Vibhuti Patel, "Women's Liberation in India," *New Left Review* 153 (September/October, 1985), pp. 75–6.

35 Radha Kumar, "Contemporary Indian Feminism," *Feminist Review* 33 (Autumn 1989), pp. 20–9.

36 *Ibid.*, p. 20.

37 *Ibid.*

38 *Ibid.*, p. 21.

39 For more recent scholarship on the women's movement in India, see Nandita Gandhi and Nandita Shah, *The Issues at Stake: Theory and Practice in the Contemporary Women's Movement in India* (New Delhi: Kali for Women, 1992). Also see Radha Kumar, *The History of Doing: An Illustrated Account of Movements for Women's Rights and Feminism in India, 1800–1990* (New Delhi: Kali for Women, 1993).

40 A fact that is important (especially in the present context of assessing women's literature) is that women's activism in post-independence India flourishes quite independently of creative writing by women, especially that written in English. The key players of these movements are not literary writers, literary critics or literary journals. Nor does academia play as decisive a role as it appears to in the US.

41 See "Preface," in Susie Tharu and K. Lalitha, eds., *Women Writing in India, Volume 2: The Twentieth Century* (New York: The Feminist Press, 1992), p. xxiii.

42 For biographical information and details of the literary careers of Deshpande, Desai and Sahgal, see William Walsh, *Indian Literature in English* (London: Longman, 1990). See especially: "Chronology," pp. 187–95, "Select Bibliography," pp. 196–202, and "Individual Authors," pp. 203–14.

43 K. Krishnamoorty, "The All-Time Relevance of Bharata's Literary Canons," in C. D. Narasimhaiah and C. N. Srinath, eds., *A Common Poetics For Indian Literatures* (Mysore: Dhvanyaloka, 1984), pp. 11–17.

44 *Ibid.*, p. 15.

45 *Ibid.*, p. 17.

46 *Ibid.*, p. 165.

47 *Ibid.*, p. 3.
48 *Ibid.*, p. 167.
49 A passage from "End of Another Home Holiday" by D. H. Lawrence is quoted in Desai's novel at this point in the narrative (p. 150).
50 Sahgal, *The Day in Shadow*, pp. 14–15. Cited hereafter as *DS* in the text.
51 Meena Alexander, "Outcaste Power: Ritual Displacement and Virile Maternity in Indian Women Writers" *The Journal of Commonwealth Literature* 14, 1 (1990), p. 13.
52 *Ibid.*, p. 14.
53 *Ibid.*
54 For a detailed discussion of the complaints against Indian literature in English, see Meenakshi Mukherjee, *The Twice Born Fiction: Themes and Techniques of the Indian Novel in English* (New Delhi: Heinemann, 1971). The Introduction to G. P. Sarma's *Nationalism In Indo-Anglian Fiction* (New Delhi: Sterling, 1978), pp. xi–xxiii, defends Indo-Anglian literature from charges such as Gordon Bottomley's description of Indian poetry in English as "Matthew Arnold in a sari" (p. xii).
55 Alexander, "Outcaste Power," p. 16. In the very next sentence, Alexander displays her own reliance on the Romantic rhetoric that I have repeatedly identified in the literary genre under discussion. She writes: "The questions of a lasting freedom, of a sublime transcendence that so often haunt the imagination do not vanish." Alexander is a poet and writer based in New York. Her first novel, *Nampally Road* (San Francisco: Mercury House, 1991), is an interesting assessment of the politics of teaching Wordsworth in a postcolonial context, in present day Hyderabad. Once again we have as a heroine, a sensitive, poetic young woman in search for a role that will accommodate all her selves. She is not, however, in search of a suitable domestic role but of a place from which she and others can operate as free, independent subjects of a decolonized country. In the concluding pages of this chapter, I introduce a novel by Rohini (no last name is provided), entitled *To Do Something Beautiful* (London: Sheba Press, 1990). This novel, I believe, lives up to Alexander's expectations of the "female effort at decolonization," that this passage from her article calls for. Furthermore, *To Do Something Beautiful* does this in English.
56 Gayatri Chakravorty Spivak, "Feminism and Decolonization," *differences* 3.3 (1991), p. 142.
57 Some of the work (especially the short stories) of these women writers in Indian languages other than English has been translated and anthologized in the last five years. The first of these selections of English and translated stories was published in 1986: *Truth-Tales: Contemporary Writing By Indian Women* (New Delhi: Kali, 1986). This successful collection was followed by: *The Slate of Life: An Anthology of stories by Indian Women* (New Delhi: Kali, 1990); Lakshmi Holmstrom, ed., *The Inner Courtyard: Stories By Indian Women* (New Delhi: Rupa, 1991). Also see the recent collection of

Ismat Chugtai's stories in translation – Tahira Naqvi and Syeda S. Hameed, eds. and trans., *The Quilt and Other Stories*, (New Delhi: Kali for Women, 1990). Other recent anthologies include: Stephen Alter and Wimal Dissanayake, eds., *The Penguin Book of Modern Indian Short Stories* (New Delhi: Penguin, 1989); and Nissim Ezekiel and Meenakshi Mukherjee, eds., *Another India: An Anthology of Contemporary Indian Fiction and Poetry* (New Delhi: Penguin, 1990). The earlier cited two-volume anthology edited by Susie Tharu and K. Lalitha (*Women Writing in India, Volume 1: 600 BC to Early Twentieth Century*, and *Women Writing in India, Volume 2: The Twentieth Century*) has established itself as the single most comprehensive and carefully researched work in this area.

58 What further complicates matters is the fact that in their recent work, both Desai and Sahgal move beyond the domestic crises of elite Indian women, (see *Baumgartner's Bombay* [New York, Knopf, 1988] and *In Custody* [Harmondsworth: Penguin, 1985] by Desai and *Rich Like Us* by Sahgal). Deshpande, a relatively young writer, may well move beyond this subject in books to come.

59 See "Landmarks in Official Educational Policy: Some Facts and Figures," compiled by Lola Chatterjee, in *The Lie of the Land: English Literary Studies in English*.

60 See Lola Chatterji, *The Lie of the Land*, for further data on this issue.

61 I would like to thank Gautam Padmanabhanam and Subhashree Krishnaswamy of Affiliated East West Press, Madras for answering my many questions on the details of the publishing and marketing aspects of Indian women's writing in English. A first novel in English by a fairly unknown Indian woman writer would have an initial printing of about a thousand copies. Around ten thousand copies are printed in the first edition of books that are expected to be "best sellers." (Shobha Dé is the only Indian woman writer whose books have sold so widely.)

62 Gayatri Chakravorty Spivak, "Feminism and Decolonization," p. 143.

63 Viswanathan, *Masks of Conquest*, p. 6.

64 See Lola Chatterji, *The Lie of the Land*, p. 308. In recent months the influx of multinational media corporations into the Indian telecommunications industry (especially television) has resulted in a substantial increase of English language programs on privately owned and operated TV channels.

65 The term "commercial" cinema refers to one of the two categories ("commercial" or "formula" and "art" or "parallel" cinema) that is used to differentiate between the two kinds of films produced in post-independence India. "Commercial" films are the raucous, musical, star-studded extravaganzas which cause Indian intellectuals to throw up their hands in despair. The ruling philosophy behind these films is that entertainment is that which best provides a means of escaping the harsh realities of everyday life. "Parallel" or "new wave" cinema is that which deals directly with social issues usually from a leftist political stance. There are of

course other films that fall somewhere in between the two categories as well as the extremely popular "theological" melodramas.

66 *Subhah* would be categorized as an "alternative" film, that did cross over to a mainstream audience. The film was made with some concessions to this regular audience, such as the use of musical numbers at periodic intervals in the narrative and some slapstick comedy. Directed and produced by Jabbar Patel, the screenplay was written by Satya Chitra, and the main protagonist Savitri acted by the late Smita Patil, the best known actress of alternate India cinema. The role of her husband Suresh was played by a versatile film and theatre actor, producer, director and writer, Girish Karnad. The film went on to sweep the Indian film awards for the year 1982. Worldwide distribution rights for this film on video cassette is held by India Sun. An English version of the screenplay for the Marathi language film *Umbartha* (The Threshold) based on the same story has been published in book form: see Jabbar Patel, *Umbartha* (Calcutta: Seagull Books, 1985).

67 See chapter 4 for a discussion of the automatic connotations of the name "Savitri."

68 Khushwant Singh, "A Generation Writing in English," *The New York Times* (February 13, 1990), p. C13.

69 *Ibid.*

70 Shobha Dé's closest predecessor is undoubtedly Namita Gokhale whose first novel *Paro: Dreams of Passion* was first published in 1984 by Chatto and Windus. Like Dé, Gokhale founded and edited a Bombay film magazine (*Super*) which was accused of being a pale imitation of Dé's magazine *Stardust*. The plot of *Paro* echoes through Dé's first novel, *Socialite Evenings*. Both novelists were accused of selling "soft porn" packaged as "respectable Literature" – both were accused of violating "decent" images of marriage, fidelity and female friendship.

71 For more on Indian English see Mulk Raj Anand, "Pigeon English," *World Literature Written in English* 21, 2 (Summer 1982), pp. 325–35. Also see Vimala Rama Rao, "Decolonization, not Disinheritance: English in India Today," in K. Ayyappa Paniker, ed., *Indian English Literature Since Independence* (New Delhi: The Indian Association for English Studies, 1991), pp. 144–8.

72 In chastising Dé for creating heroines with an "unlimited freedom to flirt" (with men, women, life, Tradition, careers, etc.), Subhash Chandra reveals what most upsets conservative critics who have written about this and other novels by this writer. See Subash Chandra, "Family and Marriage in Shobha Dé's *Socialite Evenings*," in *Indian English Literature Since Independence*, pp. 27–33. His article presents Dé as an "authentic" member of the class she portrays and hence the authority on (and champion of) the breakdown of "the traditional concept of marriage with fidelity as its cardinal principle" (p. 33). Family values crumple under the pressures put on social institutions by a "militant feminism" which is presented in

Chandra's article as little more than acquiring "all the resources to flirt ad *infinitum*" (p. 32).

73 Despite several formal and informal queries to Shebha Press and to scholars and publishers in the field, I have not located any biographical information about "Rohini." I will therefore presume that it is appropriate to discuss the plot of "her" novel in the context set up in this chapter.

74 Several short stories in English by Indian women writers such as Vishwapriya Iyengar have of course represented classes of women outside their own. The novel by Meena Alexander mentioned earlier, *Nampally Road*, also represents women outside these classes, however her concern is not so much with domestic as with national space.

75 See the earlier cited works by Patel, Kumar and Maria Mies for detailed accounts of the various issues that have been central rallying points for women's organizations in urban India. A chapter entitled "Violence Against Women and Ongoing Primitive Accumulation of Capital" in *Patriarchy and Accumulation* by Mies, is based on research conducted in India and is specially insightful on the ways in which women's groups have been formed around violent crimes against women (pp. 145–75). In Rohini's novel the bonding between women take place in a similar fashion.

76 Rohini, *To Do Something Beautiful*, p. 5.

77 *Ibid.*, pp. 5–6.

78 *Ibid.*, p. 153.

6. "TRAVELING LIGHT": HOME AND THE IMMIGRANT GENRE

1 See Barbara Harlow, "The theoretical-historical context," *Resistance Literature* (New York: Methuen, 1987), pp. 1–30. Barbara Harlow builds on the theory put forward in 1981 by Ngugi Wa Thiongo which divided literature into that of oppression and that of the struggle for liberation, thus challenging the conventional practice of distinguishing between literary texts on the bases of form.

2 In recent years, several excellent essays have centered around the examination of related issues. For an elaborate and moving discussion of the literature of exile, see Edward Said, "Reflections on Exile" in Russell Ferguson et al, eds., *Out There: Marginalization and Contemporary Cultures* (Cambridge, MA: MIT Press, 1990), pp. 357–66. Also see Fran Bartkowski, "Travelers v. Ethnics: Discourses of Displacement," *Discourse* 15, 3 (Spring 1993), pp. 158–76; Carmen Wickramagamage, "Relocation as Positive Act: The Immigrant Experience in Bharati Mukherjee's Novels," *Diaspora* 2, 2 (1992), pp. 171–200.

3 My intention is not so much to attempt a taxonomy of immigrant fictions as, enabled by the arguments formulated in the novels, to intervene in the ongoing theoretical discussions on postcolonial literature/literary theory and in the critical formulations on minorities and margins.

4 See for example, Timothy Brennan, *Salman Rushdie and the Third World: Myths of the Nation* (New York: St. Martin's Press, 1989). Brennan coins the term "Third-World Cosmopolitan" in an attempt to categorize and contextualize the works of writers such as Salman Rushdie, Derek Walcott, Isabel Allende, Gabriel Garcia Marquez, and Bharati Mukherjee.

5 Anita Desai, *ByeBye BlackBird* (New Delhi: Orient, 1985); Bharati Mukherjee, *Wife* (Canada: Penguin, 1987); Buchi Emecheta, *Second Class Citizen* (1974) (New York: Braziller, 1983); Salman Rushdie, *The Satanic Verses* (New York: Viking Press, 1988); Sara Suleri, *Meatless Days* (Illinois: University of Chicago Press, 1989); Beryl Gilroy, *Boy-Sandwich* (Oxford: Heinemann Caribbean Series, 1989).

6 Sam Selvon, *The Lonely Londoners* (London: Longman Caribbean Writers, 1956). Cited hereafter in the text as *LL*.

7 "The Liberation of the Black Intellect" was written by A. Sivanandan in 1972 for a symposium on "immigrant intellectuals" in Britain and later published as "Alien Gods" in Bhikhu Parekh, ed., *Colour, Culture and Consciousness* (London: Allen and Unwin, 1974), pp. 104–18. Also see Salman Rushdie, "The Empire Within," *Imaginary Homelands: Essays and Criticism 1981–1991* (London: Granta Books, 1991).

8 Homi Bhabha, "DissemiNation: time, narrative, and the margins of the modern nation," in Homi K. Bhabha, ed., *Nation and Narration* (London: Routledge, 1990), pp. 291–332. Cited hereafter in the text as *D*.

9 Jurgen Joachim Hesse, "Speaking with Voices of Change: Immigrant Writers and Canadian Literature," *The Journal of Ethnic Studies* 19, 1 (Spring 1991), p. 87.

10 *Ibid.*

11 Salman Rushdie, *Shame* (New York: Random House, 1984), p. 91.

12 Jamaica Kincaid, *Annie John* (New York: Plume Press [Penguin] 1986).

13 *Ibid.*, pp. 134–5.

14 *Ibid.*, p. 133.

15 *Lucy* (New York: Farrar, Straus, Giroux) written by Kincaid after *Annie John* and published in 1990, "continues" this narrative in the US, through the story of another young Antiguan girl, Lucy. In the 1990s, the US has thoroughly replaced the UK as the desired and most logical site of a "future abroad" even for persons from one-time British colonies.

16 Edward Said, *After the Last Sky: Palestinian Lives* (New York: Pantheon Books, 1986).

17 *Ibid.*, p. 14.

18 Perhaps the best way to access the political critique of cultural colonization in *Annie John* is to read it alongside Kincaid's *A Small Place* (Canada: Plume Press, 1987). In this anti-travel guide to Antigua, Kincaid exposes the unseen cultural violence in a place like Antigua where outright racism is seen by genteel colonials as a severe case of "bad manners."

19 Selvon, *The Lonely Londoners*, p. 18.

20 M. G. Vassanji, *The Gunny Sack* (London: Heinemann International, African Writers Series, 1989). Cited hereafter in the text as *GS*.
21 Salman Rushdie, *Shame*, p. 89.
22 In Beryl Gilroy's *Boy-Sandwich*, Clara Grainger, the young narrator's [Tyrone] grandmother who left the Caribbean for England in the 1950s, also carries two bags with her that she vows "no one but me [Tyrone] would inherit after her death"(p. 11). Tyrone realizes that it's "no use saying I don't want them" for his grandmother is determined that he will inherit the contents of the larger bag – an assortment of the tools of her trade as a seamstress, old jewelry, a pair of shoes she wore to a dance in Brixton in 1952, etc. The smaller linen bag that is "as sacred as her cross and her Bible" contains Island earth that she had brought with her and that she wants to be buried with (p. 13). It is important to note that eviction from their home in a part of London that was taken over by developers, makes Clara Grainger and her husband Simon, homeless exiles who rapidly disintegrate in their new abode, a home for the elderly. At the end of the novel Clara and Simon Grainger go back "home" to "the Island" and her bags are emptied out and put away.
23 In *An Immigrant Success Story: East Indians in America*, the authors Arthur Helweg and Usha Helweg note that in the early decades of this century, thousands of Indians had left India and traveled by sea and land to Africa, Europe, North and South America with "hostel gurudwaras providing refuge and support along the way" (p. 54). In a footnote on the same page, the Helwegs add "Sikh communities which held to the custom of offering in their *Gurudwaras*, food and lodging to needy travelers were scattered throughout the British Empire. Migrants often took refuge in the sikh *Gurudwaras*." Arthur W. Helweg and Usha M. Helweg, *An Immigrant Success Story: East Indians in America* (Philadelphia: University of Pennsylvania Press, 1990), p. 54.
24 For instance, the affiliations of first generation Japanese American writers and readers are very different from that of the second generation, English speaking "nisei" or third generation "sansei" writers. Similarly, for the contemporary Palestinian, the personal experience of exile is recounted in terms of whether one is "jil filastin" (those who have known and lived in Palestine before its partition) or "jil al-nakba" (those born after 1948). Memory and desire operate differently for different generations. In *Mississippi Masala*, Mira Nair's film (Goldwyn Pictures, 1992) on Indian immigrants in the US, the confrontation between the young heroine and her father on the issues of love and race, are typical of this generational difference.
25 "Holy Perversions," Benedict Anderson, "Nationalisms and Sexualities" Conference, Keynote Panel 1, June 16th, 1989. Doris Sommer's "Love and Country in Latin America: An Allegorical Speculation," *Cultural Critique* (Fall 1990) pp. 109–28, makes similar connections between erotics

and politics. Theresa Hubel, "'The Bride of his Country': Love, Marriage, and the Imperialist Paradox in the Indian Fiction of Sara Jeanette Duncan and Rudyard Kipling," *Ariel: A Review of International English Literature* 21, 1 (January 1990), pp. 3–19, examines the metaphoric marriage between Britain and India which was commonly used in the narratives written by colonial writers. Imperialism is thus represented as a marriage between the masculine Britain and the coy, mysterious India. Anderson's most recent book, *Language and Power: Exploring Political Cultures in Indonesia* (New York: Cornell University Press, 1990), reads select Indonesian cultural texts in terms of this dynamic of power and passion.

26 However, elsewhere in the novel, Kala demonstrates how malleable the English language can be in his hands if he so desires. For instance, describing the early years of his parents' marriage which were spent under the supervision of Aunt Awal, Kala writes of the Indian notion of "khandaneeath" or family position and prestige.

There were in the household then Awal's two sons, now married, and her three nieces, my aunts. Over the six young women the tall, thin-lipped, long-nosed puritan Awal ruled with an iron hand. "If your pachedis keep slipping off your heads, use a nail," she would rail, in her constant efforts to preserve her home's khandaanity: that snobbish form of respectability which every family, however crooked, lays claim to. Daughters-in-law, responsible for the khandaanity of their father's names, occupied the lowest rungs in the family hierarchy. (*GS*, 68)

The use of the term "khandaanity" here displays the transportation of concepts from one language to another that is common with bilingual individuals. "Khandaneeath" thus is "translated" or at least transformed into the more English-like "Khandaanity," so that the pause to explain the word or even the word "pachedi" (here conveniently pluralized as in the English language with an addition of an "s") is very slight.

27 Peter Nazareth, another East African Indian writer, examines this complex issue of the representation of Africa and Africans in literature in English in "Out of Darkness: Conrad and Other Third World Writers," *Conradiana* 14, 3 (1982), pp. 173–87. Claiming that the English language is "inherently racist," Nazareth goes on to exonerate Conrad and Marlow who together work to reverse the images of whiteness and blackness (p. 177). Nazareth indicts V. S. Naipaul and Shiva Naipaul for allowing their use of the English language to exhibit a racism that is sharpened by the use of a vocabulary that is "superficially Conradian ("impenetrable," "inscrutable," "frenzied") but actually anti-Conradian (and which therefore draws) racist conclusions" (p. 181).

28 "China" in Amy Tan's *Joy-Luck Club* (New York: Putnam, 1989) operates similarly for the generation of "mothers" in that novel.

29 Desai, *Bye Bye Blackbird*, pp. 12–13.

30 Leena Dhingra, *First Light* (New Delhi: Rupa, 1991). Note that Piccadilly is next to "Jail" on the Monopoly game board.

31 Benedict Anderson, *Imagined Communities: Reflections on the Origin and Spread of Nationalism*, (London: Verso, 1983), pp. 15–16. Anderson's text emphasizes the many ideological apparatuses that work toward mobilizing this sense of the nation as an imagined unity.

32 M. G. Vassanji, "South Asian Canadian Literature," *Literary Criterion* 19, 3–4 (1984), pp. 61–71. This journal is published by the Department of English, Bangalore University, in Bangalore, Karnataka State, India.

33 Gayatri Chakravorty Spivak, "Woman in Difference: Mahasweta Devi's 'Doulati the Bountiful,'" *Cultural Critique* (Winter 1989–1990), pp. 105–28.

34 Jamaica Kincaid, *A Small Place*, p. 11.

35 J. Hesse makes a somewhat similar point in "Voices of Change." His reference is however to the cultural superiority complex of Canadian immigrants who came from Europe. He states: "To be part of multi-ethnic and multicultural affairs in Europe can well breed a feeling of cultural superiority when compared to the straitlaced, unidirectional and repetitive examples of much of North American cultural products... Sure some of us immigrant writers feel superior to this banal culture" (pp. 98–9). While we are familiar with this Eurocentric dismissal of Canada and the United States as no more than faint and/or fake echoes of Europe, there is also another point being made here. Hesse argues that the immigrant, in this case from Europe, is culturally superior "as [a] result of having had intimate knowledge of several cultures simultaneously" (p. 89).

36 When Bhabha theorizes about "wandering migrants" he focuses on the "foreignness of languages," on "loss," on "voids," "death," "opacities," and "untranslatable silences" (*DissemiNation*, pp. 315–19). Enabled by Berger's work on Turkish immigrants in Germany, Bhabha sets out to examine "the desolate silences of the wandering peoples...that 'oral void' that emerges when the Turk abandons the metaphor of a *heimlich* national culture: for the Turkish immigrant the final return is mythic" (p. 316). Given the Turkish worker's unfamiliarity with the German language, Bhabha concludes that: "The object of loss is written across the bodies of the people, as it repeats in the silence that speaks the foreignness of language" (p. 315). The view from *within* the Turkish immigrant community as available in oral and written texts may be quite different. Bhabha himself somewhat alters his view of "desolate silences" when he includes Salman Rushdie's theorizing on the immigrant experience in *The Satanic Verses* into his reading of migranthood. Like Rushdie, Vassanji's narrative speaks *from* the position of the immigrant rather than *of* those at the margins.

37 Although the texts I read challenge Bhabha's assertions, clearly wandering is not always painless. Mira Nair's *Mississippi Masala* further complicates the distinctions between exile and immigration that this chapter attempts to enunciate. Set in the late 1980s in Mississippi, Nair's film narrates the story of an Indian immigrant family that had been evicted from Uganda in the early 1970s. Different members of this family view their

joint predicament differently. The father, played by Roshan Seth, suffers the anguish of exile. Uganda was and is his homeland. His wife (Sharmila Tagore) and daughter (Sarita Choudhury) view this event in their past and their much more circumscribed present condition of "homelessness" (the family rents two rooms in a relative's motel) with greater equanimity. The film follows two parallel plots: the daughter's romance with an African-American (Denzel Washington), and the father's slow rejection of the "pleasures" of absolute identification of himself with a place on the map. At the end of the film the father returns to Uganda for a short visit and finds that his growing detachment to the idea of national belonging makes an immigrant out of him. He discovers that he will be happy to live wherever his family resides. Meanwhile, back in Mississippi, the young lovers set off to wander the world together. Their first stop will be Jamaica and from there they will go to Africa, to India...

38 Also see the very similar dynamics in descriptions of various Gonzaga brothers as they shuttle between Manila and Spain in Jessica Hagedorn's *Dogeaters* (New York: Penguin, 1990). Of her father, Freddie Gonzaga, the narrator Rio writes:

> I am still not sure what sort of passport he waves in the air, if he owns one or two. Maybe Spanish, maybe British, maybe Filipino, maybe anything. It is the sort of business he keeps to himself. He believes in dual citizenships, dual passports, as many allegiances to as many countries as possible at any given time. My father is a cautious man, and refers to himself as a "guest" in his own country. My mother who carries American papers because of her father, feels more viscerally connected to the Philippines than he ever could...
>
> My father and uncles are smug, mysterious men together, especially at the dinner table. "Let's be on the safe side," my father might say to Pucha's father, Uncle Augustin. "We are not fools, and we're not cowards. But we are typical Gonzagas who want to stay alive at all costs. Nothing to be ashamed of." My father could be discussing anything – real estate or politics – it's all the same to him...
>
> My father brings up one of his favorite topics, the eldest and most successful Gonzaga brother, my Uncle Christobal who lives in Spain. Uncle Christobal flies a Falangista flag above his front door to show his allegiance to Franco during the Spanish Civila war. He flies the flag not because he really is a fascist, but because he is a wily opportunist; like my father and Uncle Augustin, he is a practical Gonzaga, a man who always knows which side is winning. After the war, Uncle Christobal is rewarded with a prosperous import–export firm based in Madrid. My father said that if Uncle Christobal had lived in Russia in 1917, he would have been a Marxist. "Adaptability is the simple secret of survival," my father always maintains. It is another of his well-worn Gonzaga clichés, but also a rule he lives by. (pp. 7–9)

39 Kincaid, *Annie John*, p. 144.
40 *Ibid.*, p. 138.

41 Said, *After the Last Sky*, p. 23.

42 Very briefly, Tanganyika was a German colony till after World War I, after which the League of Nations put the area under British administration. After World War II, it was declared a United Nations Trust Territory, again under British administration with the understanding that the British would work toward eventual independence for Tanganyika. Julius Nyerere led this independence movement. He entered politics in the early 1950s, and in 1954 pulled several factions together to form the Tanganyika African National Union. He was elected first Prime Minister and then President of Tanganyika and later of the independent Tanzania. Popularly known as "Mwalimu" (teacher), Nyerere set up a sophisticated, non-violent socialist program for Tanzania both before and after independence.

43 "Ujamaa" translated from Swahili would roughly mean "family" or "familyhood" and the word suggests the social responsibility that being part of a family entails. This filial responsibility was to be carried out through mandatory citizen service in various community and self-help projects around the nation. Nyerere's socialist project also included a two-year compulsory work program for university students, called National Service, under which scheme they were sent to work on road construction, irrigation and other rural development projects which would challenge their elitism as members of an educated class. This, and other reforms were to ensure that the notion of the national family for which members (including the elite) took up their responsibility was to be put into material practice. See Basil Davidson, *Which Way Africa? The Search for a New Society* (1964; repr. London: Penguin, 1967) for a wider understanding of Tanzanian politics in the context of postcolonial Africa.

44 Lawrence Fellows writes that at the time of independence there were a total of four hundred thousand Indians among the thirty million Africans in Tanzania, Kenya and Uganda. The Indian population controlled about four-fifths of the commerce in these three adjacent countries – from the big trading houses to the small *dukas*. *East Africa* (London: Macmillan, 1972). In Tanzania, one of the poorer African nations, at the end of the year of independence (1961), there was no dramatic positive change in the national income or the personal wealth of individuals as had been expected. A drop in world prices of sisal fiber (used in the manufacture of rope and packaging material, such as gunny sacks) and a drop in world coffee prices, led to worker layoffs, diminishing profits and increased resentment against whites and Indians. State-sanctioned confiscations of white farms and Indian businesses were frequently enacted by youth groups. Deportation of Indians was on the rise, especially of those who had not given up their Indian or British passports. Violence and looting were commonplace as Black Africans attempted to get control over their own economies.

45 See Neil Lazarus, "Great Expectations and the Mourning After: Decolonization and African Intellectuals," in *Resistance and Post-Colonial*

African Fiction, for an account of the significance of these ceremonies of independence in the popular understanding of national history, especially as re-presented in African literature. In drawing attention to the ceremony itself, Lazarus' intention is to stress that "unless we grasp the huge significance that the (re)attainment of nationhood carried for African intellectuals in these years of decolonization, it is almost impossible for us to understand the subsequent trajectory of African literature. We cannot make sense of the problematic of postcolonialism in this literature unless we read it as relating, very concretely and immediately to the headiness of initial expectations of independence" (p. 3).

46 Correspondingly, there is not even a passing reference to the Indian struggle for independence or to the handing over of power in the context of the Indian subcontinent.

47 For instance, Bhabha writes: "The narrative of national cohesion can no longer be signified, in Anderson's words, as a 'sociological solidarity' fixed in a 'succession of plurals' – hospitals, prisons, remote villages – where the social space is clearly bounded by such repeated objects that represent a naturalistic, national horizon" (*D,* pp. 304–5).

48 In insisting that what is written at the margins not be understood as "National Discourse," my intention is to suggest that immigration and immigrants are in themselves sites that evacuate meaning from concepts such as "national discourses" and "national literatures."

49 This sentence echoes the excerpt from Agha Shahid Ali's poem, "The Previous Occupant" that is used as an epigraph to this chapter. See Arvind Krishna Mehrotra, ed., *The Oxford Anthology of Twelve Modern Indian Poets* (New Delhi: Oxford University Press, 1992), p. 147.

Index

aboriginals, 187
abortion, 150, 157
Achebe, Chinua, 91, 200
  No Longer at Ease, 238
  Things Fall Apart, 118, 238
activism, 32, 57, 143, 168
Adorno, 34
aesthetics, 53, 61, 62, 152, 153–7, 170, 240
affiliations, 11, 16, 17, 170, 178, 191, 207, 245
Africa/Africans, 42, 68, 73, 84, 89, 94, 118, 119, 176, 180–3, 187, 188, 189, 194, 246, 249
  as primitive, 20
  Belgian, 59
  British Africa, 3, 188
  East Africa, 8, 176, 184, 188, 190
  independence, 194–5, 206, 250
After the Last Sky: Palestinian Lives, see Said, Edward
Age of Empire, see Hobsbawm, Eric
agency, 142, 163, 200
Ahmad, Aijaz, 102, 104–7, 111, 113, 229, 231
Aidoo, Ama Ata, 5, 119
  Changes, 120
  No Sweetness Here, 5
  Our Sister Killjoy, 203, 233
Alexander, Meena, 157–9, 240, 243
Ali, Agha Shahid
  "The Previous Occupant," 171, 250
alien/alienation 1, 7, 33, 36, 46, 53, 62, 63, 65, 66, 74, 76, 99, 102, 103, 113, 116, 118, 121, 128, 158, 189–90, 222
allegory, 7, 15, 40
Allegories of Empire, see Sharpe, Jenny
Allende, Isabel, 244
Alter, Stephen and Wimal Dissanayake
  The Penguin Book of Modern Indian Short Stories, 241
Almayer's Folly, see Conrad, Joseph
Althusser, 225

Am I That Name? Feminism and the Category of "women" in History, see Riley, Denise
Ambai, 159
America/Americans, 32, 40, 56, 97, 111, 136, 165
Amritvela, see Dhingra, Leena
Amsterdam, 77
Anand, Mulk Raj, 164
  "Pigeon English," 242
  Untouchable, 118
Anderson, Benedict, 3, 12, 108, 181, 195, 226
  Imagined Communities Reflections on the Origin and Spread of Nationalism, 3, 12, 108, 186, 247
  Language and Power: Exploring Political Cultures in Indonesia, 246
Anderson, Perry, 7, 66, 72, 75, 76, 88, 90, 223, 225, 235
Anderson, Sherwood, 110
Annie John, see Kincaid, Jamaica
Another India: An Anthology of Contemporary Indian Fiction and Poetry, see Ezekiel, Nissim
Antharjanam, Lalithaambika, 158 anthropology, 73
Antigua, 129, 173, 174, 188, 189, 192
Anzaldua, Gloria, 29
Arabs, 75, 76, 174
Architectural Uncanny: Essays on the Modern Unhomely, The, see Vidler, Anthony
architecture, 19, 22, 183, 210
Arendt, Hannah, 89
Armah Ayi Kwei, 118
  The Beautyful Ones Are Not Yet Born, 5,118
Armstrong, Frances, 70, 224
Armstrong, Nancy
  Desire and Domestic Fiction, 37, 203, 205
art, 46, 49, 114, 115, 116, 133, 144, 145, 151–4, 162, 169, 192
  aesthetics, see aesthetics
  and women, 133
  modernist, 67
  western, 90

251

Ashcroft, Bill, Gareth Griffiths, and Helen Tiffin
  The Empire Writes Back: Theory and Practice in Postcolonial Literature, 105, 208, 230
Asians, 181
aura, 115, 175
  of home, 2, 21, 175
Aurobindo, 141, 157
Austen, Jane
  Emma, 45
  Mansfield Park, 70
Australia, 42

Bachelard, Gaston, 20
  The Poetics of Space, 21, 207
Bachelor of Arts, The, see Narayan, R. K
Balamaniamma, 158
Bangladesh, 173, 212
barbarism, 68, 74
  as gendered, 68
Barnabas, Sarla
  The Promise of Spring, 238
Barnouw, Eric, and S. Krishnaswamy
  Indian Film, 234
Barr, Pat
  The Memsahibs: In Praise of the Women of Victorian India, 215, 218
Barrett, Michele, and Anne Phillips
  Destabilizing Theory: Contemporary Feminist Debates, 203
Barthes, Roland, 225
  Mythologies, 236
Bartkowski, Fran
  "Travelers v. Ethnics: Discourses of Displacement," 243
Beautiful Ones are Not Yet Born, The, see Armah, Ayi Kwei
Beck, Evelyn Torton
  Nice Jewish Girls, 204
becoming minor, 28, 29, 35, 103, 112
Beghar, see Nisal, Shanta
Beirut, 174
belonging, 1, 2, 8, 15, 62, 73, 75, 83, 170, 173, 193, 196, 197, 199
Below the Peacock Fan: First Ladies of the Raj, see Fowler, Marian
Bengal, 219
Ben-Jalud, Tahir, 209
Benjamin, Walter, 74, 105, 113, 114–17, 230
  "The Storyteller," 113, 114, 116
  "The Work of Art in the Age of Mechanical Reproductions," 232
Berlin conference (1884), 73
Bhabha, Homi, 75, 104, 183, 230, 247, 250
  "DissemiNation: time, narrative, and the margins of the modern nation," 8, 105, 173, 183, 186, 187, 190, 195, 197
  "Postcolonial Criticism," 225
  "Signs taken for Wonders: Questions of Ambivalence and Authority under a Tree Outside Delhi, May 1817," 230
Bharata
  Natyasastra, 151
Bhattacharjee, Annaya
  "The Habit of Ex-Nomination," 236
Bhattacharya, Bhabani, 140
bilingualism, 90
Birmingham, 208
Blackwoods, 76, 86
Boehmer, Elleke, 230
Bombay, 145, 149, 151, 153, 154, 164–6, 167, 169, 185, 208, 215
boredom, 132–3, 135, 145–57
Bottomley, Gordon, 240
Boy-Sandwich. See Gilroy, Beryl
Breeze, Jean "Binta", 91
Brennan, Timothy
  Salman Rushdie and the Third World: Myths of the Nation, 104–5, 244
Britain/British, 1, 66,74–5, 249, see also England
  subjects, *see* subject/subjecthood: British
  colonialism, *see* colonialism: British
  culture, 64, 66, 90, 222, 223, 235
  empire, 35–60, 90, 191, 218
  imperialism, *see* imperialism: British
  occupation of India, 35–64
  colonists, 183
  in Conrad, 7, 94
  intelligentsia, 66, 72
Brittain, Vera, 217
Bronte, Charlotte
  Jane Eyre, 32, 40, 70, 71
Brussels, 85
Bulkin, Elly, 204
Bungalow: The Production of a Global Culture, The, see King, Anthony
Burma, 63
Burmese Days, see Orwell, George
Burnett, Frances Hodgson
  The Little Princess, 224
Burns, Robert, 157
Burton, Antoinette, 213, 221
Butler, Josephine, 213
ByeBye BlackBird, see Desai, Anita

Calcutta, 158, 208, 215
Callaway, Helen
  Gender, Culture and Empire: European Women in Colonial Nigeria, 222
Canada, 173, 186, 187, 197, 207, 247

Captain Desmond V.C., see Diver, Maud
Carlyle, Thomas, 73
caste system, 59, 75, 121–5, 133, 135, 136, 137, 143, 167, 181
Celebrity, see Dé, Shobha
celibacy, 58, 220
Chadha, Ramesh, 140
Chakrabarty, Dipesh
  "The Difference-Deferral of (A) Colonial Modernity: Public Debates on Domesticity in British Bengal," 219
Chandra, Subhash, 242, 243
Changes, see Aidoo, Ama Ata
Chatterjee, Partha, 12, 60, 107, 108, 117, 118
  Nationalist Thought and the Colonial World: A Derivative Discourse, 12, 117
  "The Nationalist Resolution of the Women's Question," 219
Chatterji, Lola, 161
  Woman Image Text: Feminist Readings of Literary Texts, 237
Chattopadhyay, Bankimchandra, 117
childhood/children, 21, 38, 49, 50, 51, 52, 54, 56, 59, 70, 81, 88, 91, 116, 117, 121, 126, 149, 151, 174, 180, 192, 209, 225, 227
Chinese Exclusion Act of 1882, 32
Chitra, Satya, 242
Christianity, 83, 123, 156, 206, 220
Chugtai, Ismat, 159, 241
cinema, see film
cities, 208, see also individual cities
  African, 59, 63, 73, 85, 94, 182
  colonial, 23–4, 215
  Egyptian, 60
  European, 23, 63, 94
  western, 60
citizen/citizenship, 24, 37–8, 40, 46, 62, 83, 112, 170, 178, 186, 193, 200, 218, 222
City of Quartz, see Davis, Mike
civilization, 49, 58, 64, 72, 74, 87
  and barbarism, 74
  and wilderness, 84, 226
  and gender, 226–7
Claiming an Identity They Taught Me to Despise, see Cliff, Michelle
class, 2, 6, 7, 8, 9, 16, 28, 30, 32, 33, 37, 46, 54, 59, 67, 71, 73, 74, 77, 80, 87, 88, 91, 93, 96, 122, 123, 130, 132, 133, 135, 136, 137, 144, 159, 160, 163, 166, 168, 181, 189, 193, 197, 218
  see also individual classes
  and domesticity, see domesticity and class
  and feminism, see feminism: and class
  and Indian women, see women: Indian elite

Clear Light of Day, see Desai, Anita
Cliff, Michelle, 211
  Claiming an Identity They Taught Me to Despise, 28, 29
  No Telephone to Heaven, 203
Clifford, James, 2
Coleridge, Samuel Taylor, 139
collective unconscious, 20
Collits, Terry, 223
colonial subject, see subject/subjecthood: colonial
colonialism, 4, 8, 12, 14, 17, 24, 40, 53, 75, 83, 86, 98, 107, 123, 128, 129, 144, 158, 171, 172, 189, 190, 197, 204, 208, 212, 214, 220, 222, 226, 244–5
  British, 4, 36, 96, 122, 189, 190, 191, 203, 212
colonies, 5, 6, 23, 73, 87, 96, 172, 190, 204, 214, 218, 222
  India as, 37–64
colonized, 1, 3, 4, 5, 8, 9, 15, 44, 50, 84, 88, 172, 186, 190
colonizers, 1, 88, 96, 204, 209
  German, 187, 189, 190, 191
  neo, 129, 205
Colonizing Egypt, see Mitchell, Timothy
Common Poetics For Indian Literature, A, see Narasimhaiah, C. D.
community, 3, 6, 7, 9, 11, 15, 18, 25, 26, 27, 43, 60, 62, 73, 76, 81, 108, 113, 114, 115, 123, 128, 179, 180, 181, 182, 185, 186, 188, 190, 194, 205, 209, 226
Complete Home, The, see Wright, Julia McNair
Complete Indian Housekeeper and Cook, The, see Steel, Flora Anne and Grace Gardiner
conduct books, 37, 41
Conrad in the Nineteenth Century, see Watt, Ian
Conrad, Joseph, 7, 8, 19, 63, 64, 65–99, 127, 199, 200, 223, 226, 246
  "A Glance at Two Books," 65, 76
  "Autocracy and War," 87, 88
  A Personal Record, 75
  Almayer's Folly, 7, 68, 75, 76–80, 77, 78, 79, 91, 93
  and England, 74, 75
  and gender, 64, 67–9
  Heart of Darkness, 7, 9, 19, 68, 69, 76, 83–8, 89, 92, 93, 94, 96, 97, 226–7, 228
  Lord Jim, 7, 68, 69, 76, 80–3, 80, 81, 82, 83, 86, 97
  The Nigger of Narcissus, 68
  The Secret Agent, 68, 87, 88
  Typhoon, 68
  Under Western Eyes, 68, 88
  Victory, 68
consumerism, 136, 166

Contemporary Indian Literature, 233
Cooper, Clara, 20, 207, 209
Criticism and Ideology. *See* Eagleton, Terry
Cvetkovich, Ann and Avery Gordon
"Not in Our Names: Women, War,
AIDS," 229

Dark Room, The, *see* Narayan, R. K.
Das, Kamala, 147, 164
"The Sunshine Cat," 131, 135
*Daughters of Independence: Gender, Caste and Class
in India*, *see* Liddle, Joanna
Davidson, Basil
*Which Way Africa? The Search for a New
Society*, 249
Davin, Anna
"Imperialism and Motherhood," 38, 221
Davis, Mike
City of Quartz, 209
Day in Shadow, The, *see* Sahgal, Nayantara
de Lauretis, Theresa
Feminist Studies/Critical Studies, 210
Dé, Shobha, 164, 165, 166, 241, 242
Celebrity, 165
Sisters, 164
Socialite Evenings, 134, 164, 165, 242
Society, 165
Stardust, 165, 166, 242
Starry Nights, 164
Sultry Days, 164
Obsession, 164
Dean, Michael, 204
decolonization, 93, 94, 159, 250
Deleuze, Gilles, and Felix Guattari, 28, 29,
35, 111, 112, 210
Dell, Ethel, 221
The Lamp in the Desert, 61
Delusions and Discoveries, *see* Parry, Benita
Desai, Anita, 131–67, 240, 241
ByeBye BlackBird, 172, 175, 183
Clear Light of Day, 238
Where Shall We Go This Summer?, 131, 132,
145–54, 155, 156, 157, 167
Desani, G.V., 91
Deshpande, Shashi, 131–67, 241
Roots and Shadows, 238
That Long Silence, 131, 133, 134, 145–9,
153, 154
*Desire and Domestic Fiction: A Political History of
the Novel*, *see* Armstrong, Nancy
*Destabilizing Theory: Contemporary Feminist
Debates*, *see* Barrett, Michele
deterritorialization, 28, 30, 35, 112, 210
Devi, Mahashweta, 159
"Doulati the Bountiful," 187
Dhareshwar, Vivek, 107

Dhingra, Leena
First Light/Amritvela, 183, 231, 237
Dickens, Charles, 70
Great Expectations, 71
Dickinson, Emily, 238
Die Englanders in Indien, *see* Konigsmark,
Count John
*Disappearance of God: Five Nineteenth-Century
Writers, The*, *see* Miller, J. Hillis
Dissanayake, Wimal, 241
Diver, Maud, 6, 40, 43–56, 58–61, 63, 64,
69, 215, 217, 219, 220, 222
Captain Desmond V.C., 43–4, 47–8, 53, 63,
216, 222
The Englishwoman in India, 39, 42, 47, 49–50,
51, 53, 54, 55, 56, 58–60, 215, 219
Unconquered: A Romance, 44–7, 54, 63
domestic crisis, 132, 135, 145, 155, 157, 165,
167, 168
domestic fiction, *see* literature: domestic
domestic violence, 21, 143, 167, 211, 236,
243
domesticity, 3, 4, 13, 21, 36, 40, 41, 50–60,
65, 69, 72, 80, 86, 90, 91, 124, 126,
127, 132, 133, 140, 161–3, 199, 200,
219, 221, 223, 224, 241
Dogeaters, *see* Hagedorn, Jessica
Doob, Leonard, 109, 205
Dostoevsky, 105, 116
Dublin, 63
Dubois, Ellen, 37, 40, 213
Dufferin, Lady, 59, 219, 221
Dutt, Toru, 141, 158, 235

Eagleton, Terry, 66, 67, 68, 74
Criticism and Ideology, 68
Exiles and Emigres, 66, 68, 222
"Form, Idealogy and *The Secret Agent*," 222
"Idealogy and Literary Form," 222
East India Company, 212, 214
Eberhardt, Isabelle, 222
economics, 17, 18, 23, 41, 66, 67, 72, 103,
104, 132, 133, 137, 143, 205, 210
education
colonial subjects', 51, 57, 58, 59, 119
legacy of colonial, 122, 136, 138–9,
158–60, 172, 174, 231
postcolonial, 119, 133, 134, 138, 159–60,
170, 172, 240
servants', 52
wives', 72
Eliot, T.S., 139, 157, 238
The Family Reunion, 238
"The Hollow Men," 238
"elite," 15, 129–30, 132, 133, 135, 136, 137,
164–5

Emecheta, Buchi, 209
  Second Class Citizen, 172
emigres, 7, 66, 67, 74, 75, 90
Emma. See Austen, Jane
Empire Writes Back, The, see Ashcroft, Bill
England/English, 9, 37, 74, 94, 95, 96, 183,
  215, *see also* Britain
  17th and 18th century, 37, 70
  as home, *see* home: England as
  Edwardian, 70
  Englishness, 43, 75, 76, 95–6
  and Conrad, 65, 75, 76
  history, 65
  home, *see* home: English
  literature, *see* literature: English
  rural, 73
  Victorian, 70–3
  women, *see* women: English
English language, 1, 7, 8, 14, 53, 62, 88–91,
  98, 121, 122, 138, 159–60, 163, 166,
  172, 182, 185, 222, 237, 246
  global, 1, 3, 6, 8, 14, 89–91, 121, 159,
  160, 197, 200, 203, 241, 242, 246
Englishwoman in India, The. See Diver, Maud
epic, 113–4, 116
etiquette, 45
Europe, 12, 18, 61, 63, 64, 77, 80, 86, 94, 247
Everson, Norma
  The Indian Metropolis: A View to the West, 24
exile, 28, 35, 36, 61–2, 67, 74, 88, 89, 105,
  171, 172, 174, 193, 222, 245, 248
Exiles and Emigres, see, Eagleton, Terry
Ezekiel, Nissim, and Meenakshi Mukherjee
  *Another India: An Anthology of Contemporary
  Indian Fiction and Poetry*, 241

Fabian, Johannes, 102
fairy tales, 116
family, 18, 21, 27, 40, 58, 71–2, 80–1, 88,
  145–9, 161–2, 174–5, 176–7, 189,
  195–6, 207, 208, 209, 246
  and Hinduism, 124–6
  and home, 21
  and immigrants, 190, 191, 196
  in immigrant literature, 173–4, 178–82,
  185, 192
  national, 194, 249
  nuclear, 55
Family Reunion, The, see Eliot, T. S.
family values, 243
Fellows, Lawrence, 249
Female Medical Aid Fund (Dufferin Fund),
  59, 221
Feminine Mystique, The, see Friedan, Betty.
femininity, 7, 68, 69, 70, 85, 158, 199, 226
feminism, 20, 25–34, 35–6, 40–1, 44, 45, 62,

126, 128, 130, 131–8, 142–5, 159, 163,
  166, 167, 169, 199, 200, 212, 213, 215,
  218, 220, 239, 243
  and home, 25–34
  and imperialism, 38–9, 214
  feminist theory, 25–35, 199
Feminism and Geography, see Rose, Gillian
Feminism and Nationalism, see Jayawardene,
  Kumari
Feminist Studies/Critical Studies, see de Lauretis,
  Theresa
fiction, *see* literature
filiations, 16–7, 18, 191, 207
film, 122, 123, 149, 208, 245
  Indian, 122–3, 161–3, 166, 234, 238, 241–2
First Light. See Dhingra, Leena
first world, 18, 28, 30, 98, 103, 105, 107,
  108, 110
foreignness, 90
Forster, E.M., 43, 63, 69
  A Passage to India, 24, 63
Forty, Adrian, 20, 204
Foucault, Michel, 25, 26, 54, 128, 204
  "The Subject and Power," 25, 210
  "Why Study Power: The Question of the
  Subject," 209
Fox-Genovese, Elizabeth, 6, 35, 36
Fowler, Marian
  Below the Peacock Fan: First Ladies of the Raj,
  215
Frankenburg, Ruth
  *White Woman, Race Matters: The Social
  Construction of Whiteness*, 230
Freud, Sigmund, 22, 23
Friedan, Betty
  The Feminine Mystique, 136
Frost, Robert, 21, 26
Froude, James 224
Futehally, Shama, 164
  "Portrait of a Childhood," 132

Gandhi, Indira, 139, 143, 166
Gandhi, Nandita and Nandita Shah
  *The Issues at Stake: Theory and Practice in the
  Contemporary Women's Movement in India*, 239
Gandhi, M.K., 117
Gardiner, Grace. *See* Steel, Flora Anne
gender, 68, 93, 170, 182, 208, 212, 214, 216,
  218, 220, 234
  and imperialism, 35–42, 43, 45, 56–8,
  62–4, 214, 246
  in Conrad, 67–9
*Gender, Culture and Empire: European Women in
  Colonial Nigeria, see* Callaway, Helen
generations, 245
genre, 65, 67, 69

gentrification, 15
geography, 30, 67
Ghose, Aurobindo, 235
Ghosh, Amitava, 164, 209
Gidé, Andre, 89
Gikuyu, 17, 230
Gillman, Charlott Perkins
 The Yellow Wallpaper, 32–3
Gilroy, Beryl
 Boy-Sandwich, 118, 172, 245
global English, *see* English language:
 global
Gokhale, Namita, 242
 Paro: Dreams of Passion, 242
Gordon, Avery, *see* Ann Cvetkovich
Gramsci, 118
Great Expectations, see Dickens, Charles
Great Indian Novel, The, see Tharoor, Shashi
Greene, Graham, 89, 127, 128
Greer, Germain, 136
Grewal, Inderpal and Caren Kaplan, 212
Grimus, see Rushdie, Salman
Guattari, Felix, *see* Deleuze, Gilles
Gunny Sack, The, see Vassanji, M. G.

Hagedorn, Jessica
 Dogeaters, 118
Haraway, Donna, 203
Hariharan, Githa, 164
 The Thousand Faces of Night, 164
Harlow, Barbara, 206, 207, 243
Harris, Wilson, 91
 The Palace of the Peacock, 91
Harrod, Roy, 72
Hayes, Carlton, 109
 Nationalism, A Religion, 205, 207
Head, Bessie
 Maru, 209
Helweg, Arthur and Usha
 *An Immigrant Success Story: East Indians in
 America*, 245
Heart of Darkness, see Conrad, Joseph
Heinemann African Writers Series, 176
Hesse, Jurgen, 173
 "Voices of Change," 247
Hindi language, 161, 166, 169, 193, 218,
 219, 234, 246
Hindu/Hinduism, 57, 58, 124–6, 135, 136,
 142, 144, 147, 156–7, 220–1, 234, 235,
 238
 nationalism, *see* nationalism: Hindu
 women, *see* women: and Hinduism
Hindu Women: Narrative Models, see Mukherjee,
 Prabhati
History and Class Consciousness, see Lukács,
 Georg

*History of Doing: An Illustrated Account of
 Movements for Women's
 Rights and Feminism in India, 1800–1990,
 The, see* Kumar, Radha
Hobsbawm Eric, 23
 The Age of Empire 1875–1924, 208
Hoffman, F.T.A., 22
home, 1, 2, 6, 8, 12, 13, 14, 15, 16, 18,
 21, 22, 23, 24, 25, 26, 28–9, 31, 33,
 35, 45, 46, 49, 83, 85, 87, 88, 95, 98,
 101, 130, 147, 158, 167, 170, 171,
 173, 179, 180, 195, 199, 201, 205,
 210, 218, 227, 229
 and civilization, 20, 74, 86
 and feminism, *see* feminism: and home
 and immigrants, 175, 179, 180, 189, 196,
 197, 200
 and nation/nationalism, 7, 14, 15, 16, 211
 and self/selfhood, *see* self/selfhood: and
 home
 and subject/subjecthood, *see* subject/sub-
 jecthood: and home
 and violence, 21, 27
 as private space, 17, 18, 19–25, 48–9, 71–2
 as uncanny, 22
 as womb, 22, 31
 definitions/constructions of, 1–3, 4, 9, 11,
 15, 16, 17, 18, 21, 22, 23, 26–7, 31, 70,
 71, 82, 85, 86, 88, 196, 203, 205
 England as, 3, 4, 49, 73, 76, 82, 84, 86,
 97
 English, 70, 71, 72, 76
 in colonies, 7, 22, 36, 39, 40, 41, 209,
 213
 in India, 35–63, 217, 218, 220
 English working class, 59, 71
 feel at home, 33, 75, 86, 98, 128, 170,
 184, 197
 going home, 80, 82, 245
 home-country/homeland, 1–3, 6, 8, 11,
 17, 19, 33, 39, 49, 61, 83, 170, 192,
 203, 207, 248
 houses, 19, 20, 22, 23–4, 31, 33, 36, 41,
 46, 49, 50–1, 53, 55, 77–9, 188–9, 205,
 217, 220
 in literature, 1–3, 16, 23–5, 77–88, 91–3,
 95, 131–70, 173–91
 leaving, 35–6, 130, 132, 149, 191–7
 of the "native," 23, 24, 55–6, 59–60
 second, 127
 sentimentalization of, 13, 70, 71, 199, 203
 Victorian, 70–3, 77, 78, 224
Home: A Short History of An Idea, see
 Rybczynski, Witold
Home Girls: A Black Feminist Anthology, see
 Smith, Barbara.

home industries, 46
home management guides, 36, 37, 39, 40,
　41, 42, 47, 49–55, 58, 59, 60, 61, 220
Home Rule for Ireland Party, 225
Home to India, see Rau, Shanta Rama.
Homecoming, see Ngugi, Wa Thiong'o
homelessness, 8, 61, 62, 90, 170, 171, 175,
　179, 193, 197, 226, 245, 248
homesickness, 1, 3, 22, 27, 114, 175, 199,
　224
hooks, bell, 1, 30, 56, 101
Houghton, Walter E.
　The Victorian Frame of Mind, 224
House for Mister Biswas, A, see Naipaul, V. S.
housewives, 41, 136, 161, 238
　in Indian women's fiction, 145–57, 237
Howe, Susan
　Novels of Empire, 42, 222
Hubel, Theresa
　"The Bride of his Country: Love,
　Marriage and the Imperialist Paradox in
　the Indian
　Fiction of Sara Jeanette Duncan and
　Rudyard Kipling. ," 216, 246
Hunt, Nancy Rose, 59
Hurston, Zora Neale
　Their Eyes Were Watching God, 32
Hussain, Attia, 164
　Sunlight on a Broken Column, 139, 238

identity, *see* self/selfhood
Ilbert Bill (1883), 216
*Imagined Communities Reflections on the Origin and
　Spread of Nationalism, see* Anderson,
　Benedict
immigrants/immigration, 170, 171–99, 200,
　236, 247–8
　and nationalism, *see* nationalism: and
　immigrants
　and the nation, 194–5
　European in Canada, 247
　Greek immigrants in Africa, 188
　in World War I, 190
　Indian in the West, 245
　Indian immigrants in Africa, 188–9, 190,
　191, 196
　Lebanese immigrants in Africa, 188
　literature, *see* literature: immigrant
　luggage in immigrant literature, 8, 171,
　173, 175, 176, 177, 178, 186, 188, 196,
　197, 211
　Syrian in Antigua, 188, 189
　Turkish in Germany, 247
　wandering, 28, 176, 177, 184–5, 190, 197,
　200, 247
An Immigrant Success Story: East Indians in

America, An, see Helweg, Arthur and
　Usha.
imperialism, 2–3, 4, 5, 28, 51, 53, 61, 63, 65,
　68, 69, 72, 73, 74, 76, 90, 94, 137, 173,
　187, 199,
　203, 213, 214, 216, 223, 246
　and English women, 35–64
　British, 2, 3, 4, 41, 48, 61, 62, 65, 73, 137,
　139, 187, 188
　German, 187, 191
In My Own Name, see Shan, Sharan-jeet
India/Indians, 24, 130, 137, 138, 139, 166,
　187, 189–90, 193, 194, 197, 214, 234,
　239, *see* also individual cities
　British India, 3, 37, 42, 54, 61, 138, 199,
　208, 212, 216, 217, 218
　Emergency (1975), 143
　in English literature, 35–64
　in Indian literature, 121–8, 131–70
　independence, 121, 138–9, 250
　immigrants, *see* immigrants: Indian
　Mother India, 137
　mythology, 158
　Nationalist movement, 117
　urban, 24, 136, 154, 159, 165, 205, 243
　women, *see* women: Indian
　women writers, *see* literature: Indian: by
　women
Indian Film, see Barnouw, Eric
Indian languages, 52, 180, 233
Indian Literature in English, see Walsh, William
Indian Metropolis: A View to the West, The, see
　Everson, Norma
Indian sub-continent, 212
Indira, M.A (film), 234
individualism, 24, 26, 39, 41, 56, 69, 140
Indo-Anglian, 237
Infant Mortality, see Newman, George
Inner Courtyard: Stories By Indian Women, The,
　241
Irigaray, Luce
　"Any Theory of the Subject Has Always
　Been Appropriated by the Masculine,"
　224
Ishiguro, Kazuo, 88, 93, 94, 200
　and Joseph Conrad, 68, 93–8
　Remains of the Day, 67, 93–8, 228
*The Issues at Stake: Theory and Practice in the
　Contemporary Women's Movement in India, see*
　Gandhi, Nandita.
Iyengar, K.R. Srinivasa, 138, 237
　"English Literature," 237
Iyengar, Vishwapriya, 243

Jamaica, 175
James, Henry, 127

Jameson, Fredric, 7, 66, 67, 89, 90, 99,
102–20, 127, 128, 129, 228, 229, 230,
231, 232
Marxism and Form, 115
"Modernism and Imperialism," 225
"Postmodernism, or The Cultural Logic of
late Capitalism," 128
"Romance and Reification," 223
The Political Unconscious, 89, 225
"Third World Literature in the Era of
Multinational Capitalism," 7, 99, 102–17
Jane Eyre, see Bronte, Charlotte
JanMohamed, Abdul, 103, 111, 112
Jay, Martin, 113
Marxism and Totality, 232
Jayawardena, Kumari
Feminism and Nationalism in the Third World,
219
Jha, Rama, 142
Jhabvala, Ruth Prawer, 140, 216
Joshee, Dr. Anandbai, 219
Joshi, Rama, 238
Joshi, Svati
*Rethinking English: Essays in Literature,
Language, History*, 237
Joy Luck Club, The, see Tan, Amy
Joyce, James, 63, 105, 110, 221
Jung, Anees, 131, 139, 142
Jung, Carl, 207
Memories, Dreams, and Reflections, 19
jungle, *see* wilderness

Kafka, 112
Kafka, Franz, 88
Kaplan, Caren, 27, 28, 29, 30, 204, 210, 212
"Deterritorializations: The Rewriting of
Home and Exile in Western Feminist
Discourse," 28, 35, 210
Karnad, Girish, 242
Kaye, Mary, 246
Keats, John, 139, 157
Kedourie, Elia, 109
Kenya, 14, 15, 249
Kenyatta, Jomo, 17
Keynes, John, 72
Khanafani, Ghassan
Men in the Sun (Rajal fi al-shams), 61
khandaneeath, 246
Kincaid, Jamaica, 209
A Small Place, 129, 188, 244
Annie John, 8, 9, 173, 174, 175, 192, 197,
244
Lucy, 197, 244
King, Anthony
*The Bungalow: The Production of a Global
Culture*, 204

kinship, 9, 85, 97, 122, 207, 228
Kipling, Rudyard, 43, 61, 217
"The Song of Cities," 24
Kohn, Hans
Nationalism: Its Meaning and History, 205
Konigsmark, Count John
Die Englanders in Indien, 215
Krishnamoorty, K., 151–2
Krishnaswamy, Shanta, 234, 239
The Woman in Indian Fiction in English, 140,
234, 239
Kristeva, Julia, 105
Kumar, Radha, 143, 144
*The History of Doing: An Illustrated Account of
Movements for Women's Rights and Feminism
in India, 1800–1990*, 239

Lakshmi, C.S., 159
Lalitha, K., 144, 145, 241
Lamp in the Desert, The, see Dell, Ethel
language, 5, 14, 42, 51, 52, 53, 61, 62, 63,
79, 80, 81, 88, 111, 112, 159, 161, 170,
181, 182, 185, 187, 193, 218, *see also*
individual languages
*Language and Power: Exploring Political Cultures in
Indonesia, see* Anderson, Benedict
Lanser, Susan S., 32
Larrain, Jorge, 70, 93
Latin America, 105, 106
Lawrence, D.H., 19, 153, 157
"End of Another Home," 240
Sons and Lovers, 19, 160
Layoun, Mary, 13, 15, 62, 226, 228
*Travels of a Genre: The Modern Novel and
Ideology*, 61
Lazarus, Neil
Resistance and Postcolonial African Fiction, 233,
249
Le Corbusier, 22
Lebanon, 193
lesbians/lesbianism, 27, 45, 162, 165
Leskov, Nikolai, 116
Lewis, Jared, 215
Liddle, Joanna and Rama Joshi
*Daughters of Independence: Gender, Caste and
Class in India*, 238
*Lie of the Land: English Literary Studies in India,
The, see* SunderRajan, Rajeshwari
literacy, 160
literature, 2, 4–5, 7, 108, 138, 172, 197, 200,
205, 216, 232, 234
about English in India, 42–50, 55–8, 212,
216
African, 24, 118, 119, 120, 195, 250
and imperialism, 76
and nationalism, 16

colonial/imperial, 4, 24, 37, 43, 62, 63, 65, 79, 93, 104, 199, 219, 238, 246
domestic, 63, 67, 75, 131–70
Edwardian, 72
English, 1, 5, 62, 64, 66, 70, 71, 73, 90, 91, 98, 138, 157, 223
  by women, 35–64
  English tradition, 5, 90–1, 138
"ethnic," 186
first world, 1, 105, 109, 113, 115, 120
global/postcolonial, 5, 7, 16, 65, 67, 89, 90, 91, 93, 99, 103, 104, 105, 107, 108, 110, 116, 120, 129, 131–70, 171, 172, 195, 197, 207, 208, 209, 219, 230, 233, 234, 239, 240, 241, 243, 244, 245, 246, 247, 250
immigrant, 8, 171–99, 200, 211, 243
  and the nation, 186–91
modernist, 66, 67
national, 67
nationalist, 104, 117, 118
realist, 2, 4, 101, 108, 138
romance, 69, 98, 167
third world, 1, 98, 99, 102–20, 124, 129, 200, 231, 232, 239
travel, 104
Victorian, 67, 72
world literature, 1, 111, 113, 135
Little Princess, The, see Burnett, Frances Hodgson
Lloyd, David, 103, 111, 112
location, 4, 8, 11, 26, 28, 29, 30, 31, 89, 91, 93, 98, 109, 120, 171, 173, 186, 197, 199, 203, 211, 248
  and home, 3, 17
  literary, 65
  politics of, 35, 74, 101, 102, 104, 108, 129, 203
Locke, John
  Second Treatise, 215
London, 63, 73, 84, 87, 88, 179, 183, 184, 192, 194
London Calling: V.S. Naipaul, Postcolonial Mandarin, see Nixon, Rob
London, Dock Strike of 1889, 225
Lonely Londoners, The, see Selvon, Sam
Lonely Planet Survival Guide, 35
Lord Jim, see Conrad, Joseph
love, 4, 5, 9, 44, 45, 58, 71, 78, 120, 124, 125, 127, 185, 216, 217, 227, 235
  and caste system, 181
  and class, 181
  and colonialism, 79, 181
  and race, 79, 180, 181, 182
lower class, 87, 88

Lucy, see Kincaid, Jamaica
Lukács, Georg, 232
  History and Class Consciousness, 129
  The Theory of the Novel, 113, 114, 116

MacMillan, Margaret, 214, 218
Maharani of Kuch Behar, 219
Mallah, Indu K.
  Shadows in Dream-Time, 238
Mansfield Park, see Austen, Jane
Manusmriti, 126
margins/marginality, 8–9, 28, 158, 170, 177, 178, 180, 184, 186–91, 194, 195, 200, 210, 247, 250
Markandaya, Kamala, 140, 142, 164
  Nectar in a Sieve, 166
  Some Inner Fury, 142, 164, 209
Marquez, Gabriel Garcia, 244
marriage, 45, 49, 77, 86, 91, 121, 127, 132, 140, 145–57, 165, 166, 167, 214, 216, 217, 220, 227, 234
  and race, 180–2, 216
  in Conrad, 76–80
  companionate, 72, 77
  European, 63, 80
  wife/husband, 44, 46, 47, 48, 49, 57, 58, 62, 71–2, 78, 79, 121, 122, 124, 125, 126, 127, 132, 133, 134, 145–57, 161, 162, 164, 165, 168, 180
Martin, Biddy, and Chandra Mohanty
  "Feminist Politics: What's Home Got to Do With It?," 26–7
Maru, see Head, Bessie
Marx, Karl, 236
Marxism, 66, 223
  western, 108, 113
Marxism and Form, see Jameson, Fredric
Marxism and Totality, see Jay, Martin
masculinity, 22, 43, 68, 69
  failure of, 85, 93
Masks of Conquest: Literary Study and British Rule in India, see Vishwanathan, Gauri
Mau Mau movement, 179
Meatless Days, see Suleri, Sara
Melbourne, 208
Melville, Herman, 22
Memories, Dreams and Reflections, see Jung, Carl
memory, 70, 73, 76, 97, 153, 173–80, 183–5, 196, 245
memsahib, 35–63, 130, 168, 212, 217, 218, 219
Memsahibs: In Praise of the Women of Victorian India, The, see Barr, Patt
men, 19, 22, 38, 45, 46, 47, 48, 50, 57, 58, 62, 64, 69, 72, 83, 84, 86, 93, 123, 124, 126, 131, 137, 138, 167, 215

Men in the Sun (Rajal fi al-shams), see
    Khanafani, Ghassan
Mexico, 207
middle class, 71, 133, 136, 144, 147, 162, 237
Midnight's Children, see Rushdie, Salman
Mies, Maria, 237, 243
    Patriarchy and Accumulation on a World Scale,
    204
migrants/migration, 105, 172, 173, 186, 187,
    245, 247
Milan, 208
Mill, John Stuart
    Subjection of Women, 72
Miller, Christopher, 107
Miller, J. Hillis
    "Repetition as Subversive of Organic
    Form," 226
    The Disappearance of God: Five Nineteenth-
    Century Writers, 226
mimicry, 75, 89, 226
Minh-ha, Trinh T., 103, 104, 112
Mississippi Masala (film), 245, 247
Mister Sampath, see Narayan, R. K.
Mitchell, Timothy
    Colonizing Egypt, 54, 60–1
Miyoshi, Masao, 207
mobile home park, 24
Modern World System, see Wallerstein,
    Immanuel
modernism, 62, 63, 65–7, 89–90, 98, 109,
    110, 139
    literature, *see* literature: modernist
Mohanty, Chandra, 18, 26, 29, 128, 131,
    203, 204, 207, 231, *see also* Martin,
    Biddy: and Chandra Mohanty
    "Feminist Encounters: Locating the Politics
    of Experience," 30, 203
    Third World Women and the Politics of
    Feminism, 104, 131, 236
Mohanty, S.P., 101, 103
Moraes, Dom, 164
mother-country, 174, 192
motherhood, 22, 45, 77–9, 133, 174, 189,
    193, 227
    and country, 174
    and imperialism, 38
    Victorian, 79
    Victorian/Edwardian, 78
Mukherjee, Bharati, 244
    Wife, 19, 172
Mukherjee, Meenakshi, 241
    The Twice Born Fiction: Themes and Techniques
    of the Indian Novel in English, 240
Mukherjee, Prabhati
    Hindu Women: Narrative Models, 235
Munich, 208

My Indian Family: A Story of East and West Within
    an Indian Home, see Wernher, Hilda
myth-making, 189
Mythologies, see Barthes, Roland

Nabokov, V. 221
Naidu, Sarojini, 141
Naipaul, Shiva, 246
Naipaul, V.S., 75, 88, 91, 200, 226, 246
    A House for Mister Biswas, 67, 91
    and Joseph Conrad, 67, 88–93, 98
    travel literature, 104
Nair, Janaki
    "Uncovering the *Zenana*: Visions of Indian
    Womanhood in Englishwomen's
    Writings, 1813–1840," 212
Nair, Mira, 245, 247
Narasimhaiah, C.D.and C.N. Srinath
    A Common Poetics For Indian Literatures, 152
Narayan, R.K., 7, 123, 127, 140, 164, 232,
    234
    Mr. Sampath, The Printer of Malgudi, 235
    Swami and Friends, 208
    The Bachelor of Arts, 235
    The Dark Room, 7, 108, 121–8, 234
national allegory, 7, 102, 103, 105, 106, 107,
    110, 115, 118, 121, 124, 128, 129, 130,
    172
nationalism, 3, 5, 6, 7, 11, 12–19, 60,
    102–05, 108, 116–20, 123, 124, 127,
    134, 141–2, 144, 187–8, 206, 229,
    231
    and home, 19
    and immigrants, 172, 186–91, 194, 250
    brahmin, 128
    colonial, 13
    Hindu, 122, 124, 127, 128
    in literature, 102–30, 186–91
    Indian, 13, 60, 141, 142, 219
    and gender, 136
    and women, 141–2
    non-western, 12, 108, 205, 206, 231
    African, 195, 206
Nationalism: A Religion, see Hayes, Carlton
Nationalism: Its Meaning and History, see Kohn,
    Hans
Nationalism in Indo-Anglian Fiction, see Sarma,
    G.P.
Nationalism in the Twentieth Century, see Smith,
    Anthony
Nationalisms and Sexualities Conference
    (1989), 181
Nationalist Thought and the Colonial World: A
    Derivative Discourse, see Chatterjee, Partha.
Natyasastra, see Bharata.
Nazareth, Peter

"Out of Darkness: Conrad and Other Third World Writers," 246
Ndebele, Njabulo
"Redefining relevance," 119
Nectar in a Sieve, see Markandaya, Kamala
Nehru, Jawaharlal, 117
Nepal, 212
New Guinea, 217
Newman, George
Infant Mortality, 218
New York, 35, 193, 207
New York Times, 55
Ngugi Wa Thiong'o, 209, 243
Petals of Blood, 118
Homecoming, 14
Nice Jewish Girls, see Beck, Evelyn Torton
Nigger of Narcissus, The, see Conrad, Joseph
Niranjana, Tejaswini, 205
Siting Translation: History, Post-Structuralism, and the Colonial Context, 204
Nisal, Shanta
Beghar, 161
Nixon, Rob, 93
London Calling: V.S. Naipaul, Postcolonial Mandarin, 88
No Longer at Ease, see Achebe, Chinua
No Telephone to Heaven, see Cliff, Michele
No Sweetness Here, see Aidoo, Ama Ata
nomadism, 28, 29, 36
Non-Resident Indians (NRIs), 161
North America, 8, 68, 176
nostalgia, 16, 22, 113, 116, 178, 183
Novalis, 1
Novels of Empire, see Howe, Susan
Nyerere, Julius, 194, 249

Orientalism, see Said, Edward
Orwell, George, 5, 63
Burmese Days, 63
Other/Otherness, 21, 27, 32, 36, 57, 102, 109, 115, 204, 220, 224, 232
Ottoman Empire, 54
Our Sister Killjoy, see Aidoo, Ama Ata

p'Bitek, Okot
The Song of Lawino, 233
Padmanabhanam, Gautam, 241
Paintal, Veena
Spring Returns, 238
Palace of the Peacock, The, see Harris, Wilson
Pakistan, 118, 169, 191, 192
Palestine/Palestinians, 61, 174, 193, 245
panopticon, 54
Paro: Dreams of Passion, see Gokhale, Namita
Parry, Benita, 42, 43, 106, 215, 216
Delusions and Discoveries, 42

Passage to India, A, see Forster, E. M.
Patel, Jabbar, 242
Patel, Vibhuti, 143
Pateman, Carole, 213, 215
Pater, Walter, 22
Pathak, Zakia
"The Prisonhouse of Orientalism," 237
Patil, Smita, 242
patriarchy, 1, 23, 32, 33, 40, 58, 72, 88, 121, 126, 133, 134, 157, 220, 221
British, 137
Patriarchy and Accumulation on a World Scale, see Mies, Maria
patriotism, 15, 166, 200, 201, 207
Penguin Book of Modern Indian Short Stories, The, see Alter, Stephen
Perrin, Alice, 40, 43, 216
Personal Record, A, see Conrad, Joseph
Petals of Blood, see Ngugi, Wa Thiong'o
Phillips, Anne, 203
place, 208, 212
gendering of, 22
notion of, 15
Places and Placelessness, see Relph, E.
Poe, Edgar Allen, 22
poetics, 28, 29, 145, 152
feminist, 29
in Indian literature, 138–41, 144
Poetics of Space, The, see Bachelard, Gaston
poetry/poets, 24, 93, 135, 138, 139, 151, 153, 154, 162, 163, 235, 240
English, 139, 156
Romantic, 67, 138, 139, 151, 152, 158, 238
Political Unconscious, The, see Jameson, Fredric
Porteous, Douglas, 13, 20
"Home: The Territoral Core," 21, 207
postcolonialism, 8, 9, 24, 106, 130, 135, 136, 172–93, 205, 223
postcolonial literature, *see* literature: postcolonial
postcolonial theory/theorists, 65, 102, 104, 118, 225, 230
postmodernism, 107, 220
Power of Geography, The, see Wolch, Jennifer
Pratt, Minnie Bruce, 27, 29, 211
"Identity: Skin Blood Heart," 26, 229
Price, Martin, 226
Pritam, Amrita, 159, 235
private
privacy, 41, 54, 55, 95
sphere, 1, 3, 19, 40, 41, 48, 49, 213, 215
Promise of Space, The, see Barnabas, Sarla
Proust, 89, 105, 110
psychoanalysis, 12, 20, 22

public
  space, 36, 39, 40, 56, 59
  sphere, 3, 41, 49, 213, 215, 222

race, 2, 4, 6, 9, 14, 30, 32–3, 36, 38, 44, 49,
    50, 58, 61, 63, 76, 77, 79, 80, 90, 93,
    181, 187, 189, 197, 200, 204, 209, 214,
    216
  and love, *see* love: and race
racism, 33, 35, 56, 181, 189, 245, 246
Ramabai, Pundita, 219
Rao, Raja, 140, 141, 164
  The Serpent and the Rope, 235
Rao, Vimala Rama
  "Decolonization, not Disinheritance," 242
rape, 143, 167, 194
Rau, Rama
  Home to India, 209
  Remember This House, 164, 209
reader/readers, 101, 107, 109, 110, 129,
    166, 172, 231, 232
Reagon, Bernice Johnson, 31
Recasting Women: Essays in Colonial History, see
    Sangari, Kumkum
refugees, 62
religion, 7, 9, 46, 81, 87, 127, 134, 166, 169,
    170, 181
religious sects, 179
Relph, E., 20
  Places and Placelessness, 208
Remains of the Day, The, see Ishiguro, Kazuo
resistance, 26, 30, 54, 102, 103, 118, 135, 137
  passive, 118
  peasant, 135
Resistance and Postcolonial African Fiction, see
    Lazarus, Neil
Rethinking English: Essays in Literature, Language,
    History, see Joshi, Svati
Rhetoric of Indian English, The, see Suleri, Sara
Rich, Adrienne, 30
Richard, Cliff, 194
  "Travelling Light," 171, 194
Riley, Denise
  Am I that Name?: Feminism and the Category of
    "women" in History, 38, 213
Rohini
  To Do Something Beautiful, 164, 166, 167,
    168, 169
romanticism, 114, 138, 139, 151, 152, 157,
    158
  novels, 43, 98
  poetry/poets, *see* poetry/poets: Romantic
Room of One's Own, A, see Woolf, Virgina
Roots and Shadows, see Deshpande, Shashi
Rose, Gillian, 21, 22, 23, 33
  Feminism and Geography, 30

Rushdie, Salman, 91, 104, 117, 164, 176,
    199, 209
  "'Commonwealth Literature' Does Not
    Exist," 233
  Grimus, 238
  Midnight's Children, 117
  Satanic Verses, 65, 118, 172
  Shame, 107, 173, 176
  "The Empire Within," 244
Ruskin, John, 71, 225
  Sesame and Lilies, 71
Rybczynski, Witold, 20
  Home: A Short History of an Idea, 210

Sahgal, Nayantara, 135–67, 241
  The Day in the Shadow, 131, 145, 153, 154–7
  The Time of Morning, 140
Sahitya Akademi, 233
Said, Edward, 15, 88, 89, 98, 105, 106, 107,
    111, 200, 207
  After the Last Sky: Palestinian Lives, 8, 174,
    193
  Orientalism, 204, 232, 237
  "Reflections on Exile," 221
  The World, The Text and the Critic, 16, 229
Salman Rushdie and the Third World: Myths of the
    Nation, see Brennan, Timothy
Sam, Agnes, 119
  What Passing Bells, 119
Sandoval, Chela, 29
Sangari, Kumkum, and Sudesh Vaid, 104
  Recasting Women: Essays in Colonial History,
    204
Sarabji, Cornelia, 220
Sarma, G.P.
  Nationalism in Indo-Anglian Fiction, 240
Sartre, Jean-Paul, 115, 116
Satanic Verses, see Rushdie, Salman
Saunders, Rebecca
  "Gender, Colonialism, and Exile: Flora
    Anne Steel and Sara Jeanette Duncan
    in India," 61
Savitri (film), 234
Scott, James C.
  Weapons of the Weak: Everyday forms of Peasant
    Resistance, 135
Second Class Citizen, see Emecheta, Buchi
Second Treatise, The, see Locke, John
Secret Agent, The, see Conrad, Joseph
self/selfhood, 1, 6, 8, 18, 19, 21, 27, 29, 58,
    62, 66, 84, 91, 123, 129, 130, 134, 144,
    158, 159, 175, 192, 196, 203, 234, *see also*
    subject/subjecthood
  and home, 2, 3, 12, 19–25, 19, 20, 24, 25,
    26, 27, 34, 170, 200, 209
  European, 64

immigrants, 177, 193
women, 6, 35, 36, 38, 58, 132, 136, 140,
  141, 158, 159, 209, 214, 236
  English as imperialist, 35–64
  Indian, 133, 137, 138, 141, 142, 144,
  147, 166
Selvon, Sam, 91
  The Lonely Londoners, 172, 175
sentimentalism, 11, 22, 79, 166, 199
Serpent and the Rope, The, see Rao, Raja
servants, 6, 38, 41, 46, 47, 49, 50–5, 121,
  132, 143, 147, 149, 161, 164, 167, 168,
  218
  butlers, 94, 96
Sesame and Lilies, see Ruskin, John
sexism, 35, 56, 162
sexuality, 33, 97, 181, 210, 220
Shadows in Dream-Time, see Mallah, Indu K.
Shame, see Rushdie, Salman
Shan, Sharan-jeet
  In My Own Name, 231
shanty towns, 24
Sharpe, Jenny, 212
  Allegories of Empire, 214, 216
Sherwood, Mary, 216
*Simians, Cyborgs and Women: The Reinvention of
  Nature, see* Haraway, Donna
Singh, Khushwant, 163, 164
Sinha, Mrinalini
  "'Chathams, Pitts and Gladstones in
  Petticoats' The Politics of Gender and
  Race in the Ilbert Bill Controversy," 216
*Siting Translation: History, Post-Structuralism, and
  the Colonial Context, see* Niranjana,
  Tejaswini
Sivanandan, A., 172, 244
*Slate of Life: An Anthology of Stories by Indian
  Women, The*, 240
slums, 24, 143
Small Place, A, see Kincaid, Jamaica
Smith, Anthony D.
  Nationalism in the Twentieth Century, 205
Smith, Barbara, 204
  Home Girls: A Black Feminist Anthology, 204
social reform, 40, 56, 60, 163, *see also*
  women's social work
  English, 72
Socialite Evenings, see Dé, Shobha
Some Inner Fury, see Markandaya, Kamala
Sommers, Doris, 105, 246
Song of Lawino, The, see p'Bitek, Okot
Sons and Lovers, see Lawrence, D. H.
Sopher, David
  "The Landscape of Home," 20, 21, 26
South Africa, 24, 119, 120
Space and Place, see Tuan, Yi-Fu

Spivak, Gayatri, 25, 39, 40, 104, 160
  "Can the Subaltern Speak?" 230
  "Feminism and Decolonization," 159, 160
  "French Feminism in an International
  Frame," 220
  "The Burden of English," 231
  "Three Women's Texts and a Critique of
  Imperialism," 39
  "Women in Difference," 187
Sprinker, Michael, 111
Srinath, C.N., 152
Srinivas, Mysore N.
  "The Changing Position of Indian
  Women," 238
Steel, Flora Anne, 6, 40, 43, 49, 61, 64, 69,
  216 ,218
  and Grace Gardiner
  The Complete Indian Housekeeper and Cook, 49,
  51, 52, 55, 218
Steinem, Gloria, 136
Stevenson, Robert Louis, 89
Strobel, Margaret, 218
  European Women and the Second British Empire,
  214, 217
subaltern, 15, 25, 161, 187, 188, 206
Subhah (film), 161, 163, 242
subject/subjecthood, 6, 24–5, 27, 34, 62, 79,
  119, 130, 204, 209, 210, 224, *see also*
  self/selfhood
  and home, 17, 18, 23, 199, 230, 231
  and the "native," 24
  colonial, 3, 5, 24, 40, 183, 191, 192, 199,
  204, 209
  definition of, 3–4, 25
  English, 39, 64
  immigrants, 170, 190
  minority, 112
  national subject, 6, 33, 38, 42, 49, 50, 186,
  190, 194, 195
  postcolonial, 170, 200
  postmodern, 200
  subaltern, 25
  women, 6, 39, 61, 143, 159, 169, 209, 229
Subjection of Women, The, see Mill.
suffrage, 37, 40, 57, 58, 213
Suleri, Sara, 14, 106, 191
  Meatless Days, 172, 191
  The Rhetoric of Indian English, 230
SunderRajan, Rajeshwari
  *The Lie of the Land,: Engish Literary Studies in
  India*, 237
Sunlight on a Broken Column, see Hussain, Attia
Swami and Friends, see Narayan, R. K.
Syria/Syrian, 189, 193

Tamil, 159

Tan, Amy
  The Joy Luck Club, 246
Tanzania, 187, 192, 194, 195, 197, 249
Thackeray, William Makepeace
  Vanity Fair, 71
Tharoor, Shashi, 164
  The Great Indian Novel, 163
Tharu, Susie, 141, 142, 145
  "Tracing Savitri's Pedigree: Victorian
    racism and the Image of Women in
    Indo-Anglian Literature," 141
  and K. Lalitha
  *Women Writing in India: The Twentieth
    Century, Volume I*, 241
  *Women Writing in India: The Twentieth
    Century, Volume II*, 144
That Long Silence, see Deshpande, Shashi
Their Eyes Were Watching God, see Hurston,
  Zora Neale
Theory of the Novel, The, see Lukács
Theroux, Paul, 91
they, *see* us
Things Fall Apart, see Achebe, Chinua
third world, 7, 89, 99, 103–17, 133, 135,
  231, 244
  culture, 111
  definition of, 103
  versus first world, 1, 111, 113, 115
third world literature, *see* literature: third world
*Third World Women and the Politics of Feminism,
  see* Mohanty, Chandra
Thousand Faces of Night, The, see Hariharan,
  Githa
Tiffin, Helen, 208, 230
Time of Morning, The, see Sahgal, Nayantara
To Do Something Beautiful, see Rohini
Tolstoy, 127
topophilia, 22
tourism, 28, 29, 35, 36, 129, 175
  textual, 29
trade unions, 143, 167
translation, 14, 15, 102, 206
transnational corporations, 18, 231
travel/traveling, 2, 73, 83, 171, 173, 196
*Travels of a Genre: The Modern Novel and Ideology,
  see* Layoun, Mary
Trinidad, 175
*Truth-Tales: Contemporary Writing By Indian
  Women*, 240
Tuan, Yi-Fu, 20
  Space and Place, 20, 22
  *Topophilia: A Study of Environment, Perception,
    Attitudes and Values*, 22, 208
*Twice Born Fiction: Themes and Techniques of the
  Indian Novel in English, The, see*
  Mukherjee, M.

Typhoon, see Conrad, Joseph

Uganda, 248, 249
Ujamaa, 194, 249
Umbartha (film), 242
Unconquered: A Romance, see Diver, Maud
Under Western Eyes, see Conrad, Joseph
United States, 18, 24, 33, 107, 118, 187,
  193, 207, 223, 230, 247
Untouchable, see Anand, Mulk Raj
Up The Ghat, see Whitaker, Zai
Upanishads, 157
upper class, 63, 73, 98, 133, 142, 159, 167,
  168, 237
Urdu, 159
us versus them, 101, 102, 103, 108, 112,
  129

Vaid, Sudesh, 204
Vanity Fair, see Thackeray, W. M.
Varnasramadharma, 124
Vassanji, M.G., 8, 170, 176, 182, 247
  "South Asian Canadian Literature," 187
  The Gunny Sack, 8, 170, 176–97, 226
Verma, Mahadevi, 159
Victorian Frame of Mind, The, see Houghton,
  Walter E.
Victory, see Conrad, Joseph
Vidler, Anthony
  *The Architectural Uncanny: Essays on the
    Modern Unhomely*, 22
Viswanathan, Gauri
  *Masks of Conquest: Literary Study and British
    Rule in India*, 138, 160, 204

Walcott, Derek, 244
  "The Fortunate Traveller," 93
Wallerstein, Immanuel
  The Modern World System, 210
Walsh, Willian, 234
  Indian Literature in English, 239
Walter, Pater, 224
war, 45, 46, 47, 48, 87, 88, 95, 146, 155
Ware, Vron, 213
Watt, Ian, 75
  Conrad in the Nineteenth Century, 74
we, *see* us
Weapons of the Weak, see Scott, James
Wedding Banquet, The, (film) 18
Weil, Simone, 199
Wernher, Hilda
  *My Indian Family: A Story of East and West
    Within an Indian Home*, 55, 57, 63, 220
Where Shall We Go This Summer? See Desai,
  Anita Whitaker, Zai, 164
Up The Ghat, 164

White Woman's Protective Ordinance (1926),
217
*White Woman, Race Matters: The Social
Construction of Whiteness, see* Frankenburg,
Ruth
whiteness, 43, 62, 76, 80
Wickramagamage, Carmen
"Relocation as Positive Act: The
Immigrant Experience in Bharati
Mukherjee's Novels," 243
Wife, see Mukherjee, Bharati
wilderness, 84, 85, 86, 94
Williams, Raymond, 73, 88
Wolch, Jennifer and Michael Dean
*The Power of Georgraphy: How Territory Shapes
Social Life*, 204
Woman in Indian Fiction, see Krishnaswamy,
Shanta
women, 7, 13, 14, 15, 19, 22, 23, 31, 33, 35,
38, 39, 45, 49, 72, 83, 123, 128, 138,
191, 222
African, 59, 120
and Hinduism, 57, 124, 126, 145
and nationalism, 15
as consumers, 41
as marginal, 186
as wilderness, 84, 85, 86
brahmin, 124
colonized, 158
English, 33, 36, 37, 47, 49, 56, 212, 214,
218, 221
in India, 6, 35–64, 36, 41, 53, 130, 137,
199, 214, 216, 217, 221, 222, 229
European, 158
in Conrad, *see* Conrad: and gender
in social sphere, 40
Indian, 7, 36, 37, 40, 56, 57, 59, 130,
131–70, 187, 193, 200, 209, 212, 220,
236, 237, 238
and art, 152
elite, 131–70, 237, 241

as symbols of nationalism, 141–42
in film, 161–63
lower class, 168
Muslim, 153
postcolonial, 134
subjecthood, *see* subject/subjecthood:
women
Saudi, 220
third world, 128, 131, 134, 220, 233
Victorian, 71
western, 35, 36, 56, 57, 58, 62, 143, 229
white, 35, 57, 58, 69, 85, 212, 220
Women for Immigration and Nationalist
Group (WING), 222
women's movements, 31, 137
Indian, 136, 143, 144, 167, 239, 243
women's social work, 40
in British India, 56–60, 219
*Women's Writing in India: The Twentieth Century,
Volume I, see* Tharu, Susie
*Women's Writing in India: The Twentieth Century,
Volume II, see* Tharu, Susie
Woolf, Virginia, 62, 63, 211
A Room of One's Own, 32
Wordsworth, William, 139, 240
working class, 7, 59, 69, 71, 143, 160, 222
world exhibitions, 60
world systems theory, 210
World, Text and the Critic, The, see Said, Edward
World War I, 44, 190, 191, 249
World War II, 95, 206, 249
Wright, Julia McNair
The Complete Home, 70
writers, 112, *see also* literature, Romanticism,
poetry/poets

Yeats, William Butler
"The Second Coming," 238
Yellow Peril, 32
Yellow Wallpaper, The, see Gillman, Charlotte
Perkins